M000101964

WINNIPEG
WITHDRAWN
APR 8 2002
PUBLIC LIBRARY

—— The ——
ASSINIBOINE

—— The ——
ASSINIBOINE

by Edwin Thompson Denig
edited by J.N.B. Hewitt
Introduction by David R. Miller

—— Canadian Plains Research Center, 2000 ——

Copyright: © Canadian Plains Research Center

Copyright Notice

All rights reserved. No part of this work covered by the copyrights hereon may be reproduced or used in any form or by any means — graphic, electronic or mechanical — without the prior written permission of the publisher. Any request for photocopying, recording, taping or information storage and retrieval systems of any part of this book shall be directed to the Canadian Reprography Collective.

Canadian Plains Research Center
University of Regina
Regina, Saskatchewan S4S 0A2
www.cprc.uregina.ca

Canadian Cataloguing in Publication Data
Denig, Edwin Thompson, 1812-1862?
   The Assiniboine
   (Canadian Plains reprint series, ISSN 1208-9680 ; 5)
   Includes bibliographical references and index. ISNB 0-88977-132-4
1. Assiniboine Indians.   I. University of Regina. Canadian Plains Research Center. II. Title. III. Series.

E99.A84D45 2000   978'.0049752   C00-920143-2

Cover design: Donna Achtzehner, Canadian Plains Research Center
Cover illustration: Karl Bodmer's *Fort Union on the Missouri*, reproduced courtesy of the Josyln Art Museum, Omaha, Nebraska

Printed and bound in Canada by Hignell Printing, Winnipeg

Printed on acid-free paper

—— Contents ——

—— Introduction to the 2000 Edition——

by David Reed Miller

The Assiniboine, by Edwin Thompson Denig, is a remarkable document, the finest and most detailed description of a Plains Indian tribe written during the buffalo-hunting days. In 1837 Denig was assigned by the American Fur Company to duty at Fort Union, on the Upper Missouri, where over the course of two decades he came to know the Assiniboine intimately. The writings that became this book date from about 1854 and were composed as answers to a circular designed by Henry Rowe Schoolcraft to collect systematic information about the Indian tribes of the United States. Denig's detailed report prepared in response to the circular constitutes the first ethnography of a Plains Indian people.

The Assiniboine are a Siouan-speaking people who, in the mid-nineteenth century, were one of the most populous tribes of the Northern Plains. Their closest relatives are the Stoney, who live in Alberta, and the Sioux, whose various divisions are scattered from Minnesota to Montana and from Saskatchewan and Manitoba to Nebraska. In Denig's time, Assiniboine territory stretched east to west in Saskatchewan from Wood Mountain to the Cypress Hills, and north to south from the North Saskatchewan River to the Milk and Missouri rivers in northern Montana. By the twentieth century Assiniboine reservations and reserves were located in Montana and Saskatchewan, within the area they occupied in the previous century.

Denig's report mainly concerns the Assiniboine, who are presented as representative of Upper Missouri tribes, but it also includes comparative information on many other tribes of the region, including the Sioux, Crow, Blackfoot, and Plains Cree, as well as the earth-lodge dwelling tribes of the Missouri, the Arikara, Hidatsa (whom he calls "Gros Ventre"), and Mandan. For that reason, when first published in edited form by J.N.B. Hewitt in 1930 in the *Forty-Sixth Annual Report of the Bureau of American Ethnology*, it was given the somewhat misleading title "Indian Tribes of the Upper Missouri."[1] Denig himself gave no title to his report; the title *The Assiniboine* has been chosen to reflect the focus of the work. The 1930 edition, following the conventions of the Bureau of American Ethnology, used the spelling "Assiniboin." The title of the present edition restores the final "e," which was Denig's spelling and which continues to be the preferred contemporary spelling of the Assiniboine people.

Denig's writings constitute the historical baseline for Assiniboine culture.

Subsequent studies provide supplementary cultural detail and document Assiniboine culture changes in the century and a half since Denig wrote. In 1909 Robert H. Lowie published an ethnography based on fieldwork during the summer of 1908 among the Assiniboine on the Fort Belknap Reservation in Montana and the Stoney on the Morley Reserve in Alberta.[2] Lowie's most important contribution was in documenting oral literature, a topic in which Denig had little interest. In 1938 David Rodnick published a study of culture change among the Fort Belknap Assiniboine, based on four and one-half months of field study. He drew extensively on Denig's report for his composite description of "The Aboriginal Background," the baseline against which he measured change.[3] In the summer of 1953, John C. Ewers did limited fieldwork at Fort Peck and Fort Belknap reservations, working with Joshua Wetsit and Henry Black Tail among others. Using Denig's writings as the point of reference, Ewers documented details of the Bear and Horse medicine societies.[4] Other more recent contributions to the ethnographic record of the Assiniboine have also drawn to varying degrees upon Denig's invaluable account.[5]

Edwin Thompson Denig

Born in McConnellstown, Huntingdon County, Pennsylvania on 10 March 1812, Denig was the son of Dr. George Denig, a physician. Nothing is known of his life prior to joining the fur trade at the age of twenty-one. He was probably recruited into the American Fur Company by Alexander Culbertson, from nearby Chambersburg, who had already finished a three-year stint on the Minnesota River when he returned to Pennsylvania to visit his family in the summer of 1832. The American Fur Company records show Denig's first-term contract dated 10 April 1833, for one year of service at $400 per annum. Beginning in that year he was assigned as a clerk at Fort Pierre, and spent one winter managing a trading house on Cherry Creek, sixty miles northwest. By 1837 he was reassigned to Fort Union where he rose through the ranks; in 1843 he became chief clerk and in 1848 he was appointed bourgeois, the superintending officer of the post.[6]

Fort Union was built in 1829 at the confluence of the Missouri and Yellowstone rivers to support the expansion of the fur trade on the Upper Missouri. Its site was said to have been selected by the chief of the Rock band of the Assiniboine.[7] It was located in the country of the Assiniboine, who served as middlemen between American traders on the Missouri and their northern competitors on the Saskatchewan, Assiniboine, and Souris rivers in British North America. The American Fur Company sought to capitalize on the trade networks of the Assiniboine and soon extended the trade up both the Missouri and Yellowstone rivers directly to other Indian nations whom they encouraged to bind their trade to the Americans.[8]

Denig's situation at Fort Union put him in a position to become an authority on the Assiniboine and other Indians of the region. The knowledge, both cultural and linguistic, that he acquired in his role as a trader allowed him to understand

Indians as producers and consumers. However, another critical source of knowledge emanated from his role as an affinal kinsman. Officers in the fur trade regularly formed domestic unions ("marriages of the country") with daughters or sisters of local headmen, which provided both partners and their families and associates influence and access to information.[9] Denig was married to two Assiniboine women. Little is known of his first wife, other than she was the mother of his son Robert (birth date unknown) and a daughter, Sarah (born 10 August 1844). She was reported to have been sickly, which may explain why Denig took as a second wife Deer Little Woman, daughter of Iron Arrow Point, chief of the Rock band of the Assiniboine, and sister to First To Fly, who after a power struggle with several of his brothers emerged as a major leader among the Lower Assiniboine. Deer Little Woman was the mother of Denig's other two children: Alexander (born 17 May 1852) and Ida (born 22 August 1854). Denig did his best to give his wives amenities fitting their station, importing clothes for them and toys for the children from St. Louis.[10]

Denig became increasingly aware of the uniqueness of his vantage point. While at Fort Union he met the scientist-travelers who visited there with the annual steamboats that brought supplies from downriver and carried furs and robes back to St. Louis. In the summer of 1843 John James Audubon, the artist and naturalist, visited Fort Union. Denig learned much from this encounter, helping Audubon to collect and prepare bird and animal specimens, which prompted Denig to begin his own collection. At Audubon's request, Denig wrote a description of Fort Union and its history, dated 30 July 1843, the earliest surviving example of Denig's writing.[11] In 1850 Alexander Culbertson's younger half-brother Thaddeus, a naturalist engaged to collect material for the Smithsonian Institution, visited the fort. Denig offered him advice and helped him in the collection of specimens. Denig, together with Alexander Culbertson and others of their associates in the fur trade, continued to collect in the 1850s, shipping downriver crates of minerals, fossils, stuffed animals, and other natural history specimens for the Academy of Science of St. Louis, the Smithsonian Institution, and other museums in the east.[12]

Denig may have met Pierre-Jean De Smet, S.J., in the 1840s when the itinerant priest made his first visits to Fort Union. In any case, in his role as bourgeois, Denig was able to extend hospitality to De Smet in the summer of 1851. The priest spent two weeks at the fort, organizing Indian leaders for the trip to Fort Laramie to attend the great treaty council called by the government. During his stay, De Smet spoke at length with Denig, exchanging facts and ideas and establishing what was to be a lasting friendship.[13]

De Smet was impressed with Denig's knowledge of the Upper Missouri tribes as well as his favorable disposition toward Indian perspectives. He encouraged the trader to write cultural descriptions of the Assiniboine and neighboring tribes, and Denig apparently lost no time in working on this assignment. In September 1852 De Smet acknowledged receipt of Denig's completed manuscript.[14] De Smet incorporated this material into a series of letters originally published in French, then in English, to arouse public interest in the Indian missions and to raise money for their support. In acknowledging Denig as his source, De Smet wrote: "I cite the authority of Mr. Denig, an intimate friend, and a man of high probity, from whom I have received all the information that I have offered you concerning the Assiniboins."[15]

The Swiss artist Rudolph Friederich Kurz spent seven months visiting Fort Union, from September 1851 until April 1852. His journal documents the daily life of the fort and makes frequent reference to Denig. In fact, Kurz noted on 21 September 1851 that Denig read to him from the manuscript that he was preparing for De Smet.[16] Kurz was particularly interested in Denig's collection of animal specimens, natural history, and ethnographic objects, which he used as models for a number of his sketches. Meanwhile, Denig gave Kurz various tasks in exchange for his board and room, including decorating the main administration building, painting portraits, and overseeing the preparation of an inventory, during which Kurz found out how exacting Denig could be. At one point, due to an injury to his hand, Denig enlisted Kurz to serve as his secretary, taking dictation as he worked on his manuscripts and other correspondence.[17]

By 1850, the American Fur Company had established 140 fur posts, some as hubs and many more as satellites. Because of its size and its complete dependence on Indians as suppliers and consumers, this enterprise had tremendous impact on Plains Indians. But by mid-century epidemics among Indian populations, reorganizations to meet supply and demand by producers and consumers, and the vicissitudes of capitalism and competitors converged to crisis proportions, creating doubt about the continued profitability of the trade.[18]

In 1854 Denig contemplated his future prospects. During his twenty-one-year tenure at Fort Union he had only once, in 1845, left his post to make a journey east to visit relatives. His personal sacrifice, perseverance, diligence, and ability had contributed to his successful rise through the ranks. His partnership in the American Fur Company yielded him one twenty-fourth of the annual profits from the trade. Facing an uncertain future, Denig decided to leave the Upper Missouri. His retirement from the company was effective in 1855. That summer Denig took Deer Little Woman and his children to visit his brother, Augustus, in Columbus, Ohio. They traveled much of the way by steamboat and while en route in St. Louis, Denig and his wife were married by a Father Daemen and their children were baptized. Denig's daughter Sarah remembered that, although they had intended to relocate there, the family found the climate in Columbus too warm. Seeking a place to settle, Denig chose to return to Fort Union by a circuitous route, traveling from St. Louis to St. Paul and by Red River cart to the Red River Settlement in Rupert's Land. They arrived back at Fort Union on 28 November 1855 after a trip of nearly three months.[19]

Denig and his family spent the winter at Fort Union, during which he apparently continued his writing of Indian ethnography. Packed and ready to leave, Denig received payment from P. Chouteau, Jr. and Company at Fort Union on 13 July 1856. He arrived on the White Horse Plains west of the Red River Settlement in late summer of 1856 with four cartloads of goods, and set himself up as an independent trader.[20] Denig's reasons for choosing Red River are undocumented, but it is likely that they related to his mixed-blood family.

There is very little information about the closing years of Denig's life. On 12 September 1856 Denig presented his will to the clerk of the Hudson's Bay Company for notarization.[21] In it he declared himself a resident of the "Red River Settlement of the North" and made provision for the education of his children in a Catholic school. Denig's diligence to detail in ordering his affairs foreshadowed his death on 4 September 1858, when he succumbed to an inflammation thought to have been appendicitis. He died at the age of forty-six on the White Horse Plains, and was buried in the Anglican cemetery at Pilot Mound, near present Headingly, Manitoba.[22]

Denig's Ethnological Writings

Denig's writings concerning the Assiniboine and other tribes of the Upper Missouri comprise three major manuscripts. First is the manuscript sent to Father De Smet in 1852, which the Jesuit directly incorporated into some of his letters published under the title *Western Missions and Missionaries*. Denig's material — concerning Assiniboine religion, hunting, warfare, and a biographical sketch of Old Gauche, a prominent chief — appears in letters 10 through 13, comprising more than seventy pages of that volume.[23] This work is only known through De Smet's publication; apparently the original manuscript was not preserved.

Second is the report published here, probably completed in 1854, based on Denig's answers to the Schoolcraft circular. The manuscript is preserved in the Bureau of American Ethnology (BAE) collection, National Anthropological Archives, Smithsonian Institution, Washington, and was published by the BAE in 1930 under the editorship of J.N.B. Hewitt. Denig, transmitting his report to Governor Isaac I. Stevens, indicated that the governor had requested him to "answer the Inquiries published by act of Congress regarding the history, present condition, and future prospects of the Indian tribes with which I am acquainted." Denig asserted that he might have organized a "perhaps more interesting work [that] might have been presented to the general reader" but that he was replying "in conformity to the instructions laid down in the document," referring to the 348 topics outlined in the circular. He asserted his qualifications for writing the report by citing "a constant residence of 21 years among the prairie tribes in every situation," and noting that "I have on all occasions had the advice of intelligent Indians as to the least important of these queries, so as to avoid, if possible, the introduction of error." Denig was emphatic that he did not want his manuscript "published in a mutilated form or made to coincide with any histories of the same people from others who have not had like opportunities of acquiring information" (p. xxxiii).

Denig emphasized that one of his challenges had been to present Indian "customs and opinions ... although very plain and common to us who are in their daily observance" accurately and comprehensively to readers "who are a stranger to these things." Denig explained that "the following pages exhibit a miniutiæ of information on those subjects not to be obtained either by transient visitors or a residence of a few years in the country"; rather he indicates that the "whole has been well digested, the different subjects pursued in company with the Indians for an entire year, until satisfactory answers have been obtained, and their motives of speech or action well understood" (pp. xxxiii-xxxiv).

Denig was obviously concerned that readers understand his dedication to accurate representation of the peoples with whom he had spent well over half of his life. Moreover, he wrote, "I shall rejoice if I have contributed in any degree toward opening a course of policy on the part of Government that may result in the amelioration of the sad condition of the savages" (p. xxxiv).

Denig's third work is an unfinished manuscript for a book on the Indian tribes of the Upper Missouri, probably written in 1855-56. Found among the papers of Alexander Culbertson's family, the manuscript is preserved in the Missouri Historical Society, St. Louis. Although the manuscript was anonymous, John C. Ewers of the Smithsonian Institution identified Denig as the author. It was published under Ewers' editorship as *Five Indian Tribes of the Upper Missouri* (1961).[24] In the introduction that Denig had begun to draft, he explained that his intention was to present

> the different traits of Indian character ... first, to give a short history of each tribe, its geographical position and other peculiarities; after which an inquiry will be instituted into their government, condition, manners, and customs as a body. Most customs and opinions are common to all tribes, but wherever any great difference is observable, or marked traits to be noticed, they will be found in the compendiums of their separate histories.[25]

The manuscript includes sketches of five tribes: Sioux, Arikara, Assiniboine, Cree, and Crow.

This manuscript probably originated in a joint project with Culbertson. In 1856 Ferdinand V. Hayden, of the United States Geological Survey, wrote to Spencer F. Baird, of the Smithsonian Institution in Washington, that Culbertson was preparing for publication a two-volume work on the Upper Missouri, all or part of which was undoubtedly to be written by Denig.[26] That project was never completed and after Denig's death Hayden incorporated much of it verbatim in his monograph, *Contributions to the Ethnology and Philology of the Indian Tribes of the Missouri Valley*.[27] Although Hayden expressed his indebtedness to members of the American Fur Company for assistance in preparing his monograph, that acknowledgment fails to reflect the wholesale use he made of Denig's work.

In addition to these three major works, Denig also completed other, shorter ethnological writings during these same years. He provided a representative vocabulary of Assiniboine, which Schoolcraft published in 1854, and in 1855, Denig published a short article on medicine among the Cree.[28]

The Report on the Schoolcraft Circular

The circular that provided the stimulus for Denig's report on the Assiniboine was composed by Henry Rowe Schoolcraft. Among his credits, Schoolcraft had served as an agent for the Chippewa, carried out a survey of the Indians of New York, and published volumes on both the Chippewa and the Iroquois, making him one of the pre-eminent experts on American Indians in the mid-nineteenth century. In 1847 Schoolcraft was appointed by the secretary of war, whose office oversaw the administration of Indian affairs, to compile information on the history and present conditions of Indians in the United States. He considered the first order of business to be a census, which might be given a "systematic footing by circulating a printed form to the agents." By mid-May 1847 Schoolcraft had his circular printed and sent through government channels to agents, teachers, and "men of learning and experience."[29] The final product of his work, compiling material as he accumulated it, was a set of six huge volumes entitled *Historical and Statistical Information Respecting the History, Conditions, and Prospects of the Indian Tribes of the United States*, published between 1851 and 1857. The circular was printed as an appendix to the first volume.[30]

When Denig received a copy of the Schoolcraft circular is not known definitely. However, Governor Stevens and the Northwest Railway survey party made an eight-day layover at Fort Union in August 1853 and it is likely that on this occasion Stevens requested Denig to answer the circular, probably as much for his own information as *ex-officio* superintendent of Indian affairs for Washington Territory (including at that time all of Montana) as for Schoolcraft.[31] Consequently, Denig's letter of transmittal of his report based on the circular was submitted directly to Stevens, probably in 1855, just prior to Denig's retirement from Fort Union.

How Denig's manuscript got from Stevens to the Smithsonian is not definitely known. There is no evidence that it had ever been forwarded to Schoolcraft. When the Bureau of Ethnology (later renamed the Bureau of American Ethnology) was founded as part of the Smithsonian Institution in 1879 by John Wesley Powell, manuscripts relating to Indians from within the institution and from the government-sponsored geological surveys were forwarded to Powell.[32]

Denig's manuscript languished unpublished in the Bureau of American Ethnology (BAE) Library for many years. Discussion of the work of staff members in the *Annual Reports* of the BAE between 1919 and 1929 attest that the Denig manuscript had been considered a candidate for publication for quite some time. In 1918 James Mooney, the BAE's Plains specialist, initiated correspondence with members of the Denig family "for the purpose of gathering all available information concerning the history and personality of the author," and this "in connection with the preparation of the Denig Assiniboin[e] manuscript for publication," presumably in the role of editor.[33] However, Mooney died in 1921 without completing the project, although he did have a copy made of the manuscript for purposes of editing, assembled biographical information for an introduction, and drafted some text for footnotes. Subsequently, J.N.B. Hewitt, "custodian of manuscripts" at the BAE, assumed responsibility for editing the Denig manuscript. The BAE report for 1922-23 noted that Hewitt had worked on the project; it is next mentioned in the 1926-27 report, and the report for 1927-28 indicates that the work was completed.[34]

John Napoleon Brinton Hewitt (1858-1937) was a self-trained ethnographer, folklorist, and linguist. He was of Tuscarora descent, and virtually all of his own studies were with the Iroquois.[35] However, he had been with the BAE nearly from the time of its founding and was a veteran editor familiar with BAE style. In approaching Denig's manuscript, Hewitt's overall editorial hand was light. His main task was to transform Denig's responses to the specific inquires of the Schoolcraft circular into an ethnographic narrative. He deleted the circular section numbers that Denig has written in the margins and in most cases he added a phrase to indicate the topic of the section. These phrases, printed in capitals, serve as section headings in the published version. Hewitt imposed some standardization of terms and spelled out abbreviations. He also made grammatical corrections, occasionally adding words and changing verbs or verb tense. Sometimes for clarity a word was silently added, deleted, or substituted. Hewitt occasionally attempted to edit out Denig's personal opinions, but generally he allowed them to remain in the text.

Hewitt exercised a heavier editorial hand by imposing the BAE's ethnographic terminology on Denig's writing, following the standard set by the *Handbook of American Indians North of Mexico* (BAE Bulletin 30). For example, "tribe" replaced "nation," "kinship" replaced "clanship," and "gentes" replaced "clans."[36] Likewise, in the representation of religious concepts, when Denig explained the notion of medicine, Hewitt replaced the word "medicine" in the text with "divining"; consequently, "medicine man" became "divining man," and "medicine dog" (the Assiniboine term for horse) became "divining dog" (p. 18). However, the term "divining" distorts the Assiniboine meaning of the term as a pervasive form of power manifested in visions and given to particular individuals.

In introducing the concept of a Creator spirit, Denig used the term "the Great Spirit" followed immediately by the phrase "who is imaginary"; Hewitt replaced this expression with the words "Wakoñda, who is a spirit" (p. 18). This initial mention of the Creator occurred in the description of how, following the hunt, hunting medicine was invoked to propitiate the spirits of slain animals. Here Hewitt added words to emphasize that it was "the spirit of" the carcass, not the carcass itself, that was addressed in the ritual. Hewitt used "Wakoñda" as a generic Siouan term, but this proves particularly confusing because it is orthographically closer to the Omaha and Osage term than to the Assiniboine "wakan."[37]

Again, in a discussion of Assiniboine and Sioux concepts of creation (p. 20), Hewitt excised the heading "Creation" and Denig's opening two sentences: "Their knowledge on this subject is very limited. They believe the earth to be a great plain." Hewitt left the following sentence in place: "They believe that Wakoñda created all things and this one idea appears original and universal, further than which, however, they are at a loss." Denig's original has "Great Spirit" in place of Wakoñda and *"all things"* is underlined for emphasis. In these instances, Hewitt's editing distorts Denig's meaning.

The Significance of Denig's Report

Denig wrote his report from the perspective of Fort Union, using the Assiniboine as a prism to look outward at the similarities and differences of other tribes in the Upper Missouri trade network. His description of Assiniboine politics and social organization was particularly insightful, one of the most definitive for any Plains group in the mid-nineteenth century. Denig considered his report to be a service to the government, providing detailed responses to questions formulated by the circular to generate detailed information on particular tribes and regions in order to gauge the successes and failures of federal Indian policy. Denig hoped that his primary audience would be policy makers and only secondarily scientists and general readers.

Denig's report did not go beyond detailed answers to the topics outlined in the circular, but he sought to be as thorough and definitive in his responses as possible. Remarking that he spent a year talking with Indians about material for the report, Denig revealed a sense of pride in this fieldwork and the authenticity with which he felt it imbued his report. In it, Denig consciously sought to counter popular misinformation and the superficial accounts of travelers. Denig wrote from the perspective of a resident among the Assiniboine and their contemporaries and constructed his report much the same as twentieth-century anthropologists would, focusing on the native point of view. This documented and demonstrated knowledge was, for Denig, the basis of a cultural relativity foreshadowing the intellectual struggle for the acceptance of that concept a century later.

Assessing Denig's contribution in the introduction he wrote to the publication of *Five Indian Tribes of the Upper Missouri*, John C. Ewers wrote: "Denig was both the most prolific and the most knowledgeable writer on the Indian tribes of the Upper Missouri in the mid-nineteenth century."[38] Denig's responses to the inquiries in the Schoolcraft circular were fittingly encyclopedic. Ranging from the pragmatics of political order to religious thought and practice, Denig's work is the pre-eminent ethnographic compendium about a Plains Indian people, based on fieldwork. It attests to Denig's unique abilities as an observer and participant in the life of the people of the Upper Missouri in the early to mid-nineteenth century. Historically, Denig was aware of the local contingencies and the political and economic realities that were building in the early 1850s. He anticipated the degree to which change would alter the lives of the individuals, families, and groups with whom he had been so intimately connected. Driven by his own intellectual interest, and convinced of the intrinsic worth of Indian cultures, Denig sought to preserve a record of Assiniboine society and culture. His particular contribution to the cultural history of the Assiniboine was substantial even by today's standards, and this work remains a most important baseline study, providing an unparalleled portrait of the Northern Plains before the imposition of reservations and reserves.

The present reprint will bring Denig's work to a new generation of readers, who will find here an incomparable wealth of detail on nineteenth-century Plains Indian cultures.

Notes

The author of this introduction acknowledges the generous research support of the Short Term Visitor Grant Program, Office of Fellowships and Grants of the Smithsonian Institution in 1996 and 1999, for visits to the National Anthropological Archives for work with the original manuscript that constituted the original publication, and to the Friends of Fort Union Association for the 1999 Fort Union Research Fellowship enabling a visit to utilize the research collection at the Fort Union Trading Post National Historic Site, National Park Service, Trenton, North Dakota, for details of Denig's tenure there.

1. The only printing prior to this reprint was Edwin Thompson Denig, "Indian Tribes of the Upper Missouri," edited with notes and biographical sketch, by J.N.B. Hewitt, *Forty-sixth Annual Report of the Bureau of American Ethnology to the Secretary of the Smithsonian Institution, 1928-29* (Washington, DC: United States Government Printing Office, 1930), 375-628.

2. Robert H. Lowie, *The Assiniboine, Anthropological Papers of the American Museum of Natural History*, vol. 4 (New York: American Museum of Natural History, November 1909), 1.

3. David Rodnick, *The Fort Belknap Assiniboine of Montana: A Study in Culture Change* (New Haven: Yale University Press, 1938). Other articles by Rodnick based on this research include: "Political Structure and Status Among the Assiniboine Indians," *American Anthropologist* 39 (1937): 408-16; "An Assiniboine Horse-Raiding Expedition," *American Anthropologist* 41 (1939): 611-16; "The Effect of Culture Change Upon the Personalities of Second-Generation Reservation Indians," *Yivo Annual of Jewish Social Science* 2 and 3 (1947-48): 252-61.

4. John C. Ewers, "The Bear Cult Among the Assiniboin and Their Neighbors of the Northern Plains," *Southwestern Journal of Anthropology* 11 (1955): 1-14; "The Assiniboin Horse Medicine Cult," *Anthropological Quarterly* 29 (1956): 57-68.

5. Gary Blake Doige, "Warfare Patterns of the Assiniboine to 1809" (Master's thesis, University of Manitoba, 1989); Verne Dusenberry, "Notes on the Material Culture of the Assiniboine Indians," *Ethnos* 25 (1960): 44-62, and "Some Unrecorded Ethnology of the Assiniboine Indians of Montana" (unpublished, undated manuscript, Dusenberry Papers, Calgary: Glenbow Museum Archives); Brenda Farnell, *Do You See What I Mean: Plains Indian Sign Talk and the Embodiment of Action* (Austin: University of Texas Press, 1995); and David Reed Miller, "Montana Assiniboine Identity: A Cultural Account of an American Indian Ethnicity" (Ph.D. dissertation, Indiana University, 1987). Also see Raymond J. DeMallie and David R. Miller, "Assiniboine," *Plains* 13, and Raymond J. DeMallie (ed.), *Handbook of North American Indians* (Washington, DC, Smithsonian Institution Press, in press).

6. Denig's family history and his own biographical beginnings were related in greater detail by J.N.B. Hewitt, editor of the monograph, and in two further elaborations: Chris Vickers, "Denig of Fort Union," *North Dakota History* 15 (1948): 134-43; and John C. Ewers, "Literate Fur Trader Edwin Thompson Denig," *Montana: The Magazine of Western History* 6, no. 4 (1956): 1-12.

7. Charles Larpenteur, *Forty Years a Fur Trader on the Upper Missouri: The Personal Journal of Charles Larpenteur 1833-1872*, ed. Elliot Coues, 2 vols. (New York: Francis P. Harper,1898), 1: 109.

8. For the history of Fort Union see Ray H. Mattison, "Fort Union: Its Role in the Upper Missouri Fur Trade," *North Dakota History* 29 (1969): 181-208; Erwin N. Thompson, *Fort Union Trading Post: Fur Trade Empire on the Upper Missouri* (Williston: Fort Union Association, 1994), originally published as Part I of the work entitled *Fort Union Trading Post Historic Structures Report, Part II, Historical Data Section*, National Technical Information Service, Document PB-203901 (Washington, DC: United States Department of Commerce, 1968).

The history of the Missouri River fur trade is best summarized by William R. Swagerty, "Indian Trade in the Trans-Mississippi West to 1870," *History of Indian White Relations*, Vol. 4 of *Handbook of North American Indians*, ed. Wilcomb E. Washburn (Washington, DC: Smithsonian Institution Press, 1988), 351-74; John E. Sunder, *The Fur Trade on the Upper Missouri, 1840-1865* (Norman: University of Oklahoma Press, 1965; David J. Wishart, *The Fur Trade of the American West, 1807-1840* (Lincoln: University of Nebraska Press, 1979).

For the northern spheres of trade influencing the Assiniboine and other northern Plains Indian groups see Arthur J. Ray, *Indians in the Fur Trade: Their Role as Trappers, Hunters, and Middlemen in the Lands Southwest of Hudson Bay, 1660-1870* (Toronto: University of Toronto Press, 1974) and "The Hudson's Bay Company and Native People," *History of Indian White Relations*, 335-50.

9. For discussion of "marriages of the country" in the fur trade see Sylvia Van Kirk, *"Many Tender Ties": Women in Fur-Trade Society, 1670-1870* (Winnipeg: Watson & Dwyer, 1980): 28-29.

10. Rudolph Friedrich Kurz, a visitor to Fort Union wrote: "Owing to an accident, his [Denig's] old wife is of no service; so according to customs in this part of the world, he might be divorced. For the sake of his kind feeling toward her and of keeping her here as companion for his younger wife, so that the latter may not seek amusement at the homes of the clerks' or *engagés*' wives, he will not cast her off. Furthermore, he has a son and a daughter by her. His boy is being educated in Chicago, but the girl is at home with her mother." *Journal of Rudolph Friedrich Kurz: An Account of His Experiences Among Fur Traders and American Indians on the Mississippi and the Upper Missouri Rivers During the Years 1846 to 1852*, trans. Myrtis Jarrell, ed. J.N.B. Hewitt, *Bulletin 115, Bureau of American Ethnology* (Washington, DC: United States Government Printing Office, 1937), 136. Note that Hewitt also edited this important journal of the artist's sojourn on the Upper Missouri.

See further biographical detail in John C. Ewers, "Introduction," in Edwin Thompson Denig, *Five Indian Tribes of the Upper Missouri: Sioux, Arickaras, Assiniboines, Crees, Crows* (Norman: University of Oklahoma Press, 1961), xiii-xxxvii; also see the discussion about Deer Little Woman in John C. Ewers, "Mothers of the Mixed-Bloods," *Indian Life on the Upper Missouri* (Norman: University of Oklahoma Press, 1968): 57-67.

11. Edwin T. Denig, "Description of Fort Union (July 30, 1843)," in Maria R. Audubon and Elliott Coues (eds.), *Audubon and His Journals*, 2 vols. (New York: Charles Scribner's Sons, 1897), 2: 180-88; Ewers, "Introduction," xv-xvi; Sunder, *Fur Trade on the Upper Missouri*, 130.

12. Sunder, *Fur Trade on the Upper Missouri*, 130; also see Ewers, "Introduction," xvii-xviii.

13. Robert C. Carriker, *Father Peter John De Smet: Jesuit in the West* (Norman: University of Oklahoma Press, 1995), 41, 61, 62, 104. Carriker noted that De Smet visited Fort Union a total of ten times between 1842 and 1867, detailed in his article "Entertainment for the Evening: Father Peter John De Smet, S.J., Recounts His Missionary Travels to the Citizens of Fort Union," *Fort Union Fur Trade Symposium Proceedings, September 13-15, 1990* (Williston: Friends of Fort Union Trading Post, 1994), 60.

14. Father Pierre Jean De Smet, *Life, Letters, and Travels of Father Pierre Jean De Smet*, 4 vols., ed. H.M. Chittenden and A.T. Richardson (New York: Francis P. Harper, 1905), 4: 1215-16.

15. Father P.J. De Smet, *Western Missions and Missionaries: A Series of Letters* (New York: James B. Kirker, 1863), 202.

16. Kurz, *Journal of Rudolph Friedrich Kurz*, 133, 136.

17. Ibid., 258.

18. See chapters in Sunder, *Fur Trade on the Upper Missouri*, about the decline in the trade and various factors attributed.

19. Ewers, "Introduction," xxiii-xxv.

20. Ibid., xxv.

21. Edwin Thompson Denig, Last Will and Testament, 12 September 1856, Photostat, 5 pp., Manitoba Provincial Archives, Winnipeg, Manitoba; Vickers, "Denig of Fort Union," 139-43.

22. Ewers, "Introduction," xxv; Vickers, "Denig of Fort Union," 136.

23. See Chapter 10, "Religious Opinions of the Assiniboins;" Chapter 11, "Indian Hunts;" Chapter 12, "Indian Warfare;" and Chapter 13, "Tchatka, the Poisoner, an Assiniboin Chief;" in De Smet, *Western Missions and Missionaries*, 134-205. Denig probably facilitated the communication from Crazy Bear to De Smet, also published in this volume, Chapter 9, "The letter of Crazy Bear, Assiniboin Chief," 130-33.

24. John C. Ewers edited and published each of the five Denig sketches prior to all being republished in *Five Indian Tribes of the Upper Missouri*: "Of the Arickaras," *Bulletin of the Missouri Historical Society* 6, no. 2 (January 1950): 198-215; "Of the Sioux," *Bulletin of the Missouri Historical Society* 7, no. 2 (January 1951): 185-215; "Of the Assiniboines," *Bulletin of the Missouri Historical Society* 8, no. 2 (January 1952): 121-50; "Of the Crees or Knistenau," *Bulletin of the Missouri Historical Society* 9, no. 1 (October 1952); and "Of the Crow Nation" "With Biographical Sketch and Footnotes by John C. Ewers," Anthropological Paper No. 33, *Bulletin 151, Bureau of American Ethnology* (Washington, DC: Government Printing Office, 1953), 1-80.

Ewers also published a biographical sketch, "Literate Fur Trader Edwin Thompson Denig," *Montana: The Magazine of Western History* 4, no. 2 (Spring 1954):1-12 which is elaborated on in his introduction to the publication of the entire manuscript, *Five Indian Tribes of the Upper Missouri*.

25. Quoted by Ewers, "Introduction," xxviii-xxix; the Denig manuscript introduction was not included in the 1961 publication of *Five Indian Tribes of the Upper Missouri*.

26. Ewers, "Introduction," xxxv; see Ewers footnote 21 for reference to the Hayden letter to Baird, 9 January 1856, "Letter in Archives of the Smithsonian Institution, Washington, D.C."

27. F.V. Hayden, "Contributions to the Ethnography and Philology of the Indian Tribes of the Missouri Valley," *Transactions, American Philosophical Society* (n.p., n.d.), 12; see

the detailed discussion of Hayden's career, and also the expeditions of John Wesley Powell and George M. Wheeler in William H. Goetzmann, *Exploration & Empire: The Explorer and Scientist in the Winning of the American West* (New York: Alfred A. Knopf, 1966), 489-529.

28. An Assiniboine vocabulary included in Henry Rowe Schoolcraft, *Historical and Statistical Information Respecting the History, Condition, and Prospects of the Indian Tribes of the United States...* Part 4 (Philadelphia: Lippincott, Grandbo & Co., 1854), 416-32, was attributed to Denig, without any further explanation; Edwin Thompson Denig, "An Account of Medicine and Surgery as it exists among the Cree Indians. By a non-professional observer, who has resided for a number of years among them and is familiar with their language, habits and customs," *The Medical and Surgical Journal* 13 (1855): 312-18.

29. Brian W. Dippie, *Catlin and His Contemporaries: The Politics of Patronage* (Lincoln: University of Nebraska Press, 1990), 173, 476.

30. The Schoolcraft questionnaire, which appeared as an appendix to the first volume of Henry Rowe Schoolcraft, *Historical and Statistical Information Respecting the History, Condition, and Prospects of the Indian Tribes of the United States*, 6 vols. (Philadelphia: Lippincott, Grambo & Co., 1851-57) is reprinted as an appendix in this volume.

31. Isaac. I. Stevens, *Narrative and Final Report of Explorations for a Route for a Pacific Railroad near the Forty-Seventh and Forty-Ninth Parallels of North Latitude from St. Paul to Puget Sound*, Pacific Railroad Reports, Vol. 12 (Washington, DC: Beverly Tucker, 1860), 78-87.

32. James R. Glenn, *Guide to the National Anthropological Archives* (Washington, DC: National Anthropological Archives, 1996), xiii.

33. J. Walter Fewkes, "Report for Fiscal Year ending 30 June 1920," *41st Annual Report, Bureau of American Ethnology* (Washington, DC: Government Printing Office, 1928), 6.

34. J. Walter Fewkes, "Report for Fiscal Year ending 30 June 1923," *41st Annual Report, Bureau of American Ethnology*, 86; J. Walter Fewkes, "Report for Fiscal Year ending 30 June 1927," *44th Annual Report, Bureau of American Ethnology* (Washington, DC: Government Printing Office, 1928), 6-7; J. Walter Fewkes, "Report for Fiscal year ending 30 June 1928," *45th Annual Report, Bureau of American Ethnology* (Washington, DC: Government Printing Office, 1930), 6.

35. Blair A. Rudes, "John Napoleon Brinton Hewitt: Tuscarora Linguist," *Anthropological Linguistics* 36, no. 4 (1994): 467-81.

36. Frederick Webb Hodge (ed.), *Handbook of American Indians North of Mexico*, 2 vols., *Bulletin 30, Bureau of American Ethnology* (Washington, DC: Government Printing Office, 1907). See Hewitt's final paragraph in his introduction to this volume, where he delineates his use of such terms; also see instances in published form, compared with editorial copy of the manuscript, 398. As an example of where these terms were changed, Hewitt heavily edited the segment, "Intertribal [Denig used "International"] Rank and Relations" and elsewhere, see below, 9-11, and in the editorial manuscript copy, National Anthropological Archives, "2600-a-1, Assiniboin," beginning at page 586.

37. *Handbook of American Indian North of Mexico*, 2: 897-98.

38. Ewers, "Introduction," xxxvii.

—— Publisher's Note ——

Readers will note that two different sets of pagination are to be found in *The Assiniboine*. This was an editorial decision necessitated by the fact that, when E.T. Denig's report was first published in 1930, it appeared as the second section of the *Forty-sixth Annual Report of the Bureau of American Ethnology to the Secretary of the Smithsonian Institution*, and as such began on page 375. *The Assiniboine* begins on page 1, but the original pagination has been retained on the facsimile version contained herein. Pagination for entries in the index, however, has been changed, since the material found between pages 1-374 in the first section of the original *Forty-sixth Annual Report* has not been reproduced here.

— Preface to the 1930 Edition —

This manuscript is entitled "A Report to the Hon. Isaac I. Stevens, Governor of Washington Territory, on the Indian Tribes of the Upper Missouri, by Edwin Thompson Denig." It has been edited and arranged with an introduction, notes, a biographical sketch of the author, and a brief bibliography of the tribes mentioned in the report.

The report consists of 451 pages of foolscap size; closely written in a clear and fine script with 15 pages of excellent pen sketches and one small drawing, to which illustrations the editor has added two photographs of Edwin Thompson Denig and his Assiniboin wife, Hai-kees-kak-wee-läh, Deer Little Woman, and a view of Old Fort Union taken from "The Manoe-Denigs," a family chronicle, New York, 1924.

The manuscript is undated, but from internal evidence it seems safe to assign it to about the year 1854.

The editor has not attempted to verify the statements of the author as embodied in the report; he has, however, where feasible, re-arranged some portions of its contents by bringing together under a single rubric remarks upon a common topic which appeared in various parts of the report as replies to closely related but widely placed questions; and he has attempted to do this without changing the phraseology or the terminology of Mr. Denig, except in very rare instances, and then only to clarify a statement. For example, the substitution of the native term for the ordinary English expression, the Great Spirit, and divining in the place of " medicine " in medicine man, practically displacing *medicine man* by the word *diviner*.

In his letter of transmittal " To his Excellency, Isaac I. Stevens, Governor of Washington Territory," Mr. Denig writes: " Being stimulated with the desire to meet your wishes and forward the views of government, I have in the following pages endeavored to answer the ' Inquiries ' published by act of Congress, regarding the ' History, Present Condition, and Future Prospects of the Indian Tribes ' with which I am acquainted. * * * Independent of my own personal observation and knowledge acquired by a constant residence of 21 years among the prairie tribes, in every situation, I have on all occasions had the advice of intelligent Indians as to the least important of these inquiries, so as to avoid, if possible, the introduction of error. * * *

88253°—30——25

377

"It is presumed the following pages exhibit a minutiæ of information on those subjects not to be obtained either by transient visitors or a residence of a few years in the country, without being, as is the case with myself, intimately acquainted with their camp regulations, understanding their language, and in many instances entering into their feelings and actions.

" The whole has been well digested, the different subjects pursued in company with the Indians for an entire year, until satisfactory answers have been obtained, and their motives of speech or action well understood before placing the same as a guide and instruction to others.

" The answers refer to the Sioux, Arikara, Mandan, Gros Ventres, Cree, Crow, Assiniboin, and Blackfeet Nations, who are designated as prairie, roving, or wild tribes—further than whom our knowledge does not extend.

" I am aware of your capacity to judge the merits of the work and will consider myself highly honored if I have had the good fortune to meet your approbation; moreover I shall rejoice if I have contributed in any degree toward opening a course of policy on the part of the Government that may result in the amelioration of the sad condition of the savages. Should the facts herein recorded ever be published or embodied in other work it is hoped the errors of language may be corrected, but in no instance is it desired that the meaning should miscarry."

Elsewhere in this letter Mr. Denig writes: "Some of their customs and opinions now presented, although very plain and common to us who are in their daily observance, may not have been rendered in comprehensible language to those who are strangers to these things, and the number of queries, the diversity of subjects, etc., have necessarily curtailed each answer to as few words as possible."

The report was made in response to a circular of "Inquiries, Respecting the History, Present Condition, and Future Prospects of the Indian Tribes of the United States," by Henry R. Schoolcraft, Office of Indian Affairs, Washington, D. C., printed in Philadelphia, Pa., in 1851. This circular is a reprint of the circular issued in July, 1847, in accordance with the provisions of section 5, chapter 66, of the Laws of the Twenty-ninth Congress, second session, and approved March 3, 1847, which read, " *And be it further enacted*, That in aid of the means now possessed by the Department of Indian Affairs through its existing organization, there be, and hereby is, appropriated the sum of five thousand dollars to enable the said department, under the direction of the Secretary of War, to collect and digest such statistics and material as may illustrate the history, the present condition, and future prospects of the Indian tribes of the United States."

The original circular recites that it was addressed to four classes of individuals, namely, " I. Persons holding positions under the department, who are believed to have it in their power to impart much practical information respecting the tribes who are, respectively, under their charge. II. Persons who have retired from similar situations, travelers in the Indian Territory, or partners and factors on the American frontiers. III. Men of learning or research who have perused the best writers on the subject and who may feel willing to communicate the results of their reading or reflections. IV. Teachers and missionaries to the aborigines."

The circular closes with an expression of the " anxiety which is felt to give to the materials collected the character of entire authenticity, and to be apprised of any erroneous views in the actual manners and customs, character, and condition of our Indian tribes which may have been promulgated. The Government, it is believed, owes it to itself to originate a body of facts on this subject of an entirely authentic character, from which the race at large may be correctly judged by all classes of citizens, and its policy respecting the tribes under its guardianship, and its treatment of them, properly understood and appreciated."

The 348 inquiries in the circular embrace the history (and archeology), the tribal organization, the religion, the manners and customs, the intellectual capacity and character, the present condition, the future prospects, and the language, of the Indian tribes of the United States.

But the report of Mr. Denig consists of brief and greatly condensed replies to as many of the questions propounded in the circular in question as concerned the native tribes of the upper Missouri River, to wit, the Arikara, the Mandan, the Sioux, the Gros Ventres, the Cree, the Crows, the Assiniboin, and the Blackfeet, tribes with whom he was thoroughly acquainted, although the Assiniboin seem to have been the chief subjects of his observations. It should be noted that the answers to some of the questions, if adequately treated, would have required nearly as much space as was devoted to the entire report.

While the facts embodied in the replies of Mr. Denig are, when unqualified, affirmed of all the eight tribes mentioned in his letter of transmittal, he is nevertheless careful, when needful, to restrict many of his answers to the specific tribes to which their subject matter particularly related. But, of course, all the tribes mentioned belonged measurably to a single cultural area at that time.

That Mr. Denig made use of the circular issued by Mr. Schoolcraft is clearly evident from the fact that on the left-hand margin of the manuscript he usually wrote the number of the question to which he was giving an answer.

In the manuscript there appear two quite distinct handwritings, and so it is possible that this particular manuscript is a copy of an original which was retained by the author.

Dr. F. V. Hayden made extensive use of this report in preparation of his " Contributions to the Ethnography and Philology of the Indian Tribes of the Missouri Valley," Philadelphia, C. Sherman & Son, 1862. But he did not give Mr. Denig proper credit for using verbatim numbers of pages of the manuscript without any indication that he was copying a manuscript work from another writer whose position and long experience among them made him an authority on the tribes in question. This piece of plagiarism was not concealed by the bald statement of Doctor Hayden that he was " especially indebted to Mr. Alexander Culbertson, the well-known agent of the American Fur Co., who has spent 30 years of his life among the wild tribes of the Northwest and speaks several of their languages with great ease. To Mr. Andrew Dawson, superintendent of Fort Benton; Mr. Charles E. Galpin, of Fort Pierre; and E. T. Denig, of Fort Union, I am under great obligations for assistance freely granted at all times."

Mr. Edwin Thompson Denig, the author of this manuscript report, was the son of Dr. George Denig and was born March 10, 1812, in McConnellstown, Huntingdon County, Pa., and died in 1862 or 1863 in Manitoba, probably in the town of Pilot Mound, in the vicinity of which his daughters live, or did live in 1910. His legally married wife was the daughter of an Assiniboin chief, by whom he had two daughters, Sara, who was born August 10, 1844, and Ida, who was born August 22, 1854, and one son, Alexander, who was born May 17, 1852, and who was killed by lightning in 1904.

To his early associates Mr. Denig was a myth, more or less, having gone West as a young man and having died there. He lost caste with his family because of his marriage with the Assiniboin woman.

Mr. Denig entered the fur trade in 1833 and became very influential among the tribes of the upper Missouri River. He was for a time a Government scout; then a bookkeeper for the American Fur Co. Earlier he had gone to St. Louis and became connected with the Choteaus and the American Fur Co. Before he was 30 years of age he was living among the Indians as the representative of these two companies in that vast and almost unknown region between the headwaters of the Mississippi and the Missouri Rivers inhabited by tribes of the Sioux.

Mr. Denig became a bookkeeper for the American Fur Co. at Fort Union, situated near the mouth of the Yellowstone River, of the offices of which for a time, about 1843, he was superintendent. Because of his thorough and comprehensive knowledge of the Indians of his adopted tribe, their language, customs, and tribal relations, he was consulted by most of the noted Indian investigators of that period—Schoolcraft, Hayden, and others.

Being a Government scout, Mr. Denig was able to conciliate the Indians during the expedition of Audubon in 1843, making it possible for the great Frenchman to collect his wonderful specimens. A very colorful description of Fort Union was written by Mr. Denig July 30, 1843. This description is found in Volume II, page 180, of "Audubon and His Journals." In it Mr. Denig writes: "Fort Union, the principal and handsomest trading post on the Missouri River, is situated on the north side, about 6½ miles above the mouth of the Yellowstone River; the country around it is beautiful and well chosen for an establishment of the kind." Then after describing in detail the structure and furnishings of the fort, he says: "The principal building in the establishment, and that of the gentleman in charge, or bourgeois, is now occupied by Mr. Culbertson, one of the partners of the company," and farther on, "Next to this is the office, which is devoted exclusively to the business of the company. * * * This department is now under my supervision [viz, E. T. Denig]."

During this period Audubon sojourned with him for some time and spoke of him not only as an agreeable companion but also as a friend who gave him valuable information and enthusiastic assistance. One of his frequent companions at Fort Union was the Belgian priest, Father De Smet. Their correspondence was continued after De Smet had returned to Belgium. (See Life, Letters and Travels of Father De Smet, Chittenden and Richardson, 4 vols., New York, 1905.)

Several plausible but nevertheless quite unsatisfactory etymologic interpretations of the name, Assiniboin, have been made by a number of writers. Among these interpretations are " Stone Roasters," " Stone Warriors," " Stone Eaters," etc. These are unfortunately historically improbable. It appears that difficulty arises from a misconception of the real meaning of the limited or qualified noun it contains, namely, *boin*. This element appears in literature, dialectically varied, as *pour, pouar, poil, poual, bwân, pwan, pwât*, etc. Evidently, it was the name of a group of people, well known to the Cree and the Chippewa tribes, whom they held in contempt and so applied this noun, *boin, bwân, pwât*, etc., to them. The signification of its root *bwâ*(n) or *pwâ*(t) is " to be powerless, incapable, weak." So that *Pwâtak* or *Bwânŭg* (animate plurals) is a term of contempt or derision, meaning " The Weaklings, The Incapable Ones." This name was in large measure restricted to the nomadic group of Siouan tribes in contradistinction from the sedentary or eastern group of

Siouan peoples who were called Nadowesiwŭg, a term appearing in literature in many variant spellings. The name Dakota in its restricted use is the appellation of the group of tribes to which the name *Bwânŭg*, etc., was applied. This fact indicates that the *Assiniboin*, or *Assinibwânŭg*, were recognized as a kind of Dakota or Nakota peoples. Nakota is their own name for themselves. The rupture of the Dakota tribal hegemony thrust some of these peoples northward to the rocky regions about Lake. Winnipeg and the Saskachewan and Assiniboin rivers. So it was these who were called Rock or Stone Dakota (i. e., *Bwânŭg*). It would thus appear that the rupture occurred after there were recognized the two groups of Siouan tribes in the past, namely, the nomadic or western, the Dakota, and the sedentary or eastern, the *Nadowesiwŭg* of literature.

Traditionally, the Assiniboin people are an offshoot of the Wazikute gens of the Yanktonai (Ihañktoⁿwaⁿna) Dakota.

Dr. F. V. Hayden in his " Contributions to the Ethnography and Philology of the Indian Tribes of the Missouri Valley " says that Mr. Denig was " an intelligent trader, who resided for many years at the junction of the Yellowstone and Missouri Rivers as superintendent of Fort Union, the trading post for the Assiniboins." Of the vocabulary of the Assiniboin language, recorded by Mr. Denig, Doctor Hayden wrote that it is " the most important " one theretofore collected. From the citation from Mr. Denig's description of Fort Union in a preceding paragraph it appears that Doctor Hayden is in error in making Mr. Denig superintendent of the fort rather than of the office of the American Fur Co. at that point.

In one of his letters Reverend Father Terwecoren wrote that Mr. Denig, of the St. Louis Fur Co., is " a man of tried probity and veracity."

From references in Audubon, Kurtz, De Smet, Hayden, and Schoolcraft, and as well from a perusal of this manuscript, it is evident that Mr. Denig was an exceptional man, and for more than 20 years was a prominent figure in the fur trade of the upper Missouri River.

In this summary report to Governor Stevens Mr. Denig has succinctly embodied in large measure the culture, the activities, the customs, and the beliefs of the native tribes who occupied the upper Missouri River 75 years ago, more than 75 per cent of which has been lost beyond recovery by contact with the white man. For more than 40 years the native life with which Mr. Denig was in contact has been largely a thing of the past, so that it is futile to attempt to recover it from the remnants of the tribes who formerly traded with Mr. Denig at Fort Union.

In addition to preparing this report to Governor Stevens Mr. Denig also recorded a Blackfoot Algonquian vocabulary of about 70 words, a Gros Ventres Siouan vocabulary, and an Assiniboin Siouan vocabulary of more than 400 words, which was published by School-craft in his fourth volume.

From a letter written February 27, 1923, by Dr. Rudolph Denig, of 56 East Fifty-eighth Street, New York, N. Y., the following interesting biographical matter relating to the ancestry of Mr. Denig is taken:

The Denigs, or "Deneges," trace their descent from one Herald Ericksen, a chieftain, or "smaa kongen," of the Danish island of Manoe in the North Sea, from whose descendant Red Vilmar, about 1460, they derive an unbroken lineage. They were seafarers, commanding their own vessels, and engaged in trade in the North and Baltic Seas.

About 1570 Thorvald Christiansen changed the tradition of the family by becoming a tiller of the soil, having obtained possession of a large farm near Ribe in northern Slesvig, which to this day bears its ancient name of Volling gaard. Christian Thomsen, 1636–1704, was the first of the family to take up a learned profession; he studied theology, and being ordained a minister in the Lutheran Church, he was also the first biographer of the family, in that he left a kind of genealogy inscribed on the flyleaves of his Bible.

His grandson, Frederick Svensen, took part as corporal in a Danish auxiliary corps at the age of 17 in Marlborough's operations in the Netherlands in the war of the Spanish Succession. Following the disbanding of his corps he took up his residence in Cologne, and after a few years he found a permanent home, about 1720, in Biebrich-Mosbach, opposite Mayence.

The two branches of the family at present are the descendants of Philip George and Johan Peter, both sons of Frederick. Johan Peter emigrated to America in 1745, leaving among his descendants Edwin Thompson Denig, the subject of this treatise; Commodore Robert Gracie Denig, United States Navy, his son; Major Robert Livingston Denig, United States Marine Corps, a distinguished soldier of the World War, and Dr. Blanche Denig, a well-known woman physician of Boston.

The descendants of Philip George include Dr. Rudolph C. Denig, professor of clinical ophthalmology in Columbia University, New York, N. Y.

Ethnologically, it may be of more than passing interest to know that the name Denig was originally Denek(e), then Deneg, which was taken as a family name by Frederick Svensen at the time he left Denmark in 1709. Until then the family had followed the old Scandinavian custom of the son taking his father's first name with the suffix sen or son as his family name.

The Denigs came to their present name in the following manner:
After the Kalmar War, 1611–1613, conditions in Denmark became
critical, and the Danes were hard pressed for all the necessaries of
life, especially foodstuffs. They were therefore forced to import
grain from neighboring countries. So it happened that Ludvig
Thorvaldsen, born in 1590, was sent by his father, Thorvald Christiansen, to Valen in Westphalia, a district still renowned for its
agriculture, to buy corn.

Ludvig went there every fall for three or four successive years.
Eventually the Westphalians nicknamed him Deneke; "Den" meaning Dane, and the suffix "eke," like "ike," "ing," and "ig," a diminu-
tive, derivative, or patronymic. Naturally this surname was not
used at home, but it became useful when occasional trips took members of the family outside of Denmark.

The use of such a nom de guerre has always been popular with
Scandinavian and kindred races like the Friesians. As the supply
of available names did not meet the demand, frequent similarity
of names made it difficult to avoid losing one's identity.

When Frederick Svensen Deneg had settled in Biebrich-Mosbach
the name Deneg had to undergo another change. While in the north
the syllable "eg" is pronounced like "ek," the Chatto-Franconian
dialect around Mayence pronounces it like "esh." Automatically,
for euphonic reasons the name was dialectically changed to Denig.
In former times such capricious changes in names were frequently
made. In perusing old chronicles many names are found written
in three or four different ways within one century. An instance to
the point is the Frankish name of King Meroveg, who was also
called Merovig, and his descendants were called Meroveger, Mero-
viger, and Merovinger, according to dialects spoken in the different
regions of the former Frankish empire. This parallels the change
of Deneg to Denig.

Upon his arrival, September 5, 1851, at Fort Union, 3 miles
above the mouth of the Yellowstone River on the Missouri, Mr.
Frederick Kurz, the Swiss artist, of Berne, Switzerland, who had
heard some ugly rumors about Mr. Denig, wrote in his Journal
(yet in manuscript): "Bellange delivered the letter he brought to
a small, hard-featured man, wearing a straw hat, the brim of which
was turned up in the back. He was my new *bourgeois*, Mr. Denig.
He impressed me as a rather prosy fellow. . . . He ordered supper delayed on our account that we might have a better and more
plentiful meal. A bell summoned me to the first table with Mr.
Denig and the clerks. My eyes almost ran over with tears. There
was chocolate, milk, butter, omelet, fresh meat, hot bread—what
a magnificent spread. I changed my opinion at once concerning

this new chief; a hard, niggardly person could not have reconciled himself to such a hospitable reception in behalf of a subordinate who was a total stranger to him" (pp. 205–206). Kurz remained with Denig three years.

Again, Kurz wrote: "In his relations with me he is most kind and agreeable. Every evening he sits with me either in my room or in front of the gate and relates experiences of his earlier life. As he has held his position in this locality for 19 years already, his life has been full of adventure with Indians—particularly since the advent of the whisky flask. He wishes me to paint, also, a portrait of himself and his dog, Natah (Bear), a commission I am very glad to execute" (p. 211).

Again, in speaking of the duties of Mr. Denig, Kurz wrote: "It goes without saying that a *bourgeois* who occupies the position of responsible warden, chief tradesman, and person in highest authority at a trading-post far removed, where he has fifty men under his direction, may regard himself of more importance than a man who directs five men" (p. 213).

Again Kurz wrote: "As a matter of course, Denig keeps the subordinate workmen strictly under his thumb—what is more, he has to, if he is to prevent their overreaching him. He feels, however, that one man alone is not sufficient to enforce good order among these underlings, for every one of them is armed and, though not courageous in general, are, nevertheless, touchy and revengeful. So, for purposes of order and protection he has attached to himself the clerks who stand more nearly on the same level with him in birth and education and afford, besides, the only support, moral as well as physical, upon which he can reckon" (p. 216).

Again Kurz wrote: "He talks to me continually about Indian legends and usages. As he writes the best of these stories for Pere De Smet, by whom they are published, there is no need of my preserving more than some bits of memoranda" (p. 238). This explains why the writings on these matters of Father De Smet have a close family resemblance with those of Mr. Denig.

Again Kurz wrote: "Mr. Denig has been reading to me again from his manuscript, which is extremely interesting. He is very well educated and he has made a thorough study of Indian life—a distinct advantage to him in trade. He is so fond of the life in this part of the country that he is averse to any thought of going back to his Pennsylvania home in the United States. For the reason, as he says, that he may avoid political carryings-on that disgust him" (p. 242).

Another entry in the Kurz Journal reads: "September the 24th. Began a portrait of Mr. Denig—life-size, knee-length. This work is to be finished before Mr. Culbertson's return from Fort Laramie" (p. 254).

The following citation is from the Kurz Journal at page 577: "February the 26th, Mr. Denig is a Swedenborgian and at the same time he is a Freemason. He mentioned to me that it would be of great advantage on my travels if I were a Freemason."

It seems appropriate to insert here briefly what another intimate friend of Mr. Denig, the Reverend Father De Smet, thought of the knowledge and attainments of our author. Father De Smet in speaking of the source of his information in a particular instance wrote: "I have it from two most reliable sources—that is to say, from a man of tried probity and veracity, Mr. Denig of the Saint Louis Fur Company . . ."[1]

On page 1215 of this same work Father De Smet in a personal letter to Mr. Denig, dated September 30, 1852, wrote: "I do not know how to express my gratitude for your very interesting series of narratives concerning the aborigines of the Far West. . . . Nothing could be more gratifying to me than the beautiful and graphic details which you have given me of the religion, manners, customs, and transactions of an unfortunate race of human beings."

It is hoped that these excerpts from the writings of Frederick Kurz and Father De Smet, both intimately associated with Mr. Denig, will supply some data concerning our author not otherwise accessible.

The Swiss artist, Friedrich Kurz, who painted many pictures of the region around Fort Union, lived with Denig for some time, and in 1851 painted his portrait.

The Indians called Mr. Denig "The Long Knife," which simply meant that they knew him as "an American."

In the manuscript Mr. Denig employs the word "band" to denote "a gens of a tribe," the word "clans" to denote "societies" or "corporations," and the "orders of doctors" he calls "shamans or theurgists." To understand Mr. Denig these meanings must be kept in mind.

THE EDITOR.

---

[1] Chittenden, H. M., and Richardson, A. T. Life, letters, and travels of Father Pierre-Jean De Smet, S. J., 1801–1873. Vol. IV, p. 1111. New York, 1905.

LETTER OF TRANSMITTAL

To His Excellency Isaac I. Stevens,
    Governor of Washington Territory.

Sir: Being stimulated with a desire to meet your wishes and forward the views of Government, I have in the following pages endeavored to answer the Inquiries published by act of Congress regarding the history, present condition, and future prospects of the Indian tribes with which I am acquainted.

Had I been called upon to illustrate the facts herein recorded by reference to their different individual histories and actions, a more voluminous and perhaps interesting work might have been presented the general reader, but in conformity to the instructions laid down in the document referred to, have only replied to the various queries, limiting the answers to plain statements of facts.

Independent of my own personal observation and knowledge acquired by a constant residence of 21 years among the prairie tribes in every situation, I have on all occasions had the advice of intelligent Indians as to the least important of these queries, so as to avoid, if possible, the introduction of error. Should there be new ideas presented, and the organization, customs, or present condition of the Indians made public in the following manuscript differ either materially or immaterially from any other now extant I would beg leave to say I would much rather have the same rejected than to see it published in a mutilated form or made to coincide with any histories of the same people from others who have not had like opportunities of acquiring information.

Some of their customs and opinions now presented, although very plain and common to us who are in their daily observance, may not have been rendered in comprehensible language to those who are stranger to these things, and the number of queries, the diversity of subjects, etc., have necessarily curtailed each answer to as few words as possible. In the event, therefore, of not being understood or of apparent discrepancies presenting, it would be but justice done the author and patron to have the same explained, which would be cheerfully done.

It is presumed the following pages exhibit a minutiæ of information on those subjects not to be obtained either by transient visitors or a residence of a few years in the country, without being, as is the

88253°—30——26   393

case with myself, intimately acquainted with their camp regulations, understanding their language, and in many instances entering into their feelings and actions. The whole has been well digested, the different subjects pursued in company with the Indians for an entire year, until satisfactory answers have been obtained, and their motives of speech or action well understood before placing the same as a guide and instruction to others. The answers refer to the Sioux, Arikara, Mandan, Gros Ventres, Cree, Crow, Assiniboin, and Blackfeet Nations, who are designated as prairie roving or wild tribes, further than whom our knowledge does not extend.

I am aware of your capacity to judge the merits of the work, and will consider myself highly honored if I have had the good fortune to meet your approbation. Moreover, I shall rejoice if I have contributed in any degree toward opening a course of policy on the part of Government that may result in the amelioration of the sad condition of the savages. Should the facts herein recorded ever be published or embodied in other works, it is hoped the errors of language may be corrected, but in no instance is it desired that the meaning should miscarry.

Should any references be required by the department for whom this is written I beg leave to name as my friends and personal acquaintances in addition to your Excellency, Col. D. D. Mitchell, Kenneth Mackruger, Esq., Rev. P. I. De Smet, Messrs. P. Chouteau, Jr., & Co., and Alex. Culbertson, Esq., all of St. Louis, and Dr. John Evans, United States geologist, any of whom will satisfy inquiries on this head.

Permit me, my dear friend, to remain with great respect and high consideration, truly your most obedient servant,

Edwin T. Denig.

INDIAN TRIBES OF THE UPPER MISSOURI

By Edwin T. Denig

THE ASSINIBOIN [1]

HISTORY

ORIGIN.—But little traditionary can be stated by these Indians as authentic of their origin which would be entitled to record in history, though many singular and fabulous tales are told concerning it. As a portion of people, however, once inhabiting another district and being incorporated with another nation, their history presents a connected and credible chain of circumstances. The Assiniboin were once a part of the great Sioux or Dacotah Nation, residing on the tributary streams of the Mississippi; say, the head of the Des Moines, St. Peters, and other rivers. This is evident, as their language with but little variation is the same, and also but a few years back there lived a very old chief, known to all of us as Le Gros François, though his Indian name was Wah-he' Muzza or the "Iron Arrow-point," who recollected perfectly the time of their separation from the Sioux, which, according to his data, must have been about the year 1760.[2] He stated that when Lewis and Clark came up the Missouri in 1805 his band of about 60 lodges (called Les Gens des Roches) had after a severe war made peace with the Sioux, who at that time resided on the Missouri, and that he saw the expedition referred to near White Earth River, these being the first body of whites ever seen by them, although they were accustomed to be dealt with by the fur traders of the Mississippi. After their first separation from the Sioux they moved northward, making a peace with the Cree and Chippewa, took possession of an uninhabited country on or near the Saskatchewan and Assiniboin Rivers, in which district some 250 or 300 lodges still reside. Some time after the expedition of Lewis and Clark, or at least after the year 1777, the rest of the Assiniboin, at that time about 1,200 lodges, migrated toward the Missouri, and as soon as they found superior advantages regarding game and trade, made

[1] Consult Preface for etymologic analysis of this word and for its objective meaning.
[2] This traditional date given by Denig is evidently much too late, for as early as the middle of the seventeenth century they were known to the Jesuit missionaries of Canada.

the latter country their home. One principal incident in their history which they have every reason to remember and by which many
of the foregoing data are ascertained is a visitation of the smallpox
in 1780 (see Mackenzie's travels), when they occupied the British
territory. Even yet there are two or three Indians living who are
marked by the disease of that period and which greatly thinned their
population, though owing to their being separated through an immense district, some bands entirely escaped. Upon the whole it does
not appear to have been as destructive as the same disease on the
Missouri in 1838, which I will have occasion to mention in its proper
place in these pages and which reduced them from 1,200 lodges to
about 400 lodges.

NAME AND GEOGRAPHICAL POSITION.—The name of the Assiniboin
among themselves is Da-co-tah, same as the Sioux, which means " our
people." By the Sioux they are called Ho'-hai or "Fish-eaters,"
perhaps from the fact that they lived principally on fish while on
the British grounds, as most of those Indians do. By the Cree
and Chippewa they are called As-see-nee-poi-tuc or Stone Indians;
hence the English name of Assiniboin arises. As has been stated,
at the earliest date known they roved about the head of St. Peters,
Des Moines, Lac du Diable, and Lac qui Parle; and they were then
joined with the Sioux Indians, who inhabited and claimed all the
lands between the Mississippi and the Missouri as low down as Big
Sioux River and as high up as the head of Rivier à Jacques, thence
northward toward Lac du Diable, other bands of Sioux (Teton)
residing west of the Missouri. The number of Assiniboin when they
separated must have been at least 1,500 lodges, averaging six souls
to a lodge [or about 9,000 persons]. Their migration has been
referred to and the extent of land they occupied in the British territory on the Saskatchewan, etc., was very large, but at present their
habitat is entirely different, and it may be as well to state it here.
The northern Assiniboin, 250 or 300 lodges, rove the country from
the west banks of the Saskatchewan, Assiniboin, and Red Rivers
in a westward direction to the Woody Mountains north and west
among small spurs of the Rocky Mountains east of the Missouri, and
among chains of small lakes through this immense region. Occasionally making peace with some of the northern bands of Blackfeet
enables them to come a little farther west and deal with those Indians,
but, these " peaces " being of short duration, they are for the most
part limited to the prairies east and north of the Blackfeet range.
The rest of the Assiniboin, say 500 to 520 lodges [who may be called
the Southern Assiniboin], occupy the following district, viz, commencing at the mouth of the White Earth River on the east, extending up that river to its head, thence northwest along the Couteau

de Prairie, or Divide, as far as the Cyprus Mountains on the North Fork of the Milk River, thence down Milk River to its junction with the Missouri River, thence down the Missouri River to the mouth of White Earth River, or the starting point. Formerly they inhabited a portion of country on the south side of the Missouri River along the Yellowstone River, but of late years, having met with great losses by Blackfeet, Sioux, and Crow war parties, they have been obliged to abandon this region and now they never go there. As before remarked, the Assiniboin still numbered 1,000 to 1,200 lodges, trading on the Missouri until the year 1838, when the smallpox reduced their numbers to less than 400 lodges. Also, being surrounded by large and hostile tribes, war has had its share in their destruction, though now they are increasing slowly.

ANCIENT AND MODERN HABITAT.—Before proceeding further it would be well to state and bear in mind that of all the Indians now residing on the Missouri River the Assiniboin appear to have made the least progress toward acquiring civilized ideas or knowledge of any kind. Superstitious, lazy, and indisposed to thought, they make no attempt to improve themselves in any way. Neither are they anxious that others should teach them; consequently they are far behind the other tribes even as regards their own savage manner of life. This will receive further explanation. They do not think the Great Spirit created them on or for a particular portion of country, but that he made the whole prairie for the sole use of the Indian, and the Indian to suit the prairie, giving among other reasons the fact that the buffalo is so well adapted to their wants as to meat and clothing, even for their lodges and bowstrings. To the Indian is allotted legs to run, eyes to see far, bravery, instinct, watchfulness, and other capacities not developed in the same degree in the whites. The Indian, therefore, occupies any section of prairie where game is plentiful and he can protect himself from enemies. With regard to any other kind of right than that of possession and ability to defend, besides the general right granted by the Great Spirit, they have not the most distant idea. The Assiniboin conquered nothing to come into possession of their habitat, they had their difficulties with surrounding tribes and still have, as others have, and continue as they commenced, fighting and hunting alternately. Their first interview with Europeans (now spoken of) was when the traders of the Mississippi pushed their traffic as far as their camps, and from whom they obtained firearms, woolen clothing, utensils, etc. Afterwards these supplies were had from the Hudson Bay Co. and, latterly, from the Americans on the Missouri River. There is every reason to believe that the introduction of ardent spirits among them was coeval, if not antecedent, to that of any other article of trade.

Before the trade was opened with them by the whites they say they used knives made of the hump rib of the buffalo, hatchets made of flint stone, mallets of the same, cooking utensils of clay and wood, bones for awls, and sinew for thread, all of which articles can yet be found among them.   They made with these rude tools their bows and arrows, pointing the latter with stone, and, as game was abundant, hunted them on foot or threw them into pens built for the purpose, which method they continue to use to this day.   In this way they had no difficulty in supporting themselves, and so contend that they have gained nothing by intimacy with the whites but diseases which kill them off in numbers and wants which they are unable at all times to gratify.   They have never sold lands by treaty, and the only treaty (with the exception of that at Laramie, 1851) was made by them through an Indian agent of the United States named Wilson, at the Mandan village in 1825.   But this was merely an amicable alliance for the protection of American traders and an inducement held out to the Indians to leave off trading at the Hudson Bay Co.'s posts and establish themselves on the Missouri, without, however, any remuneration on the part of the United States.

VESTIGES OF EARLY TRADITION.—They have no creditable tradition of the Mosaic account of the creation or deluge, neither of their ancestors having lived in other lands nor knowledge of foreign quadrupeds nor any idea of whites or other races occupying the country before the Indians.   It is easy to perceive in converse with them that whites have from time to time endeavored to explain the Mosaic account of the creation and deluge, together with other scriptural records, but instead of comprehending the same they have mixed with their own superstitions and childish notions in so many various and nonsensical forms that none is worthy of record.

They have no name for America, neither do they know of its extent, for the most part believing that the lands occupied by themselves and the surrounding tribes compose the greatest part of the world, and certainly contain the greatest reputed number of people. It vexes and grieves them to be told of large tracts of land elsewhere, and they do not or will not believe the whites to be as human as they are.

There is nothing in this subject any Assiniboin could either comprehend or answer, except that there is a mound about 50 miles above the mouth of the Yellowstone on the west side and near the Missouri consisting of an immense pile of elk horns, covering an area of about an acre of ground, and in height about 30 feet.   We have frequently inquired of these and the surrounding nations as to its origin, but it was raised previous to the knowledge or even tradition of any tribe now living in these parts.   From the state of decay the horns are in it must be very ancient.

NAMES AND EVENTS IN HISTORY.—There is no great event in the history of the Assiniboin that gives them cause to rejoice. True, they have occasionally gained a battle, but at other times have lost greatly by wars. Upon the whole they have had the worst of it; at least they, being a smaller nation than the Blackfeet and Sioux (their enemies) have felt the loss more severely. The principal calamity that first overtook them, and by which they suffered greatly, was the smallpox in 1780. (See Mackenzie's travels and other authors.) On this occasion they lost about 300 lodges of their people, and it is to this day mentioned by them as their greatest first misfortune. In the spring of 1838 this disease was again communicated to them, being brought up the Missouri by a steamboat, and although every precaution had been used, the boat cleansed, and no appearance of disease for a long time aboard, yet it in some way broke out among the Indians, beginning with the Sioux tribes and ending with the Blackfeet. Being an eyewitness to this, we can with certainty give an account of its ravages. When the disease first appeared in Fort Union we did everything in our power to prevent the Indians from coming to it, trading with them a considerable distance out in the prairie and representing to them the danger of going near the infection. All efforts of the kind, however, proved unavailing, for they would not listen, and 250 lodges contracted the disease at one time, who in the course of the summer and fall were reduced to 65 men, young and old, or about 30 lodges in all. Other bands coming from time to time caught the infection and remained at the fort, where the dead were daily thrown into the river by cartloads. The disease was very virulent, most of the Indians dying through delirium and hemorrhage from the mouth and ears before any spots appeared. Some killed themselves.

On one occasion an Indian near the fort after losing his favorite child deliberately killed his wife, his two remaining children, his horses and dogs, and then blew his own brains out. In all this the Indians behaved extremely well toward the whites, although aware they brought the disease among them, yet nothing in the way of revenge took place, either at the time or afterwards. Being obliged to be all the time with them, helping as much as possible to save a few, they had plenty of opportunities should they have wished to do damage. Every kind of treatment appeared to be of no avail, and they continued dying until near the ensuing spring, when the disease, having spent itself, ceased. The result was that out of 1,000 lodges and upward of the Assiniboin then in existence but 400 lodges or less remained, and even these but thinly peopled. Relationship by blood or adoption was nearly annihilated, all property lost or sacrificed, and a few very young and very old left to

mourn the loss. Most of the principal men having died, it took years
to recover from the shock. Young men had to grow up, new leaders
to be developed, remnants of bands to be gathered together, property
to be had—in fact, under all these adverse circumstances, so slow
has been the increase that during the interim of 17 years but 100
lodges have accumulated. In times like this no leader can be effective. All counsel was rejected; their chiefs and divining men
shared the fate of the others. With the Mandan the disease was even
more destructive. Before it they numbered 600 warriors and inhabited two large villages where the Arikara are now stationed,
and when the disease ceased about 30 men remained, from which
remnant have since sprung about 25 lodges. All this time an Assiniboin chief named The Gauche, or by the Indians " He who holds
the knife," was the principal man in the band which bore his name,
consisting of 250 lodges.

These died in greater proportion than the others and after the
disease had disappeared the old chief found himself at the head of
about 60 fighting men. The Gauche was a very old man and had
had the smallpox in the north; he was also famed in their annals
as a leader and divining man. He had been very successful in his
expeditions against the Blackfeet, and by the use of poisons administered occasionally to his people, while predicting their death, he
had inspired in all the fear of a sorcerer. His life contains a history
which our limits do not admit of describing, although well known,
singular, interesting, and authentic. On this occasion he understood that the Mandan were rendered totally helpless by the effects
of the smallpox, and conceived the idea of taking their village and in
a measure retrieving his losses by the horses and other property of
these Indians. Gathering together the remnant of his band, about 50
men, he proceeded thither. The writer saw him pass with the pipe
of peace to lull suspicion, in order to enter their village in a friendly
way, and then at a given signal each one with knife in hand to rush
upon and destroy the unsuspecting friends. The whole was well
planned, managed, and kept secret, and it would have succeeded but
for an occurrence of which the Assiniboin was not then aware. The
Arikara, a tolerably numerous people, having left the Missouri, had
been for years residing on the Platte River, and having previously
had the smallpox did not contract the disease to any extent. About
the same time The Gauche was on his way to the Mandan, they returned suddenly from the Platte and took possession of their village
a short distance from the Mandan. Now the Arikara numbered
about 500 men, all deadly enemies to the Assiniboin, so that when the
latter presented their pipe of peace the ceremonies were interrupted
by an attack of the Arikara. The Assiniboin were routed, and
about 20 of them killed.

The old chief, as usual, escaped, though his day of power was over. Shortly afterwards he predicted the day and hour of his own death at the fort—days beforehand, without any appearance of disease or approaching dissolution, and the writer with other gentlemen at the fort saw the same fulfilled to the letter. The conclusion was that he took poison, which he was long supposed to have received from the whites in the north and kept a dose for the fullness of time.

This man had more renown than any other leader spoken of, although several have done gallant actions. His success may be attributed to great cunning and the large force he always headed, together with the power his fetishes gave him over his fellows, who blindly followed his instructions and fought desperately under his prophecies, though his life shows the anomaly of a great leader being entirely destitute of every particle of personal intrepidity. Many other events have happened which form data in their history; indeed it is composed of reference to certain remarkable occurrences, such as the year of the smallpox, year of the deep snow, year of massacre of 30 lodges of Blackfeet, year of great rise of waters, and other natural phenomena.

PRESENT RULERS AND CONDITION.—Their present ruling chief is Man-to-was-ko, or the Crazy Bear, made chief by Colonel Mitchell, Commissioner of the United States, at the Laramie treaty in 1851. The choice could not have been better. The Crazy Bear has always been a respectable and brave man, greatly elevated above all the rest in intelligence but not ranking with some in military exploits, having never been a great warrior, though on some small occasions he has shown an utter contempt of death before his enemies. He is a mild, politic man, looking after his people's interest, and viewing with a jealous eye anything inconsistent with them. Even when a very young man his opinions were always honored with a hearing in council, and he now bears his honors with great credit to himself and service to his people, endeavoring to carry out to the letter the stipulations of the treaty to which he is a party.

Among the principal soldiers and war captains may be mentioned To-ka′-ke-a-na, or the " First Who Flies." This man is a son of the old chief, Wah-hé Muzza, or "Iron Arrowpoint," mentioned before. The whole of that old man's numerous family have been, and those living still are, desperate men, proud and overbearing with their people, though good to the whites. From the eldest, named " The Sight," who visited Washington City by General Jackson's orders, to the one now mentioned, five in number have been killed by their own people in personal quarrels.

The one now spoken of has frequently led parties to battle and showed such a recklessness of danger that his name stands high as a warrior; has also killed two of his own people who were concerned in the murder of his brothers; was at the Laramie treaty and since behaves himself with great moderation; is one of the Crazy Bear's principal soldiers and supports; and should the Bear die would undoubtedly take his place as chief of the tribe.

Wa-ké-un-to, or the Blue Thunder, is another warrior and partisan in a band of 200 lodges, is not over 25 years of age, but has raised himself to distinction by going to war alone on the Sioux and bringing home scalps and horses; he has also headed several war excursions with great success and is generally liked by his own people.

Wo'-a-see'-chah, or Bad Animal, known to traders by the name of Le Serpent, is a war leader and chief of Les Gens des Canots Band, the same 200 lodges of which Blue Thunder is one of the warriors and camp soldiers. I believe he has never killed many enemies but has murdered in quarrels two of his own people, is considered a sensible man, very friendly to the whites, judicious in his government of his band, and also is a person whom it is not desirable to aggravate too much. Me-nah (The Knife), A-wah-min-ne-o-min-ne (The Whirlwind), Ish-ta-o-ghe-nah (Gray Eyes), He-boom-an-doo (La Poudrière), and others are soldiers and warriors whose histories are known to us and would present the usual features of savage life and warfare.

The Assiniboin speak but one dialect, being radically the same as the Sioux; no other is incorporated in it, though some few can in addition speak Cree and others of the northern bands of Blackfeet, but no more than one interpreter is required in transacting any business with each or all of them. A person who can speak the Sioux language well could interpret for the Assiniboin, or vice versa.

There are many elderly persons capable of stating their traditions and willing to impart any information they are in possession of regarding their history; but what is heard from them in this respect is so mingled with fable and superstition as seldom to admit of its serving as a basis for truth or knowledge or for a correct representation of their past condition. They do not exhibit any chain of connected facts; and though these oral tales have been preserved entire, transmitted in their original form through successive generations, and may possibly have been the belief of their ancestors, yet at the present day are regarded more as a source of amusement than a medium of instruction or means of perpetuating their history. Too much error has been the result of depending for knowledge on these traditions by people who only understand them in their literal sense or have been badly interpreted. All facts among the nations with whom we profess an intimate acquaintance and minute knowledge farther than a century back are involved in obscurity, mingled with fable, or embodied in their superstitions.

The time when the tribe reached its present location was from 1804 to 1825, when the most of them might be considered as established on the waters of the Missouri, the boundaries of which have been pointed out, though in 1839, 60 lodges of Assiniboin came over from the British northern possessions and joined those of the Missouri, since which time they have resided together.

INTERTRIBAL RANK AND RELATIONS.—As to the question, what rank and relationship does the tribe bear to other tribes, we are not aware of any political scale of superiority or inferiority existing among any of the tribes along the Missouri; neither do their traditions point out or assign any such particular position to each other. Being well acquainted with the manners and customs of the Sioux, the Arikara, the Mandan, the Gros Ventres, the Crow, the Assiniboin, the Cree, and the Blackfeet tribes we can safely say that no such distinction exists that would receive the sanction of all parties. There is, however, this: Each nation has vanity enough to think itself superior to its neighbors, but all think the same, and the more ignorant they are the more obstinately they adhere to their own opinions. All tribes are pretty much independent of one another in their thoughts and actions, and, indeed with the exception of the Gros Ventres, the Mandan and the Arikara, who are stationary and live in a manner together, neighboring tribes usually are completely in the dark regarding one another's government, not even knowing the names of the principal chiefs and warriors unless told them or recognizing them when pointed out. In all the above-mentioned tribes there is no such thing as pretensions to original rank. Rank is the growth of the present, as often acquired as lost. The greatest chief any of these tribes ever produced would become a mere toy, a butt, a ridicule, in a few days after he lost his eyes or sense of sight.

Neither has affinity of blood in this sense anything to do with rank as to succession. If the son for want of bravery or other qualifications can not equal or follow the steps of his father chief, he is nothing more than an ordinary Indian. There are consequently no discordant pretensions to original rank, though it may be a matter of dispute which of two or three chiefs ranks at present the highest, and in this case it would be immediately decided in council by the principal men. In fact the rank or standing of each Indian, be he chief or warrior, is so well known, and his character so well judged by the vox populi that he takes his place spontaneously. A higher step than his acts and past conduct confer, imprudently taken, would have the effect of injuring him in their eyes as a leader. Every chief, warrior, or brave carves his own way to fame, and if recognized as one by the general voice becomes popular and is supported; if not, he mixes with hundreds of others who are in the same situation, waiting an opportunity to rise. There is no relative rank among tribes bearing the name of uncle, grandfather, etc. The names of the different bands among themselves or the surrounding tribes have no such signification. There are, of course, affinities of blood and relationship among the Indians as well as among whites. People have their fathers, uncles, grandfathers, brothers-in-law, etc., but this personal or family relationship has nothing to do with the clanship, nor has it any bearing on other tribes. As to the relations above alluded to we will have occasion to refer to them under the head of tribal organization and government. Among eastern or southern tribes such distinctions may exist, but we can vouch they have no name nor interest in all the tribes mentioned in the beginning of this answer. To prevent misunderstanding, it should be observed that when we speak of a tribe we mean the whole group who speak that language. Different tribes are different groups. Portions of these groups or tribes are called gentes, and portions or societies of these gentes are designated as subgentes, and the next or most minute subdivision of gentes would be into families.

"Peaces" are made between wild tribes by the ceremony of smoking and exchanging presents of horses and other property; sometimes women. The advantages and disadvantages are well calculated on both sides before overtures for peace are made. It is a question of loss and gain and often takes years to accomplish. The Crows, a rich nation, five years ago, through the writer as the medium made peace with the Assiniboin after half a century of bloody warfare. Why? The Crows being a rich nation and the Assiniboin poor, how could the former gain? The points the Crows gained were these: First, liberty to hunt in the Assiniboin country unmolested and secure from the Blackfeet; second, two enemies less to contend with and from whom they need not guard their numerous herds of horses; third, the privilege of passing through the Assiniboin country to the Gros Ventres village in quest of corn. Now for the other party. The Crows having large herds of horses and the Assiniboin but few, the former give them a good many every year to preserve the peace. The Crows winter with the Assiniboin, run buffalo with their own horses, and give the latter plenty of meat and skins without the trouble of killing it. The Crows are superior warriors and the others have enough to contend with the Blackfeet. Again, one enemy less, and jointly the numerical force is so augmented as to make them formidable to all surrounding tribes, while separately they would prey upon each other. It is in this case evident the peace must last, there being sufficient inducements on both sides to keep it, although upon the whole any of their "peaces" are liable to sudden and violent interruptions and are not to be depended upon.

MAGNITUDE AND RESOURCES OF TERRITORY A CAUSE OF THE MULTIPLI- CATION OF TRIBES.—There can be no doubt that magnitude and re- sources of territory are the principal causes of an increase of popula- tion. All roving tribes live by hunting, and scarcity of animals produces distress, famine, disease, and danger by forcing them to hunt in countries occupied by their enemies, when game is not found in their own. Such a state of things happened in this district in 1841, when during a total disappearance of buffalo and other game some of the Assiniboin and Cree were under the necessity of eating their own children, of leaving others to perish, and many men and women died from fatigue and exhaustion. Although the above posi- tion is evident, yet we do not see how it could multiply tribes, much less dialects. A large territory with much game might induce por- tions of other tribes not having these advantages to migrate, make peace with the residing nation, and perhaps increase in a greater ratio than they otherwise would have done, but the language would remain the same, neither would it produce a separate tribe, but only a portion of the tribe who migrated.

The Gros Ventres of the Prairie were once Arapaho and lived on the Arkansas. They have for a century past resided with the Black- feet, yet have preserved their own language. True, by these means they learn to speak each other's language, but they do not commingle and make a separate dialect of the two. The Assiniboin from the Sioux, the Cree from the Chippewa, the Crows from the Gros Ventres are three other cases of separation, and in each the language is so well preserved that they understand without any difficulty the people whence they emanated. The causes of these separations, whether feuds, family discords, or in quest of better hunting grounds, does not now appear. Most probably it was dissatisfaction of some sort. From all appearances we may reasonably expect to see ere long a portion of the Sioux occupying the large disputed territory south of the Missouri and along the Yellowstone, as game is becoming scarce in their district since white emigration through it and Indians are thronging there from St. Peters and elsewhere.

The Sioux regard the Mississippi as once their home, and it is very certain that nation came from thence, also the Cree and Assiniboin, and perhaps others. It does not appear that the track of migration pursued any direct course. From certain facts, similitude of lan- guage and customs, it would seem some nations traveled from south to north or northwest, such as the Gros Ventres of the Prairie who were once Arapaho. The Arikara speak the same as the Pawnee and must have migrated westward. The Blackfeet moved from north to southwest, and the Crows, Cree, and Assiniboin west and north. It is reasonable to believe they spread out over these immense plains from all points and at different times as circumstances favored or forced them. The habits of the prairie Indian differ essentially from the Indian of the forest, and those of stationary and cultivating habits from both. It is impossible for us now to state with any degree of certainty the time of their first location on these plains, or to point out any one general course of emigration pursued by them.

GEOGRAPHY

FIGURE OF THE GLOBE.—It can not be expected that these Indians who are in a complete savage and unenlightened state should have any knowledge of the configuration of the globe or of its natural divisions. They know what a small lake or small island is and have names for the same as they are to be met with through their country. They think the earth to be a great plain bounded by the Rocky Mountains on one side and the sea on the other, but have no idea of its extent nor of any other lands except those they are acquainted with. Although told frequently, they can not realize extent of lands in any great measure, and without troubling themselves to think or inquire are content with believing there are few lands better or larger than their own. It is not in their nature to acknowledge inferiority, which would follow were they convinced of the extent of the territory and power of the whites. Of the sea they have a vague idea from information offered them by the traders, and would not believe there is such a body of water had not the same received a sort of sanction through the Cree and Chippewa, some of whom, having seen Lake Superior, represent it as the ocean.

LOCAL FEATURES OF THE HABITAT.—The chief rivers running through the Assiniboin country are, first, the Missouri, which is so well known as to need no description here. The next is Milk River, on the northwest boundary, a very long and narrow stream; heads in some of the spurs of the Rocky Mountains east of the Missouri and lakes on the plains, runs a southwest course, and empties into the Missouri about 100 miles above the Yellowstone. Its bed is about 200 yards wide at the mouth, though the waters seldom occupy more than one-third of that space, except during the spring thaw, when, for a week or two, it fills the whole bed; is fordable on horseback all the year except at the time above alluded to and when swollen by continuous rains.

Rivière aux Tremble, or Quaking Aspen River, empties into the Missouri about 50 miles below Milk River, is about half the length and breadth of the others, and heads in the range of hills constituting the divide, called "Les Montaignes des Bois." It is fordable at all times except during spring freshets and when swollen by rain. Neither of these streams is navigable by any craft larger than a wooden canoe except at the high stages of water above referred to, and then navigation would be difficult and dangerous owing to floating ice and driftwood. There are no rapids or falls in either of them.

Several creeks fall into the Missouri below the point on the east side called Big Muddy, Little Muddy, Knife River, etc., all of which contain but little water and are of no consequence.

White Earth River, the last, is about 100 miles in length and at the mouth a little more than 100 yards wide, contains but little water, always fordable, and not navigable by anything, empties into the Missouri near the commencement of the Great Bend. None of these rivers being navigable except the Missouri, goods are only landed at the following points along that river, viz: Fort Pierre (Sioux), mouth of the Teton River; Fort Clarke (Arikara) at their village; Fort Berthold (Gros Ventres village); Fort Union (Assiniboin), mouth of Yellowstone. Steamboats have gone up the Missouri as high as the mouth of Milk River, but heretofore goods for Fort Benton (Blackfeet), near the mouth of Maria River, have been transported by keel boats from Fort Union.

We know of no large navigable lakes in this district, though along the northern boundary there are many small ones, or rather large ponds of water, without any river running through them or visible outlet, being fed by snows, rain, and springs, and diminished by evaporation and saturation. Lakes of this kind are to be met with in many places on the plains and differ in size from 100 yards to 2 or 3 miles or even more in circumference, are not wooded, and contain tolerably good water. Small springs are also common, most of them having a mineral taste, though none are large enough to afford water power.

SURFACE OF THE COUNTRY.—The whole country occupied by the Assiniboin is one great plain, hills and timber only occurring where rivers run, in the valleys of which good land for cultivation is found, but the general feature appears to be sterile as regards arable land, producing, however, grasses of different kinds, some of which are very nutritious, and particularly adapted to raising horses, cattle, and sheep. The prairies may be said to be interminable and destitute of the least particle of timber except along the banks of the few streams before mentioned, and even these but thinly wooded. Water, however, can always be found in the small lakes and rivers spoken of. The Assiniboin do not cultivate the soil in any way, though the Gros Ventres and Arikara raise corn and pumpkins to some extent on the Missouri bottoms. By experiments made at or near Fort Union,

we find that oats, potatoes, corn, and all garden vegetables grow
well if the season be favorable. The soil, being light and sandy,
requires frequent rains to produce good crops, which happens about
one year in three; the others fail from drought and destruction by
grasshoppers, bugs, and other insects. The natural productions of
the country are few and such as no one but an Indian could relish.
A wild turnip called by them teep-see-na, and by the French pomme
blanche, when boiled is eatable, is found in quantity everywhere on
the plains, will sustain life alone for a great length of time either
cooked or in its raw state, can be dried and preserved for years, or
pulverized and made into passable bread.

Wild rhubarb is found and eaten either raw or cooked. It has
rather a pleasant sweetish taste. Artichokes grow in quantites near
marshes. Chokecherries, bullberries, service berries, buds of the
wild rose, red plums, and sour grapes are the principal fruits and
are greatly sought after by the Indians, preserved, dried, cooked, and
eaten in various ways, and considered by them great luxuries. Wild
hops are in abundance which possess all the properties of the culti-
vated hop. These are all of any note the country produces.

FACILITIES FOR GRAZING.—These Indians raise no stock of any
kind, though judging from that raised at Fort Union it is one of the
best grazing countries in the world. The supply of grasses of spontaneous growth is inexhaustible and very nutritious. The only difficulty is the severe cold winter and depth of snow, though if animals
were provided for and housed during the severe cold we know that
a hardier and better stock can be raised than in the States. As yet,
however, no market being open for surplus stock and but few raised
for the use of the fort, our attention has not been much directed to
that business, but have no hesitation in advancing the opinion that
horses, horned cattle, and sheep would thrive and increase well with
proper care. We are not able to say whether water could at all
times be had by digging on the high prairie and in the absence of
springs or creeks, never having tried the experiment, though the
country abounds in small lakes, cool springs, and creeks where good
localities for grazing purposes could always be chosen. In the
winter animals appear to want very little water and generally eat
snow in its place.

EFFECTS OF FIRING THE PRAIRIES.—We presume there must be
some mistake that any of the tribes residing on the plains set them
on fire to facilitate the purposes of hunting. It has the contrary
effect, driving the game out of their own country into that of their
neighbors. Buffalo may pass through a burnt country covered with
snow, but can not remain, and travel until they meet with suitable
grazing. Consequently the greatest precautions are used by both
Indians and whites to prevent their taking fire in the fall, when the

grass is dry (the only time it will burn), and the most severe penalties short of death are imposed on any person, either white or red,
who even by accident sets the prairie on fire. A good thrashing with
bows and sometimes tomahawking is in store for the poor traveler
who has been so forgetful as not to put out his camp fires and they
extend to the plains. These fires are made mostly by returning war
parties, either with the view of driving the buffalo out of their
enemy's country or as signals to their own people of success in their
expedition, though sometimes they originate in accident or petty
malice of individuals. With regard to its injuring the soil it has no
such effects; on the contrary, the next crop of grass is more beautiful
than the other, as the undergrowth and briars are by that means
destroyed. The same, unfortunately, is not the case with the timber.
There are no forests on the plains to burn, though where the fire
passes through the bottoms of the Missouri it consumes and kills
great quantities of timber, which dries and decays and is only replaced in time by younger saplings. Fruit bushes are also destroyed,
though they recover its effects in three or four years.

WASTE LANDS.—In this section there are no deserts or barren land
of any extent; though there are some marshes, pools, and swamps
which, however, are not so close together or extensive as to form
any formidable obstruction to roads. Even if they could not be
drained or otherwise disposed of, they could be left on either side
of the way. Neither do these appear to affect the health of any of
the Indians more than being the cause of producing hosts of mos-
quitoes, which are very annoying to man and beast.

EFFECTS OF VOLCANIC ACTION.—We are not aware of any remarkable appearances of this kind,[3] neither are there to be found extensive sand plains or other tracts entirely destitute of herbage. The
cactus is found everywhere, but not in such quantity as to destroy
herbage or be a hindrance to animals traveling. A mile or two
may occasionally be found where herbage is comparatively scarce.
Still, even in these places there is sufficient for animals for a short
time.

SALINE PRODUCTIONS.—We do not feel ourselves competent to state
the properties of the mineral springs so common throughout all
this country. Some of them no doubt contain Glauber salt, as they
operate as a violent cathartic; others have the taste of copper, sul-
phur, etc. What the country would produce in the way of gypsum,
saltpeter, etc., we can not say, never having witnessed any geological
or mineral researches and being personally completely uninformed
regarding this branch of science.

---

[3] There are portions of pumice stone and other things occasionally picked up that have
undergone volcanic action; also burning hills, but no eruptions.

COAL AND MINERAL PRODUCTS.—Dr. J. Evans, who lately traveled through this country, can enlighten you on this subject. As for us, we must plead unadulterated ignorance.

CLIMATE

The climate is pure and dry and perhaps the healthiest in the world. In the months of May and June, when east winds prevail, much rain falls, but during the rest of summer and fall the season is generally dry and moderately warm, except a short time in July and August, when intensely hot. There are occasionally severe thunderstorms accompanied by rain or hail; not more, however, than three or four in a summer, and these in a few hours swell the smallest streams so as to overflow their banks, but with the ceasing of the rain they fall as suddenly as they rise, and do no damage, as there are neither crops nor fences to injure. Tornadoes we have never seen here, although they do happen on the Missouri far below this place. Severe gales are occasionally met with, lasting but a few minutes. With regard to temperature and other natural phenomena I refer you to the accompanying tables.

WILD ANIMALS

The most numerous and useful animal in this country is unquestionably the buffalo, both as regards the sustenance of all the Indians and gain of the traders. Any important decrease of this animal would have the effect of leaving the Indians without traders, no returns of smaller skins being sufficient to pay the enormous expense of bringing supplies so far and employing such a number of people. Buffalo are very numerous, and we do not, after 20 years' experience, find that they decrease in this quarter, although upward of 150,000 are killed annually throughout the extent of our trade, without taking into consideration those swamped, drowned, calves frozen to death, destroyed by wolves, or in embryo, etc. It yet would appear that their increase is still greater than their destruction, as during last winter (1852–53) there were more found in this quarter, and indeed in the whole extent of our trade, than had been seen for many years before.

The buffalo is the Indian's whole dependence. It serves him for all his purposes—meat, clothing and lodging, powder horns, bowstrings, thread and hair to make saddles. In the winter season the hides are dressed, made into robes and traded to whites, by which means they are able to buy all their necessaries and even some luxuries. Robes are worth about $3 each, and although the number sent to market is great, yet the high price paid for them to Indians and the danger of transportation is such that fortunes are more easily and often lost than made at the business. Beaver were formerly numerous and valuable, therefore much hunted by whites and Indians, but of late years the price of that fur being greatly reduced, and the danger of hunting considerable, does not induce either whites or Indians to hunt them. This animal has been trapped and killed to such an extent as to threaten their entire extinction, though for the last 10 or 12 years, since beaver trapping by large bodies of men has been abandoned, they have greatly increased, and are now to be found tolerably plentiful in all the small streams and in the Missouri and Yellowstone. These Indians do not and never did trap them much; though the Crow and the Cree still make good beaver hunts, they do not rely much on this either as a source of profit or food.

Elk, deer, bighorn, and antelope are numerous and afford a means of living and profit to the Indians although they are not hunted to any extent except in a great scarcity of buffalo. From this circumstance they do not diminish and are found now in much the same numbers as 20 years back.

Wolves are very plentiful and of three kinds, the large white wolf, the large grayback wolf, and the small prairie wolf, all a good deal hunted and many killed, though they continue to increase. They follow the buffalo in large bands, waiting an opportunity to pounce upon one that has been wounded or mired. They also destroy a great many small calves in the month of May when they are brought forth. The skins of the larger kind are worth 70 cents to $1 each; the smaller about 50 cents each.

Red and gray foxes, hares, badgers, skunks, wild cats, otters, ermines, and muskrats are found and killed when opportunity offers. Of all these the red fox appears to be the only one that has diminished in numbers. We are not aware that any animals have disappeared altogether, nor of any perceptible decrease of any except the beaver and red fox. The Indians kill only as many buffalo as are wanted for meat and hides. Taking only as many hides as their women can dress, they do not destroy them wantonly to any extent; consequently the destruction is limited, and that not being equivalent to the increase, but little diminution, if any, is perceptible, and the trade as long as this is the case can not have the effect of exterminating them. It is different as regards the beaver and fox. Their skins require no labor except drying, and being slower to increase must of course be the first to disappear if hunted. Grizzly bears are tolerably numerous on the Missouri and Yellowstone and are not hunted often, although killed occasionally. The animal being ferocious is not much sought after by the Indians.

ANCIENT BONES AND TRADITIONS OF THE MONSTER ERA.—The Indians know from bones found that such animals existed and were of immense size, but their traditions never make mention of the living animal. To these bones, etc., they assign the general name of Wanwan-kah, which is a creature of their own imagination, half spirit, half animal. Any whirlwind or great tempest would be attributed to the movements of the Wan-wan-kah, also any other natural phenomenon. Many stories are told of its actions, but all are fabulous, although they profess to believe in the existence of its powers, some even stating they have seen it crossing the Missouri in the form of a large fish covering half the breadth of that river.[4]

ANIMALS USED AS ARMORIAL MARKS.—These armorial marks or symbols, such as the eagle, owl, bear, serpent, etc., do not represent any tribal organization but kinship occasionally. Neither do they refer to any traditions of any early date, but are insignia adopted by themselves as their medicine or charm. Most Indians have a charm of this kind, either in consequence of some dream or of an idea that the figure has some effect in carrying out his views regarding war, the chase, or the health of his family. These are assumed for his own purposes, whether real or imaginary, to operate on his own actions or to influence those of other Indians. To these tangible objects, after Wakoñda, who is a spirit, they address their prayers and invocations. Neither do these symbols affect them regarding the killing of the same animals on all occasions, though after he has killed it he will smoke and propitiate [the spirit of] the dead carcass, and even offer the head small sacrifices of tobacco and provisions.

THE HORSE

ERA OF THE IMPORTATION OF THE HORSE.—When the horse was first introduced among them does not appear by any of the traditions of these ignorant people. The name of the horse in Assiniboin is shunga (dog) tunga (large), i. e., large dog. Among the Sioux it is named shunka (dog) wakan (divining), i. e., divining dog, which would only prove that the dog was anterior to the horse, inasmuch as they were obliged to make a name for the strange animal resembling some known object with which it could be afterwards compared.

PICTOGRAPHS

CHARTS ON BARK.—Their drawings of maps and sections of country are in execution miserable to us but explanatory among themselves. Most Indians can carve on a tree, or paint, who they are, where going, whence come, how many men, horses, and guns the party is composed of, whether they have killed enemies, or lost friends, and, if so, how many, etc., and all Indians passing by, either

---

[4] See page 617 at the end of their oral tales.

friends or foes, will have no difficulty in reading the same, though such representations would be quite unintelligible to whites unless instructed. (Pl. 64.) Some Indians have good ideas of proportion and can immediately arrive at the meaning of a picture, pointing out the objects in the background, though others can not distinguish the figure of a man from that of a horse, and as to their executions of any drawing they are rude in the extreme. Where the natural talent exists, however, there is no doubt they could be instructed.

ANTIQUITIES

From the Sioux to the Blackfeet, inclusive, there is not in all that country any mounds, teocalli, or appearances of former works of defense bearing the character of forts or any other antique structure. Not a vestige or relic of anything that would form data, or be an inducement to believe their grounds have ever been occupied by any other than roving tribes of wild Indians; nor in the shape of tools, ornaments, or missiles that would lead to any such inference. We have not been more fortunate in searching their traditions in the hope of finding some clue relative to these things. They do not believe that any persons ever occupied their country except their own people (Indians), and we can not say we have ever seen or heard anything to justify any other conclusion regarding the extent of territory mentioned.

The elk-horn mound, mentioned elsewhere, is evidently of remote date and the work of Indians, but proves nothing sought by these researches. It might be stated that although no antique vessels of clay are found, yet the Arikara now, and as long as the whites have known them, have manufactured tolerably good and well-shaped clay vessels for cooking, wrought by hand without the aid of any machinery, and baked in the fire. They are not glazed, are of a gray color, and will answer for pots, pans, etc., equally as well as those made by the whites, standing well the action of fire and being as strong as ordinary potter's ware. They also have the art of melting beads of different colors and casting them in molds of clay for ear and other ornaments of various shapes, some of which are very ingeniously done. We have seen some in shape and size as drawn in Plate 65, the groundwork blue, the figure white, the whole about one-eighth inch thick, and presenting a uniform glazed surface.

PIPES

No antique pipes are found, but many and various are now made by all Indians.

VESSELS AND IMPLEMENTS

The Arikara and Gros Ventres, who raise corn, have other vessels as alluded to, but not the roving tribes, except the utensils furnished by whites. None of these things denote anything more than a people in the rudest state of nature, whose only boiling pot was once a hollow stone, or the paunch of a buffalo in which meat can be boiled and still is on occasions, by filling the paunch with water and casting therein red-hot stones until the water attains a boiling point, after which the stones are taken out, and one added occasionally to continue the heat, or the paunch suspended above a blaze at such a distance that the fire, though heating, does not touch it. Their spoons are yet made of the horns of the bighorn and buffalo, wrought into a good shape, some of which will hold half a gallon with ease. These are dippers. Others for eating are made smaller of horn and wood, yet large enough to suit their capacious mouths. (Pl. 65.) In all this and in everything they do, but one idea presents itself—that of crude, untutored children of nature, who have never been anything else.

The only ancient stone implements we have ever seen are the hatchet, stone war club, arrow point, buffalo shoulder-blade ax, hump-rib knife, and elk-horn bow, the shapes of which we have endeavored to draw in Plate 66, and all of which, except the knife, can yet occasionally be seen among them.

There is a total absence of anything antique, any shell, metal, wampum, or other thing formerly possessed by inhabitants supposed to have occupied this country. Neither are there any hieroglyphics or traditions to denote anything of the kind.

ASTRONOMY AND GEOLOGY

EARTH AND ITS MOTIONS.—Their knowledge on this subject is very limited. They believe the earth to be a great plain containing perhaps double the extent of country with which they are acquainted, and that it is void of motion. They do not believe the stars are inhabited by other people, but admit they may be abiding places of ghosts or spirits of the departed. They are not fond of talking about these things, neither do their opinions agree, each man's story differing materially from the other and all showing extreme ignorance and superstition.

They believe that Wakoñda created all things and this one idea appears original and universal, further than which, however, they are at a loss.

If they can not be made to comprehend the extent of the earth and its laws of motion, etc., there is much less likelihood that they can have any reasonable idea of the field of space or other creations therein further than superstitious notions according to the fancy of the individual.

THE SUN.—They take the sun to be a large body of fire, making its daily journey across the plains for the purpose of giving light and heat to all, and admit it may be the residence of Wakoñda; consequently it is worshiped, venerated, smoked, and invocated on all solemn occasions. We have often endeavored to explain the diurnal revolution of the earth, representing the sun as stationary, but always failed. They must first be brought to understand the attractions of cohesion and gravitation, for, as a sensible Indian stated on one of these occasions, " If at midnight we are all on the under side, what is to hinder the Missouri from spilling out, and us from falling off the earth? Flies, spiders, birds, etc., have small claws by which they adhere to the ceiling and other places, though man and water have no such support."

THE SKY.—Those who take the trouble to explain state the sky to be a material mass of a blue color, the composition of which they do not pretend to say, and think it has an oval or convex form, as apparent to the eye, resting for its basis on the extreme boundaries of the great plain, the earth. Hence their drawing, which is almost the only form in which they could represent it. Stars are small suns set therein, though they think they may be large bodies appearing small by seeing through space. Space is the intervening distance between earthly and heavenly bodies.

The Indians can not rationally account for an eclipse, supposing it to be a cloud, hand, or some other thing shadowing the moon, caused by Wakoñda to intimate some great pending calamity. Many are the prophecies on these occasions of war, pestilence, or famine, and their predictions are often verified. Predicting an eclipse does not appear to excite their wonder as much as would be supposed. The writer predicted the eclipse of the moon on December 25, 1852, months before, but received no further credit than that of having knowledge enough from books to find out it was to take place.

Their year is composed of four man-ko'-cha or seasons, viz, wai-too (spring), min-do-ka'-too (summer), pe-ti-e-too (autumn), wah-nee-e-too (winter). These are only seasons and do not each contain a certain number of days, but times—a growing time, a hot time, a leaf-falling time, and a snow time. These four seasons make a year which again becomes man-ko'-cha or the same as a season. This is difficult to explain. They count by the moon itself and its different phases, not computing so many days to make a moon, nor so many moons to a year.

They give each moon its name, beginning, say, with the March moon whenever it appears either in February or March, when it would be wee-che'-ish-ta-aza, sore eye moon; next would follow Ta-pa'-ghe-na-ho-to, frog moon; next pe-tai-chin-cha'-ton, buffalo calf moon; next wee-mush-tu, hot moon; next wah-pa'-ze-ze, yellow-leaf moon; next wah-pa-ich-pa'-ah, leaf-falling moon; next yo-ka'-wah-how-wee, first snow moon; next we-cho-kun, middle moon; next om-hos-ka-sun-ka-koo, lengthening days moon's brother; and next om-has-ka, lengthening of days moon. Their year has no beginning nor end. They count and name the moons as they come, and these names are also varied. Any annual remarkably known fact respecting the season can be applied to the name of the same moon. Thus the sore-eyed moon can be called the snow-melting moon, and the falling-leaf moon be termed the moon when the buffaloes become fat. These moons suffer no divisions of time except their phases, viz, new moon, increasing moon (first quarter), round moon (full moon), eaten moon (second quarter), half moon, dead moon (invisible). Among themselves they have no division of time equal to a week, although they are aware that we count by weeks, or divining days (Sundays), and will often ask how many divining days (or Sundays) there are to a given period.

An Indian in counting any period less than a year will say 3 moons and a full (3½ moons), 4 moons and an eaten one (4¾ moons), 6 moons and an increasing one (6½ moons), etc. These serve all his purposes and when wishing to be more minute and exact he must notch each day on a stick. For a year or four seasons they say a winter. A man may say " I am 40 winters old and one summer." Yet sometimes the same man will say, " I am 40 seasons old." This is still right. He will also say that he is 80 seasons old, or 160 seasons old. All of these are correct and understood immediately, as in the one case you mentally take the half, and in the other the quarter. This is often done among themselves, but with whites they generally name the winter only to designate the year, yet man-ko-cha (season) is the right name for a year and would be received as such by all the Assiniboin. The day is divided into the following parts: hi-ak-kane (daylight), umpa (morning), wee-he-num-pa (sunrise), wee-wa-kan-too (forenoon), wi-cho-kun (midday), we-coo-cha-nu (afternoon), we-coh-pa-ya (sunset), hhtie-too (twilight), eoch-puz-za (dark), and haw-ha-pip-cho-kun (midnight). Any intermediate space of time would be indicated by pointing the finger to the place the sun is supposed to have been at that time. They know nothing of the division of hours and minutes, yet some of the squaws living a long time in the fort can tell the hour and minute by the clock.

They know that the minute hand makes the revolution of the dial plate before it strikes and know the figures from 1 to 12; also that each figure is five minutes apart, and will say it wants so many fives to strike 9, or it has struck 10 and is 5 fives past. This they pick up nearly of their own accord, which proves that some are susceptible of intelligence and education. They know nothing of the solstices nor have any period such as a cycle or century, neither do they believe the world will come to an end or that their priests or any others have the power to destroy or rebuild it.

They know and name the North Star the same as we do—wa-se-a-ure-chah-pe (north star)—and also know the Ursa Major, sometimes calling it the " seven stars " and " the wagon." They are aware that it makes its revolution around the polar star, pointing toward it, and this is the secret of their traveling by night when there is no moon. They call no other stars by name. The Milky Way is said to be moch-pe-achan-ka-hoo (the backbone of the sky). It is known by them to be composed of clusters of small stars, but they suppose it to bear the same relative position to the arch of the heavens, and to be as necessary to its support as the backbone of any animal to its body. Meteors are falling stars which become extinguished as they fall. They attract but little attention as their effects are never perceived. Aurora borealis is believed to be clouds of fire or something the same as electricity. Being very common and brilliant it creates neither wonder nor inquiry.

The moon is not believed to influence men or vegetables nor to have any other properties than to give light by night.[5] They suppose it to be made of some body wasting away during a given period. Some say it is eaten up by a number of small animals (moles) and Wakoñda makes a new one on the destruction of the old. They know very well that all this is error and that the whites have a better philosophy, but will not take the trouble or can not comprehend our views of the motions of heavenly bodies. Having nothing else better explained to them, they adhere to their own ideas, which are of the simplest and most primitive kind, and do not appear to wish them superseded by others which they can not understand. The same remark would apply to all their astronomical and geographical opinions. They have a correct knowledge of the cardinal points, and honor the east as the first from the fact that the sun rises there. The pipe is first presented to the east, then to the south, supposed to be the power of the spirits of their departed friends, then west, then north, and lastly to the earth as the great grandfather of all. The amount of facts or real information they can give are mentioned and as for further explanations, as observed before, they

---

[5] It is considered a fetish as a light at night and sacrificed to on this account.

do not delight to talk about these matters but appear to think them sacred or forbidden fields through which their thoughts ought not to roam. The subject affords no scope for research unless a writer is disposed to collect a number of fables, which would serve no purpose unless it be to develop their ignorance and superstition.

FUTURE LIFE

INDIAN PARADISE.—The Paradise of these Indians is in the south in warm regions (not necessarily in the heavens, yet in some imaginary country not belonging to earth), where perpetual summer, abundance of game, handsome women, and, in short, every comfort awaits them; also the satisfaction of seeing their friends and relatives. No quarrels, wars, disturbances, or bodily pain are allowed to exist, but all live in perfect harmony. Departed spirits have the power to revisit their native lands, manifest themselves to their friends in dreams, and if they have been neglectful in crying for or feasting them can trouble them with whistling sounds and startling apparitions, many of which are said to be seen and heard and are most religiously believed in by all. Consequently, the dead are feasted (a long ceremony), smoked, sacrificed to, and invoked, besides being cried for years after they are gone, perhaps as long as any of the relatives are living. The heavenly bodies they think may also be residences for spirits, but we think this idea is derived from the whites. The other is the most ancient and original tradition, if not the only one, and is universally believed. This subject will meet with further notice in the course of these pages.

ARITHMETIC

NUMERATION.—All these prairie tribes count by decimals and in no other way. The names of the digits are:

One—washe'nah.
Two—noom'pah.
Three—yam'ine.
Four—topah.
Five—ta'ptah.

Six—sha'kpah.
Seven—shakkowee.
Eight—sha'kkando'gha.
Nine—noo'mpchewo'oukkah.
Ten—wixchemenah.

After ten the word akkai, dropping the name of the ten, serves until twenty, thus:

Eleven—akka'i washe.
Twelve—akkai noompah.
Thirteen—akkai yammene.
Fourteen—akkai topah.
Fifteen—akkai zaptah.
Sixteen—akkai sha'kpah.

Seventeen—akkai shakko'.
Eighteen—akkai sha'kando'gha.
Nineteen—akkai noompchewoukkah.
Twenty—wixche'mmene noompa; i. e. for twenty, literally two tens.

From twenty to thirty the word "sum" or "more" (plus) is added, thus:

21—wixchemmena noompa sum washena (two tens plus one).

22—wixchemmena noompa sum noompa (two tens plus two).

23—wixchemmena noompa sum yammene (two tens plus three),
and so on up to thirty, which is three tens or wixchemmene yam'mene.

31—wixchemmene yammene sum washena (three tens plus one).

32—wixchemmene yammene sum noompa (three tens plus two);
the same as after twenty, and the same after each succeeding ten as far
as one hundred, thus—

40—wixchemmene to'pah (four tens).

41—wixchemmene topah sum washena (four tens plus one).

50—wixchemmene zaptah (five tens).

51—wixchemmene zaptah sum washena.

52—wixchemmene zaptah sum noo'mpa.

60—wixchemmene shakpa (six tens).

61—wixchemmene shakpa sum washena.

62—wixchemmene shakpa sum noompa.

70—wixchemmene shakko (seven tens).

71—wixchemmene shakko sum washena (seven tens plus one).

72—wixchemmene shakko sum noompa.

73—wixchemmene shakko sum yammene.

74—wixchemmene shakko sum topah, etc.

80—wixchemmene shakandogha (eight tens).

90—wixchemmene noomchewouka (nine tens).

100—o-pah-wa-ghe.

101—o-pah-wa-ghe sum washea.

110—opahwaghe sum wixche'mmene.

160—opahwaghe sum wixche'mmene shakpa.

161—opahwaghe sum wixche'mmene shakpa sum washena.

170—opahwaghe sum wixche'mmene shakko.

180—opahwafihe sum wixche'mmene shakandogha.

190—opahwaghe sum wixche'mmene noomchewouka.

200—opahwaghe noompa.

300—opahwaghe yammene.

400—opahwaghe topah.

500—opahwaghe zaptah.

600—opahwaghe shakpah.

700—opahwaghe shakko.

800—opahwaghe shakandogha.

900—opahwaghe noomchewouka.

1,000—koke-to-pah-wa-ghe.

1,853—koketopahwaghe sum opahwaghe shakandoga sum wixche'mmene
zaptah sum yammene.

2,000—koketopahwaghe noompah.

3,000—koketopahwaghe yammene.

4,000—koketopahwaghe topah.

10,000—koketopahwaghe wixchemmene.

20,000—koketopahwaghe wixchemmene noompa.

50,000—koketopahwaghe wixchemmene zaptah.

100,000—opahwaghe koketopahwaghe.

500,000—opahwaghe zaptah koketopahwaghe.

600,000—opahwaghe shakpah koketopahwaghe.

10,000,000—opahwaghe wixehemmene koketopahwaghe.

Although the computation could thus be carried on to a million yet the Indian would not appreciate the number. We think that after 5,000, or at the utmost 10,000, their ideas fail them; that is, they can not realize in thought more than that amount, yet are able mechanically to count it. This is evident, as they have no distinct name for a million, but are obliged to call it ten hundred thousand, and were they requested to go further would proceed eleven, twelve, thirteen hundred thousand, etc., but not comprehending the great number as a body. They can not multiply or subtract uneven sums without the aid of small sticks or some other mark. Thus to add 40 to 60 would be done by the fingers, shutting down one for each succeeding ten, naming 70, 80, 90, 100. But to add 37 to 94 would require some time; most Indians would count 37 small sticks and beginning with 94, lay one down for each succeeding number, naming the same until all were counted. Now tell them to add 76 to 47 and substract 28. In addition to the first process, and counting the whole number of sticks, he would withdraw 28 and recount the remainder. They are easily confused when counting and consider the knowledge of figures one of the most astonishing things the whites do.

In counting with the hand, an Indian invariably begins with the little finger of the left, shutting it down forcibly with the thumb of the right; when the five fingers are thus shut he commences on the thumb of the right, shutting it with the left fist. When wishing to telegraph by signs a certain number less than 10 he holds up that number of fingers, beginning with the little finger of the left hand and keeping the others shut. Should the number be 7, then all the fingers of the left and thumb and finger of the right would be extended, holding up his hands, the rest of the fingers closed. Tens are counted by shutting and opening both hands; thus, 100 would be indicated by shutting and opening both hands 10 times in succession. The number 7 has two names, shakkowee and enshand (the odd number). They count fast enough in continuation from 1 to 100 but must not be interrupted.

Coin.—There is not now nor have we any reason to suppose there ever has been among them any coin, shells, wampum, or any other thing constituting a standard of exchange, neither are they acquainted with American money. Were a guinea and a button presented there is no question but the Indian would take the latter. They barter their furs for goods which have fixed prices, and are well acquainted with these prices, as also of the value of their robes and furs as a means of purchasing merchandise.

Keeping Accounts.—The Indians themselves keep no accounts. The manner in which accounts are kept by whites with them is as follows. We are not exactly acquainted with the minor operations in accounts kept by the Hudson's Bay Co. with the Cree and the Chippewa, but from authentic information the following appears to be their system. A plue is equal to 1 pound beaver skin or 3 shillings sterling (say 67 cents); that is, 1 pound of the fur is worth at their forts 67 cents in merchandise at their fixed prices. Therefore a large beaver skin (2 pounds) is 2 plues; 6 muskrats, which are worth from 10 to 12½ cents each, is a plue; 1 wolf skin is counted a plue, being equal in value to the standard 67 cents; an otter skin is 2 plues, a red-fox 1, and so forth.

All skins and other articles of trade acquired by Indians are reckoned into plues by the trader and the Indians and the prices of merchandise are computed in the same manner. On the Missouri the plan is somewhat different, to explain which we annex the following accounts copied from our books. It will be necessary to observe that everything is brought to the standard of buffalo robes which have an imaginary value of $3 each in the country.

THE CRAZY BEAR, ASSINIBOIN CHIEF

1851		Dr.	1852		Cr.
Dec. 3	To 1–3 pt. white blanket_____	3 robes.	Jan. 8	By 6 robes_____	6 robes.
	To 2 yards blue cloth_____	2 robes.		By 2 dressed cow skins_____	1 robe.
	To ¾ yard scarlet cloth_____	1 robe		By 30 pounds dried meat_____	1 robe.
	To 2½ pounds tobacco_____	1 robe.		By 2 red fox skins_____	1 robe.
1852				By 2 raw cowhides_____	1 robe.
Jan. 16	To 1 horse_____	10 robes.		By 1 large elk skin, raw_____	1 robe.
	To 3 knives_____	1 robe.	Feb. 10	By 4 robes_____	4 robes.
	To 1 kettle, 2 gallon_____	2 robes.		By 12 wolf skins_____	4 robes.
	To 100 loads ammunition_____	1 robe.		Balance forward_____	2 robes.
		21 robes.			21 robes.
1853					
Feb. 10	To balance on settlement_____	2 robes.			

Pictorial or other signs are not used in accounts, either by them or the white people.

ELEMENTS OF FIGURES.—A single stroke answers for 1 and each additional stroke marks the additional number as far as 100. When a stroke is made apart, the score is rubbed out and begun again. There are no written nor marked records kept, either on graves or otherwise, of ages or of events, scalps taken, or war expeditions.[5a] Their transactions, or coups, as they are called in this country, are pictured on their robes, lodges, and shields, but these wearing out are seldom renewed, particularly when the man becomes old. Also these coups are recounted publicly by the performer on occasions appointed for the purpose, which we shall notice hereafter, and moreover, are

[5a] It is not intended by this that they make no use of picture writing, but that these records are not preserved. For further explanation see picture writing, p. 603. The devices on their robes are not renewed after they have arrived at a very advanced age, or in other words after their influence and standing has been destroyed by age and helplessness.

talked of often enough around their firesides. Ages are numbered by particular events that took place at the time they could first recollect, and afterwards by certain remarkable years from time to time. Though no Indian can be sure as to his exact age, yet he will not vary more than a year or two as to the time. The cross ($\times$) is not used in counting or for any other purpose, neither does the dot or full comma signify a moon or anything else.

MEDICINE

GENERAL PRACTICE.—They are careful of their sick relatives and particularly so in regard to their children or men in the prime of life. Very aged persons do not, however, meet with such kindness even from their own children, having become useless as a help in camp. Besides being a burden in traveling and a bore and expense, they are anxious to get rid of them and leave them on the plains to die. It must, by no means, be inferred from this that the Indian has no paternal feelings or affection; from several instances of the kind that have come under my observation I am assured it is their inability to carry about and along with them aged people. These Indians are poor, have but few horses and are constantly on the move, in all weather, sometimes requiring flight; therefore everything that might encumber in the way of baggage is thrown aside, and among other rubbish is classed the aged of both sexes. I am also told that it is often the desire of the aged to be left to die. To keep up appearances with his people, the Indian will generally pay a small doctor's bill for the relief of his aged relatives, but nothing like the amount the same man would pay for his wife or child. To explain their mode of practicing medicine, surgery, etc., we must be somewhat prolix.

In every camp there are several doctors, both men and women, called by them divining men, who have the double reputation of physicians and sorcerers. This is generally some old wretch who is very ugly, of great experience, and who has art enough to induce others to believe in his knowledge, and can drum, sing, and act his part well.

The present great doctor and soothsayer is named " Bull's Dry Bones," a very old man who is now with me. This man was once sick and died while the camp was traveling. His friends packed and tied him up in several envelopes of raw hides, blankets, etc., and, after duly crying over him, placed the body in the fork of a tree as is their custom. By some means, however, the man came to life and after great difficulty worked himself out of his bonds, traveled and overtook the camp some days after they had left him. He stated to them that during his decease he had been in other worlds, seen much, knew everything, past, present, and future, and from this circumstance he has ever after been considered a great divining man and prophet. We will now state how they proceed in case of sickness. A child falls sick. The father or some other near relative immediately sends a gun or a horse to the divining man to secure his services. Sometimes smaller articles are sent, and the doctor, thinking them beneath his notice, will not pay a visit until enough is offered, which amount varies in proportion as the patient's relatives are rich or poor. He then enters the lodge of the sick person in his medical capacity. His instruments are a drum, a chi-chi-quoin, or gourd rattle, and, perhaps, a horn cupping apparatus. He must have (although not perceptible) some things concealed in his mouth or about his person, as will presently appear, although they go usually through their operations entirely naked (except the breech-cloth) and not in a hideous costume as has been represented. The doctor is accompanied by five or six others as old and ugly as himself, bearing drums, bells, rattles, and other noisy instruments.

All sing to the extent of their voices and make a terrible noise with the instruments spoken of. The doctor slowly approaches the patient, applying his mouth to his naked breast or belly, draws or appears to draw therefrom by suction a worm, sometimes a bug, a wolf hair, or even a small snake, making at the same time horrible gestures, grunts, and grimaces. This object he displays to the lookers-on, stating he has extracted the cause of the disease. This operation is repeated several times with like results, and after he and the accompanying band of music partake largely of a dog or other feast provided for them they leave for the time. The whole performance, with the music, incantations, preparations, and feast included, would occupy perhaps from two to three hours and often the whole night, if the performers are paid high. Frequently their diseases are colic from eating unripe fruits and berries or overloading the stomach, which, of course, get well in a short time and the credit is given to the doctor, each recovery aiding to raise his reputation and enlarge his practice. But if the case is serious and the patient gets worse, the doctor is then paid again and another visit takes place. The forms are always somewhat similar, but on this occasion, in addition to the full band of music and cupping with the horn, besides the usual grimaces, noises, etc., the patient is made to drink decoctions of roots or powders made by the doctors of pulverized roots, rattles of the rattlesnake, calcined bones, etc., the properties of which he is entirely ignorant, and probably the smallness of the dose preventing them from doing any harm. This, with the noise of the instruments and feast, concludes the second visit.

Sometimes the doctor performs alone and keeps up the drumming, etc., all night. In this way by a repetition of visits, if the case is

of long duration, the whole of the property of the relatives of the
sick person falls to the doctor and his assistants, who are also slightly
paid for the music. And this is the cause of great individual distress and poverty, though the property given does not go out of the
nation, but only changes hands and is liable in like manner to revert
to others should the divining man fall sick. In case, after all, the
patient dies, it is then the doctor who is in danger, and runs great
risk of losing his life, by the parents or relatives of the deceased.
Indeed, being aware of this they generally abscond to other camps
when death approaches, and whatever property they leave behind
is taken from them. No later than last winter the writer paid an
Indian to prevent his killing the " Bull's Dry Bones " (doctor) who
the man said had poisoned his two children six years ago. But the
old doctor, although a humbug, is an innocent man and would harm
no one.

They have various forms of doctoring, in all of which the drum
forms a principal figure, and songs and incantations, all of which
are most religiously believed in by the Indians. Old women are
as often practitioners as old men and of as great celebrity. There
is also another reason why these Indians give away so much of their
property to the divining man. Independent of these payments
securing the doctor's services, they are considered as sacrifices; that
is, the man makes himself poor with a view of propitiating the Great
Spirit.

Also it is considered and spoken of as a great honor to give away
large articles to the divining man, such as horses, guns, etc., and
goes to prove the affection with which they regard their sick relatives. For a long time afterwards the giver will boast of his liberality in these respects and is also looked upon as a man with a " large
heart." We must, at the risk of not being believed, state that on
two particular occasions, and before witnesses, we have examined
the divining man's mouth, hands, and all his person, which was
entirely naked, with the view of discovering where these worms,
snakes, etc., were hidden, and that these examinations were made
without any previous intimations to him who, never having been
subject to examinations of the kind by Indians, was completely unpre-
pared for the trial, yet he acquiesced cheerfully, afterwards continued
his performance, and repeated it in our presence, drawing and
spitting out large worms, clots of blood, tufts of hair, skin, etc., too
large to be easily secreted, and leaving no visible mark on the
patient's body. The trick was well done and not yet known to any
of us.

Their knowledge of anatomy consists in being acquainted with the
larger bones and joints. They can set a broken arm or simple frac-

ture tolerably well, and even replace a dislocated shoulder, which they do by pulling and outward pressure from the armpit, but this knowledge is not confined to the divining man nor is it his business more than any other who happens to be present. Most men of middle age have witnessed so many accidents of the kind that they can do this.

They are, however, unacquainted with the circulation of the blood and with any judicious treatment of internal diseases, for all of which they resort to incantations and drumming. They do, however, indiscriminately use the vapor bath or sweat house for various complaints. This construction is a small lodge thrown over a basket-work of willows stuck in the ground and bent in an oval or round form, the skins well pinned down and every aperture well closed. The doctor after heating some large stones red hot and putting them into the lodge enters with the patient, both entirely naked and taking along a kettle of water and, as usual, his drum. The lodge is then shut tight by the people on the outside. A brisk singing and drumming is kept up in the lodge by the doctor, who at intervals throws water on the stones and steam is raised. A violent heat and perspiration takes place, which they endure as long as they can; as soon as the patient is taken out he is immersed in cold water, which in nine cases out of ten results in his death. In this way the Crow Indians lost nearly 200 persons three years since during a prevailing influenza. The Mandan and Gros Ventres, however, being accustomed to cold bathing from their youth, are said seldom to suffer any inconvenience but often receive benefit from the vapor bath and immediate cold immersion. They have no names for fevers, consumptions, obstructions of the liver, etc., and can not explain further than by pointing out that part of their body which is in a state of pain.

Indeed, in this climate, except consumption, rheumatism and quinsy, diseases are extremely rare; and no febrile symptoms seen except in cases of wounds and parturition when puerperal fever often occurs, and assuming a typhoid form is generally fatal. They are also exempt from paralysis, toothache, and almost all the thousand nervous complaints to which the whites are subject, among which might be mentioned baldness or failure of eyesight from age. Their materia medica is consequently in a very primitive state. They have no medicine except some roots, some of which are known to be good for the bite of the rattlesnake, frozen parts, and inflammatory wounds. The principal of these is the black root, called by them the comb root (pl. 67, *a*), from the pod on the top being composed of a stiff surface that can be used as a comb. It is called by the French racine noir, and grows everywhere in the prairie throughout the Indian country. It is chewed and applied in a raw state with a

88253°—30——28

bandage to the part affected. We can bear witness to the efficacy of this root in the cure of the bite of the rattlesnake or in alleviating the pain and reducing the tension and inflammation of frozen parts, gunshot wounds, etc. It has a slightly pungent taste resembling black pepper, and produces a great deal of saliva while chewing it. Its virtues are known to all the tribes with which we are acquainted, and it is often used with success. A decoction of the root of cat-tail (pl. 67, *b*) is also used to reduce inflammation, and given internally to produce perspiration, but mostly as an external application for wounds, sprains, and pains of all kinds, as also the inner bark of the red willow; both of which are said to be beneficial, and are much used by the Indians and French voyageurs in all the Indian country.

At the risk of a smile and perhaps something more from the enlightened civilized medical fraternity we will now state how they absolutely can and do cure hydrophobia, in hopes of furnishing them with a hint that may be improved upon. We have never actually seen this operation, but are as certain of its being done as we can be of anything not seen but in all other respects well authenticated. Although Indians are often bitten by mad wolves, yet they never die from the disease if operated upon. After it is known that the patient has hydrophobia, the symptoms of which they are well acquainted with, and has had a fit or two, he is sewed up in a fresh rawhide of a buffalo. With two cords attached to the head and foot of the bale the man is swung backward and forward through a hot fire until the skin is burnt to cinders and the patient is burned and suffocated [sic]. He is brought to the brink of the grave by the operation; taken out in a state of profuse perspiration and plunged into cold water; and if he survives the treatment the disease disappears. The remedy is terrible. Now, if the poison of the rattlesnake is expelled by perspiration by administering ammonia and other remedies, might not the poison communicated by the rabid animal undergo a like process by the violent treatment mentioned, or intense heat produce the desired constitutional revolution and effect a cure.

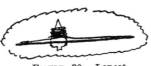

FIGURE 30.—Lancet

DEPLETION BY BLEEDING.—They bleed often, both when the pulse is full from sickness and at any time they think it beneficial.

The instrument is a sharpened arrow point or any other small piece of pointed iron. (Fig. 30.) They wrap the whole of this with sinew except as much as they wish to enter the vein. It is then tied into a split stick and secured firmly with sinew and being laid on the vein is knocked in suddenly with the thumb and middle finger. They also open the veins of their legs and arms while crying over dead relatives, making large transverse cuts with knives, arrow points, or flints. When they bleed they generally let the blood flow as long as it will without bandage. Cupping is done with a part of the upper end of a buffalo horn, about 2½ inches long, and a vacuum is produced by suction with the mouth which, with their powerful muscles and exertions, is, of course, double force. It is said to be useful in drawing out the poison of snake bites and is also used for pains and cramps in the stomach, besides for extracting worms, bugs, snakes, etc., as mentioned in the general practice. We believe it may have something of the effect of dry cupping with glasses; they do not, however, scarify before cupping except in cases of snake bites.

STOPPAGE OF BLOOD AND HEALING ART.—For stopping of blood they use cobwebs, dried pulpy fungus, or very fine inner bark of trees. When these are not to be had finely pulverized rotton wood is used. These answer tolerably well when the divided artery is small. They have no good plasters or healing salves.

Bandages are mostly tied on too tight, with the view of stopping the bleeding and are left too long before being removed, which frequently results in gangrene. They are not skillful nor clean in these things, seldom washing a wound. From actual observation, which has been pretty extensive with regard to cuts and wounds of all kinds, we are disposed to believe that their cure does not depend upon any skill in treatment nor care taken of them, but upon their vigorous constitutions, extremely healthy climate, and strictly temperate mode of life, with perhaps a disposition to heal naturally in the absence of scientific knowledge vouchsafed to the ignorant Indian by an all-wise Creator.

AMPUTATION.—They never amputate a limb, though fingers and toes often undergo that operation.[6] The Assiniboin run a sharp knife around the joint of the finger and snap it off. The Crows do the same, but on other occasions take them off by placing a sharp tomahawk on the finger, it being laid on a block and the tomahawk being struck with a mallet. Whenever a Crow Indian dies his near relatives, male and female, sacrifice each a finger and sometimes two, and the loss of these people by sickness and enemies the last few years having been great, there is scarcely such a thing as a whole hand to be found in the Crow Nation. The men reserve the thumb and middle finger on the left and the thumb and two forefingers of the right hand to use the bow and gun, but all the rest are sacrificed.

They mostly take them off at the first and second joints, though occasionally lower down. These small amputations are seldom at-

---

[6] In the few cases where the Indians have an arm or leg missing, they have been shot off, or so nearly off as not to come under the head of amputation, as but little skin or nerve were to be cut.

tended with any serious effect, but from their awkward operations the bone frequently projects and requires a long time to heal. They use splints and bark in fractures and lacerated bones, but are not skillful in applying them, nor attentive in removing them, and in a short time the wound smells bad. Their wounded are carried from the field in a blanket, robe, or skin, by four men each holding a corner, who are relieved by others when fatigued, in which way they transport them for days and sometimes weeks together. When very badly wounded in an enemy's country and supposed to be mortally wounded they are left in some point of timber to die. A small stock of provisions and ammunition is left with them. They sometimes recover almost by miracle. Instances of this kind are not uncommon and serve to show the suffering an Indian will undergo and the different means he will use to preserve life.

THEORY OF DISEASES AND THEIR REMEDY.—They understand nothing of the properties of mineral medicines except a few simple ones given them by whites of later years, neither are they acquainted with the theory of diseases, being for the most part unable to describe their complaint so that any person could prescribe. They are as ignorant of any true knowledge of diseases or medicines as they are of astronomy or any other science.

It is hardly conceivable how the smallpox among Indians could be cured by any physician. All remedies fail. The disease kills a greater part of them before any eruption appears. We have personally tried experiments on nearly 200 cases according to Thomas's Domestic Medicine, varying the treatment in every possible form, but have always failed, or in the few instances of success the disease had assumed such a mild form that medicines were unnecessary. It generally takes the confluent turn of the most malignant kind (when the patient does not die before the eruption), which in 95 cases out of 100 is fatal. It appears to be the natural curse of the red men, and here we leave it, perfectly willing others should do more. We have from year to year tried to introduce general vaccination with kinepock among them, and have even paid them to vaccinate their own children, but they will not have it done to any extent, and the few who will do it more to please us than to benefit themselves. Moreover, should any accident happen to the child or even should the Indian miss his hunt, or any casualty befall him or his family, the vaccination would be blamed for it and the good-hearted operator would find himself in a position of danger and expense. There is also great risk in giving them medicines, for should the patient die the whites would be blamed for poisoning him, and should he live the Indian drummer or doctor will get both the credit and the pay. Therefore, as their customs at present stand but little can be done for them, however willing people are to attempt it.

PARTURITION.—Men never interpose their services in cases of parturition.

When there is danger a midwife is called, and the deobstruents administered are castoreum and pulverized rattles of the rattlesnake, either of which have the effect of the ergot. Shampooing is also resorted to with the view of detaching the fetus or expelling the envelope. Nevertheless strangulation and consequently death of both mother and child often happens, not so much in the natural course as when destroyed expressly in utero, as is done by the Crow women and sometimes by the Assiniboin, though not to such an extent by the latter. This is accomplished by violent pressure on the abdomen, by leaning on a stick planted in the ground, and, swinging the whole weight of their body, they run backward and forward, or by violent blows administered by some other person called for the purpose, in all which operations, if the time be not well calculated for expelling the fetus, death is the consequence.

Their vapor baths have been alluded to and might prove efficacious in some cases of chronic rheumatism, catarrh, etc., if proper care was taken, but are very pernicious owing to their negligence afterwards, or cold immersion during perspiration. In conclusion we would remark that with regard to any judicious treatment of any disease whatever (that is, any such treatment as would meet medical approbation) they are entirely in the dark. The most of their dependence is on the drumming, singing, and incantations which perhaps sometimes have some little effect on the mind of youthful patients, though in these cases the probability is they are more frightened than sick.

In a large camp the drum can be heard at all hours of the day and night, as there is always some one who is sick, or thinks he is. What appears singular is that the doctor, knowing his art to be deception, should he fall sick calls for another divining man and pays for the drumming the same as his patients have paid him. This would seem to prove they actually have faith in their own incantations, etc. They can not distinguish between an artery and a vein. They call both by the same name, though they say the arteries are large veins. Arteries are compressed, not taken up when cut, and if a large one is cut, the consequence is either mortification from the ligature or, if loosely tied, death by bleeding, which invariably happens when the large artery of the thigh is separated.

Indians will receive extensive wounds, apparently mortal, and yet recover. Some years ago an Assiniboin was surrounded by three Blackfeet a few miles from this place. He had fired at a prairie hen, and the moment his gun was discharged the three enemies fired on him. The three balls took effect. One broke his thigh, another the shin bone of the other leg, and the third entered his abdomen and came out near the kidney and backbone. They then ran in upon and endeavored to scalp him, running a knife around the cranium and partially withdrawing the scalp. Finding that he struggled they stabbed him with a long lance downward under the collar bone, the lance running along the inside and against the right ribs about 12 inches. They also gave him several more stabs in the body with their knives.

In the struggle the man got out the lance and plunging it at them alternately they retired a few paces. The camp in the meantime having heard the firing and suspecting the cause, turned out. The enemies seeing this, decamped, and the Assiniboin carried the wounded man to his lodge. In a few days afterwards the camp passed by the fort and the writer saw this man in so helpless a state that, expecting him to die, nothing was done. The weather was very hot, the wounds had a purple color, smelt bad, and had every appearance of gangrene. The camp moved off and the man in time recovered. The scalp was replaced and grew on again. Here was no judicious treatment, not even ordinary care, for in traveling that is impossible, and very unfavorable weather. This man is yet living and is said by the Indians to bear a charmed life, is respected as a warrior and brave, called "He who was many times wounded," and can be seen any time in the Band des Canots of the Assiniboin.

GOVERNMENT

TRIBAL ORGANIZATION AND GOVERNMENT.—The tribe of Indians called Assiniboin is separated into the following distinct bands, viz, Wah-to′-pah-han-da′-tok, or "Those who propel boats," by the whites Gens du Gauche, from the circumstance of the old Gauche (chief) spoken of before who for a half century governed this band. It now numbers 100 lodges. The second band, Wah-ze-ab-we-chas-ta, or Gens du Nord, thus named because they came from that direction in 1839 as already represented, though their original appellation was Gens du Lac. These count 60 lodges. Third band, Wah-to-pan-ah, or Canoe Indians, Gens des Canots, who may be recorded at 220 lodges that trade on the Missouri, and 30 lodges more who deal with American and British traders near the mouth of Pembina and Red Rivers, occasionally visiting the Missouri. Fourth band, We-che-ap-pe-nah, or Gens des Filles, literally the "Girls Band"; these can be put down at 60 lodges. Fifth, E-an-to-ah or Gens des Roches, literally "Stone Indians," comprising 50 lodges. The original name for the whole nation given them by the Chippewa (As-see-ni-pai-tuck) has the same [7] signification. Within the last 10 years another division has again arisen, called Hoo-tai-sha-pah or "Lower End Red," alias

[7] For correct meaning see footnote 1.

"Red Root." These are a branch from the Gens des Canots and odds and ends of other bands and consist of 30 lodges.

RECAPITULATION

Indian name	French name	Lodges	Chiefs of bands	Head chief
Wah-to-pah-han-da-toh____	Gens du Gauche_____	100	La Main que tremble___	
Wah-ze-ab-we-chas-tah____	Gens du Nord_____	60	Le Robe de vent_____	
Wah-to-pan-ah_____	Gens des Canot_____	220	Le Serpent_____	L'ours Fou or
We-che-ap-pe-nah_____	Gens des Filles_____	60	Les Yeux Gris_____	Crazy Bear.
E-an-to-ah_____	Gens des Roches_____	50	Premier qui volle_____	
Hoo-tai-sha-pah_____	Le Bas Rouge_____	30	Le Garçon bleu_____	
		520		

Average, four and one half persons per lodge. Total, 2,340 souls.

These 520 lodges form the nation, with the exception of those residing in the north, whom they never visit. The bands named are distinct and usually encamped in different sections of country, though they mingle for a short time when circumstances require it, such as scarcity of buffalo in some part of their lands or on an approach of a numerous enemy. When these causes for combination cease they separate and occupy their customary grounds severally, within three or four days' travel of each other. The chief of the whole nation is Crazy Bear, made so by the commissioner of the United States at the Laramie treaty in 1851, not having as yet, however, that popular rule which will follow in due time if the treaty stipulations on both sides are complied with.

CHIEFS.—In each and all the bands mentioned there are several men bearing the character, rank, and name of chiefs. But he only is considered as chief of the band who heads and leads it. Yet this power does not give him a right to tyrannize over any of the other chiefs, or dictate to them any course they would not willingly follow; neither does it detract from their dignity and standing to acknowledge him as the head. Some one must be the nominal leader, and as this place involves some trouble and action and is not repaid with any extra honors or gifts it is not in general much envied. Moreover, this leader is mostly, if not always, supported by numerous connections who second his views and hence his authority. In fact, these bands are nothing more than large families, the chiefs resembling the old patriarchs, being intermarried and connected in such a way as to preclude the probability of clashing of interests or separation. These are the elements of the bands. The chief is little more than the nominal father of all and addresses them as his children in a body.

Now, although some of these children may be as brave as he, and have accomplished greater feats in war and the chase, yet they do not feel disposed to dispute his acknowledged authority, neither would such insubordinate conduct be submitted to by the mass of the people, without some great mismanagement on the part of the chief, rendering such a course necessary and inevitable.

The process of arriving at the chieftaincy—an instance of which was exemplified in the formation of the Red Root Band and of which we were an eyewitness—has always been the same and is as follows: Some ambitious brave young man with extensive relations separate from another band with 8 or 10 lodges of his connections and rove and hunt in a portion of the country by themselves, acknowledging this man as their head on account of his known bravery and successful management of large war expeditions. From time to time additions are made to this band from other bands of persons with their families who from different causes of dissatisfaction choose to leave their leaders and submit to the government of the new chief. This chief, wishing to rise, does all in his power to benefit his small band by protecting them, choosing good hunting grounds, giving to them all horses and other property taken by him from his enemies, and, if necessary, fearlessly risking his life to strike or kill one of his own people to preserve order or their sense of justice. In the course of some years around this nucleus is assembled a body which assumes the form and name of a band and the leader, rising in power and support, increases in respect, and the standing and name of chief rewards his perseverance. It will be thus seen that the title and position of chief is neither hereditary nor elective, but being assumed by the right and upon the principles above explained, is voluntarily granted him by his followers.

And this is the correct representation of the origin of Assiniboin chieftainship and different bands being the same in all the roving tribes of which we attempt to treat in these pages. This high officer does not, however, at all times wear his honors securely. It is a known impossibility for any man in high station to please everybody, and although surrounded by numerous and strong friends yet he must have some enemies, and it does happen, though rarely, that he is assassinated. But this is more the consequence of some personal quarrel than ambitious designs, for although by assassination the chief is destroyed yet it does not follow that the assassin would take his place. Generally the reverse is the case and he is obliged to fly or the relatives of the deceased chief would kill him. In the event of the decease of a leader or chief, most likely some one of his relatives would succeed him, but whether brother, cousin, or uncle would not matter. The successor must absolutely possess the requisite governing powers, viz, known and acknowledged bravery and wisdom, moderation, and justice. If the relative be thus constituted, he would become the chief, not because he is a relative, or that he is the only brave man in camp—there are many such—but simply by being such and having a stronger family connection than any other he would consequently be acknowledged by the greater part of the band. Should there be two candidates for the chieftainship equally capable and related, the question would be decided the first day the camp moved.

Each would follow the leader he liked best, and the smaller portion would soon revert to the larger, or if they were equally divided and both parties intractable, a new band would be formed subject to increase under their new leader or to dissolve and mix up with other bands. Viewing things in this light, it is easily comprehended how some personal defect, such as loss of sight or constitutional debility, would depose a chief, but that these unfortunate circumstances should render him a laughingstock and butt for others who before feared and respected him is a trait in their character not to be admired. We have said enough to give a general idea of the origin, progress, and tenure of chieftainship. It is only elective so far as general consent has accorded his right to rule, and is only hereditary, or appears so, because the relatives of the chief are mostly the most numerous, and from their ranks arises a successor. Though we have witnessed the chieftainship pass into other hands when the claims of two powerful families were equal and the abilities or popularity of one of the candidates defective in some principal part.

Women are never acknowledged as chiefs, or have anything to say in councils. We know of but one anomalous instance of the kind on the whole upper Missouri which, being very remarkable, merits notice. She is a Blackfoot by birth, but having been taken prisoner when young by the Crows, was raised by and has since resided with that nation, being identified with them.

We have known this woman for 10 years, and during that time have seen her head large war parties of men against the Blackfeet, bringing away great numbers of horses, and killing several of the enemy with her own hand. She is likewise a good huntress, both on foot with the gun and on horseback with the bow and arrow, ranks as a warrior and brave and is entitled to a seat in councils of the Crow Nation. She ranked as fifth from the Crow chief in a council held by the writer with the Crows and the Cree at Fort Union on the occasion of making a peace between these two nations. She keeps up all the style of a man and chief, has her guns, bows, lances, war horses, and even two or three young women as wives, but in reality servants. In appearance she is tolerably good-looking, has been handsome, is now about 40 years of age, and still goes to war. Her name is " Woman Chief," and although dressed as a woman the devices on her robe represent some of her brave acts. She is fearless in everything, has often attacked and killed full-grown grizzly bears alone, and on one occasion rode after a war party of Blackfeet, killed and scalped one alone (within sight of our fort on the Yellowstone), and returned unharmed amid a shower of bullets and arrows. This extraordinary woman is well known to all whites and Indians. She resided at Fort Union last winter, and appears in private disposition to be modest and sensible; but she is an only instance in all the roving tribes of the Missouri. Her success induced an imitation a few years since by an Assiniboin woman, but she was killed by the enemy on her first war excursion, since which no rivals have sprung up.

Having disposed of the chieftainship for the time and separated the nation into bands, we will now proceed to describe other divisions which we shall call clans. These are clubs or societies formed by the young men of different bands or of the same band. There are not many among the Assiniboin, they being a small nation, but are numerous among the Sioux and the Blackfeet, bearing the names of Foxes, Foolish Dogs, Strong Hearts, Bulls, Pheasants, etc. Among the Assiniboin are first the braves, Na-pa'-shee-nee, Ceux qui sauvent, who are a picked body of young men, said to be bound by the most solemn promises and oath never to run from an enemy or leave one of their clan in danger. They are chosen from all the bands on account of some previous brave act, and are only known as a body at feasts of their own and on war expeditions. They wear no badges but dance completely naked in public and have different songs, different from those of other dances. The Bulls, Tah-tun-gah, are another of the same kind of clans in the band, Gens des Canots. Their badge is a bull's head and horns painted on their drums, shields, and robes, also in the Bull Dance they imitate the motions of that animal, his bellowing, and shoot at each other's feet with powder. When dancing they wear the head and horns of a bull, skinned to the neck, the bones taken out, and the skin dried. Into this the head of the man is thrust, giving him the appearance of half man and half animal.

THE SNDOO-KAH, "CIRCUMCISED."—This is a large clan of the band, Gens des Canots, consisting of at least 100 persons, young and old. They have not actually had circumcision performed, but these are called so, and belong to that class who are naturally minus the prepuce. These assemble once or twice a year and their ceremonies are kept somewhat secret. They are, however, obliged to display the part alluded to, to prevent imposition. When wishing to be known in that capacity on private occasions they paint the tip of their nose red. The end of a feather painted red or the pod of the plant sketched as the comb root stuck in their hair is equally significant.

The Fox and Wolf clans are small and only appear to differ in the manner of their dances and songs. There does not seem to be much

importance attached to these clans, neither do they appear to be of
much use, and most likely are got up for the purpose of display,
dancing, and other ceremonies, but as soon as these are over mix up
with the bands they belong to, and are very little talked of. There
are no minor subdivisions except into families. These remarks answer
nearly all search for origins of bands in badges and names of bands.
Now, as far as the roving tribes are concerned, this is error. The
names of the Assiniboin bands we have mentioned and those of the
Sioux now follow, some of which consist of two, three, and four
hundred lodges, and none of them have the least reference to Bear,
Wolf, Eagle, Fox, or Father, Grandfather, Uncle, etc., or anything
of the kind.

The names of the different bands of the Missouri and the Platte
Sioux are Lower Yanctons, Sechong-hoo (Burnt Thighs), Oglala,
Sawone,[8] Minneconzshu, Etasepecho (Sans Arcs), Honcpapa, Seah-
sappah (Blackfeet Band), Wohainoompa (Two Kettle Band), Mide-
wahconto, Esantees, Teezaptah, Zahbaxah (Tête Coupées), Waze-
cootai (Tireur dans les Pines).

As before remarked, not one of these names bears the most distant
resemblance to any living animal, bird, and so forth, neither have any
of them any general badge representing these things as symbolical of
their band.[9] The clans before referred to are of no importance in
their government and with the Sioux and with the Assiniboin are
only recognized as separate bodies during their dances and other
ceremonies.

Is each band entitled to one or more chiefs? There is, as observed
before, but one nominal chief to each band, and it is he who leads it.
Yet this position does not destroy nor militate against the will of
several others in the same band whose voices are as much entitled to
a hearing and sometimes more so than his. No man's rule over them
is absolute; their government is pure democracy. Their consent to be
governed or led by any man is voluntarily given and likewise withdrawn at the discretion of the person. But their existence as a
people depends on forming themselves into bodies capable of defense.
These bodies must have leaders and these leaders must be brave, respected, followed, and supported. In case of a treaty either with
whites or with Indians of other nations, the leading chief's voice
would have no additional weight because he is in that position. He
would be allowed to state his opinions with others of the same standing as men in the same band, but nothing more. As a good deal that
is to follow will depend upon receiving a correct idea of these chiefs
or leaders we do not like to leave any portion of these matters obscure or unanswered. There are no bands more honorable than

[8] This term is the same as Saone or Sanona.
[9] Here Denig seems to refer to what is commonly called clan totems.

others; some are more powerful, more rascally, or more tractable, but no aristocratic or honorable distinctions exist.

SOLDIERS.—Having mentioned and explained the divisions of bands and clans with the chiefs thereof, the next important body in their government is the ah-kitch-e-tah,[10] or soldiers or guard. These soldiers are picked from the band on account of their proved bravery and disposition to see things well conducted. They are men of family from 25 to 45 years old, steady, resolute, and respectable, and in them is vested the whole active power of governing the camp or rather of carrying out the decrees and decisions of councils. In a camp of 200 lodges they would number 50 to 60 men, and in a camp of 60 lodges 10 to 15 men. The soldiers' lodge is pitched in the center of the camp and occupied by some of them all the time, although the whole body are only called when the chief wishes a public meeting or when their hunting regulations are to be decided upon. This is their statehouse; all business relative to the camp and other nations is transacted there, and all strangers or visitors, white or red, are lodged therein.

Neither women, children, nor even young men are allowed to enter in business hours and seldom are seen there at any time. All tongues of animals killed in hunting belong to this lodge if they wish them, and the choicest parts of meat are furnished them by the young hunters all the time. A tax is also laid on the camp for the tobacco smoked here, which is no small quantity, and the women are each obliged to furnish some wood and water daily.

What are the general powers of chiefs in council? To explain this, it will be necessary to describe a council as witnessed by me a few years since. The camp when I was a visitor consisted of about 110 lodges and in the neighborhood, say, 10 or 15 miles off were two other camps, respectively 50 and 60 lodges, all being of the band Gens des Canots. The council was held in the soldiers' lodge, where, being a stranger, I had a right to be, though having nothing to say regarding the question. This question was, Will we make peace with the Crow Nation? A few days previous the leading chief had received an intimation through me that overtures for a peace were made to them by the Crow Nation, and that the Crow tobacco sent for that purpose was in my possession at any time the council assembled; also that a deputation of Crow Indians was at the Fort, who had commissioned me to bear the tobacco with their request and to await a reply prior to their visiting the camp in person.

To decide this runners were sent immediately to the two camps mentioned with a message from the chief requesting the attendance of all chiefs, counsellors, soldiers, and warriors who felt an interest

---

[10] In form and sense this term *ah-kitch-e-tah* is identical with the Chippewa *kitchitwa*, "sacred, holy, honorable," and with the Cree *okitchitaw*, "a brave, a soldier, un soldat)."

in the affair in question, who in due time arrived and took up their residence in the different lodges around about until the hour for business arrived. When it was ascertained that all or a sufficient number had come the haranguer or public crier of the camp made the circle of the village, speaking at the extent of his voice the object of the meeting and inviting all soldiers, chiefs, and braves or warriors to attend and hear what their chief would bring before them for their

Lodge door

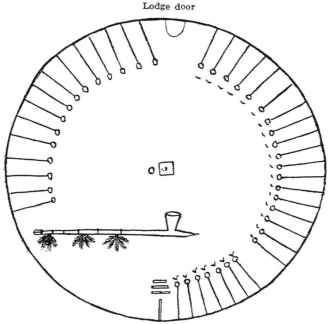

FIGURE 31.—Diagram of a council lodge, representing the interior of a council lodge in which Mr. Denig met the Assiniboin leaders to discuss peace overtures made by the Crow Indians to the Assiniboin at the instigation of Mr. Denig. At a point directly opposite the doorway Mr. Denig is seated with the proffered tobacco of the Crow Indians lying in front of him, denoted by 3 parallel marks; at Mr. Denig's right sits the leading Assiniboin chief; to his right sit 6 other chiefs and councillors; next are seated 18 so-called "soldiers," i. e., official guards of the camp; the next 15 figures are 15 principal young warriors. The small square figure with a central dot is a small fire; and the small circlet beside the fire is a flagstaff running up through the lodge top, flying a United States flag. The calumet pipe lies in front of the leading chief.

consideration. This was repeated over and over again in different parts of the camp, and shortly afterwards they began to assemble in the soldiers' lodge. Three skin lodges had been formed into one, making an area 24 feet in diameter, which could with ease accommodate 60 to 80 persons. On this occasion about 46 people presented themselves and when the whole had entered the interior exhibited the form shown in Figure 31.

It was nearly sunset when they had assembled and no feast had
been prepared in this lodge, though after the council was over they
were feasted elsewhere. We have here the represented authority of
220 lodges, for the chiefs are largely connected, having from 10 to
20 or more lodges of their immediate relatives each. The soldiers
are the most respectable heads of families in camp, and the warriors
are the sons and relations of these and others of the camp. If this
body decides on carrying a point who are to object? Those about
are also related to those present and these being the principal leave
only young rabble, very old men, women, and children not represented, all of whom combined could do nothing against the decision
of this body. We will now proceed with the ceremony. For nearly
a half hour the pipe was passed around in silence, it being filled with
their own tobacco and handed from mouth to mouth, making its
circuit on the right-hand, after which it was laid down by the leading chief and he opened the meeting by thus stating its object, the
words of whom and others were taken down by us at the time and
preserved. It will be necessary to state here that the Crow Indians
had massacred about 30 lodges of this same band two years previous
on the banks of the Yellowstone, yet had succeeded in making a peace
with some of the upper bands of Assiniboin who had not suffered by
them.

The leading chief spoke thus from where he sat:

" My children, I am a mild man. For upward of 20 years I have
herded you together like a band of horses. If it had not been for
me, you would long ago have been scattered like wolves over the
prairies. Good men and wise men are scarce; and, being so, they
should be listened to, loved, and obeyed. My tongue has been worn
thin and my teeth loosened in giving you advice and instruction. I
am aware I speak to men as wise as myself, many braver, but none
older or of more experience. I have called you together to state
that our enemies (the Crows) have sent tobacco, through the medium of the whites at the big fort, to me and my children, to see
if they could smoke it with pleasure, or if it tasted badly. For my
part I am willing to smoke. We are but a handful of men surrounded by large and powerful nations, all our enemies. Let us
therefore by making a peace reduce this number of foes and increase
our number of friends. I am aware that many here have lost relatives by these people, so have we by the Gros Ventres, and yet we
have peace with them. If it be to our interest to make peace all
old enmities must be laid aside and forgotten. I am getting old,
and have not many more winters to see, and am tired seeing my
children gradually decrease by incessant war. We are poor in
horses—from the herds the Crows own we will replenish. They

will pay high and give many horses for peace. The Crows are good warriors, and the whites say good people and will keep their word. Whatever is decided upon let it be manly. We are men; others can speak. I listen—I have said."

This speech was received by a slight response by some of Hoo-o-o-o and by the majority in silence. After a few minutes' interval he was replied to by another chief, the third or fourth from where he sat. This was a savage, warlike, one-eyed Indian, and his speech was characteristic. He said: " He differed from all the old chief had said regarding their enemies. Individually as a man and as their leader he liked his father, the chief, but he must be growing old and childish to advise them to take to smoke the tobacco of their enemies, the Crows. Tell the whites to take it back to them. It stinks, and if smoked would taste of the blood of our nearest relations. He thought (he said) his old father (the chief) should make a journey to the banks of the Yellowstone, and speak to the grinning skulls of 30 lodges of his children, and hear their answer. Would they laugh? Would they dance? Would they beg for Crow tobacco or cry for Crow horses? If horses were wanted in camp, let the young men go to war and steal and take them as he had done—as he intended to do as long as a Crow Indian had a horse. What if in the attempt they left their bones to bleach on the prairie? It would be but dying like men! For his part it always pleased him to see a young man's skull; the teeth were sound and beautiful, appearing to smile and say, ' I have died when I should and not waited at home until my teeth were worn to the gums by eating dried meat.' The young men (he said) will make war—must have war—and, as far as his influence went, should have war. I have spoken."

This speech was received with a loud and prolonged grunt of approbation by more than two-thirds of the assembly.

Other speeches followed on both sides of the question, some long, some short, until the council became somewhat heated and turbulent; not, however, interrupting one another, but mixing a good deal of private invective and satire with the question in their speeches. At a point of violent debate and personal abuse, two soldiers advanced to the middle of the lodge and laid two swords crosswise on the ground, which signal immediately restored order and quiet. The debate was carried on with spirit for about two hours but it was easily to be perceived long before it terminated, by their responses and gestures, that the war faction greatly predominated. The chief, after asking if all had spoken and receiving an affirmative answer, remarked they could go and eat the feast that had been prepared for them. The warriors gave a loud yell and when out commenced

singing their war song. We asked the old chief what was the decision. He said, "It is plain enough; listen to that war cry." He then
desired me to send the Crow tobacco back without delay and tell
them to leave the fort immediately and go home. A few days after
a large war party started to the Crow village. The morning after
the council's decision was made known by the haranguer or public
crier, at the break of day, walking through the village and crying it
out at the top of his voice. From the foregoing it will be seen that
the chief only expressed his opinion as the others, yet the large majority or rather the feeling evinced for war by the leaders of the war
parties, warriors, heads of families, soldiers, and all who could make
war, left none to contend with.

Had the same general exhibition for peace prevailed, the same
powers could make it, or rather force would be unnecessary when a
unanimity of such a body prevailed. Had the parties or feeling been
equally manifest the question would have been laid aside for another
time, perhaps years, and each went to war or remained at home as
he pleased.

Most councils have this feature and termination, that is, if the
measure is not at once visibly popular, it is abandoned. This pre-
cludes the necessity of vote and none is taken. Besides, except for
camp regulations, hunting, etc., they are not obliged to decide. Time
is not valuable to them. There is no constituent power in the rest of
the band, whose voices are not asked, nor required, to force a decision, nor actual power to operate against any measures, that may
be decided upon by their parents, and soldiers of the camp. Wherever force is necessary, however, to carry out these decisions, as in
hunting regulations, the soldiers are pledged to act in a body to
effect it, even at the risk of their lives. But should the decision be
for a peace and afterwards a war party be raised to go against the
nation with which peace has been made, the soldiers would not use
force to prevent it. They have too much good sense to strike or kill
any of their own people to benefit their enemies, and in this case the
peace party being the most numerous, and consequently the richer,
would pay the partisan, or leader of the party, to remain at home
and a collection of horses, guns, and other property made among
them for that purpose, which being handed the partisan and by
him divided among his warriors, stops the expedition.

This is done often among them, particularly at this time when
"peaces" have become tolerably general through the Laramie treaty.
There are cases, however, where force is necessary, and the soldiers
are brought to act, which we will shortly mention. To present any
idea of their government so that it can be understood, we must first
proceed to describe the component parts of a large camp, after which
it will be easy to perceive their principles of government. The regu-

lations kept up in the following description is only in large camps: Smaller ones, from 10 to 20 lodges, hunt, every man when he pleases, and, as there are but few persons to feed, they can always have meat in this way; but where the camp is composed of from 50 to 100 or 200 lodges this is not the case, as will presently appear.

COMPONENT PARTS OF A LARGE CAMP

1. The leading chief.
2. The other chiefs.
3. Chief of the soldiers.
4. Cook of the soldiers' lodge.
5. The soldiers.
6. The elderly men.
7. The haranguer.
8. The master of the Park.
9. Warriors and hunters.
10. Partisans.[11]
11. Doctors and conjurors.
12. Very old men.
13. Young women.
14. Old women.
15. Middle-aged women.
16. Boys and girls.
17. Very small chlidren.

The ordinary occupations of these several divisions of the camp will now be taken up in order.

1. The leading Chief, Hoon-gah, being the head, is expected to devote his time to studying the welfare of his people. It is for him to determine where the camp shall be placed and when it should move; if war parties are advisable, and with whom, how many, and at what time; where soldiers' camps and the soldiers' lodge should be established; when traders are wanted in camp, or when they shall go to the fort to trade; to call councils on these and all other affairs of general interest.

2. The other Chiefs, Hoo-gap-pe. These are sometimes counselled privately in their lodges by their leader and their advice followed if correct and according to his views. They sit in council when called, and rank equally with the leader as men, warriors, counsellors, etc., except they do not publicly attempt to lead or act without his knowledge and consent.

3. Chief of the soldiers, Ah-kitche-tah Hoon-gah. This is the head man in the soldiers' lodge; sees to their property therein, whether there is wood, water, tobacco, and meat enough; opens councils; sometimes sends invitations for the others to assemble when the Chief requests, and on small occasions of his own accord; makes feasts; lights the pipe in large assemblies, and is the nominal head of this active body; is a highly respected and useful officer in camp. He has much influence with the young warriors and is selected from among the bravest of them.

4. Cook of the soldiers' lodge. First, Wo-ha-nah; second, Wah-yu-tena. This functionary is also a soldier and a highly respectable officer, ranking next to the Chief of the soldiers.

---

[11] Denig employs the word partisan in the sense of "a leader of a war party."

Eating being one of the Indian's most important occupations, the care of the meat, choice of the parts, and separation of the whole depending upon him, the station becomes at once of consequence and requires a determined man. On feasting, which in that lodge is going on every night, if not every day, he dishes out the meat into wooden bowls and gives to each the parts he chooses. Of a dog, the head, paws, and grease—bouillon—are the most honorable parts. There is great etiquette shown in this respect, and it is too long a story to record when there is so much yet to be written.

5. The soldiers, Ah-kitche-tah. These are the bravest and most orderly men of from 25 to 35 years of age. They have been and are still warriors and leaders of parties to war, are chosen expressly to carry out the decrees of the council, even at the risk of their lives, to punish people for raising the buffalo, setting the prairie on fire, govern the camp, protect whites and strangers of other nations in camp, entertain and feast the same, arrange preliminaries of peace, trade, and generally to aid their chief in carrying out his views and decisions of council.

6. Elderly men, We-chap-pe. These may be called the body of the camp, being men of family, about 40 years old, have been warriors and soldiers when younger, but have abandoned these occupations, devote their time to hunting, are still good hunters, try to amass horses and other property by making robes, endeavor to get their daughters married well, send their sons to hunt or to war.

They are respectable, quiet, peaceable men, among their own people, content to follow their leader and obey the council, rank as councillors when they wish, are always invited though but few attend except on interesting occasions.

7. The Public Crier. First name, Ponkewichakeah; second, Hoon-kee-yah. This is some elderly or middle-aged man who has a strong voice and a talent for haranguing. He answers the purpose of the daily newspaper of the whites. A little before daybreak he walks around and through the camp different times every morning, calling upon the young men to get up and look after their horses and arms, to go on the hills and look for buffaloes, watch if there be any signs of enemies about—to the women to get up to bring wood and water, cook, dress hides, etc. If any news has been received in camp the day before or any councils held, he now states the results. Whenever the camp is to be moved or hunts made, or enemies seen, or councils to be held, this man publishes it in this way. He is in fact their publisher and a useful man, doing more to preserve order and induce unanimity of action than any other, is entitled to eat and smoke in any lodge he happens to enter without invitation, receives many small presents, and is a general favorite for the trouble he gives himself.

8. Master of the Park, Wo-wee-nah. A park or pen to catch buffalo is not at all times made, though almost every winter there is one or two among the Assiniboin. We will have occasion to refer to this original method of hunting in another place; at present it suffices to say that the person who superintends that employment is some old conjuror or medicine man who is said to make the buffalo appear and to bring them toward the pen. He makes sacrifices to the Wind, the Sun, and to Wakoñda, etc., of tobacco, scarlet cloth, and other things; he is a necromancer and is supposed to be possessed of supernatural powers and knowledge; he has from four to six runners under his command whose business it is to discover the buffalo within 20 or 30 miles around, and to report to him.

9. Young men, Ko-ash-kah-pe. These are a numerous body, some warriors, some hunters, some neither. Those who have killed or struck enemies or stolen many horses from their foes are entitled to sit in the council and are always invited, principally to hear and give their assent or dissent in responses, gestures, etc. They, no doubt, would be allowed to speak but they never do, because those who are older speak, and they are generally the fathers and relations of these young men. In this modesty of deportment they are much to be admired. They always conform to the decisions of the soldiers and the chiefs. The partisans or leaders of war parties are chosen sometimes from these young men, when by their acts they have proved a capacity to lead, though mostly it is one of the soldiers who raises and leads the war expedition.

The Partisan is in command during the entire expedition, directs their movements, possesses the power of a military captain among the whites, and receives the honors or bears the disgrace of success or failure, his authority in' that capacity ceasing on his return to camp from the war.

10. Doctors, alias conjurors, alias priests, alias soothsayers, alias prophets, Wah-con-we-chasta. These have been alluded to under the head of " General Practice " in their medical capacity. They are not numerous, form no distinct body, and unite the above talents in the same person. They do many tricks well, also foretell events, interpret dreams, utter incantations, medicine speeches and prayers, and cry for the dead, etc. They are believed sincerely by all to possess supernatural powers. The males of this class are sometimes in councils but they have little influence there. Councils are matters of fact and do not admit of their noise and flummery, without which they are ciphers. They are tolerated because somewhat feared, are paid for their services, and by no means rank as very respectable and efficient councillors, warriors, or men.

11. Very old men, We-chah-chape. These are few. Indians are not long-lived. These are countenanced in private feasts and or-

dinary conversation, principally on account of their talent in reciting fables and creating mirth for the rest. They also sing for the doctors and cry for the dead when paid, are poor, not respected, and manage to rub through the rest of their days the best way they can. They never sit in council when very old, are neglected, and serve for a butt and ridicule for the young. They stay at home, make pipes, smoke, and eat constantly and are ready at all times to offer their services when something is to be gained.

12. Young women, We-kosh-kap-pi, do little work before they are married and have their first child, after which time they commence a laborious life. Before this they go for wood and water, garnish with beads and porcupine quills, and other light work. They gather berries, assist in dances, paint, and show themselves.

13. Middle-aged Women, Wé-yah-pe. These are the wives of the soldiers or middle-aged men, and their time is employed in dressing skins, cooking, drying meat, taking care of their children, making cloth for their family. They are always busy, but can not be said to lead a too laborious or miserable life.

14. Very Old Women, We-noh-chah (Sioux), Wa-kun-kun-ah (Assiniboin). On these fall all drudging and scullionry, some of their occupations being too disgusting to relate. They also pound meat and berries, make pemmican, carry burdens, and are used pretty much as one of their dogs. They are thrown into the fort or left on the prairie to die by their own relatives.

15. Boys and Girls, Och-she-pe wechin chap-pe. The boys hunt rabbits, set traps for foxes, play, but they seldom quarrel; they are great pests and nuisances, both in camp and in the fort; they are spoiled by their parents—forward, officious, tormenting, and impudent. The girls are modest, timid, and exceedingly well behaved.

Very Small Children, Yaque-ske-pe-nah, are carried about on the backs of their mothers, or packed on dogs; they stand severe cold well, do not cry much, and are suckled for two or three years. The children are as well taken care of as they can be in the roving mode of life of their parents, but being subject to exposure in all weather and accidents. About two out of five are raised.

The ahkitchetah regulate the hunt. The buffalo are not hunted by a large camp as each individual chooses, but surrounded by the whole camp at one time, which we will describe in that part of the report which refers to hunting and to game laws. The dogs for these hunts are determined by the chief and soldiers in the soldiers' lodge, and the people are individually forbidden to hunt or in any manner to raise the buffalo before that time. The reason is that by going in a body and hemming in or surrounding them, some hundreds of the animals are slain in a short time, whereas by one man's individual hunting the whole herd would be frightened and run away and the camp thereby be always in a starving condition, instead of having abundance of meat as is the case when the laws respecting the surround are enforced. Should any person or persons violate these laws, after the decree of the soldiers' lodge has been published, they (the soldiers) meet him on his return home, take his meat, kill his dogs, or horses, cut his hides up, cut his lodge to pieces, break his gun and bow, etc. If the individual resists or attempts to revenge any of these things he is shot down on the spot by the soldiers, or struck down by a tomahawk and pounded to death. Occasionally they are also thrashed with bows, in addition to the breaking of the gun, etc. The writer has seen two killed and many severely thrashed for these misdemeanors. The consequences of destroying the hunts are serious to the whole camp, hence the violent penalty and examples are made occasionally which serve to increase the respect and fear of the soldiers as a body, and enables that business to proceed with order.

In all this the soldiers are supported by the whole camp, and it is in them as a body that decisions are invested with a binding force, if force be necessary. We may state that the power is tacitly committed to the chief as a common and general function of the office, to be held as long as he governs with general satisfaction, subject, however, to the advice and consent of the soldiers and other bodies in camp, as has been explained. They are at all times open to popular opinion and are only the exponents of it, and although distinguished deeds were the cause or some of the causes of their exaltation to this high office, and that they have since been and generally are discontinued, when the chief becomes of middle age, yet so long as the capacity and ability of the incumbent exists and coincides with the popular will, he is retained in office. Old age, debility, or other natural defect, and incapacity to act, advise, and command, induces the necessity of change in his position, and though not formally deposed, he voluntarily retires and resigns in favor of some growing and popular soldier and warrior. The disapproval of the mass of the body of soldiers, warriors, etc., as represented in the council of war, would also be an effectual barrier to the existence of his power or functions in every respect and at any and all times. It should be remembered that all the remarks in these pages, although written primarily for the tribe called the Assiniboin, apply equally well to all the roving tribes of the Missouri River from and including the Sioux to the Blackfeet, our limits not admitting separate descriptions for each tribe. Where there is any important difference, however, we will not fail to mention it.

Is the democratic element strongly implanted? Very. The whole is a pure democracy, as has by this been developed. There are also

consultations in private lodges previous to meeting in councils, but
these do not appear to influence the opinions of any, further than
thereby getting a thorough acquaintance of the subject, and preparing their minds for a speech, and not much idea can be formed in
this way of the popularity of the question until it meets public discussion in the council.   Neither are these private councils held with
that view but are merely conversations regarding the importance of
the subject and something to talk about, which is always desirable in
an Indian camp.   They are obstinate in adhering to a formed opinion and not easily moved by oratory or extraneous remarks, are
shrewd and pursue the subject with intensity and perseverance until
decided or abandoned.   They are liable also to be carried away by
the excitement of debate and lose sight of the subject in personal
abuse and recrimination until called to order by some more cool.
There is no vote taken, though the prevailing feeling is manifest and
those who do not exhibit any of this feeling are quietly asked their
opinion, which they as quietly give.   All this has met with sufficient
explanation.   The leading chief does nothing in advance of public
opinion.   His business is rather to think of their welfare and interests, bringing those subjects under discussion which appear to
him of sufficient importance and which he sees merit consideration
by the excitement they occasion in private lodges, or if smaller matters they are left to the decision of the soldiers.   In councils held
in the soldiers' lodge for hunting the chief does not always appear.
When the camp is placed for the winter he assists in forming the
body of soldiers and in giving general instructions which they carry
out.   Afterwards he seldom goes for these purposes.   The business
of these soldiers will meet with further notice in these pages and
it is worth while considering their powers, as they are the active
force of all large camps.

Councils.—Councils are opened in a very sedate and orderly form.
The pipe is the principal of all ceremonies, and its motions vary
with the occasions.   Councils between two nations for a peace, deputations of both being present, are very solemn and take a long time.
It is likely these ceremonies are very ancient, being nearly the same
among all the roving tribes.   The real calumet used on this occasion
with its accompaniments presents the form as sketched and explained
in Plate 68.   This instrument is always kept packed up in many
envelopes of cloth, skin, etc., the whole making a roll as thick as
a man's thigh, sometimes as large as a piece of common stovepipe, 5
or 6 feet long, is laid in the middle of the soldiers' lodge on a piece
of scarlet cloth in that way before the deputation has arrived, or
immediately on its arrival, is not opened, however, until a full council has been assembled.   The chief (who owns the pipe) then com-

mences the ceremony of unrolling it, and at the taking off of each envelope says a few words equivalent to " Peace we wish," " Look over us, Wakoñda," " This to the Sun," " This to the Earth," etc., giving, as it were, some distinction or value to each envelope. After a long time and the untying of many knots, the pipe and stem appear, with a tobacco sack, a bunch of sweet-smelling grass, a probe for the pipe, and a small sack containing a charm or amulet. The pipe is on this occasion filled from the tobacco (or mixture) sack by the chief of the soldiers, though not lit, and in this way handed to his own chief. He (the chief) now stands up, the different deputations of nations sitting opposite each other on either side of the lodge. He first presents the pipe to the East, singing a gentle and harmonious song for about a minute, then presents it South, West, North, to the Sky and lastly to the Earth, repeating the song at each presentation.

In conclusion he turns it slowly three times round, and lays it down, all responding hoo-o-oo as the pipe is placed on the ground. The chief now sits down in his place, and the Chief of the soldiers rises. He lights the pipe with a piece of the sweet-smelling grass—if the strangers are of the Crow nation a piece of dried buffalo dung is used to light it—stands up and presents it precisely to the same points as the chief had done without singing, giving three puffs or whiffs of the pipe to every presentation, finishing in the same way the chief had done, and, receiving a loud prolonged universal hoo-o-oo or grunt of approbation, he then resumes his seat. The chief now rises the second time and having had the pipe relighted, holding the stem in his hand advances and presents it, or rather places it in the mouth of the head man of the strange deputation, allowing him to take a few whiffs, passes to the next and the next, they sitting and he moving round from one to another until all the strangers have been smoked, then he hands the pipe to the chief of the soldiers and sits down. This officer now presents the pipe in the same way to his own chief and going round the other side smokes all his people, and hands the pipe to another soldier, who goes the whole round again, and this is repeated over in silence for at least two hours, when the pipe is laid down by the chief, and speeches or signs begin by which they arrange the preliminaries of a peace. After all is settled the pipe undergoes the ceremony of rolling up, which is fully as long, though not in silence, conversation becoming general and ordinary pipes being introduced. The termination on this occasion is a grand feast in the soldiers' lodge to the strangers, and invitations to 50 or more other feasts in camp, to all of which they must go, and when all is finished the strangers are accommodated with temporary wives during their short residence.

There is generally order observed in the breaking up of councils, the chief saying " We are done," when all retire. Occasionally, however, it breaks up turbulently, and they separate in passion, but the subject is recouncilled and settled in order the next time. Different councils have different ceremonies. Some open and some close with feasts of dog meat. The pipe is never omitted, though the real calumet is never opened except in dealings with strangers. In all other councils soldiers' pipes are used. The duties of the public crier we have already mentioned. Questions are well debated, and generally decided on the spot or abandoned as already explained on the principle of large majorities, or rather general approbation, though absolute unanimity is not required. The few who oppose say nothing against the affairs when once decided, and although they do not relinquish their opinions, yet can not or will not go contrary to the wishes of the many. But the voice of the leading chief is in no instance taken as the expression of the will of even a single band, much less a whole tribe.

SCOPE OF CIVIL JURISDICTION.—A decision by the body of the council is carried into effect by the soldiers, by force if necessary, as in the case of hunting by the surround, removing neighboring lodges of their own people who are so placed as to bar the passage of the buffalo toward the camp. Lodges thus situated are invariably forced to come and join the camp or to remove so far as to be no obstruction to the passage and advance of the buffalo, and to move them against their will is often a serious and always a dangerous undertaking. They do it, however; that is, the soldiers turn out in a body, kill their dogs, and keep doing damage until they leave. The power of taking life is not invested in any body of Indians, neither has the council any right to take cognizance of or legislate on the subject. If a soldier is killed in doing his duty the body of soldiers would immediately fall upon the murderer or on any of his relatives, should he have absconded. Crimes of this kind are privately redressed and revenged by the relatives of the deceased, and as the murderer always flies, it is often years before they can get an opportunity to kill him, yet vengeance only slumbers. All these things will be fully explained under the head of " Crime." It might, however, be as well to state here that there is no public body among them whose duty it is to punish crime of any kind, nor any authority equivalent to or resembling a court of justice. Consequently, there are no public or stated executions, neither is there any person who exercises the functions of public executioner. All this will be fully explained, as also the restoration of property, in the place where rights of property are considered.

CHIEFSHIP.—How are rank and succession in office regulated? The circumstances of the decease of the leading chief and the succession has already been referred to. If not yet sufficiently explicit, we may in addition state that it would be a subject of earnest debate in council, not so much with the view of choosing the successor, as this individual had long before been tacitly acknowledged, being the next most popular leader of the right kind, and of the most numerous connections, but to install that person into office, intimating their desire that he should lead and govern the camp. This might be called election, although no vote is taken, yet if a general feeling in his favor prevails he becomes their leader; if not, those who dissent have the privilege of leaving that band and joining another, or if numerous enough for the general purposes of hunting and defense can form a band of their own and choose a leader from among themselves. In all this we hope to have been sufficiently explicit as not to present any idea of a distinct line of hereditary succession.

A chief would be deposed from his office by being guilty of any conduct that would bring upon him general disgust and dissatisfaction. Though crimes in the abstract could not have this tendency, yet if he murdered a man without cause whose relations were numerous, a skirmish between the two families and immediate separation would be the consequence. If the murdered man was friendless nothing would be done and the rest would fear him the more. The offenses that would most likely lead to his overthrow would be remarkable meanness, parsimony, or incest. A chief must give away all to preserve his popularity and is always the poorest in the band, yet he takes good care to distribute his gifts among his own relatives or the rich, upon whom he can draw at any time should he be in need.

We take the custom of wearing medals to be a modern one, at least they say so, introduced by the whites. The ancient mark of distinction was, and still is, the feathers of the eagle's tail, wrought into headdresses of various forms, which to this day is the badge denoting the chief and great warrior, and are not allowed the ordinary class to wear. Tattooing also is a mark of dignity.

We have already named the principal chiefs of bands, though there are others, but by no means a numerous body. But few Indians go through war enough to arrive at that position, more especially as the same individual must be possessed of other natural talents and wisdom. The number is not limited but is from 3 to 6 or 8 in bands respectively of 50, 100, and 200 lodges. It makes no difference in their government whether they be few or many; if many, so much the better, as they are wise, brave, and responsible men.

POWER OF THE WAR CHIEF.—No chiefs are war chiefs in contradistinction to their being civil chiefs. If it is desirable to go to war and so decided, any chief, soldier, or brave warrior has a right to

raise and lead a war party, provided he can get followers. He then
comes under the head of partisan or captain of the expedition, his
powers in this capacity only lasting during the excursion and termi-
nating on his return to camp and resuming his civil place and duties.
The powers of war and civil chief are united in the same, also those
of warrior and hunter, soldier and hunter, soldier and partisan, chief
and partisan. The leading chief could also and often does guide the
whole band to war; in fact in the event of any general turnout, he
must be the head. Any man, however, in whom the young men
have confidence to follow, may raise and lead a war party, if war
is going on and the time suits the chiefs and soldiers in council
assembled. But as the chiefs and soldiers are the most experienced
in this occupation, and are better acquainted with their enemies'
country, they are generally chosen as leaders in these expeditions.
Yet from among the warrior class, occasionally a young partisan
arises who is neither chief nor soldier, but whose character for bravery, caution, and all the necessary talents is established. There is
no specified age when a young man may rightfully express his opinion. This depends on his success in war, his general good behavior,
activity in hunting, etc. When he becomes remarkable for these
things he is noticed by the soldiers, invited to feasts, to councils,
where being of sufficient consequence his opinion is asked and is
given. We have known men not over 22 to 24 years of age being
called upon to speak in council, and others to arrive at extreme old
age without ever opening their lips there. An Indian soon sees and
feels his standing with the others, and acts accordingly; to do otherwise, or force his presence and opinions prematurely, would only
incur ridicule, contempt, and disgrace.

POWER OF THE PRIESTS IN COUNCIL.—The power of priests is con-
joined with that of doctors, sorcerers, and prophets, to which is occasionally added that of councillors, as they are sometimes shrewd
old men and somewhat feared on account of their supposed supernatural powers; but they do not influence councils in any great degree, seldom attending at all. Whatever influence they have on
public questions must be exercised in council, and not as a separate
body. They do not constitute a body and only rank as councillors
when their former exploits have been of a nature to entitle them to
that position, and their age is not too far advanced. Being generally
very old, their opinions in council are not much regarded. Their
forte is at the bed of the sick or in other operations where something
is to be gained. In making war or peace they would have little to
say, in a cession of lands still less, and in conducting war parties nothing at all. The old Gauché mentioned before, although a divining
man, was a warrior, not old at that time, and feared because he had
the power over their lives by the use of poisons which he made no

scruple to administer; besides he was no doctor nor sorcerer on other occasions, and was one of the greatest chiefs the Assiniboin ever had. He was uniformly successful in his young and middle time of life, although he failed in age and died as recorded. This extraordinary man does not present a correct sample of a priest or sorcerer as now considered, and is an anomalous case.

MATRONS IN COUNCIL.—Neither matrons nor any other women whatever sit in council with the men of any of the Missouri tribes, nor have they privately any influence over men in their public affairs, and take but little interest in them. Their domestic duties occupy most of their time and their social position is inferior to that of men in every respect. We have heard of only one instance where a woman was admitted in council, during a period of 21 years' constant residence with all these tribes.

GENERAL COUNCILS.—The roving tribes call no general councils with other nations. Even those with whom they have for a long time been at peace they look upon suspiciously and seldom act together in a large body. We have known, however, a combination of Cree, Chippewa, and Assiniboin, consisting of 1,100 men, who, having met in council, went to war upon the Blackfeet. The council was formed by the Cree and Chippewa sending tobacco to the Assiniboin during the winter, to meet them at a certain place the ensuing spring, where, after deliberating the matter at home, they went and formed the above-named expedition. It is the misfortune of all large bodies of Indians formed of different nations to meet with failure. They can not act in a body. Jealousies arise between the soldiers of the different nations, often quarrels, and always separations and defeat of the object. The evil appears to be the want of a commander in chief whom all are content to follow and obey; also their ignorance and unwillingness to submit to discipline, restraint, or subordination. Opinions clash, rank is interfered with, rebellion, dissatisfaction, and consequent separation follows; or should any considerable body keep on, their march is conducted in such a disorderly manner that their enemies have time and notice to enable them to hide or prepare for them. These tribes are not yet far enough advanced in civil organization to enable them to unite for any great purpose, excepting their mutual and general interest require it. The only way they could and do accomplish anything of importance at war by combination is by each nation being headed and commanded by their own leaders and going to war upon the general enemy at different times and entirely independent of each other. This increases the number of war expeditions and annoys the enemy from different quarters, but does not give them the advantage of bringing large armies into the field.

PRIVATE RIGHT TO TAKE LIFE.—Every Indian believes he has a
right to his own life and consequently to defend it. There being no
persons or body whose duty it is to punish crime, trespass, or insult,
each individual is taught when a boy, and by experience when a
man, to rely entirely on himself for redress or protecting his person,
family, and property. Every one is thus constituted his own judge,
jury, and executioner. Whether the person wronged is right in his
means of redress does not matter. He thinks he is right and risks the
consequences of retaliation. Every Indian being armed induces the
necessity of each using arms; therefore when an Indian strikes, stabs,
shoots, or attempts to do these things it is always with an intent to
kill, knowing if he misses his aim or only wounds, the other revenges
either on the spot or after, as occasion requires or opportunity offers.
Therefore he can not act otherwise. This being the state of things,
quarrels are not so common as might be supposed. When it is universally known that a blow or a trespass would entail death as its
consequence they are avoided, or if unavoidable each endeavors to
gain an advantage over the other by acting treacherously or waiting
a favorable time when he least expects it to kill or strike him, stating
for his reason that if he had not killed him the other only waited
the same opportunity against himself. A fair chance to kill or strike
does not always present itself. The relations may be too numerous
on one side, and the object of contention (be it a horse or a woman)
is given up for the time by the weaker party, apparently willingly,
yet he only waits until their situations are reversed to seek redress.
When a man has killed another, if the relatives of the deceased are
more numerous than his own, he flies to a distant part of the country,
joins another band and seeks protection there, where he is not sought
by the next of kin at the time, but will be killed whenever they
meet. In the meantime the relatives of the offender pay much to
stop the quarrel.

If the killed and the killer are both of the same band and equally
strong in relationship perhaps nothing would be done at the time as
the rest of camp would endeavor to stop a skirmish, and a good many
guns, horses, and other property would be raised and presented the
relatives of the deceased to stop further bloodshed. This generally
concludes an amnesty or respite for the time, but the revenge must
be accomplished at some time by the next of kin, otherwise it would
be a great disgrace to him or them. An opportunity to kill the
offender with comparative safety is then sought, perhaps for years,
or as long as any of that generation lives. Time and absence may
have the effect of giving the murderer a chance to die in some other
way or of diminishing the force of the revenge so that he does not
find himself in a position to act with any degree of safety when an

occasion offers. Yet, if of standing in camp, and a brother, father, or brother-in-law to the deceased, he is bound to revenge at some time, though they make no scruple to receive presents of horses, etc., to refrain in the meantime. Thus the death of a man is never paid for by that generation, though by that means the revenge may be delayed for some years, which is all they can do except surrendering up their relative to the incensed party, which would not for a moment be thought of. We have known three or four horses to be given on the instant by the friends of the offender to those of the deceased and the same to be repeated yearly for two to six years and more, yet still revenge was consummated. On one occasion I asked the man why he killed the other after so long a time and taking property as payment from his relatives and friends. He answered that the pay was well enough as long as the culprit kept out of his sight; that remuneration only destroyed the disposition to seek him out and kill him, although it did not affect the right to revenge if he was fool enough to thrust himself in his way.

When he saw him his blood boiled, his heart rose up, and he could not help it. Besides (he observed) he was obliged to kill him, as the other, being afraid of him, would do the same to him to save his own life. Thus the killing of one induces the necessity of killing another, and there is no end to the affair. The other party are obliged to retaliate and so on through several generations. In this way a good many of the family of the chief, Wah-he Muzza, have been killed, and the smallpox settled the affair by taking off the offenders on the other side. It will be inferred from this that vengeance is not appeased by payment, absence, or the lapse of time, and in the instances where retaliation has not followed after payment we believe they may be ascribed to a decrease in the relationship of the deceased or other domestic changes or reverses which render vengeance out of their power, or too dangerous to accomplish, in which case the relatives get over it by saying they have been paid or forgotten it, yet at the same time would revenge, could they act with safety, or even a chance of comparative safety. Sometimes, however, large offers of recompense are rejected by the father or brothers of the deceased, and the tender is then made to relatives not so closely connected, who generally accept. Herein the cunning of the Indian is manifest. This is a point gained. A negotiation is opened in the family of the deceased and a difference of feeling established with regard to the offender, slight to be sure, but it is there, and is worked by these distant relatives to his advantage and their own, and opens a way through which presents and overtures of compromise may be offered the brothers, etc. But there is no dependence to be placed on anything a wild Indian does.

Neither do they depend on one another. They are suspicious in everything, and more particularly so when life is at stake. In these compromises no one is deceived—either he who takes or he who receives—the minds of both are perfectly known to each other, the object of the one party being to gain time, and of the other to lull suspicion and make the offender and his relatives poor by accepting their property.

We think we have presented their customs in this respect in their true light, viz, that although the compromise be effected and vengeance for the time suspended, yet the feeling is not changed or the right to punish relinquished; but time may make such a change on either part as to render revenge impracticable. There is no recognized principle or means of escape for the murderer unless it be to flee and join another nation with whom they are at peace, marry and remain there.

It will now be necessary to state that the Crow Indians are better regulated in this respect than any of the prairie tribes. Private murders are nearly unknown among them. Our knowledge of this nation from certain sources extends through a period of 40 years and in all that time but one Indian was killed by his own people. The offender absconded and remained with the Snake Nation for 12 years, when he returned, but was obliged again to leave, and since has not been heard of. Stealing women or otherwise seducing others' wives is revenged by the party offended taking every horse and all private property the offender owns, and in this he meets with no contention. It is considered a point of honor to let everything be taken but keep the woman. Now this nation has from 40 to 80 and sometimes 100 horses to a lodge, and a large haul is made by the husband of the woman, in company with his relatives. If the transgressor has no property that of his nearest relatives is taken, and is suffered to be taken away unmolested. After the excitement is somewhat over, these horses are bought back by the relatives of the offender, each giving two, three, or more as the case happens, which they hand over to him, who in the course of time gets the most of his property returned.

All smaller quarrels or misdemeanors are paid in the same way, though not so high, but they never strike or kill each other, yet are addicted to using personal abuse and invective freely. Our gentleman in charge of that nation states that he has seen the two principal bands of Crow Indians, over 200 lodges, abusing and throwing stones at each other all day, the Yellowstone River being between them. No damage could happen, as the missiles could not be thrown a fourth of the distance, yet not a shot was fired, although balls would reach, and this force was headed by the two principal chiefs of that nation. In all the regulations of these Indians (the Crows) we can discern great natural goodness of heart, and absence of any useless barbarity and bloodshed except with regard to their enemies, the males of whom they kill and cut to pieces, but never kill women and children, whereas the Assiniboin, Sioux, and Blackfeet kill everything. Very few feuds from polygamy result in death, but should it so happen the other would be punished. If the favorite wife had been killed, the least the other wife expected would be a tomahawking, or an arrow shot into her, perfectly regardless as to whether death would be the consequence or not. Women among Indians are bought, paid for, and are the property of the purchaser the same as his horses. Their lives are of course more valuable than those of animals, and every Indian regrets the loss of his woman. Yet when he has bought them he expects them to do their duty, not quarrel nor render his lodge disagreeable, or if so they must expect to be severely punished.

Their lives are not, however, considered as valuable as men, nor are they ever so much mourned for. When not bought, or unmarried, the killing of a woman never happens and would be a great disgrace to any man, though after marriage they are subject to the penalty of death from different causes in which the man thinks he is justified.

Private debts are never settled by the chief, nor private disputes by council. Advice may be given and taken, frequently is, though the usual mode of settling trivial quarrels is by payment, and an invitation to a feast. Everything except loss of life or personal chastisement can be paid for among these Indians.

GAME LAWS, OR RIGHTS OF THE CHASE.—The roving tribes subsist by hunting buffalo, and these animals being constantly on the move, they are obliged to move after them. Therefore no particular section of country is appointed to each as a hunting district.[12] There are, however, certain regulations with regard to the hunting of these animals which may as well be recorded here. A lodge or a few lodges have no right to establish and hunt within 6, 8, or 10 miles from a large camp, as by this the buffalo would be continually kept out of the range of the latter, and a few people be the cause of distress and starvation to the many. Therefore these obstructions are removed by the soldiers. When hunting by surround has been agreed upon, individual hunting is stopped for the same reason, and has met with explanation. This is also the duty of the soldiers. Hunting deer, elk, beaver, etc., being of little consequence to these Indians, each one exercises his pleasure in regard to these occupations. No right to any section of country is claimed by any person to the ex-

---

[12] The statement here militates against any claim of private ownership of hunting grounds among these tribes.

clusion of others. Should an Indian wound a deer and not follow, and another pursue and kill it, the former would have no right to either skin or meat, having relinquished that right by abandoning the wounded animal. But should he be following and arrive where the other has killed it, the hide and half the meat would be his share. As a general rule he who draws the first blood of the animal is entitled to the hide. This is often difficult to settle when large buffalo surrounds are made on horseback with the bow and arrow. Several hundreds of animals are slain in the course of an hour or so, and some have the arrows of different Indians in them. Each Indian, by his own mark, knows his arrow, but the matter of dispute is whose arrow struck first? Therefore who is entitled to the hide?

All that prevents this from being often the cause of serious quarrels is that in large hunts a sufficient number or more is generally killed than they can or do skin, and in smaller hunts the same confusion does not occur. A wounded animal is also mostly pursued until killed, and others usually pass by those that are stopped or have arrows sticking into them. With regard to the meat all Indians are liberal. In a large camp at least one-third of the men have no horses that they can catch. There are also a good many old, infirm widows, etc., all of whom must be fed. Every one who can, men and women, turn out and follow the horsemen to the hunt; and, even while the hunt is going on at a distance, commence cutting up the first buffalo they come to. The hide is taken off, and laid aside with the arrow found in it. The tongue and four of the choicest pieces are laid on the hide. This is the portion of him who killed it; and the rest, which is the greater part of the animal, is divided among those who skin it. This operation is going on with numbers of buffalo at the same time, and by this division of labor the hunters and all are ready to pack home their hides and meat nearly as soon as the hunt is finished. In this way the hunters get as many hides and as much meat as they can pack, and those who have not killed, as much meat as they want. Whatever hides are remaining are given away to those who have no horses to hunt with, and other poor people, and all are satisfied and provided for. The soldiers' lodge and others in camp who have remained to guard the property in the absence of the greater body of people are each supplied with meat by those who have been at the hunt. Feasting is then commenced, and kept up day and night until meat has become scarce, when another hunt follows. This method of hunting is continued until they have hides and meat enough.

INDIAN TRADE

There is no doubt that the Indian trade has promoted the general cause of civilization. Even within our recollection, tribes of Indians, from being bloodthirsty robbers, have changed to orderly and civil people. A foundation has been laid, and the road paved toward the civilization of the prairie tribes, but nothing more. Stationary Indians have been still further advanced. The few ideas of justice that are beginning to be developed and the very first dawn of the light of knowledge perceptible are in consequence of their traffic and communication with the white trader. The introduction of firearms, articles of clothing, utensils, and other articles manufactured by the whites must tend to enlarge their ideas, set them to thinking, to show them their uncultivated state, and to implant a desire to improve. Nevertheless their progress is slow, more so with the Assiniboin than with any other nations. They adhere with tenacity to old customs and superstitions, which is vexatious and discouraging; but the Sioux, Mandan, Gros Ventres, Cree, and Chippewa are undoubtedly much improved. The firm of Pierre Chouteau, Jr., & Co., formerly the American Fur Co., has for many years conducted the trade with all the Indians of the Missouri and its tributaries, from Council Bluffs to the headwaters of the Missouri and Yellowstone Rivers. The supplies for the trade are brought up each spring and summer from St. Louis by steamboat and distributed at the different forts along the Missouri River as far as Fort Union, mouth of the Yellowstone; from which point they are transported with keel boats to Fort Benton, near the mouth of Maria River, in the Blackfoot country. From these forts or depots the merchandise is carried into the interior in different ways, to wherever the Indians request trading houses to be established.

The traders generally bear the character of trustworthy men and the nature of the barter for robes and other skins is such that the Indian receives what he considers an equivalent for his labor or he would not hunt. There is no way in the nature of the business by which an Indian can be made to hunt, nor any means of getting his skins without paying a fair price. Should the merchandise be placed too high to be easily purchased by them they would and can dispense with nearly all the articles of trade. On the contrary should the price be too low the business could not be continued; the prospects of gain not being equivalent to the risk of the adventure or capital employed it would be abandoned. Consequently a medium is and must be established whereby are secured the advantage and comfort of the Indian and a tolerably fair prospect of gain for the trader. The trade, when carried on without competition, is in many respects a highly respectable and important occupation. Therefore the Hudson's Bay Co. have received the title of honorable from the way in which they conduct it; but it is only because they are alone that they are able to conduct it in this orderly manner.[12a] The Indian trade does not admit of competition. The effects of strong rival companies have been more injurious and demoralizing to the Indians than any other circumstance that has come within our knowledge, not even excepting the sale of ardent spirits among them. This we could easily prove, but as no monopoly can be allowed by the nature of our government it is useless. When the American Fur Co. were alone in the country a trader's word or promise to the Indians was sacred, the Indians loved and respected their traders, and still do some of the old stock, but since corruption has been carried on we look in vain for that reliance on and good feeling toward traders which was once the pride of both Indian and white.

The manner in which the trade is conducted in its operations is this:

A party of Indians, many or few, leave their camp for the trading post, packing on dogs and horses all their buffalo robes and other skins. When within a mile or two of the houses, they stop and send a few persons to the trader with an account of how many persons their party is composed of, how many skins, etc., they have, and all general news. These are furnished with tobacco and sent back with an invitation for the party to come to the house or fort. If a leading chief is then with a large party, the American flag is raised in the fort and cannon fired when he arrives. On arrival they are received at the fort gate by the interpreter, who conducts them to a large reception room. The dogs, horses, etc., are unpacked and each Indian takes charge of his own skins in the same room. They are then smoked (with the pipe), feasted on coffee, bread, corn, etc., after which the principal men and chiefs are called into the public office, when they are counciled with by the gentleman in charge. Speeches on both sides are made, and if the Indians have any complaints to make they now state them. The general situation of the camp and trade is adverted to, prospects mentioned, and prices of goods stated, with all other matters relating to their affairs. When this is finished the store is opened and the trade commenced. Several Indians can trade at the same time with different traders, handing their robes and skins over the counter, and receiving immediate payment in such articles as they wish. When all are done, a small present of ammunition and tobacco is given them and in a day or two they leave for their camp.

The place of outfit being in St. Louis, all returns of buffalo robes and other furs are taken there also every spring and summer in

[12a] Perhaps this title has been bought, but at all events they deserve it.

Mackinaw boats made at each fort for the purpose, and manned by
the voyageurs who came up on the steamboat the year previous. The
risks are numerous, both in bringing up the supplies in steamers and
in taking down the returns in Mackinaws. In the spring of 1819 this
company lost two steamboats in bringing up the supplies, one burned
with the cargo at St. Louis and the other snagged and sunk. Also
the Mackinaws down are often snagged and sunk, swamped, or the
robes wetted by rain and leakage. The loss of an ordinary boatload
of robes would be $10,000, and every year losses more or less are in-
curred in some way. From experience we know that the chance of
loss is equal to that of gain in a given period of 10 years, yet should
everything prove fortunate for a length of time money would be
made.

All men of family who turn their attention to hunting and collecting skins and robes are shrewd and sensible enough in the trading
of them, sometimes too much so for some of the traders. Knowing
the value of merchandise and of what kind they stand in need, they
make their calculations of purchases before they leave their homes
and any additional article they can beg or otherwise get is so much
additional gain. They do not purchase useless articles. Goods of
all kinds having stated prices enables them to deal to a fraction,
nevertheless they will quibble and beat down the price if possible,
even in the least thing, and are generally successful in getting something out of the trader in this way.

As for their debts, they will not pay. An Indian does not contract a debt actually with the intention of deceiving; but before he
has the means to pay, new wants arise, his family wants clothing,
he, ammunition, etc.; in short, he is always in need, consequently
never in a situation to pay. Therefore they use every argument to
get clear of the debt, many of which are very ingenious, and if none
will answer, say they will not pay and that the trader has no business
to trust them. This being the case, but few credits are made. Whenever their wants are too great, or means too small to enable them to
hunt, the articles are given them, though not credited. In the few
instances where credits are made the Indians keep no accounts whatever of them, their object being to forget them as soon as possible;
until they have their memory refreshed of the disagreeable fact by
a reference of the clerk to his blotter. Our books are full of unpaid
debts of 20 years' standing, which would make a handsome fortune
if the value could be realized. There is no worse pay in the world,
and a credit is considered lost as soon as given, or if afterwards the
trader receives half pay he considers himself very fortunate. This
being the case, no runners are employed to collect, as in the Mississippi trade. As they (the Indians) are not honest, neither are they
sober, nor moral, but have discretion for their own advantage.

The tariff of exchanges is made with the double view of securing the profit of the trader and encouraging the Indians to hunt. Were a gun, an ax, or a kettle, for instance, rated at too high a price, then one of these articles would be made to serve the purposes of several lodges by turns, or should ammunition be sold too dear only as many animals would be killed as would be sufficient to feed their families, and no more skins traded than sufficient to meet their most pressing necessities. Such proceedings would lead to the abandonment of the trade as not profitable. The expenses of this business are enormous, the risk great, the capital invested half a million dollars, and more than 300 people employed; and yet a good northwest gun is sold for six robes or $18, the cost of which is $9.67. As a general rule, all goods are sold at an average profit of 200 per cent on original cost. The cost of buffalo robes in merchandise is about $1.35 in cash and we estimate the expenses in men, forts, animals, and other disbursements at $1.20 more each robe, which would bring them to $2.55. Now the best sale made of a large quantity is $3 each. Therefore, a loss of one or two boats loaded with robes must show a loss on the outfit.

Traders are very much subject to calls on their charity, both by persons who really are in want and almost everyone else. All the roving tribes are great beggars, even if they do not actually stand in need. But viewing the question only in the light of an act of charity they are numerous indeed. Unskillful in the treatment of diseases, the different demands for medicines and attendance are great, which at all times it is not safe nor expedient to comply with. The forts are the depositions of all the old, lame, sick, poor, and feeble; in fact, every one who can not follow the camp, or is of no use there, is thrown on the hands of the traders, and his house has often more the appearance of a hospital than a trading establishment. For all this there is no pay, not even thanks nor kind words, but frequently reproach and revenge if they are told to move off after recovery. It would' appear that the feeling of gratitude is unknown to the Indian. We believe this to be the case among these.

It does not appear from our actual observation of 21 years, and pretty correct information of as many more of still an earlier date, that the principal animals have suffered diminution in the district of which we treat, viz, from the Sioux country to the Blackfoot, inclusive. How numerous they were in former years we do not know, but understand from old Indians that more buffalo have been seen in late years than were noticed 50 or 60 years since. It may be that the range of these animals is becoming more limited from the pressure of emigration westward. Yet this range is very extensive, reaching from the Platte to the Saskatchewan and from Red River to the Rocky Mountains, through all which immense district buffalo are found in great numbers. Out of this question appears to us to arise another, viz, Is not the decrease of the Indians from diseases communicated to them through white immigration and commerce, thereby reducing the number of hunters, equivalent to increasing the number of buffalo? And does not the remnant of the Indians at this time require fewer animals to feed, clothe, and provide all their necessaries, than the multitudes before commerce was established with them? We think this view merits consideration.

If the buffaloes diminish, so do the Indians, and the diminution is not felt. The manner in which they hunted before firearms were introduced (by driving the buffaloes into pens) was infinitely more destructive than at present. Hundreds, perhaps thousands, were necessarily killed when a camp of a few Indians was stationed and when a small number would have sufficed. That commerce stimulates them to hunt is true, and a great many buffaloes are annually destroyed expressly for the hides. Yet even this destruction is limited. An Indian's family can only dress a certain number of hides during the hunting season. The hides in their raw state are of no value, and not traded, and can not be packed and carried when they move, which they are obliged to do in the spring; therefore no more are killed than the Indians can handle. Besides, there are but four or five months when the hair or fur of any animal is seasonable or merchantable and the rest of the year only enough are killed for meat, clothing, and lodges for their families. As far as we can be allowed to express an opinion, would say that the Indians by diseases brought about by commerce, and of late years by white immigration, will diminish and perhaps be destroyed as formidable bodies long before their game. The loss of Indians from smallpox, cholera, measles, scarlet fever, venereal, fluxes, etc., within our own recollection can not be estimated at less than 15,000 to 20,000, without taking into consideration the consequent loss of propagation.

Were the destruction less we think it would have the effect of increasing these animals so that many must die for want of proper grazing or be forced to seek other lands for food. This would reinstate us in our first position, that it is more probable the small number of Indians now in existence will disappear before their game, or at least will be so reduced as not to retard their increase. Immigration in settling the country would banish the buffalo from that part of it where these movements were going on, and force them to the alternative of scattering through the settlements and thus be destroyed; or, being confined and limited in their grazing, they would die for want of sufficient nourishment. They are a shy animal and will not remain where they are much troubled. Indian hunting has not this effect. The Indians do not occupy the proportionate space of a town of 100 houses to a county, and in some places not more to a State of the United States. Moreover, they herd with order, and in the winter, not being able to remain on the plains where there is no fuel, and very deep snow, are obliged to place their camps on the banks of streams and hunt merely the outskirts of these immense herds.

The increases of buffaloes must be very great. Each cow has a calf yearly and the fourth year these also have calves. Now, supposing a band of 4,000 cows to increase for eight years without accident. The computation would be as follows:

	Say increase one-half cows	One-half bulls
	$4 \times 4 = 16 \div 2 = 8$	8
One-half increase	8	
Old stock	4	
	$12 \times 4 = 48$	
Old stock	12	
One-half bulls	8	
Total in 8 years	68,000	

Now supposing the whole number of buffalo cows in existence to be 3,000,000, which is certainly not an overestimate, then—

	One-half cows	One-half bulls
	$3 \times 4 = 12 \div 2 = 6$	6
One-half increase in 4 years	6	
Old stock	3	
	$9 \times 4 = 36$	
Stock	9	
Bulls	6	
Total in 8 years	51,000,000	

Making every calculation for their reduction in the many ways they are killed, or die by accident, and the consequent loss by propagation, yet being so numerous their ratio of increase is too great to diminish the whole number much by any of these means.

The conclusion is that, in our opinion, both Indians and buffaloes, with all other game, would disappear in consequence of white immigration and occupation, though the Indians, being the smaller number, would be the first to vanish. Also that commerce, by stimulating the exertions of the hunters, can not increase their labor beyond what they now perform, and that, being limited, is too small to hasten the destruction or even diminution of any game as plentiful as the buffalo. The same argument does not apply to beaver, foxes, or even elk and deer. Should all the Indians be obliged to live on elk and deer only, and have no resources but the furs of the beaver and fox to get their supplies, a diminution of these animals would

soon be perceived and destruction follow, because their increase is
not so great, neither were they ever so numerous. They are smaller,
and as more would be required they would therefore soon disappear
before the united hunts of all the Indians. But as they are not as
yet driven to hunt them they do not diminish, except the beaver,
which has been, in this district, destroyed by large bodies of white
trappers. Red foxes are not, we think, so numerous as formerly,
though it may be they are not so much hunted. The trading posts
or houses do not have the effect of diminishing or frightening away
the buffalo any more than the Indian camps.

Their locations are few and hundreds of miles apart, and their
operations confined to within a few miles of their houses. Even
while we are writing thousands of buffalo can be seen by looking out
of the fort gates, which are quietly grazing on the opposite bluffs
of the Missouri, and yet this post (Fort Union) has been established
27 years. The only good hunting grounds for elk and deer are on
the Yellowstone from 4 to 30 miles from the fort, beyond which
though there are but few Indians they are not nearly so numerous.
Beaver and foxes are caught every few days within one-half mile
to 6 miles of the fort, not in numbers, certainly, neither are they
very plentiful anywhere in this district. A trading post in a new
country may have but few buffalo the first and second years and innumerable herds the third, or vice versa. There is no rule for this.
The buffalo migrate and return. The other animals are scattered
over an immense region of country, are difficult to kill, must be
hunted separately, which is dangerous on account of enemies, consequently not followed, therefore they are not diminished. Thus no
person can say to a certainty which are the first to disappear.

Perhaps the entire destruction of game would lead to the Indians
devoting their time to agricultural pursuits. It would force them
to do that or starve, but judging from their present indisposition to
work, and tribal organization, great distress would follow the sudden disappearance of their game and starvation thin their ranks
before they would apply themselves to hard labor. The Indians who
raise corn, etc. (Mandan, Gros Ventres, and Arikara), do not do so
from any scarcity of game or apprehensions on that score, but have
done so beyond the recollection of any trader, or even of themselves.
It appears to be a desire to possess something else to eat besides meat,
and a custom handed down to them by their forefathers. Their corn
is entirely different from any raised in the States, and is the real
original maize discovered with the continent, the seed still kept in
its original purity. The labor attendant on planting and raising
these crops is performed by the women, while the men hunt like the
surrounding tribes, work of this description as their present ideas
exist being a disgrace to the males. Several of the other wild

464   TRIBES OF THE UPPER MISSOURI   [ETH. ANN. 46

tribes have for years entertained a desire to cultivate, not because
they apprehend any failure of game, but having become fond of corn,
potatoes, etc., wish to have them, but can not exert themselves enough
for the purpose.

Commerce not as yet having reached the tribes of whom we write
except in the form of trade for their furs and skins, the question as
to its ultimate effects, as a cause of civilization, can not by us be
determined, but the effects produced by traffic have had a decided
tendency toward their improvement and advancement by stimulating
their exertions and increasing their knowledge. It must be obvious
to every one who is acquainted with the character and history of
Indians that they have an antipathy to work, that as long as they
can support themselves by hunting they will do so; for through these
means they are enabled to avail themselves of the labor and arts of
Europeans in procuring articles necessary for their subsistence, in
exchange for their furs and skins. This method being more con-
sonant with their fixed habits, is less toilsome though more dangerous
than civilized occupations. Having clothing, utensils, arms, amuni-
tion, and all kinds of provisions furnished them by the traders
certainly increases their desire to obtain these things, stimulates
them to greater exertions in hunting, but does not lead to a sufficient energy of mind to endeavor to produce these things by a slower
though more certain employment. In the event of a sudden disappearance of game they would be driven to extreme want and thousands would perhaps perish before they would of their own accord
apply themselves to agricultural pursuits.

If no human exertions be made by those in power to instruct them
in the superior advantages of such labors over their present precarious life, they must by a sudden pressure of emigration, and a consequent annihilation of game, become the drudges of the whites, destroyed and degraded by their great banes, whiskey and smallpox.
It is impossible to conceal the rapid strides made by emigration or
its immoral tendency on the Indians, and it would be very unreasonable to conclude that its destroying effects would so revolutionize the
habits of an uneducated Indian as to meet the emergency.   The change
from savage to civilized life and occupations must be gradual, accompanied by instruction, education, and practical experiment illustrative of its utility.

The introduction of woolen goods has been of some advantage to
the Indians. It has added to their comfort, cleanliness, and pride,
and has had other good effects; but these alone can not be said to have
much increased their means of subsistence, though other things have.
As long as an Indian is a hunter, his dress must answer that purpose.
There is no fabric of European manufacture clothed in which he
could crawl after game over the plains covered with cactus in summer

or that would protect his body from freezing in winter. Blankets can not supply the place of buffalo robes, cloth the place of skin, boots that of moccasins, in these high latitudes and terrible snow-storms.

These things are bought for summer and fall wear in their homes or when traveling, are preferred because they are not damaged by wet, are gay, soft, and handsome, will make tolerably good undercoats in winter, will serve for traveling horseback in summer and fall. But the real hunter of the plains must have his buffalo robe coats, moccasins, mittens, and cap, skin leggings, his extra buffalo robe on his back and his snowshoes on his feet, or the cold and wind would prove more destructive to his person than he to the game. The articles introduced by commerce that have increased their means of subsistence are firearms, horses, knives, kettles, awls, fire, steel, and metallic instruments for dressing hides. Besides, the conversation and instruction received from the traders has increased their knowledge, elevated their desires, and stimulated their industry. These are some of the effects of commerce, and this subject will meet with further discussion through these pages.

We are not aware of any great moral evils consequent on the trade with Indians in this section. The variations from truth and deceptions practiced by rival companies are, however, the greatest. The introduction of ardent spirits has been demoralizing and debasing, but has in no great degree tended to the depopulation of the tribes of whom we write. From a long period of actual observation and experience can safely say that the whole number of deaths arising from the consequences of intoxicating drink does not amount to 100 during the past 20 years, from and including the Sioux to the Blackfeet. That it is morally wrong no one will doubt, but this has been much exaggerated, and can not be reckoned among the causes of their depopulation. If that cause is sought for it is very plain in the history of the smallpox, which even while we write is sweeping off the Crow and Snake Indians, upward of 1,200 of whom have died from that disease contracted on the Platte emigrant trail last summer. The destruction of Indians from cholera, measles, and smallpox since that road has been opened has been incredible and there is no probability of its decreasing. These are the causes of their depopulation and will be of their entire extinction. The introduction of firearms has been beneficial to the trade, and in some respects to the Indians. Deer, elk, and smaller game can be killed when buffalo are not found, and in default of horses to run them the Indians can support themselves with the gun.

The gun is a useful though not an indispensable implement. The loss of an Indian horse is easier replaced than that of his gun, as he could at any time steal the former from his enemies, and to get the latter would require means to purchase, which have been destroyed by its loss. Also the accident might happen when skins were of no value or unseasonable. Another advantage in having a gun is that the means of making a fire are thereby possessed, which on the plains is a matter of great consequence, and a gun often saves the lives of several travelers. In short, an Indian with a gun has double the chances of support that one without has. Should his horse be stolen he can use his gun, and if that is broken he can use his horse. By firearms a great many smaller animals are killed, and skins traded which would not otherwise be the case, though in hunting in bodies or large camps the gun is not much used, except when there are but few horses that they can catch. The possession of firearms has unquestionably promoted war. Many arrows may be shot, perhaps all the Indian has, without doing any damage unless at very close quarters, whereas at a distance or in the night guns are effective. It also facilitates waylaying and killing their enemies, a manner of which they are remarkably fond, and could not well be accomplished with arrows, lances, etc., without nearly equal danger to both parties. Guns and ammunition are considered the soul of warfare, more so than of the chase, and a few Indians thus armed are more efficient than a crowd with bows, lances, and war clubs. So much is this the case that the want of a sufficient number of guns often delays, and sometimes entirely stops, a war party.

There is only one way we know of by which the trade could be placed on a better basis, and that being inconsistent with the principles of our Government, is scarcely worth considering. It is that it should be a monopoly. A charter granted to a body of efficient people who could give bond to a large amount for their lawful prosecution of the trade, and their operations subject to the revision and examination of a competent board of directors.

EDUCATION

There are no serious or valid objections on the part of any Indians with whom we are acquainted to the introduction of schools, agriculture, the mechanical arts, or Christianity. We have examined the subject in all its bearings for upward of 20 years; counseled with Indians about it; and it appears to us very singular that as yet the Department or some charitable persons have done nothing in this respect for the Indians. It is the only way they can be really benefited, saved, recompensed for territory bought, or rendered useful. It is the only way by which they could eventually be brought to have some certain source or means of subsistence. They have often pressed upon us their desire that we should use our exertions to get some mission or school opened among them to instruct their children in agriculture and the mechanical arts. With this view we have for years corresponded with the Rev. G. I. De Smet of the St. Louis University (Jesuit), who intended and perhaps still intend to commence operations of the kind among them. Not being of the Catholic persuasion, it is not on that account that the Jesuits were thought by us the most competent for such a purpose, but that they have more zeal, knowledge, perseverance, and tact to manage Indians than any others we know of. Their religion is peculiarly adapted to that purpose.

The imposing rites and ceremonies of the Catholic Church would at once attract their attention and excite their interest; afterwards they could be made to comprehend. However, it is not with the grown Indians the commencement must be made. The first step to be taken is to stop, as much as possible, their internal wars, and this is rapidly being accomplished by the treaty made at Laramie in 1851, which has had the effect of making a general peace between all nations except the Blackfeet. This peace may suffer interruptions occasionally, by a few being killed, or horses stolen, but these things will be settled among themselves, and the peace continue, especially if the Indian agents are particular in enforcing the treaty stipulations. With the Blackfeet a peace must be made in some way and that at Laramie having proved successful, why not in the same way? They are very numerous and hostile, and nothing but a large appropriation judiciously distributed in merchandise could gain the point. Afterwards it might be kept up for a series of years by smaller annuities, and when the general end is gained these could be discontinued. The only way to work upon the wild Indian is through his cupidity and necessities; force is not to be thought of.

This point being gained, establishments should be formed among each tribe, at the same time receiving a number of their children and giving them a common English education and as soon as practicable bringing up these children in agricultural and pastoral pursuits.

Habits of industry should be inculcated as they grow up, and the field of their operations enlarged when they are grown, by portioning out lands and providing a market for their surplus stock and produce. Some of the useful mechanical arts could also be introduced, but only those that are useful in their present condition and growing state. A century or two may elapse before watchmakers, glass blowers, or even tailors and shoemakers would be necessary, though a few gunsmiths, blacksmiths, carpenters, and weavers would find immediate

468   TRIBES OF THE UPPER MISSOURI   [ETH. ANN. 46

employment. The principles of the Christian religion would of
course at the same time be taught, but the principal feature of these
establishments, as soon as the boys and girls were able to work, should
be industry, principally in agricultural and pastoral pursuits. The
great errors into which missionaries have fallen are that they make
the observance of religious duties the sole object and neglect the
others.[13] Also their zeal in this induces them to interfere with the
present government, domestic arrangements, and superstitions of the
grown Indians, thereby incurring their enmity, disgust, or revenge.
The present grown-up generation should be left entirely alone, not
interfered with, no attempt made to convert them, or even induce
them to work. It is useless, inexpedient, and subverts the general
ends. The first thing a missionary does is to abuse the Indian for
having a plurality of wives.

Would the good missionary be so charitable as to clothe, feed,
and shelter the supernumerary woman; should all the Indians follow
his advice and have but one wife? Will the Indian consent to separate his children from their mothers, or to turn both adrift to please
the whim of any man? This advice is uncharitable, unjust, and can
only be excused on the plea of ignorance of their customs and feeling. The next difference that arises is that the priests take away
all their charms, medicines, and idols, and present them their cross
instead. Now as far as any of these old Indian reprobates can
conceive the idea of the cross, it is nothing more than a different
kind of idol in exchange for theirs. What in the name of common
sense could induce old priests, in every other respect sane and well
informed, to think that by administering baptism and giving an
Indian the symbol of the cross they have thus converted them, we
can not imagine. If the Indians believe anything thereby, it is that
the image or medal possesses some intrinsic supernatural power to prevent them from personal harm or give them success in war, known
to be efficacious by the whites, and is to them in fact nothing more
than a different kind of medicine bird or medicine ball. Can they
(the priests) suppose that an Indian, only a grade above the level
of the brute in intelligence, could without education form a correct
idea of the ordinance of Baptism, the Incarnation, the Trinity, the
Crucifixion and Atonement and other abstruse points in which even
whites, with all their education, can not agree?

These grown Indians are too ignorant and obstinate to think, too
lazy to work, too proud to be instructed, and their formed habits
too savage and firmly rooted to give way before the meek truths of
the gospel. All such attempts must prove abortive; it is anticipat-

---

[13] Here Denig mildly protests against the unreasonable emphasis placed on the observance of religious rites by the missionaries to the exclusion of other duties.

ing by an age what should be their present course among the children. We would say let all the grown generation die as they have lived, though before that event took place many of them would have the satisfaction of seeing their children in comparatively happy and improved conditions. This is the only right beginning. Bring them up in the proper way, impressing moral truths and industrious habits when young and fostering the same in maturity. The Government can do this, should do it, and would be extending a charity to a part of the human race but few sympathize with, and opening a way for the remnant of aborigines to become a useful and intelligent people. We repeat it, there are no objections to this among the Indians. Proffers of the kind would be readily acceded to by any tribe, even the Blackfeet, and all sensible traders would assist. It would not benefit them, might perhaps hurt their business some, and would in the end lead to its discontinuance. But this is of minor consideration. We are confident that establishments on the principles we have suggested would succeed and answer great ends. But they must begin with the children as their foundation, not merely for the observances of religious duties, without combining active agricultural and pastoral pursuits, with a judicious choice of mechanical arts.

It does not follow that the Indians should abandon their hunting altogether to accomplish these ends. Those who wished to hunt could still do so, as they now do at Red River, and when hunting failed, as it eventually must when white emigration settles the country, the Indians would find themselves in a position to live fully if not more comfortably than before. Some of the money of the United States could not be applied to a better purpose. One-half of the amount Congress expends on the repairs of some old bridge would be sufficient to rear and educate several hundred children. Indeed, after the boys and girls had attained the age of 12 to 15 years they could more than support themselves by their labor. Abstruse studies or extensive mental acquirements should not be striven for except with the view of providing teachers or physicians of their own nation, but generally the rudiments of English education, such as is taught the peasantry of England, would answer better. Too much education would produce an unwillingness if not an inability to work.

Physicians of their own people would tend more to banish their superstitions and encourage these institutions than all the preaching in the world. Correct medical knowledge would be apparent in its effects, and be the greatest acquirement in the eyes of the Indian.

With its introduction would disappear the host of jugglers, conjurers, medicine men, and humbugs that now impoverish and kill most of their patients. A distinct idea of crime and the necessity of law would follow. The democratic principles of government already implanted would assume an effective form and civilization and Christianity would be the result. To accomplish this present payments of annuities should not be curtailed, as it would hazard the ill feelings of the grown Indians who, seeing no immediate benefit arising, would become dissatisfied with the appropriation of their funds. Separate appropriations or funds could be raised for the purpose.

WARFARE

The usual cause of war among the prairie tribes is the stealing of horses. Indians must have horses, can not well live without them, and will risk everything to obtain them. Moreover, horses are looked upon in a measure as public property; that is, those nations who have few think they have a right to take them from those who have many. Whether it is a right or not they do it, and in these expeditions frequently men are killed on both sides. This produces an obligation on the part of the relatives of the deceased to revenge their deaths, and war continues with various successes on both sides. The occupation of war is also the most honorable an Indian can follow. The young men are not noticed, neither can they aspire to the hand of a respectable young woman, without having distinguished themselves in war excursions. They are taught this when young, and as things now stand, it is difficult to change. Nevertheless it can be done. Not immediately, but in the course of a few years. There is always an opening to the heart of the Indian through his love of gain. Most chiefs, soldiers, and heads of families are open to bribes. The object of war in the first place is gain, and the dangers attending it make it honorable.

This object (gain) must be superseded by an equivalent and the idea of honor transferred to other sources. Take, for instance, the Blackfeet, who are the most numerous and bloodthirsty nation on the upper Missouri. Assemble them in treaty and make a distribution of $25,000 or $30,000 in merchandise among them and the deputations of other nations with whom a peace is to be concluded. How would this operate? The soldiers of the camp who would be appointed to distribute this merchandise are the most powerful party, have generally the raising and leading of war parties, and would take a liberal share of the presents for themselves. The chiefs and heads of families would also receive a large amount and the rest be divided among the young men, warriors, women, etc. The peace would be made, all would be satisfied for the present; but unless these payments were continued for a number of years, or until the benefits of peace were realized and acknowledged, nothing would be gained. An Indian does not reflect upon what he has received but what is yet in store for him. The prospects of an annual repetition of these presents would induce them to keep the treaty stipulations. Why and how? The soldiers, chiefs, and heads of families, whose voices only could make war, are held in check by the prospects of gain, and should any parties be raised would be paid to stop, or if they continued and stole horses, or killed a few of the nation with whom peace had been made, the affair would be paid for and hushed up on both sides, on account of the coming presents.

The reason why persons killed in time of peace between two nations can be paid for, and privately not, is that in the former case the voices of all, except the immediate relations of the slain, are against revenge, inasmuch as it would affect their interests with regard to the presents granted by the treaty. This operation going on in both nations at the same time leaves the relatives too few to effect a revenge, and the dishonor is evaded by the compulsion. In the course of a few years all old causes for revenge would be forgotten. By visiting each other and exchanging property, horses (the usual cause of war) would become more equally divided, by being bought by those who wish them, instead of stolen. Acquaintance with each other's language, intermarriages, and other ties would follow, and the advantage of receiving a large supply of merchandise without the labor of hunting skins for it, together with the honor and increase of power of the soldiers, by having the distribution of this merchandise, must effectually throw the popular voice against war. The voices of the women, though not consulted, would be felt. They are vain, fond of dress, and would, of course, be in favor of the treaty which enables them to gratify this passion in a greater degree by furnishing them with clothing gratis. Therefore war would be discontinued by them, and the hand of a peaceable man preferred to one whose conduct militated against their own interests and those of their parents. For we apprehend that the favor warriors find in the eyes of the women and their parents is the result of their success, not the glory in their bravery.

It is the horses stolen from their enemies that gives them wealth to purchase any woman they please, and the father-in-law is anxious to have a son-in-law who can at any time replace his loss in horses. Indians are poor; that is, they are always in need of articles they can not purchase, and getting a supply gratis is of great advantage to them. The power of these annuities is great, and could be wielded with sufficient force to bring different bands to war upon their own people, and compel them to preserve the treaty stipulations.

We do not think that the display of military force on treaty grounds is either necessary or politic. If to inspire a feeling of fear be the object, it would require the presence of three or four thousand

men to effect it with the Blackfeet, and even then, there would be
great danger of collision with the troops who would endeavor to
enforce military regulations when they can not be understood and
are not required. Neither would Indians be induced to assemble
when such a body of armed men are brought without their consent, or if they did, it would be with hostile feelings, and they
could give no assistance to the commissioners. A lesser force, or
one inadequate to present the idea of coercion, would incur their
contempt, as they would necessarily conclude that the Government
had sent all the men they could raise, and the few present would be
imposed upon.

Indians do not like to be forced into measures, the utility of which
has yet to be made apparent. Besides, the spirit of treaty is compromise, not force, as would be implied by these proceedings. It
must be a voluntary act on the part of the Indians, for and in consideration of a certain sum, to obtain the stipulations. Again it is
entirely on the present state of the Indian and their government
to carry out this treaty we depend after the military force be withdrawn. Their organization as pointed out in these pages shows them
capable of preserving order among themselves on these occasions,
and a few good, patient commissioners and sensible traders and interpreters would secure what is necessary when force or appearance
of it would fail. If anything more was added it might be a few
military officers in full uniform and a good band of music. After
satisfaction the treaty would operate in detail as has been mentioned,
and the next best thing would be to take deputations of the principal
men of each nation to Washington, where they could council with
their Great Father (the President), and at this time the power and
disposition of the Government could be exhibited without giving
offense, which in their return among their people would be made public and the proper feeling instilled. But Indians should never be
treated with at the seat of Government for many reasons.

The principal is that no deputation of prairie tribes could be
taken as the general voice, and even then would not think themselves
treated with on fair grounds—would agree to any and everything
and afterwards say they were forced to do it. Large bodies of
whites in the interior and on treaty grounds would necessarily be
very expensive, and are inexpedient, as pointed out, though the support of a great many Indians would be very little. They bring their
supplies along, hunt their way back, and but a few groceries would
be sufficient to feed them during the short stay the business required.
Another thing not to be overlooked is that the assembling of different nations in a body at a certain point is a great affair to them.
It forms an epoch, a date, an event, to be talked of for years. Each

nation on these occasions feel themselves bound to be polite, liberal, and attentive to strangers. Hostilities for the time are laid aside or forgotten, and the whole active force of the nations on whose ground the treaty is held is put in motion to keep order. If the question of buying their lands is not introduced, all goes on well, but on this subject they are jealous and suspicious to a great degree.

In no instance should the principal of an Indian fund be placed in the hands of any member of these prairie tribes to be distributed by him to his people. They can not appreciate the use and expenditure of money; neither could they with safety be placed in charge of any large amount of goods for distribution.

If handed to the chief, they would be given by him to a few of his immediate relations and friends, and the rest of the camp would get nothing. The present way of distributing annuities is the best, if not the only one that could give general satisfaction, and is thus conducted. The whole amount of merchandise is separated into as many portions as there are bands in the nation, according to the number of lodges in each band. One of the bands is then visited by the Indian agent, who, with the advice and consent of the chief of the nation, chooses therefrom four to six soldiers and dresses them. The whole band, men, women, and children, are formed into a semicircle with these soldiers in front, and that portion of the annuities intended for the band is laid in front of the soldiers, who separate it equally among all, retaining, however, a reasonable share for themselves. This appears to give general satisfaction. We can suggest no change in the existing laws that might benefit the Indians, unless it be that Indian agents should be people who have a correct knowledge of Indian character. If it be really the object of the Government to benefit this race of people their agents should be chosen from experienced traders or others who have and still reside with them and are well acquainted with their manners and customs.

How can a stranger who perhaps never saw an Indian, merely by counseling with a few during his short annual visit, know their wants, study their welfare, or make satisfactory reports to headquarters? Besides, so much being dependent on these agents, their term of office should not be limited to a change in the administration, as at present. It is unlike other offices and requires many years' close application and constant residence among Indians to be of any real benefit to learn in what manner they can be better regulated or to carry out any series of measures the Government may wish to introduce. The pay of these agents is also inadequate, and there are too few to be of much service. The Sioux Nation alone is numerous and widely extended enough to admit of an agency; the Mandan, Gros Ventres, and Arikara another; the As-

siniboin and Crows a third, and the Blackfeet a fourth. As it at
present stands, one man is appointed for all this, and the consequence
is some of them are neglected, if not the greater number. It can
not be otherwise. The nations are situated hundreds of miles apart
and each scattered over an immense district. Even one nation can
not be collected, consulted with, annuities distributed, and all business settled in a less time than six months and often more. Should
the present officer do nothing but travel he could not make the round
of the whole in a year.

PROPERTY

The personal property of these tribes consists chiefly of horses.
A man's wealth is estimated by the number of these animals he owns.
Besides which they have their lodges, guns, clothing, and cooking
utensils. Possession of an article of small value is a right seldom
disputed, if the article has been honestly obtained, as their laws of
retaliation are too severe to admit of constant quarrels. But horses
being their principal aim, possessing them is nothing without force
to defend. To explain this fully it will be necessary to give a few
examples of the different kinds of rights and their tenure. Rights
to property are of the following description: Articles found, articles
made by themselves, stolen from enemies, given them, and bought.
Two Indians traveling together, one discovers a lost horse and points
it out to the other, who pursues and succeeds in catching it. Now
the one who made the discovery claims a portion of the horse on the
ground that had he not seen it or not shown it to the other most likely
it would not be in his possession. The other, therefore, to extinguish
this claim, would be obliged to pay some article equivalent to half the
value of the horse, which in case he refused to do would end in the
horse being killed on the spot, and the dispute terminated. The same
rule would apply to finding a gun, but smaller articles would not
attract attention enough to produce a quarrel. An article is considered lost when the owner has abandoned the search.

All clothing, skins, arms, etc., made by themselves are the sole
property of those who made them, and this is the only general right
among them that admits of no dispute. To take away such things
by force would be reckoned a mean action; would be discountenanced
individually by all; and the perpetrator would fall into general disgrace, among both men and women. When horses are stolen from
enemies the case is different. Suppose seven Indians conjointly steal
45 horses in the night from their enemies. They would drive them
off in a body until beyond reach of pursuit and then each would lay
claim, catch, and keep as many as he could manage and defend.
No equal division or anything like it would take place. Men of
desperate character would take the greater part and leave milder

or less strongly supported Indians with one or two and some would get none. To do this sometimes two to four will combine against the others and take the largest share, but one or two men seldom carry this so far as to incur the resentment of the rest of the party. It generally depends upon the number of relatives each has with him, or his force in camp, before either of which those not so strongly supported must give way. Quarrels often occur about these divisions, and horses in dispute are killed or stolen in the night by those who have few from those who have many before their return home.

An Indian never gives away anything without some expectation of a return or some other interested motive. If one observes another in possession of a fine horse he would like to have he will take the occasion of some feast or dance and publicly present him with a gun or something of value, flattering his bravery, praising his liberality, and throwing out general hints as to his object, though not directly mentioning it. He will let the matter rest thus for some days, and if the other does not present him with the horse will demand his gift returned, which is done.

One will sometimes give a horse to another for some purpose or equivalent and allow him to keep it; but should the receiver give the horse to a third person the original owner will often claim him and take him back, giving for his reason that he did not bestow him on that person, and although he had presented him to the first, he should have kept him and not given him away to another. Smaller gifts are regarded in the light of loans and generally paid for in some way. They may be considered as exchanges of necessities which they take this way to effect.

One would think that an article bought by them or of them should be the property of the purchaser, but this is not always the case. If an Indian buys a horse from another and it is stolen the first night or two afterwards, or lamed the first race, part, and sometimes the whole, of the payment must be returned to pacify the loser.

If a gun is bought and it bursts or is broken shortly afterwards, in like manner a refund of a portion of the purchase money would be required. And worse still if the gun in the act of bursting had crippled the man's hands, which is often the case, the accident would also be paid for by him who sold the gun. These things are so well known and anticipated among them that the vendor immediately after the accident or loss invites the loser to a feast and by the payment of something settles the matter. This has the effect of their having but few bargains or dealings with each other, so much so that a horse bought and paid for by us from them can not be resold to one of their own people if they know it, because the original owner will take it if he sees it in the hands of one of his own people and that person is in a situation to be thus imposed upon. Most of their horses having had several owners, they are always a precarious gift or purchase. Property obtained by gambling is also held by a very slight tenure, so much so that the loser has many chances in his favor and these operations are much fairer among them than among whites.

Robberies of each other on any large scale are seldom attempted. They would attract the notice and induce the interference of the camp soldiers and relations of the robbed, and bloodshed would be the consequence. Infractions of smaller rights are left to individual settlement and are paid for. What prevents impositions in smaller matters is the disgrace and disgust that would fall upon any man guilty of petty infringements of personal rights.

With regard to the Indian of the British dominions applying to an agent of the United States for the payment of a private debt contracted by a north Briton, a resident of Hudson Bay, the probable operation of his mind was as follows: " All whites are very particular in endeavoring to collect their debts from Indians, and the richer are less generous. White traders are interlopers. The country, game, and all else in the territory belong to the Indians. The whites have no claims upon our generosity; are entitled to nothing without paying for it. Now a white man owes me, and from him I can get nothing. Indian agents are sent expressly to see justice done the Indians, are responsible and sensible, besides being rich and powerful. He will perhaps allow me my claim, or interpose his authority with the Hudson Bay people to make them pay. It is at least worthy of a trial, for if I gain nothing I lose nothing."

Most Indians of the British possessions in America, at least the Cree and Chippewa, are a great deal farther advanced in knowledge of every kind than those of whom we write. They have tolerably correct ideas of right and wrong and are famed for the shrewdness they exhibit in all kinds of dealings, to their own advantage. It is not even likely that if this Indian claim was not settled by the agent spoken to, he therefore abandoned it, but it is more probable that he dunned every one of the Hudson Bay traders for years until he got some remuneration. We have known an Indian at Fort Union to claim payment for carrying out three bundles belonging to one of our people when the fort was on fire. This demand was made 12 years after the circumstance happened. They never forget a claim on whites, but never recollect one upon themselves.

TERRITORIAL RIGHTS

How right to territory originally accrued can perhaps be learned by the way in which it is here discussed. None of these prairie tribes claim a special right to any circumscribed or limited territory. Their arguments are these, and have been before mentioned. All the prairie or territory in the West (known to them) and now occupied by all the Indians was created by Wakoñda for their sole use and habitation. To maintain this they state the entire fitness of the Indian for the life of a hunter; his good legs, eyes, and other qualifications which they do not allow to any other persons. The suitableness of the prairie for the support of great numbers of buffalo, and the wooded streams for smaller game, together with the adaptness of the game to their wants in meat, clothing, lodges, etc. All this is to prove their general right to the whole of the hunting grounds, where buffalo are to be found and Indians stationed. Now each nation finds themselves in possession of a portion of these lands, necessary for their preservation. They are therefore determined to keep them from aggression by every means in their power. Should the game fail, they have a right to hunt it in any of their enemies' country, in which they are able to protect themselves.

It is not land or territory they seek in this but the means of subsistence, which every Indian deems himself entitled to, even should he be compelled to destroy his enemies or risk his own life to obtain it. Moreover, they are well aware that the surrounding nations would do the same and sweep them off entirely if they could with impunity, and each claims the same right. Possession is nothing without power to retain, and force to repel, and to defend with success they must limit themselves to a certain extent of territory, for by separating their force too widely they would be cut off in detail. By these different necessary locations the country has been parceled out, each holding what they can with safety occupy, and making any encroachments they are able. They claim the land as theirs because that portion affords the means of subsistence with more security than by moving elsewhere they could procure. To sell their lands, they say, would be the same as to sell their means of living, for by moving elsewhere large bodies of enemies would require to be displaced, which could not be effected without great loss and perhaps failure. Indians who cultivate, such as the Mandan, Gros Ventres, and Arikara, only claim as their own the small patches that they till, and their right even to these (individually) only exists as long as they are occupied by the crops of the cultivator.

Should he fence it in and work it every year no one would dispute his right to do so, but if the land be left idle some other would plant upon it. It is in fact merely loaned from the general district for the purpose of him who wishes to cultivate. There being no scarcity of land, however, no difficulties occur on this point. From this view it would appear that their right to territory is nothing more than defending that portion on which they are located as necessary for

their support. Invasion of a neighboring tribe's country would only
be the consequence of famine or scarcity of game in their own and
would be looked upon by them in the light of extending their hunting
after the buffalo (which is the property of all Indians) into another
part of the great plains intended by Wakoñda for their support, being aware at the same time that they risk their lives by so
doing. The foregoing are the outlines of the arguments they use.
It is because they are at war that their lands appear to be distinct
portions assigned to each nation, although between each there are
several hundred miles of neutral ground, the nature of their forces
not admitting of closer approximation. Were all at peace it would
present the feature of one great estate on which each would rove and
hunt when and where he pleased, and what is now neutral would become hunting grounds. But as long as hunting was their sole occupation no claims would be set up by any man to a certain portion of
land.

They must become stationary, acquire property, real estate, before
land becomes of any value in their estimation, further than the space
it affords to game of all kinds to live and increase for their benefit.

PRIMOGENITURE

There is no general or fixed law of primogeniture. The eldest
son is, however, mostly a favorite, and although the custom is not
universal we have known instances of legacies left. If the parent
be a chief he will, if time permits, present his eldest son with his
medal when he anticipates death, if his son is of sufficient age to
wear it. They are anxious to be succeeded in their office by some
of their children, and the eldest would soonest be of sufficient age
to take upon himself the responsibility. But unfortunately for the
wishes of the parent the office or station of chief does not depend
upon the law of primogeniture, or any other, but upon the will of
the greater part to be ruled by him who is thus designated, and the
capacities and standing of the applicant. The chief whose speech
is recorded on page 598 presented his medal to his eldest son when
on his death bed in the presence of 20 or 30 persons of his band,
intimating his desire that his son should take his place and " follow
in the footsteps of his father." The son not being the popular choice,
another was appointed and the medal was left in our possession,
where it yet remains, though his son was of age at his father's (la-
Chef-qui-parle) death six years ago, and is living yet, and has pro-
gressed no further than becoming a camp soldier.

Most of these Indians die violent deaths, either by war, accidents
of the chase, or rapid diseases, and thus have no opportunity to
dispose of their property, yet even when they have time do not often

do it, owing to the difficulty of having these requests fulfilled after their demise. The dying request of a chief or warrior, if he makes any, is that his favorite horse, or sometimes two or three horses, shall be killed at his grave. Other horses, his gun, etc., are sometimes given to his relatives as bequests, and this gift contains an intimation to go to war after his death. The death of a warrior entails revenge, from whatever cause his death arises—sickness or accident. The horses, therefore, there bequeathed are put in mourning by having their mane, tail, and ears cut off and their body smeared over with white clay. These, with the guns and other weapons bequeathed, are taken on the first war expedition by the persons who received them. We have been appointed executor of the will of an Indian who died at Fort Union some years since from a wound through the bowels. A short time before his death (about three hours) he called us to his bedside and made a distribution of some horses and other property to be kept for his children's use, and desired his best running horse to be shot on the spot where he was to be buried, while he was yet living, which with the other requests were attended to.

There can be no doubt that if they were certain their dying requests would be fulfilled the custom of bequeathing their property when the circumstances of their death admitted it would be more general; but they know that the customs are such that after death all property must pass into the hands of strangers, as will be stated under the head of Death and Its Consequences. Even when dying bequests are made they are not always carried out. The horses and other property thus given to their families are given to others who cut their legs and bodies and cry a great deal at the interment, or rather on the occasion of their placing the body in a tree, as they usually do. When the great chief of the Crows, Long Hair, died no less than four hands were held out by four different Crow Indians, each offering to cut off two fingers to obtain the chief's war horse that he ordered to be killed upon his grave, but their offers were rejected and the horse was killed.

CRIME

Crime of any and all kinds among them is considered an offense to the individual and as such liable to punishment by the person offended. But no idea of a moral offense toward the Great Spirit is exhibited or consequent future punishment feared. All our endeavors to extract from them even an acknowledgment of the greatest crimes being morally wrong have been unavailing. They can not see that any act of theirs should meet with punishment after death because they think they have just cause for these acts, and also they

do not believe in future punishments at all. To illustrate the first
position, we will present their arguments on the greatest of crimes,
murder. An Indian never commits what in his mind would be equal
to murder in our estimation. There is no inducement in any case for
them to murder a man for his horses, wife, or any other property
they possess, for this step, instead of securing these advantages,
would operate in quite an opposite direction, making it necessary
for the murderer to relinquish his own property and that of his nearest relatives to pay the damage; also forfeiting his own life and
becoming an outcast. And this is the reason why their disputes so
seldom terminate in bloodshed, as the prospect of loss is far greater
than that of gain. When they do kill among themselves it is in
consequence of some quarrel about property, or about something,
and this they are then in a manner obliged to do, to save their own
life. It then becomes self-defense or a necessary action induced by
the principle of fear and their constant habit of carrying and raising
arms. In no instance does an Indian take life, except that of his
enemies, without provocation.

A horse, a woman, a gun, or any other article may be the cause
of a quarrel, and threats and menaces pass which place each under
the necessity of destroying the other to save himself. They say
they can not do otherwise, and often regret the necessity. To kill
an enemy, instead of being reckoned an act ungrateful to Wakoñda,
is thought by them to be highly pleasing, therefore his aid
to accomplish this and even private revenge is sought in prayers,
fasts, sacrifices, etc. All mankind have, they think, an equal right
to live, and an equal right to preserve that right, and it is the sense
of this self-preservation that compels them to remove any danger
in their way, such as wild beasts, enemies, or any of their own
people whom they are aware are only waiting an opportunity
against themselves; and it is also this right to life and fear of being
assassinated that compels them to take every advantage to accomplish the destruction of the danger pending. We have questioned
several Indians on this subject who have killed their own people
and all have led to the same subject, viz, the necessity imposed upon
them by quarrels to kill or be killed. To act otherwise when all
peaceful means have failed would be considered as the height of
foolishness and cowardice. An Indian does not take life from mere
thirst for blood, nor, as has been stated, to acquire property, as in
either case no advantage would be gained. When they waylay and
murder whites they believe they are doing right; that whites have
no business in their country, and are therefore looked upon in the
light of enemies.

They do not kill the white traders among each nation, or in the
few instances they have done so it was from some motive of revenge,

right in their estimation and in conformity to their law of retaliation. When the Blackfeet kill the whites at the Crow Fort it is from no enmity to the whites as a people, for they could if they wished kill plenty in their own country; it is that they do not wish the Crows, their enemies, to have traders who supply them with the means of killing them, by trading guns, ammunition, etc. The same reasoning on their own side is the cause of their friendship toward their own traders. Revenge, the great principle of destroying life, is strongly contended for by the Indians as necessary to their existence, both individually and as a body. The fear of the consequences of dispute prevents it, or generally is settled amicably by payment. There being no competent judiciary to try and punish crime renders it necessary for each one to retaliate, or they would be liable to constant imposition. That revenge among them supplies the want of courts of justice, prisons, and public executions. If the revenge is disproportionate to the offense, it can not be helped; their habits, customs, and organization all have that tendency. In all this they see no offense to Wakoñda nor any idea of moral wrong, even if they did believe in future punishment, which they do not, yet they know it is an offense to the individual and all his relatives, incurring their retaliation, which is the only punishment they expect.

Inasmuch as the warrior believes that by prayers, fasts, personal inflictions of pain and sacrifices they can secure the aid of Wakoñda to effect the death of their enemies or for the gratification of private revenge, by the same train of reasoning it must be manifest that the soul of a warrior must occupy a high degree of happiness in Indian paradise for accomplishing these acts through his instrumentality.

The death of a man who killed another would suffice if it were possible to stop there, but we have said enough on this subject to show they have no power to stop. The taking of the second life produces an obligation on the part of the kindred of the deceased to revenge, and retaliation is continued. The original cause of quarrel is lost in the greater necessity of defending life on either side. Therefore in their yet deplorable state of ignorance the crime of murder as an act of the same nature in our ideas can have no existence among them, neither can anything be morally wrong in which the aid of Wakoñda is invoked and if successful obtained. Robbery or theft is also an individual offense though not by them considered as such to Wakoñda. An Indian gives for his reason for stealing an article that his necessities required it and he could not get it any other way. He will not steal an article he does not want or can not use and run useless risk of detection, but a horse, gun, knife, or other things will sometimes be taken and the act excused on the plea of his necessities.

The risk attending the extraction of large articles or the disgrace incurred by pilfering is, they grant, all the punishment necessary, and these seldom are attended with any serious consequences. All must live some way and the right to property not being well defined— besides each being accustomed to frequent reverses—stealing is looked upon more as a means of subsistence necessitated by the state of their peculiar wants, and does not present the idea of theft to them as an immoral act or one tending to aggravate Wakoñda. Robberies to the extent of depriving another of his means of living are seldom if ever attempted, though retaliation would of course be severe in proportion, and in the progress of this retaliation the property thus acquired, be it horses or women, would be destroyed, besides the risk attending the robber personally.

Fornication and adultery are not considered offenses to Wakoñda. If the consent of the woman has been obtained, punishment is seldom inflicted on the man unless caught in the act. The woman, however, is punished in various ways, sometimes, though not usually, by death. The property of the offender is taken or destroyed for his trespass on the property of the offended. The chastity of any woman not the property of another man may be violated without any moral sense of wrong presenting itself, though the seducer would be liable to be made to pay or in default of doing so his horses would be killed by the relatives of the woman. Moreover, they look upon women as intended for this purpose, and only take into consideration the different claims upon them as an article of property.

Rapes on virgins are nearly unknown. Were such a crime accomplished the law would be death to the perpetrator, not because it is morally wrong, but because it depreciates the price of the woman and lessens her chance of marriage. It is also considered as an insult to her relatives, intimating a contempt of their feelings and power of protection.

The evils arising from falsehood or lying are with them of small importance. Any lies an Indian could invent would not be productive of any great evil, and owing to their associations the falsehood would soon appear. This being the case it is not regarded as a great offense even to the individual, much less Wakoñda. They all lie occasionally, and the custom is so common as scarcely to attract any further notice than their ridicule. Therefore there is no punishment attending on it further than the person famed for lying would be neglected and despised by the others. To call an Indian a liar would be insult certainly, but not in the same degree as the same epithet among whites. It would not be aggravation enough alone to merit a blow or any revenge. There is no such thing as profane swearing among any of these prairie tribes, nor is there a word in their language equivalent to even the smallest profane oaths in such general use among whites. The name of Wakoñda is never mentioned without manifestations of awe and reverence. In this respect at least they are far superior to their Christian brethren. In conclusion of this answer we come again to the starting point.

What in their estimation is crime, is wrong, is an offense to Wakoñda? Crime and wrong can be nothing more than offenses to persons subject to their law of retaliation, the punishment being greater or less according to the object which entails it. Although they do not believe in future punishments, yet they think that Wakoñda can be offended and does punish in this life; not for crimes, as they have no existence, but for neglect of proper fasts, sacrifices, and personal privations and inflictions necessary to propitiate his anger. They believe that they are under obligations to worship Wakoñda, not from the fact of their creation or even as to the author of all good, but through fear of his power. In almost every emergency an Indian can be placed, the cause of which is not visible or the result doubtful, that is, where his own powers fail, he applies to Wakoñda. These applications are made by presenting to the Sun, Thunder, and other supernatural agencies offerings of considerable value, by fasting, by lacerating their bodies, prayers, and incantations, with the view of avoiding sickness in their families, personal harm of every description, attacks of enemies, to obtain success in war, to collect the buffalo near their camp, to avoid the attacks of bears, strokes of lightning, or even the appearance of ghosts. Where success has not followed these rites and ceremonies they believe it is caused by the offerings not being of sufficient value, or not of long duration, or their having been too seldom performed. Therefore the neglect or incompetency of these sacrifices constitutes the crime and the punishment is visible in the misfortune that occurs. This part of the subject will meet with further consideration under the head of religion.

PRAYERS

PRAYER OF A WARRIOR.[14]—" O Wakoñda, you see me a poor man; have pity upon me. I go to war to revenge the death of my brother; have pity upon me. I smoke this tobacco taken from my medicine sack, where it has been enveloped with the remains of my dead brother.[15] I smoke it to my Tutelary, to you; aid me in revenge. On my path preserve me from mad wolves. Let no enemies surprise me. I have sacrificed, I have smoked, my heart is low, have pity

---

[14] Almost every sentence is repeated over three or four times in a low running tone, with the pipe presented to the Charm, Amulet, or Sun.

[15] Meaning with a lock of his hair.

upon me. Give me the bows and arrows of my enemies. Give me their guns. Give me their horses. Give me their bodies. Let me have my face blackened on my return. Let good weather come that I can see. Good dreams give that I can judge where they are. I have suffered. I wish to live. I wish to be revenged. I am poor. I want horses. I will sacrifice. I will smoke. I will remember; have pity upon me."

PRAYER TO GHOSTS.—"Spirits of our dead relatives, I make this feast for you to call you all around me. I smoke this tobacco which has been inclosed with your hair; be near us and hear. My friends are around me, and you are called to the feast. Call on all the spirits of our dead friends to aid in giving us what we ask. Make the buffalo come near and the clouds and wind fair to approach them, that we may always have meat in camp to feed us and you. Help us in every way; let our children live. Let us live. Call on all these spirits and ask them to assist you in helping us.

"If we hunt, be with us. If we go to war, be with us. Enable us to revenge some of your deaths upon our enemies. They have killed you; they have brought our hearts low. Bring their hearts low also. Let us blacken our faces. Keep us from harm, rest quiet, we will not cease to cry for and remember you. You are remembered in this feast, eat some of it [here small bits are scattered around]. This to you, my father. This for you, my grandfather, my uncle, my brother, the relations of all present eat, rest in quiet, do not let disease trouble us. We eat for you, we cry for you, we cut ourselves for you."

In conclusion, if the spirit addressed be recently dead they will all cry, and some of the immediate relatives cut their legs and arms, but if it is a feast to the memory of those long since dead some of the concluding words are left out. There is a good deal of repetition and often a long prayer is said, but the above is in amount what they ask. For the previous ceremony before the prayer is said, see the article where feasts to the dead are described.

THE MOON

They say the moon is a hot body and derives its light from its own nature, not as a reflection of the sun's rays; that it is eaten up monthly or during a given period by a great number of moles, which they call we-as-poo-gah (moon nibblers). These moles are numerous all over the prairies, have pointed noses, no teeth, and burrow in the ground. They (the Indians) believe that in eating up the moon their noses are burned off, their teeth worn out, and for their damage have been cast down from above, where they are doomed to burrow in the earth and get nothing to eat. The same operation is going on all the time by other moles, who in their turn will be thrown down. They think Wakoñda causes a new moon to grow when the old one has been destroyed. The moon is not supposed to be an abiding place for beings, but is worshipped and sacrificed to on account of its affording light by which to travel at night. They take the dark part of the face of the moon to be a large light Man holding a kettle in each hand. Stars are other bodies of fire far off, which they admit may be the residences of spirits or beings, though no great stress is laid on the idea. They are not regarded as parts of a system. Except the Polar Star and the Ursa Major, but few of the planets, if any, are known.

PARENTAL AFFECTION

The Indians show great veneration for their parents and affection among brothers and sisters; more, perhaps, to their parents than the others; but this only continues as long as they are vigorous enough to hunt, travel, and follow the camp. When old age and helplessness come on they are neglected. In proportion as age advances, veneration diminishes, and when parents become a burden they are left in some encampment with a small supply of provisions, which being exhausted, they perish. Age is under no circumstances the object of veneration; the fate of very old brothers and sisters is the same. They excuse themselves from this unnatural act by saying they are unable to transport them and that they are of no more use; also that it is the request of the old persons. This may be true, and it is likely that the life they lead in camp or in traveling, exposed to all weather and hardship, renders death desirable. There are very few very old Indians. They are not a long-lived people, and this is the reason these acts are not of more frequent occurrence. We do not know that the striking of a parent would be deemed a crime; at least no punishment would follow from others, but it is not customary and would be considered disgraceful. Eight years since this period we were present when an Indian shot his father dead for striking his mother, but this is the only instance of the kind we ever saw or heard of, and the person is despised by all, besides being since that afflicted by an incurable disease resembling scrofula. Indian priests, doctors, or conjurors are not more venerated on account of their supposed supernatural powers, but are somewhat feared, and sometimes persecuted or killed for supposed inflictions of diseases by sorcery. This fear is general but secret, and these men are neither venerated nor associated with as much as ordinary persons. If their services be required they are paid, and afterwards let alone, at least not trifled with nor loved. We can not by close inquiry find that any of these Indians ever killed by stoning a person, though enemies are tortured in almost every other way, if taken alive.

RELIGION

All these Indians believe in a Great Power, the First Cause of Creation, though they do not attempt to embody this idea, and call it by name Wah-con-tun'-ga or Great Medicine.[16] The word " medicine " in this case has no reference to the use of drugs, but the sense of it is all that is incomprehensible, supernatural, all-powerful, etc. Everything that can not be explained, accounted for by ordinary means, or all that is above the comprehension and power of man (Indians) is called Wah-con or medicine. Thus their own priests or jugglers are named Wah-con. A steamboat, clock, machine, or even toys, of the movements of which or the principle of motion they could not account for, would likewise be termed Wah-con. Now, Waconda refers to something greater than is within the power of man to accomplish, and its effects are manifested in the elements, natural phenomena, sickness, death, great distress, or loss from enemies, famine, lightning, and any other thing to them unaccountable by any visible means. They think Wakoñda pervades all air, earth, and sky; .that it is in fact omnipresent and omnipotent, though subject to be changed and enlisted on their part in any undertaking if the proper ceremonies, sacrifices, and fasts are resorted to. They consider its power to be made applicable to either good or evil according to their observance of these ceremonies. They admit the existence of its good in years of great abundance of game, seasons of general health, triumphs over enemies, etc.; and its evil or danger is felt in every loss, infectious disease, or distress, the cause of which they are ignorant. These are the attributes of Wakoñda, and his residence is supposed by some to be in the sun, but his power everywhere.

They do not acknowledge any separate existing evil spirit or influence, though they have a name for this in their language, but the idea has been implanted by whites in later years, and can not by them be realized. All unaccountable evil is a dispensation of the anger of Wakoñda, which it is in their power to avoid by the proper fasts, sacrifices, etc., and which they all do.

Now this Supernatural Unknown Cause or Mystery created all things in the beginning. After the earth a few men and women of different colors were made, from whom descended all people. Different races were created for different pursuits. They say that to the whites was allotted education, knowledge of the mechanical arts, of machinery, etc., and therefore the whites in many things are

[16] Denig here defines the sense in which he uses the term " medicine " as applied to the objects and things to which the native Indians apply their words. *wakoñ* and *wakoñda*, meaning, " spiritual, sacred, consecrated, wonderful, incomprehensible, divine ; a spirit, a diviner, etc."

Wah-con. They were also made rich and clothed, or have the means of getting clothing, and everything they want without hardship or exposure. The Indians, they say, were made naked and with such qualifications as to suit a hunter, knowledge enough to make his arms and use them at war or in the chase, a constitution to stand severe cold, long fasting, excessive fatigue, and watchfulness, and this was their portion. The position and pursuits of people were not defined by any laws, oral or otherwise delivered, but each with the powers granted him was enabled to live. The hunter soon found out that he could make traps and weapons, and felt his superiority over the animal creation.

They believe all animals are made for the use of man and more especially for the Indians, their meat being for food and their skin for clothing, " for " say they, " if not for that use for what other purpose? " Indians must have meat, and they eat all animals and birds, even to the crow and rattlesnake.[17] The prairie (the earth) was made for grazing the buffalo, and rivers to produce fuel, etc. The whites from their superior knowledge soon found out their destiny—to make everything, subdue everything, and make even the Indians work for their benefit. People were left in this state and each pursued their different occupations.

We can not trace in any of their conversations or religion any appearance of a moral code nor any offenses they can be guilty of toward Wakoñda except the omission of worship. If they had an idea of the kind they would undoubtedly do penance and offer sacrifices for these acts, but this is not the case. There is no repentance for past deeds; all ceremonies and worship is to avoid present or future evil. What we term crime can not be an offense to Wakoñda, as its aid is invoked to commit the greatest of them. Their idea of Wakoñda or Great Unknown Power is, we believe, nothing more than the fear of evil befalling them, the averting of which is beyond the power of man. Therefore they make sacrifices, fasts, prayers, etc., to this Unknown Power which they know from actual phenomena has an existence, and think His aid can thus be secured.

But they can go no further. They have no idea of a Being whose attributes are mercy, forgiveness, benevolence, truth, justice, etc., nor will they have until these words have a signification and appreciation among themselves. This view is the correct and general one among all the prairie tribes, though it is often clothed in superstitious narrative of fable not necessary to be inserted here. War and peace would not be recognized as His special acts, as they know these

---

[17] The Assiniboin never eat the rattlesnake, but it is known that some of the St. Peter's Sioux and Cree do.

things depend upon themselves, but success or defeat would be, as that is beyond their power or knowledge when they start to war. Consequently, a successful warrior or leader is always said to be Wah-con or divine—that is, one who has by some means secured the aid of Wakoñda. Natural phenomena unattended by either good or evil results would pass by unnoticed, but destructive tornadoes, deaths by lightning, by diseases such as apoplexy or unaccountable accidents would be regarded as His special acts. Eclipses, thunder, and lightning are warnings, and to these sacrifices are made with the view of averting the danger intimated, yet unknown. From this dread of unaccountable evil arises their repugnance to talk on the subject. To do so would lay open their secrets of apprehensions, of sacrifices, and might, they think, by levity produce the evil they wish to avoid or a counterpoise of sacrifice on the part of some one else render theirs unavailing.

For the further explanation of this subject it will be proper to state some of their sacrifices and ceremonies so that a minute survey of the operations of their minds can be realized. The greatest public or national ceremony of the Assiniboin is the Sacred Lodge. The time for this is appointed by some divining man of known repute and invitations are sent to the different camps to attend. Lodges are placed in the form of a long tent by posts planted a few yards apart and others transversely, over which are stretched many lodge skins to form one building about 100 yards long and 5 or 6 yards wide. To these transverse poles are tied all offerings to Wakoñda, though principally to the Sun and Thunder. These offerings consist of skins of value, different kinds of cloth, beads, kettles, and any new articles the donator can afford and is willing to sacrifice, in proportionate value as their wishes to effect some object or to avoid some danger they apprehend exists. A mast about 40 feet high is raised in front of the building and the raising of this requires the presence of all the men and women, who all the time sing a kind of hymn or tune, though no words are used in it. This mast is painted and decked out very gaily. All are dressed in their very best raiment and the whole presents a lively and interesting appearance. The divining man who called the meeting on the first day goes through many prayers and ceremonies with the pipe, the tenor of which are invocations for general health and success both in war and the chase, and for the avoiding of any and all unknown evil or accidents.

The second day is devoted to dancing and feasting on the very best they can produce, and this is the only dance among them except the scalp dance where men and women dance together. On the third day is exhibited feats of sleight of hand and tricks, some of which

are very well done and serve to increase their belief in the supernatural powers of the divining men who perform them. On the
fourth day these sacrifices are taken down, destroyed in such manner
as to be of no use to anyone who finds them, and hung on different
trees or bushes in the neighborhood. The divining man who called
the meeting receives presents from a good many who attend, of
horses and other property, and it generally proves a good speculation
on his part. This is done but once a year and is their only form of
national worship.

The common way in which sacrifices are made by individuals is
thus: The Indian takes some article of value alone into the hills
or woods, lights the pipe, and invokes the aid of Wakoñda in
whatever he desires to succeed, promising a repetition on a certain
time.[18] This article is then damaged or destroyed and left there.
After this he returns to his lodge, kills a dog, makes a feast, and
invites his neighbors, by whom the flesh is eaten and small portions
thrown on the ground as a respect to Wakoñda. It does not
appear, however, that the killing and eating of the animal is considered as part of the sacrifice further than to add to the importance
of the ceremony.

A feast of corn, flour, or berries is as often used on these occasions
as animal flesh. The article sacrificed must be something of value,
must have caused the Indian some trouble or expense to procure;
otherwise it is of no avail. On one occasion an Indian bought at this
place the following three articles at the price of six buffalo robes,
viz, two kettle covers, a ball that had been shot out of a gun, and
a chew of tobacco that had been thrown away. Now, although he
could have procured any of these articles for nothing in his own
camp, yet according to his promise to Wakoñda he was obliged to
pay a high price and to travel a long distance to procure them.

Every warrior or man of family among them makes these sacrifices
whenever he feels disposed, or their promises to Wakoñda become
due, and if they do not fulfill these promises or neglect these
ceremonies they are punished, or at least any accident, loss, or failure
would be attributed to this cause, that could not be accounted for
by any other. Another mode resorted to of propitiating the anger
of Wakoñda or securing his aid is fasting and cutting their
bodies. This is not much practiced by the Assiniboin except for
success in war.

Several principal warriors will lie out in the cold, rain, or snow
for three or four days and nights, without eating, drinking,
smoking, or speaking, making internal prayers to Wakoñda to aid

---

[18] This fetish or amulet is also exposed and smoked to as a medium for his prayer to
reach the Great Medicine.

them in accomplishing their objects and the dreams that present themselves under these circumstances are received as favorable or unfavorable omens according to the nature of the visions presented. This is done by those who are desirous of leading a war party or becoming capable to lead by some great exploit, and the leader chosen is he whose dream appears to present the greatest appearance of success. These fasts are sometimes accompanied by cutting the breast with a knife horizontally or the arms transversely above the elbow, making incisions about 3 or 4 inches long and half an inch deep, which are not bound up. Among the Mandan and Gros Ventres these ceremonies are still more severe. Incisions are made on each side of the shoulder blade on the back and a stout stick is thrust through. A cord is then attached to the stick and they are drawn up off their feet to a post planted for the purpose. By an impetus given with their feet they throw themselves out from the post and swing themselves around violently until the cord winds and unwinds successively, for one or two days, when the hold breaks and they fall to the ground.

If not already too much weakened, new incisions are made and cords 10 or 12 feet long are tied therein. To the ends of these cords are attached three or four buffalo bulls' heads and horns, each weighing from 15 to 20 pounds, and they drag this weight over the ground, the horns plowing it up until the holds break, or fainting from exhaustion they are carried away by their relatives. Nothing is eaten or drunk during all this time.[19]

These and other ceremonies are what they think appeases the anger, averts the evil, or secures the aid of Wakoñda or Great Mystery. They are not made with the view of any atonement whatever for bad deeds, neither with the object of purifying their minds for communion with him or it, but as a payment. The idea is that he who undergoes so much voluntary punishment or pain, or destroys so much property to him valuable, entitles him to the protection of that unknown power and that it can and will favor those who thus remember and worship him.

They have no idea of national and individual atonement, nor that any person was to or has come on earth to answer for them. To make this idea reasonable to them they would first have to be taught that they are guilty of crime and a correct knowledge of the attributes of the Great Mystery, together with a moral sense of justice. To do this the entire regeneration of the grown Indian must be brought about, which it would be little less than a miracle to accomplish.

---

[19] We perceive by the printed inquiry that this is not credited, yet it is so common among these people as scarcely to attract the attention of the traders.

They would, to please any missionary, give a tacit consent to his creed, whatever it was. Knowing him to be an educated and superior man, not striving after personal gain, they would be induced to give it a trial, but would continue their own ceremonies at the same time in secret, and any failure of their expectations would be blamed on the missionary. They might actually appear to him converted by outward show, but their minds would undergo no change, unless it was to become more confused and skeptical. This is the reason why all attempts at reformation should be made with their children. Abstract truth will not admit of general application, without taking into consideration the existing state of things. The necessity of law must be felt before it would avail; their ignorance made manifest before truth could be introduced; a moral sense of justice and of their depravity implanted before moral rectitude can be expected.

Horses sacrificed on an Indian's grave are an offering to the Great Mystery to conduct the soul of the departed immediately to the south, where the Indian Paradise is said to be situated, and also includes a desire that the Great Mystery should supply the place of the deceased parent, as a father and protector. Dogs and other animals that are killed in sacrifice, are eaten by those invited, and only appear to be part of the ceremony, not of the sacrifice. The entrails of the animal thus killed are neither eaten nor burned, but thrown away as on any other occasion.

In eating these feasts small bits are thrown on the ground with these words: " This to Wakoñda to keep us from harm," " This to the Sun," " This to the Thunder," or to some of their dead relatives, and these ejaculations are uttered in a very low voice, not always audible. They offer no human sacrifices to Wakoñda, neither do their traditions mention their forefathers to have done so. Though enemies are tortured to death in many ways, yet it is only to satisfy their revenge and thirst for savage glory. Within the last year several of these acts have been committed a short distance from this place, which to convey an idea of we may mention here. Five Blackfeet were caught stealing horses from the Crow village in the spring of 1853, then at the mouth of the Yellowstone River, and the enemies were pursued a mile or so, when they took refuge in a cluster of bushes. The Crows surrounded them and by constant firing killed all except one, who was shot through the leg. This man they took out alive, scalped, and cut his hands off, gathered their boys around who fired into his body with powder, striking him in the face with his own scalp, and knocking on his head with stones and tomahawks until he died. Afterwards the five bodies were carried to camp, the heads, hands, feet, and privates cut off, paraded on poles, and thrown around the camp, some of which found their

way to the fort, and were presented by the Crows to the Cree
Indians then here.

A few weeks before the period at which we write some Blackfeet
stole horses from the Cree camp, were pursued and 11 out of the 12
of which the party consisted were killed. The remaining one was
taken alive, scalped, his right hand cut off, and thus started back to
his own nation to tell the news. Now as this man was leaving the
Cree camp he met a Cree [20] boy whom he managed to kill with his
remaining hand, was pursued and taken the second time, and was
tortured to death by slow mutilation.

The trunks are generally burned, but all the members and the head
are carried about the camp, if near, and insulted by the old women
and boys in every possible manner. The Sioux, Assiniboin, and
Cree will on occasions tear out the heart of an enemy, place it on a
stick and roast it before the fire, dance around, sing, and each bite off
and swallow a small piece. There are no religious associations attending these acts, and they are not made with the view of appeasing
the anger or of sacrifices to the Great Mystery; neither do their
words and actions on these occasions imply any such idea; all is insult to the dead enemy, and savage glory and revenge to themselves.

The moral character of their priests or doctors does not differ
in any respect from that of ordinary Indians, which have by this
time been seen to possess no such qualities as sobriety, truth, etc.
Whether they actually believe in their own powers we can not say,
but rather think they do. Perhaps some strokes of fortune or remarkable coincidences have produced this belief, or they may think
that the pains and exertions they use may induce the Wakoñda
to aid them. We have already noticed this class of priests in their
medical capacity, and will now state their other qualifications. They
wear no badge of office, are either of the male or female sex, are not
hereditary, nor is their number limited. As many as are believed
to be Wa-con, or Divine, and are willing to run the risk attending
the profession, do so. They are all called by the same general name
of Wa-con, independent of their individual or real name. They
affect to cure diseases, reveal future events, direct where lost articles
are to be found, interpret dreams, etc. The ceremony attending
any of these things (except sickness) is conducted by the medicine
man, first being paid for his services. Afterwards he enters a small
lodge built for the purpose, like the vapor bath and drums,
rattles and sings alone the greater part of the night, returning his
answer to those concerned in the morning. These answers partake
of the nature of those of the ancient oracles, are ambiguous, with
the view of evading decided failure. They do not claim the power

[20] Evidently should be Blackfeet.

of witchcraft, as this is a dangerous profession, but this power is ascribed to them by the other Indians.

The majority of these people believe, or say they believe, that some of these old conjurors can "shoot them with bad spells" (as they express it) at the distance of 100 miles off, and it is on the assumption that they are the cause of some of their deaths, that the lives of these professors are sometimes forfeited. We believe their confidence in the powers of these priests and medicine men is pretty general, though some of them (the priests) are more divine or Wa-con than others. When an Indian is sick they endeavor to cure him, as has been stated, and if unsuccessful and death ensues they usually keep out of sight until the first bursts of grief are over. Others of the same profession who have not been called to administer to the patient attend the funeral, their object being to secure whatever property they can by loud crying, cutting their hair and bodies, and other display of profound grief. Nothing resembling a prayer is said over the dead at the burial nor anything spoken. Indeed, on account of their loud lamentations it would be impossible to hear it if it were. Some weeks afterwards, however, other ceremonies take place regarding the dead which will be described in another place. The body is placed in the fork of a tree, on a scaffold, or occasionally interred on the top of a high hill. No device, inscription, or hieroglyphics are made at or near the place of interment by any of these nations.

As far as we have proceeded with their religion, belief is the general one, though it may be clothed in different language by different Indians, sometimes superstitious and fabulous, but our object has been to arrive at the philosophy of their religion by rejecting fables, etc., which do not bear upon the inquiry.

From this point all other religion diverges into different minor beliefs and superstitions according to the fancy of each individual. Many believe in certain evil spells and troubles brought on them by lesser spirits or ghosts and even of the spirits of monsters which have no existence nor ever had except in their dreams and morbid imagination. It appears that these ghosts are the cause of all petty malice, vexations, or bad luck, not being of sufficient consequence to attract the attention or induce the influence of Wakoñda. To relate the different kinds of belief in these powers as each would explain it would require the labor of years, and it is somewhat difficult to generalize, owing to the prevailing differences. Under some of the answers that will follow regarding charms, amulets, ghosts, etc., will be detailed enough in conjunction with what has already been stated to form a tolerably connected idea of this feature of their faith.

Sorcery or witchcraft has already been noticed, but we may in addition state that the witchcraft imputed to some of their doctors

is their power to do evil at a great distance from the object, to produce death or disease, though they do not believe these persons can
transform themselves into other shapes; think they can exercise the
same power to do good if they choose, and do exercise it in curing
the sick.   It is in consequence of this belief that the doctor or divining man is punished in case of failure and death, as they think it is
his unwillingness, not his inability, to cure which produces the
result.   They do not burn them, but the writer has seen several shot
at different times by the relatives of the deceased, on the supposition
they caused their death.   This custom is in as great force now as it
ever was.

The divining man has a chance to become rich in horses and other
property in a short time, as his fees depend on himself; but these
advantages are more than counterbalanced by the risk attending the
profession.   The doctor, priest, conjuror, wizard, prophet, and divining man are all united in the same person; that is, to a divining man
(Wa-con), or divining woman (Wa-can), these powers, or some
of them, are ascribed, and they are believed to possess them in proportion as their success has been developed.   Some are simply doctors
of medicine, others in addition are conjurors and do tricks.   Some
go further, interpret dreams, reveal the future, find lost articles, etc.
The whole united forms the entire divining man.   The persons who
profess and perform some of these things are tolerably numerous;
but the effective diviner of established reputation, large practice, and possessing the whole of the foregoing powers are very
few, perhaps not more than six or eight in the whole Assiniboin
Nation.   As has been observed, they form no distinct body and
have but little influence in council unless they can add that of warrior
to their many distinguished titles and degrees.

The whole of these Indians most sincerely believe in the theory
of ghosts, that departed spirits have the power to make themselves
visible and heard, that they can assume any shape they wish, of
animals or men, and many will affirm that they have actually seen
these apparitions and heard their whistlings and moanings.   They
are much afraid of these appearances, and under no consideration
will go alone near a burial place after dark.   They believe these
apparitions have the power of striking the beholder with some
disease, and many complaints are attributed to this cause.   They
therefore make feasts and prayers to them to remain quiet.   Smaller
evils and misfortunes are caused by their power, and a great many
stories are nightly recounted in their lodges of the different shapes
in which they appear.

Dreams are revelations of Great Mystery and have considerable influence over them, either in war expeditions or the chase.

A bad dream on the part of the leader of a war party would be sufficient cause for their return, even if they were within a short distance of their enemies. It would also prevent an Indian from his customary hunting and have other effects of the like nature for a short time. Good dreams are therefore always desired and courted, particularly on the eve of war excursions. Faith in amulets and charms is general among the whole of these tribes. The material of these charms is of every possible variety, as also the different degrees of influence they exercise over different minds. The idea though thoroughly realized by ourselves is difficult to explain, but may be thus stated: Although the Great Spirit is all powerful, yet His will is uncertain; He is invisible and only manifests His power in extraordinary circumstances. The want of a tangible medium is felt, therefore, through which they can offer their prayers to all ghosts, lesser influences of evil, which overrule their ordinary occupations. Each Indian selects some object for this purpose and calls it his medicine, which is invested with a sacred character by the care with which it is guarded and the prayers, invocations, etc., made through it as a medium.

This charm or fetish is chosen in consequence of some dream or incident or idea presented on some important occasion, and consists of the skin of a weasel, otter, or beaver; heads and bodies of different kinds of birds, stuffed; images of wood, stone, and beads wrought upon skin; drawings of bulls, bears, wolves, owls, serpents, monsters, who have never existed; even a bullet worn round the neck; in fact anything resembling animate, inanimate, or imaginative creation, is selected according to the superstitious fancy of the individual. This charm, whatever it is, is inclosed in several envelopes of skin, and placed in a rawhide sack which is painted and fringed in various ways. This sack is never opened in the presence of anyone unless the Indian falls sick, when he has it taken out and placed at his head. Ordinarily this object is taken out in secret, and prayers and invocations made through it as a medium to the spirits he wishes to propitiate. They are aware that the object has no intrinsic power, but its virtue lies in their faith of their ceremonies, as exhibited through this charm as a visible medium to the supernatural. It is in fact the same operation of mind (though differently exhibited) as is displayed in the charms believed in by most of the lower order of whites. Although many ignorant white persons have faith in the charms, spells, etc., of quack doctors and old women, yet this does not destroy their belief in the Supreme Being, neither does it that of the Indian. As long as he has success in his different ordinary undertakings and is not troubled with the evils he fears, he will continue to say his medicine is good, but should he be disappointed and the case reversed, he will throw the charm away and substitute some other.

Thus the writing, paintings, and pictures done by whites are considered great charms by some Indians, particularly the Crows, and are eagerly sought after as such. In the same light is regarded the medal of the crucifixion given them by Catholic priests.

What is the actual character of their worship when closely analyzed?

It is hoped that the preceding remarks have rendered this character plain. All their prayers, sacrifices, feasts and personal inflictions tend only to advance their temporal welfare and interest.

Several tunes are sung on some of these occasions when presenting the pipe to the Sun, etc., that are of a sacred character, partaking of the nature of thanksgiving for any signal success in war or otherwise. A few words are used, but the chant is solemnly performed without their usual gesticulations or levity.

The custom of holding as sacred the cult of the tobacco plant is general. No ceremony of importance takes place among them in which the pipe is not used. There are, however, several solemn occasions in which the manufactured tobacco will not answer, when they use that grown by themselves. These customs occur among the Mandan, Gros Ventres, Arikara, and Crows, the only nations who cultivate the tobacco plant. Sacrifices of small quantities of tobacco are also made on many occasions, and always a small piece is found wrapped with the medicine pipe or inclosed in the medicine sack.

Why it is considered sacred they can not explain, and the idea appears one of the most ancient and original among them.

These tribes do not worship fire in any form. The Sun is thought to be a body of fire and is worshipped next to the Great Mystery by all of them, not, however, because it is fire (though being luminous no doubt originated the idea) but because it is believed by most of them to be the residence, and by some the eye, of the Great Mystery. It is worshipped as the greatest visible symbol of the Great Mystery. No other ceremonies are in existence among them by which we would judge that fire is regarded with more reverence than water. On some occasions councils are opened with fire struck from flint, such as peace-making between two nations, ceremonies in the medicine lodge, and feasts to the dead, but in all ordinary councils among themselves this distinction is not made. In the cases where it is obtained from the flint it seems to be merely an adherence to ancient custom. No extra benefits are expected on that account, neither when questioned do they attach much importance to the fact. Fire would be nothing without the tobacco. In all these ceremonies with which we are well acquainted, we can safely say that the tobacco is the sacred material (not the fire). The rest depends on their invocations, etc., to the Great Mystery or his symbols to render the whole of an effective character in their estimation. We can not by inquiry find that there has ever been among them or their ancestors an idea of a holy or eternal fire.

Omens have great influence on them on all occasions and are of every possible variety. Storms, severe thunder, croaking of ravens, and unusual sounds in the night, or even the fall of their medicine sack or medicine pipe, would be sufficient to turn back a war party if any of these omens were considered by their leaders as unfortunate in their predictions, which they generally do. Councils would not proceed during severe thunder, an eclipse, or any unusual phenomena, though smaller omens would not be regarded. The flight of birds is seldom if ever considered ominous unless their passage be accompanied with some unusual appearances. Howlings of wolves and foxes in a peculiar manner, whistling and moanings of ghosts, and bad or bloody dreams would prevent the individual from war or the chase for a short time.

From all that has been written concerning their religion we would rather others would decide whether the Indians are in reality idolaters. That they render a species of worship to idols of almost every description is true, yet this worship only refers through these toys or charms to the great source of all power, or to supernatural interference. They do not believe in the virtue of the material of which they are made, nor do they ascribe to them an immaterial spirit, but the mind by viewing them has a resting point, a something to address in form, not for great protection and aid, but for daily favors, and averting of smaller evils.

Uneducated as they are, obliged mentally to grasp at protection from supernatural evil, in every way, from the great luminary the sun, as the most powerful, to the smallest atom that may possibly be of some aid, they, through these images or objects, endeavor to excite the interest of the Great Mystery, an Unknown Power, to whose approach no one certain way presents itself. If this be idolatry, be it so.

What else could be expected? That the Indians should be in advance of Christians, who have their charms, their chance, their fortune, and other ideas fully as repugnant to the belief in an all-wise disposer of events, as the customs of the Indians present? The very fact of the general practice of this species of idolatry appears to us to be the greatest evidence of their being true worshipers. It is in fact acknowledging a supernatural agency in everything; a belief in a ruling providence over this life in every situation. If their minds pursue wrong directions, and their prayers are for temporal, not spiritual welfare, it is not their fault. Why should they desire what they do not want? If no moral sense of right and wrong is found among them, no sins acknowledged, nor future punishments feared, it must follow that temporal welfare and personal advantage are all that remains worth praying or fasting for. If they pray and sacrifice to the sun and thunder it is nothing more than acknowledging the existence and power of God in these, His works.

If they depend on fetishes and amulets to aid them in ordinary life it is what many Christians do in a different way, yet these are not accused of idolatry. If the right ideas were instilled into the mind of the Indian he would be no more the savage, but the Christian, and would worship the same being in a different sense and form than he now does in any way his distorted imagination thinks may prove effective. Great evil or great good is evaded or invoked from the Great Spirit through great apparent mediums, as the Sun and Thunder.

Smaller evils and smaller benefits are averted or sought through the medium of charms which though not intrinsically of any virtue, yet benefits are the consequences attending on their prayers through them, their character being rendered sacred by constant care, and the importance of their position as mediums of worship. The identity of the Great Spirit as a being appears to be lost in their worship of the portions of creation capable of inspiring them with fear. His existence as a cause is admitted, but we do not observe He is often addressed except through some visible medium, which is as it were a separation of his power among these objects or animals.

The medicine sack contains the fetish or charm referred to, which with a lock of some dead relative's hair and a small piece of tobacco is inclosed in several envelopes of skins of different kinds, on which pictures of imaginary or real animals are rudely drawn.

This sack is made of raw buffalo hide (dried), the hair scraped off and painted and fringed in various ways. It is well tied up, not pried into by anyone, and mostly suspended to a pole outside the lodge in camp or carried on the back of some woman when traveling. When the owner dies it is buried with him. This is the arcanum of the medicine sack, and it possesses none of the features of an ark, either inside or out.

IMMORTALITY

That the soul lives after death is the general assent, and that this is a final state, but by pursuing the inquiry we do not arrive at any certain idea of their occupation there, as they will always say they do not know. This much, however, some acknowledged, that when they die their soul is taken to the south to a warm country, though this place does not appear to be either on the earth or in the heavens. Here is a state of pleasure and happiness, free from all disease, trouble, want, war, or accident. Some are more comfortably situated than others, particularly those who have been great warriors and those who have been attentive to their sacrifices and other ceremonies. No punishment for offenses is apprehended, though rewards are granted. If still questioned they will describe a counterpart or nearly so of the Mohammedan paradise, or a shadowy image of this life, abstracting the evil. There is no resurrection of the body, though they are presumed to have other bodies furnished them in the future state, that present the same features as in this life, yet are not subject to its vicissitudes.

Animals of all kinds are found there, though it does not appear that they are the souls of those which lived in this world. Reasoning powers and immortality are not ascribed to the brute creation. Everything referring to a future state is not made the subject of their conversations, and each man's opinions differ. Some deny any such a state and think death final to soul and body. Others that the soul never leaves the neighborhood of its burial place. All information regarding their belief in futurity is with difficulty extracted, and not much importance is placed on the fact of their being immortal beings; at their death also the greatest anxiety appears to be about their family and relations left behind. They admit its uncertainty, and fear nothing on the score of future punishment. Upon the whole there is nothing in their belief of a future state which affects much their general conduct through life and as little on the approach of death. From this fact we may conclude very reasonably that the foregoing system of their religion is the correct one, as they do not feel guilty of moral offenses toward the Great Spirit entailing future punishment, but expect to be rewarded for their devotedness in their manner of worship. These Indians will also smoke, invoke, and give small pieces of tobacco to the head of a bear after they have killed it. But this does not imply they are to meet the animal in a future state. It is a kind of thanksgiving, through the bear's head, to the powers that have enabled them to accomplish the feat of killing it without accident.

The killing of a grizzly bear by a single man is no trifling matter and deservedly ranks next to killing an enemy. A coup is counted for that action in their ceremonies where they publicly recount their brave exploits. Moreover, every year persons are torn to pieces by these animals when wounded or surprised in thickets where the person can not escape. Therefore all ceremonies to the dead animal would have the nature of invocations for aid and protection from the supernatural powers whose business it is to interfere, and indeed such their words imply on these occasions. It may have been some such ceremony the Indian on the shores of Lake Superior made which was mistaken for begging the animal's pardon.

MYTHOLOGY

This subject would not present any useful information and only tire the reader with endless fable without arriving at any important conclusions. We could fill volumes with their stories of giants, demons, transformations of men into animals and other shapes, but do not think any fact thus elicited would avail any useful purpose. There are a great many traditions that would seem to prove that the doctrine of metempsychosis has formerly been the general belief, but they do not appear to put much confidence in their reality at the present day, and these stories are told more for amusement every evening than anything else. Neither does it please absolutely to contradict or deny that such things have been. In this way beaver are said to have been once white men from the sagacity they show in building their lodges, evading traps, etc. Thunder is said to be the flapping of the wings of the large medicine bird. Piles of rocks are supposed to have been heaped up by large white giants. The rainbow is called the sun's wheel; though they are aware that the colors are formed by the sun shining through rain. All these and hundreds of others have legends of their formation which are very long and one or two generally occupy an evening to relate. Most of them, however, contain a kind of moral or double meaning and are occasionally interesting and imaginative, sometimes obscure.

To present an example we will record one recited by the "Thunder Stomach," an Assiniboin warrior at the time we write and interpreted by myself, preserving as nearly as possible all the words and actually all the ideas of the Indian.

LEGEND OF THE ORIGIN OF THE URSA MAJOR AND POLAR STAR, BY THE THUNDER STOMACH, AN ASSINIBOIN WARRIOR

In the beginning a few Indians were made far in the northern regions. No sun nor moon had yet been formed, and all was utter darkness except the light of the snow. A lodge of Indians was situated on the bleak plains inhabited by eight persons who were seven brothers and one sister. The brothers all went out hunting and left the woman at home working at raiment. In their absence a stranger came outside the lodge and called to the woman to come out, using flattering words with a sweet mouth, but she moved not, nor looked upon his face. When her brothers returned she related the circumstance, and the eldest said, " You did right, my sister—had you listened to this man's sweet words and looked upon his face, you would have been obliged to follow him wherever he went, without the power to stop or turn back." She said nothing but continued her labors and they again left to hunt.

Being anxious to ascertain the truth concerning the stranger and expecting his visit, she put on four complete suits of raiment and four pairs of moccasins, one on top of the other; also tied on a pair of snowshoes. He came and used the same flattering words, when she stepped outside and looked upon his face. He immediately departed at a swift pace and she was obliged to follow in his tracks. Onward they traveled far over the plains in a northerly direction and over immense piles of snow. A long time passed without diminishing their speed, until at length they came to a lodge full of men (beings). Her conductor entered and disappeared, she followed and not seeing him took her seat near the door. " Move to the next," said the man at her side, " I am not he whom you seek," and she moved where he directed. " Farther on," said her neighbor, and she again changed her place. " Next," said the other, and she moved in this way from one to the other, until by making the circuit of the lodge she at last found herself at the entrance without seeing the one whom she had followed hither. She was about to leave the lodge when the eldest Indian, apparently the master, said, " Remain, I will tell you a story." She stopped. " There was once a woman," he continued, " who ran off with a young man, and came to a lodge full of strangers to seek her lover. She had on four entire dresses, and not finding the man, would have left, but one of her dresses fell off."[21]

On saying this, an entire dress and pair of moccasins disappeared. He repeated the words four times and at the end of each repetition a dress was missing, which left her naked. They then took her up and cast her out into the cold snow to freeze to death.

The brothers on their return from hunting missed their sister and suspecting the cause of her departure followed the tracks and arrived outside the lodge where they found their sister nearly frozen to death. After wrapping her in a robe, and she had somewhat recovered, the eldest brother said, " Go back into the lodge and tell them a story in return." She entered and said, " I come to tell a tale. There was once a woman coaxed off and forced to follow a strange man. She came to a lodge of strangers, who instead of protecting her, robbed her of all her clothing and threw her out in the snow to die. Such men have no hearts." On concluding, the hearts of all the Indians inside flew out of their mouths and stuck to the lodge poles

---

[21] This remark recalls the story of the Babylonian Ishtar, who was represented as losing one by one her seven garments and then as receiving them back again one by one.

outside, where they were cut to pieces by the brothers. She left with her brothers for their home, but got separated from them in a snow storm and wandered every way, she know not whither. In the end, after a long time she came to a large house of iron with flames of fire coming out of the chimney. She feared to enter. "Come in," said the master of the house. "If I enter, how shall I be treated? What relation shall I bear to you?" "I will be your brother," he said. "No," was the answer. "I will be your father." "No," was again the answer. "Your uncle," "your friend," still "no" was her answer. "I will be your husband." This time she replied "Yes," the large iron doors flew open and she entered, they closing violently behind her.

The inhabitant was a large, ugly man, and the interior of the building was strewn with human carcasses half devoured in their raw state. He was the first cannibal! The woman would have fled but could not, and was compelled to become his wife according to her promise. He treated her badly and although not forcing her to eat human flesh was continually devouring it himself. They lived as man and wife for a length of time, during which she had a male child by him. The brothers had never given up the search for their lost sister, and in the course of their travels for that purpose came to the house of the cannibal during his absence. The woman let them in and recognized them. The child was beginning to speak a few words, and among the first he pronounced were: "Mother, what fine, fat men; kill one of them that I may eat some good meat." The brothers stared—the child was a cannibal! "You little fool," said the mother, "would you eat your own uncle?" The brothers held a council with their sister as to the way the cannibal being could be killed and she undertook his destruction. It appears this being had the power of coming into his house any way he chose, through the floor, through the walls, or any other manner, and the only vulnerable part of him was a cavity in the top of his head, not protected by the bone of the skull. She heated a stone red hot, and when the cannibal as usual was coming up through the floor, head foremost, she threw the stone into the hole in his head and burned up his brains, causing instant death.

She then fled to a place of rendezvous appointed by her brothers, taking her child along. They returned to their home with their sister, and when they arrived held a council and condemned the child to death, to prevent the propagation of the race of cannibals. It was killed by the mother, and on killing it she was changed into a body of fire, caught up into the heavens and placed as the first star in the north, which was the polar star. The seven brothers were also changed into stars and form the constellation known as the Great Bear and are appointed to walk around and keep guard over their sister forever.

After the narrator had concluded I inquired if it had any other meaning than a story told to excite interest. He said it had, and that it showed the woman was revenged on all her persecutors, and for her resolution and good in cutting off the first cannibal and her own son, thereby destroying the species, was rewarded by being placed as a star; likewise her brothers who had protected her through life were stars also and guard her from harm. That if she had not acted thus a great part of the Indians would be cannibals. This he said was the commencement of stars, and their traditions named many other instances of like manner in which stars were created.

Manners and Customs

Constitution of the Assiniboin Family; Kinship.—There are terms for each degree of relationship and the collateral branches. These affinities are traced as far back as the great-grandfather, and the line of descent is distinguished by their referring to the names of the grandfather, father, or parents through some of their descendants living. The names for collateral relatives are the same by the father's as by the mother's side. All stepchildren become the children of all the wives the Indian has. The terms aunt and uncle are the same on both sides. The elder brother is called Ma-chin'-ah and the rest of the brothers Mis-soon-kah; the youngest is named the last. The eldest sister is called Me-tun'k-ah and the rest of the sisters Me-choon-ah. Their names are the same on either part. The name of a dead person is seldom mentioned, or if so, in a very low voice. Usually they name some living relative, and add his or her dead father. Where confusion exists as to a distant collateral relative they are all classed under the general head of cousins, though they are generally correct. They always address one of their nation as kindred if there is reason to believe the least possible degree of relationship is acknowledged, and never use their proper names if they are of kin. The name of the mother-in-law or father-in-law is never pronounced by the son-in-law. She never speaks to him nor he to her, neither do they ever look at the face nor go into the same lodge.

Should the father-in-law happen to go into a lodge where his son-in-law is seated, the latter would cover his face with his robe and not speak while the former remained. Usually they stop the one entering by crying out, " He of whom you are ashamed is here," when the other goes away and postpones his visit. All communications on business to these people by their son-in-law is transacted through his wife or strangers. To speak to or name the father or mother of an Indian's wife would excite the ridicule and laughter of the whole camp. They refer to them in speaking by mentioning my father- or mother-in-law, as the case may be, or sometimes say " my wife's father," or " her mother." A woman does not mention the individual name of her husband nor he hers, but always say " my husband " or " my wife." Most of the bands being made up of relatives, the terms denoting kindred are in constant use in conversation.

The hunter state with all these prairie tribes is precarious and uncertain. They are often weeks and months without enough meat and not infrequently reduced to absolute famine. Whenever the buffalo are plenty they have no difficulty in procuring more meat than they can use and then do dry some, but they are very improvident and their small supplies are soon exhausted.

Indians who have numbers of horses, like the Crows and Sioux, follow the buffalo at all seasons, with their camp, but those who have but few horses, like the Assiniboin, can not follow them through the deep snow. When they are far from their lodges the men go over the snow on snowshoes and pack the hides to camp on dogs. From observation and experience they know that the buffalo approach the timber when the snow is deep on the plains to eat twigs and wild rosebuds. They therefore place their camps along some stream in the commencement of the winter and await their approach. None of these nations except the Cree are good elk and deer hunters, consequently their whole dependence is on the buffalo, which, as we have stated, is precarious. Their raiment made of skins is durable, one suit being sufficient for a year, and game is always found in sufficient number to furnish them with garments before they actually need them. There is no distress on this score. Their habits and pursuits, as will be seen through these pages, do not admit of their wearing any other material than that made of skins; except in warm weather and for show on occasions, none other is worn.

Inasmuch as women are of great advantage to the Indians by their labor, a plurality of wives is required by a good hunter. The domestic peace of a family does not suffer much on that account. There are, to be sure, quarrels among the women occasionally, but these generally end in personal abuse and recrimination, or are quelled by the master, if present.

Upon the whole the domestic arrangement is benefited by having the labor divided, which would be too much for one woman. The Indians, mostly, treat their wives well, but these women require a hard ruler and sometimes they are obliged to strike severely. Jealousies among the women of the same lodge are nothing and do not affect the actions of the man further than to stop the disturbance. But jealousy on the part of the man toward some one of his women supposed to be unfaithful are accompanied by terrible punishments, not infrequently by death. Among the Blackfeet the noses of the women are cut off for this offense; others stab, strike, or kill as it happens. Women are not interfered with by the men in their management of household affairs. Such interference would excite too much ridicule for their pride.

Are the labors of husband and wife equally divided? The occupations of the man are as follows: Setting aside that of war which he occasionally follows after having a family, though not often, he is obliged to keep the family in meat and skins, and this occupies about one-third of his time. He makes his own bows and arrows, snowshoes, powder horns, and all implements of war and the chase, not purchased. He furnishes horses, either by war, bargains, or other means; collects, waters, and guards his horses; makes traps for wolves and foxes and kills and skins them; attends councils, feasts, and ceremonies; protects his family from insult and injury, and risks his life for them in hunting in different ways; all of which should be taken into consideration as forming a portion of his time and labor.

Sometimes his women will accompany him to the hunt and aid in skinning and butchering the animal, but this is only when the buffalo are near the camp. She never participates in his labors on other occasions. The usual occupations of the women are, to prepare the skins and dress them, which is a tedious and laborious operation; to cut up the meat in thin slices and dry it; to make all the clothing for the family, make lodges, cook, take care of their children and dogs, bring wood and water, pack and unpack animals, erect the tents, strike them, arrange the interior, carry burdens in traveling, render grease, pound meat, work at garnishing with beads and porcupine quills, make dogs travailles, saddle and unsaddle the master's horse, etc. In nations where canoes are used, the men make the frame and the women sew and stitch over it the bark or skin. Men make the paddles, pans, bowls, cradles, and pipes. This is among the Cree and Chippewa. With those who plant, the labor of hoeing, planting, gathering, drying, and shelling the corn is all done by the women and children; but with these less hunting is done.

Owing to the length of time required to scrape, stretch, dry, dress, and smoke even one skin it will be seen that the labor of the woman is much greater than that of the man, and she must have help or she could not attend to the domestic affairs of a large family.

A surplus of dressed skins is also necessary to buy the supplies they can not and do not make and to replace stolen or crippled horses. Thus an Indian with but one wife can not amass property, as the whole of her time would be employed in the absolute requisite domestic labors without being able to collect any skins for trade.

The first woman an Indian marries and the last are generally his favorites, the first because he has become accustomed to her ways, has children by her, and who manages the lodge in all its domestic arrangements, and the last because she is youngest and often handsomest. The actual labor performed by either of these is not near as great as by the other women. Indeed, all the others are looked upon in the light of laborers. To support several women, of course, requires greater exertions on the part of the man in hunting, but this is more than compensated for by their labor in dressing skins, which enable him to purchase horses, guns, and other means to hunt with greater facility. When buffalo are plenty, anyone can kill. The raw hide of the animal has no value. It is the labor of putting it in the form of a robe or skin fit for sale or use that makes its worth. Women therefore are the greatest wealth an Indian possesses next to his horses. Often they are of primary consideration, as after war by their labor is the only way he could acquire horses, the only standard of their wealth.

There is never any difficulty regarding raiment. Skins are durable and during the summer (when they make it) every Indian will kill enough animals for that purpose. He must do so or die, as but a small portion of the skins of the animals requisite for food will furnish the clothing. As it stands in the winter season, the women are never idle, the men also have pretty constant employment, but from spring till fall they both have a comparatively easy life. Domestic discords are not very common in their lodges.

They do, however, happen, and jealousy on the part of the master is the principal cause. All Indians have great forbearance with their families. When not excited or disappointed in some other way they will put up with almost everything their women say or do, and endeavor to laugh it off. The women study their humor, choose their time for this, and never press it so far as to enrage their husbands. If an Indian has returned from an unsuccessful hunt, lost his horses, or any other circumstance has taken place, to sour his temper, all his family immediately perceive it, and the greatest attentions are paid to him or his wants as long as this humor lasts. Some men will on these occasions tease and find fault with everything in the lodges, but they are not contradicted nor quarreled with. It is now their time to forbear, and well they know that punishment of no trifling kind hangs on a slender thread.

Discords of a nature to bring on contention and blows are uncommon except those arising from the jealousy of the man toward some one of his women. Even a look or a word in secret to a strange man is often sufficient to produce a blow or a stab. Upon the whole, however, they live in tolerable harmony, much more so than would be supposed to exist among savages. The loss of youth and youthful attractions is not a cause of neglect, particularly if the woman has children by her husband. An Indian seldom exhibits any ill feeling toward his first wife, but on the contrary depends upon her to employ and manage the others. In this and all the domestic labors she is the principal and is addressed as such and possesses more influence over the man at middle age than ever or than any of the others. No doubt the youngest is a more attractive but not so useful an inmate, and gain is the principal object of the master. Wives are even more valuable in extreme age than parents, though but few live a great length of time. Their labors are too severe. Men of family are not very amorous; they study their interest. Children give the wife great additional power over the husband, so much so that even if afterwards they prove unfaithful or very obstinate they are punished but retained, whereas without offspring they would be cast off for the same offenses. The first wife, though not necessarily, nor always, the eldest, retains the preference, as has been stated; she is the domestic councillor.

The jealousies arising among the women are only occasional bickerings in the absence of the master, who if he perceives anything of the kind going on or anything else to mar his peace soon settles it by the argument of the tomahawk. Men of family are dignified, use great forbearance toward those under their charge, and consider it as disgraceful to be engaged in quarrels and squabbles with women, seldom interfere or abuse them, never strike their children, but evince a determination to see their home rendered pleasant and agreeable. Young women are vain, fond of dress, yet this is no source of discord. Fine dress is not sought eagerly by women of middle age. More frequently they take a pride in dressing the youngest wife, or their children, if any, even at their own expense, which greatly pleases the master and induces him to flatter them otherwise for this mark of respect.

There is order enough preserved in every Indian lodge to suit their mode of life and with a delicacy toward guests that would merit imitation elsewhere. If a child cries during conversation it is taken out. Boys and young men keep their mouths shut when the masters speak. They do not contradict, abuse, or interrupt. All have their places for sitting and sleeping, at the head of which, if men, are placed their arms and accouterments; if women, their sewing, garnishing, etc. These places are arranged by the eldest wife or by the grandmother as soon as the lodge is erected by spreading skins on the ground, and are uniformly the same in the same family. They can be and are changed whenever the necessities of the men require it, though the individual's local privileges are not thereby disturbed.

Places are reserved for strangers or visitors, and baggage, water, cooking utensils, and provisions have each their space allotted. This is not perceived immediately by casual observers, but would be realized by a short residence. To present a more lucid idea of these locations in the interior, we submit the drawings (pls. 74 and 75), with the additional remark that the skin door is locked on the inside on going to bed by the mistress of the lodge to prevent the entrance of dogs and other intruders. The fastening is made by a paddle of wood twisted in a cord attached to each end of the transverse stick that forms the support of the skin door; the ends of the paddle are then thrust through the poles of the lodge and secured by loops of cord for the purpose. The whole is so constructed that any person acquainted with it would have some trouble to shut or open the door, even in the daytime. The form as represented in general, though, of course, differs when the family circle is great or small, but the same correct appointments of places are visible in all, be the inhabitants few or many. Sometimes different families, yet some way related, in default of lodging are compelled to occupy the same lodge; in this case, although they may be somewhat crowded, yet there is always a delicacy of arrangement made to prevent the promiscuous location of the different sexes.

CAMP LIFE

In an Indian camp after one has become acquainted the very opposite of taciturnity presents itself. The evenings are devoted to jests and amusing stories, and the days to gambling. When not able to raise amusement among themselves they will invite some old man to relate fables and stories of the olden time. The soldiers' lodge when not in session is the very theater of amusement and gaming by the chiefs and soldiers, all sorts of jokes are passed, and obscene stories told. Scarcely a woman in camp escapes their ribaldry, and they, consequently, never go near there. Yet, when business is to be attended to the reverse is the case, and one would not think it was then occupied by the same set of people. Ordinarily during the day in private families there is an evenness of temper, and great cordiality exhibited, with much affection shown to their children. These traits and amusements are not more observable when situated in remote parts of the plains alone, than in a large camp, perhaps not so much so for want of sufficient sources of amusement. The Indian of the plains or real savage is not the stoic ordinarily represented. Dancing, feasting, gaming, singing, stories, jests, and merriment occupy their leisure hours, and then all is fun and humor; but when in pursuit of game, sitting in council, traveling, trading, or war they are cautious, serious, quiet, and suspicious.

The number of meals they have in each 24 hours depends altogether on the supply of meat on hand. If plenty, each lodge cooks regularly three times per day—at daybreak, midday, and dark. But in addition to this pieces are kept roasting by the fire by the women and children nearly all the time.

Feasting is also common. In all those ways in times of plenty most of the men eat six, eight, ten, and as high as twenty times during a day and night. In times of comparative scarcity but two meals are had, morning and night. When meat is very nearly exhausted one meal must suffice, and for the rest the women and children are sent to dig roots or gather berries as the season and place afford. Feasts would then be desirable, but there is no one to make them, all being in want. Some who have nothing at all to eat in their lodge will send their children to watch when cooking is going on in another lodge, who report to their parents, and the man happens to drop in at the right time. No Indian eats before guests without offering them a share, even if it is the last portion they possess.

When no meat can be found they eat up their reserve of dried berries, pomme blanche and other roots, then boil the scrapings of rawhide with the buds of the wild rose, collect old bones on the prairie, pound them and extract the grease by boiling. A still greater want produces the necessity of killing their dogs and horses for food, but this is the last resort and approach of actual famine, for by this they are destroying their means of traveling and hunting. One thing is remarkable, be they ever so much in want of food, the grown persons never murmur nor complain, though the children sometimes cry.

Their appetites are capricious. It would seem that they are always hungry. The quantity of meat an Indian can eat is incredible, and after eating at six or eight feasts in succession his appetite appears fully as good for the tenth or even the twentieth as at the first. Their power in this respect as actually witnessed by us on many occasions would not be credited if related. It is useless to endeavor to impress upon the minds of persons not accustomed to this even an approach to the truth. It can not be realized. A lean, lank Indian will eat from 3 to 10 hours nearly all the time and grow gradually larger from his breast downward until in the end he presents somewhat the appearance of the letter "S," and all this without any apparent inconvenience. At other times they are from eight to fifteen days without eating anything, and often one or two months with barely enough to support life. After being deprived of food for a great length of time, and arriving suddenly on an abundance of game, they will feast again as observed and no evil effects follow.

They make no address nor grace to Wakoñda or any other supernatural power at ordinary meals, or common feasts. This is done on stated occasions which will be mentioned hereafter.

COURTSHIP AND MARRIAGE

The way courtships are conducted is that the suitor in the first place always endeavors to induce the girl to run away with him. He has two objects in this. First, it shows her great regard for him and flatters his vanity that she leaves her parents and departs to another band, with and under his protection. Next, having the girl in his possession obviates the possibility of a refusal, and also he can afterwards pay his own price for her instead of that demanded by her relatives. To accomplish this they paint, dress, and adorn themselves extravagantly, and are always on the watch to catch the woman outside or away from the view of her parents. He dogs her steps so closely that opportunities must present themselves when he can recite to her his tale of love. Of course this consists of the usual promises and flatteries used by all men for like purposes which often prove successful. Should he obtain her consent to depart with him they will agree upon a place of rendezvous and signal, which he repeats to her in the night with his flute from outside the lodge at the appointed time to meet him, and they leave, traveling night and day until they arrive at another camp. Here they stay with some distant relative or friend three or four weeks and return as man and wife, when he looks around for some means to satisfy the parents. Or it sometimes happens that having become tired of her in the meantime he throws her on their hands and proceeds to seduce another. The young Indians are great profligates and boast of their success in this way.

If, however, by all their efforts they can not succeed in this they then marry. When this is decided upon no courtship is necessary. The suitor sends a horse by the hands of some respectable old man who ties the animal to the door of the lodge where her parents reside and, entering, presents a pan of cooked meat to the girl who is desired as a wife. Consent is asked and obtained or refused through the medium of this man. The nearest of kin are always asked (the girl's father and mother); if she have neither then the eldest brother, or uncle, etc. If the parents refuse, both the victuals and horse are sent back and negotiation ends. But if the suitor be determined to have her he will try again, sending two or three horses, guns, kettles, and all he can raise, until objection on that score is overruled and she becomes his property by going to his lodge at dark and remaining there. When the right price is paid the offer is seldom rejected, though refusals are given on other grounds, such as old family feuds, or inability on the part of the applicant as a hunter or warrior. There is no tradition of the institution of marriage. It is a bargain and looked upon in this light by both parties, not merely a contract of sale, but one of amity, friendship, and mutual support of all related and concerned. Courtships and presents are only resorted to when the possession of the girl is aimed at without the consent of the parents. Otherwise the consent of the girl is not necessary, she being obliged to obey the wishes of her parents.

Neither the priests nor doctors nor any one else is consulted on these occasions, except the nearest relatives, and the negotiator is some man of standing or relation of the applicant. There is no parade or ceremony on the occasion nor are any gifts made by the mother-in-law to her daughter. On the contrary the son-in-law is regarded as their property. All he has and does is for years to the advantage of his wife's parents. The most of the meat and skins killed by him are carried to her parents by her until she has a child and her husband commences working for himself. The foregoing is the marriage of a young man with a young woman. The son-in-law, as has been stated, never enters the lodge of his wife's parents. Even in a casual passing when they meet elsewhere he is obliged to hide his face by drawing his robe over it, being as they say " abashed by them " or abashed to name or speak to them.

The men usually marry between the ages of 20 and 25 years and the women are given away from the age of 12 years upward. We are acquainted with but two instances of men of middle age among them who have never been married. The young of both sexes are extravagantly addicted to dress, particularly the beaus, who dress, paint, feather, and adorn themselves in every way imaginable, especially about the head, and are the most consummately vain fops in existence.

Widowers and widows remarry, the former in about one year after the loss of their wife and the latter from one to two and three years after the death of their husbands, in proportion as they are grieved for their loss. After a woman has had children her chances for a young husband are few, but middle-aged men do not consider this any objection if she in other respects is able to work and has a reputation for industry. The most advantageous time for a man to purchase a wife is on his return from a successful war excursion with the horses of his enemies in his possession. The manner in which his means to purchase have been procured gives him additional favor both with the girl as a brave man and with the girl's parents as one who can at any time repair their losses in horses if it be neces-

sary. After marriage the brothers-in-law on both sides become
friendly, associate, make feasts, and exchange gifts, aiding each other
on all occasions. No quarrels take place among them, nor indeed
among any near relations. The whole forms a posse, a body, a support in times of trial, need and danger.

The right of divorce lies altogether with the husband. If a man
has children by his wife he seldom puts her away even for adultery,
the greatest offense. He will punish, but retain her on that account.
Should they separate, all the larger children—that is, those who
required no nurse and were able to take care of themselves—would
remain with the man and the smaller ones depart with the woman.
When the women have no children they are turned off without any
scruple for much less offenses, or from jealousy by young husbands.
Elder Indians require the labor of their women; therefore seldom
willingly discharge them. Should he choose to do so, however, no
one has a right to object, nor is any other consent asked; they are
his property and he can do as he pleases with them. Occasionally
they part from them a year or so and take them back afterwards.
No property is given to the woman in the event of a separation.

Music

Their music on the flute referred to herein merits some notice.
The instrument is made of wood, about the length and size of an
octave flute, and the mouth on the principle of a whistle. There
are four finger holes above and one underneath for the thumb. No
tune or anything approaching it can be produced from this instrument, yet they can sound different calls in a shrill tone. It is played
in several of their dances as an accompaniment to singing, not, however, producing any sound accordant with the voice. The principal
purpose for which it is made and used is love making. By the
various notes the following intelligence can be conveyed by the man
outside to the woman inside the lodge, without any of the inmates
except her knowing for whom they are intended, as the whistle can
be distinctly heard at the distance of 100 yards or more: " I am here
waiting for you," " I am watched," " Remain," " I will come again,"
" Meet me to-morrow," and several other communications of a like
nature. The meanings of these different sounds are agreed upon
and understood by the parties beforehand. As the instrument admits
of considerable variation in its tone and note all their calls are
different, and no other person would understand them rightly.
They might suspect some assignation to be going forward, but would
not know with or between whom. Songs and this whistle are used
in their serenades and dances.

Longevity

The changes, exposures, and deprivations attending on the life of the roving tribes are without doubt great causes of the slow increase of Indian population. We think from actual observation that not more than two out of five children live until youth is passed. Even a few days after their birth, and sometimes but a few hours after, they are packed on the backs of their mothers in all weather, exposed to cold, snow, and wet. They must be iron to stand this. Should they be so fortunate as to reach the age of 4 to 6 years they follow the camp on foot through spring thaws, exposed to rain and cold, for weeks together, and a great many thus die from cold, pleurisy, and rheumatism. No question but the uncertainty of their food also contributes to their mortality, not that they often absolutely starve to death, but are rendered weak and unable to stand the hardship the life requires. In maturity war takes off another portion of the remainder, and diseases contracted by the exposures of their youth, together with their continued exertions as required by their precarious life, places it beyond probability of many arriving at extreme age. It is evident that the hard labor the women perform after marriage ruins their constitutions. A woman is old on the plains at the age of 35 years, and seldom healthy. They have from 2 to 5 children, more are occasionally seen, but 7 or 8 is a rare occurrence. There are but few very old women. The usual diseases by which they are carried off are pains in the head, heart, and side, consumption, hemorrhages from the nose and other ducts, puerperal fever, peritoneal inflammations, deliveries, and rheumatism.

Some of these complaints are certainly produced by their continued stooping when in the act of scraping skins, others from exposure, and all aggravated by their injudicious medical treatment.

A woman ceases to bear at 40 years, often earlier. Children have been produced by women at the age of 15, though this is uncommon; from 18 to 35 is the usual period. Twins are often seen; that is as frequently as this happens among the same number of white women. It is remarkable that women who bear twins are liable to a repetition of twin bearing, and two or three pairs follow. Two instances have happened under our observation where women had three children at a delivery. Barrenness is met with, but is by no means common.

Hospitality

Entertaining visitors forms one of the Indian's chief employments. Some of these meetings partake of the nature of dinner and supper parties. They are then called feasts. But as these will meet with consideration elsewhere we will allude in this place only to the custom of private entertainment, generally ascribed to hospitality. Independent of feasts, visiting and invitations to visit, as stated, occupy a great part of their time.   Most of their private business, bargains, settling disputes, hearing news, asking advice, required loans, and indeed all their transactions with individuals are carried on when visiting, or invitations are sent with that view.   They also invite to preserve good feeling and friendly relationship, but usually there is some point to be gained, or advantage to result from these pains. After cooking and preparing ready whatever is to be offered and having the lodge swept and put in order, a boy is sent to the lodge or lodges of their guests, or he hunts them up through the camp, saying to each " You are invited " or " called," directs him to the lodge of his parents, and proceeds to pick up the others.   Being acquainted with the situation of all the lodges, they are at no loss to find the way, or if they are, inquire of any one in the neighborhood.   If strangers are invited, or whites, the boy precedes as guide and they follow.   When the guests arrive they enter one after the other, saying on entering, " I have come."   They are shown to a seat in the back part of the lodge, nearly opposite the entrance, where clean skins have been spread on the ground for their reception.

If several are expected, the first who come talk and smoke with the master until all have arrived or been heard from.   The pipe being laid aside, the woman of the lodge dishes out the meal in wooden bowls, handing one to each.   When all are served the master says " Eat ye."   They fall to, but neither he nor any of his family partake of it while their visitors remain.   The guests, however, are expected to do justice to the repast, and the more heartily they partake the better pleased the host appears.   When the meal is over and the dishes laid aside the pipe is again introduced, and during the conversation of an hour or so that follows the object of the invitation is disclosed, and whatever business it is most likely settled or whatever favor desired granted.   Such a thing as disinterested hospitality may possibly be met with, at least we have been present on some of these occasions where the object of the call was not visible, but it is entirely incompatible with a correct view of the Indian character to infer thereby that he had no object.   On stated feasts, a feather, the lower end painted red, is sent as an invitation card, but on all ordinary occasions the message is by some one of the inmates of the lodge.

Casual visits without invitations are also common, sometimes only with the view of getting a meal, but mostly to accomplish some end or acquire some information.   Guests, whether invited or not, are always awarded precedence.   Any insult or imposition on a guest, once in an Indian lodge and under his protection, would be resented with greater severity than the same toward themselves.

We can not perceive in all this seeming friendliness toward guests any feeling of pure hospitality. An Indian never willingly, or without a motive, makes an enemy. The uncertainty of their lives and of everything they possess is such that mutual reliance on each other is required. It is more than probable that these attentions have for their object the forming of a name for liberality and securing the good will of as many neighbors as possible with the view of obtaining their assistance in times of need, or which is more evident, for present favors in small matters which are nearly always made known at the close of the visit. In the instances where the real object does not appear we are obliged to conclude that it lies deeper, requires a course of entertainments to accomplish, but nevertheless exists. When whites are invited and are merely travelers through their country, nothing at the time can perhaps be gained, but the rule holds good, for the Indians will always claim the same attentions when they are in turn the visitors, besides additional demands as a compensation for their hospitality. A casual observer would believe them to be the most hospitable people in the world, but a more minute acquaintance shows an undercurrent of pure selfishness in all they do. The sharing of the meat with each other in times of scarcity is no mark of liberality, or done from any other principle than the foregoing remarks present. It is a loan, or obligation, laid upon the person, to be repaid when their situations become reversed, or whenever the claimant thinks proper to remind him of it, which sooner or later he is sure to do in some way.

Indians of different nations are not only feasted by all the principal men in camp but loaded with presents to carry home. A short time after the donators pay a visit to the homes of their guests and receive as much or more in return.

Protecting a guest from insult and injury is done partly through the fear of the ridicule that would follow were he suffered to be badly treated in his lodge; it is a contempt of their power to support, and resented as such. Very often also it lays the stranger under obligations which are expected to be paid for, and usually are. Were we not limited in our remarks we could cite hundreds of instances that would prove true hospitality to have no existence among the savages of the plains. Everything they do and all their study is for the interest of self, visible or invisible to others, according to the nature of their views. We are not aware, however, that this course of hospitality is pursued with the view of covering stratagems, evil intentions, or to lull suspicion for the purpose of committing bad acts; it appears only to operate as a furtherance to all their ordinary wishes and bring about a favorable opportunity to make requests and transact other business.

Midwifery, Childbirth, Naming

Nearly all the old women and most of those of middle age exercise the office of midwives. When a woman perceives the pains of labor approaching, the lodge is cleared of all the men and children except the small ones, and the mother of the woman with some other experienced female acquaintances are invited. The doctor is also notified to have his medicine in readiness in case of it being wanted. The woman is placed on her knees and sticks set up in this form ⊓ placed before her. She presses the abdomen on the cross stick, rubbing gently along it. The pains of labor are said to be very severe. If danger is apprehended, the doctor is sent for and administers a draft of pulverized rattles of the rattlesnake or decoction of roots. If the doctor be a man, he then retires; but if a female she remains. Cases of solitary confinement happen occasionally from lonely situations. No nurse is provided; the mother takes care of her children from their birth. The rite of circumcision is not performed, but they evince a great desire that their children should be naturally thus formed and attach an unaccountable importance to that incident.

On the birth of a child a horse is given with other property to those in attendance. After three weeks or a month has elapsed the ceremony of giving it a name takes place. There is no regular period of time for this, and sometimes five or six months pass before it is done. The probability is in this case that it is the want of means to pay for the ceremonial, as in these instances they give for a reason, "the parents are too poor."

Usually, however, it is done about the time first mentioned and this ceremony is the same whether the child be male or female. Some medicine man generally makes the name, and sends word to the parents that on a certain day he will bestow it on the child. When the time has come a dog is killed and cooked or some other good dish is provided, and invitations are sent to some 20 or 30 of their friends and relatives to attend. When they are assembled the priest makes known to them the object of the meeting in a suitable speech to the supernatural powers, but principally to the tutelaries of departed grandfathers and grandmothers, invoking them to take the child under their protection, concluding with the name of the child distinctly spoken in a loud voice so that all can hear it. The feast is then divided, small portions thrown away for the dead and the rest eaten. A horse in the meantime is tied outside as a present to the medicine man for his services. He leads the horse around the camp, singing in a loud voice the child's name and those of its parents. If the child be a male this name is borne until he kills or strikes his first enemy on their own (the enemy's) land. On his return after accomplishing this, he blackens his face and that of his relatives as a token of his triumph. Some one of the medicine men who are always on the lookout for advantage blackens himself and gives a new name to the warrior by crying it out loudly through the camp, stating the change of name has been given in consequence of his great bravery in killing his enemies.

A horse is again given the priest and the second name is attached. This name lasts until by repeated successes at war he becomes entitled to the name of his father, if the parent be dead; if living, that of his grandfather is bestowed, during a ceremony of the same kind as has been related. But this name is never given without sufficient merit on the part of the warrior. It is the highest honor that could be bestowed, is never afterwards changed, and he ranks immediately as a councillor and brave. The foregoing will account for both the plurality of names among them and the manner in which the original family name and line of descent is preserved.

The names of females are not often changed, though some have two, one affixed at the first ceremony and the other originating in some marked feature, or personal appearance unusual among them, such as fair hair, gray eyes, etc., and sometimes from any deformity, as lameness, loss of an eye, teeth, etc. Generally, however, they have but one. The names given to children are not taken from the incidents of dreams or deemed sacred, but are the manufacture of the priest according to his fancy. He endeavors to make one to please the parents in order to secure the gift of the horse. This name is told them secretly by him and if acceptable is adopted; if not, they suggest another in its place to him.

The children and boys call each other familiarly by these names as in civilized life, and when grown continue to do so, unless of kin, when the degree of relationship is mentioned instead of the name.

Herewith is a list of names, male and female. Of the warriors several have two, but only one, the leader of the party here at the time, had three. Their names were taken down for insertion in this place. Those of the women I had of a warrior present, and those of the chiefs and soldiers I have known for years, some of whom having two or three names.

518   TRIBES OF THE UPPER MISSOURI   [ETH. ANN. 46

ASSINIBOIN NAMES

Partisan, "The Back of Thunder," Ya-pa-ta Wak-keum

NAMES OF 27 ASSINIBOIN WARRIORS AT FORT UNION, DECEMBER, 1853

Interpreted name.	Indian name.
The Black Horn	Hai-sap Sap-pah.
He Who Comes Laden	Kee-hee-nah.
The War Club of Thunder	Ya-chunk-pe Wah-ke-un.
Boiling	Pe-gah.
The Backbone of Wolf	Shunk-chan-ca-hoo.
The Four War Eagles	Wah-min-de To-pah.
The Winner	O-he-an-ah.
The Standing Bear	Wah-bo-san-dah.
The Crow	Conghai.
The Little Rocky Mountains	Ean-hhai-nah.
The White Crow	Conghai-ska.
He Who Sounds the Ground	Muk-kah-na-boo-boo.
The Bear's Child	Wah-ghan-seecha Och-she.
The Iron Boy	Muzza Och-she.
The Sound of Thunder	Hhom-bo-oah Wah-ke-un.
The Grey Bull	Ya-tunga-hho-tah.
He Who Deceives Calves	Chin-chah-nah Ke-ni-ah.
The Dry Sinews	Kun-sha-chah.
The Calf with Handsome Hair	Chin-chah-nah He-wash-tai.
The Bull's Face	Etai-tah Tun-gah.
The Wolverine	Me-nazh-zhah.
The Two-horned Antelope	Yah-to-kah-hhai noom-pah.
The Large Owl	He-hun Tungah.
The Large War Eagle	Wam-min-de Tun-gah.
The Child of Two Bears	Wah-ghan-see-cha noompa och-she.
Le Pene Rouge	Chai-shah.

NAMES OF 12 CAMP SOLDIERS

He Who Wishes to Bring Them	Ekando He chin-ah.
The Red Bull	Tah-tungah Du-tah.
The Bad Bull	Tah-tungah Shee-chah.
The Red Snow	Wah Du-tah.
The Blue Thunder	Wah-ke Un-to.
The Emptying Horn	O-canah-hhai.
The Standing Water	Minne Naz-zhe.
The Rose Bud Eater	We-ze-zeet-ka Utah.
The Boy of Smoke	Sho-to-zshu Och-she.
The Spotted Horn	Hai-kan-dai Kan-dai-ghah.
Shot in the Face	Etai-o-ke Nun-ei-a.
Bear's Face	Etai Wah-ghan.

NAMES OF SOME CHIEFS, OCCASIONAL LEADERS OF BANDS

The White Head	Pah ska-nah.
The Grey Eyes	Esh-tai-o G'he-nah.
The Pouderie	Hee-boom An-doo.
The Tourbillon	Ah-wah minne o minne.

Interpreted name.	Indian name.
The Little Thunder	Wah-kee-e-nah.
The Knife	Menah.
Hair Tied Up in Front	Pai-pach Kich-tah.
He Who Wounds Dogs	Shunga Ou-nah.
The Claws	Shak-kai-nah.
The Great Traveler	Ca-wai-ghai Man-ne.
He Who is Above the Others	Wa-caun-too.
The Marksman	Coo-tai-nah.

NAMES OF 20 YOUNG ASSINIBOIN WOMEN

Interpreted name	Indian name
The Spotted Woman	Kan-dai-ghah We-yah.
The One Leg	Hoo wash e nah.
The Big Horn Woman	Hai-kees-kah We-yah.
The Glittering Lodge	Te Owah Ho-wat-tah.
The Four Thunders	Wah-ke-un Topa.
The Four Women	Topa Weyah.
The Season Maker	Man-ka-cha Ca-ghah.
The Lodge on Fire Woman	Te-ien da weyah.
She Who Makes the Clouds	Moh pe ah caghah.
The Door Scratcher	Te opah u-cai-ghah.
The Wing Bone	Hoo pah hoo.
The Crow's Cawing	Coughai a-hho-ton.
The Head Made White	Pah-kah shah-nah.
The Curled Hair	Pah-hah e-u-me-ne.
The Hawk Woman	Chai-tun We-yah.
The Red Chief	Hoon yuh shah.
The Mane of the Flying Eagle	Ap-pai Wam-min-de E-i-ah.
The Yellow Bear	Wah-ghan She-chah-ze.
The Iron Body	Chu-we Muz-zah.
The Fair-skinned Woman	We-yah Skah.

CHILDREN

Cradles are not much used by the tribes of whom we write. A few are seen among them which they procure from the Cree and Chippewa. The back is a flat board with a bow bent across the front where the head of the child is placed. (Fig. 32.) A rim runs along the inside the size of the child, cloths are attached inside this rim to the boards or back, and the whole ornamented in various ways. The child is then bundled up, inclosed in the rim, and the cloth covers strapped over it. This is carried on their back, and at any time should the cradle fall the child is protected by the bow across from touching the ground. These Indians make a kind of sack with eyed holes in front of scarlet or blue cloth ornamented with beads, and the child being well wrapped, all except the head, it is placed in the sack and strapped up. There is no doubt but this is the cause of their feet being straight, although they are not intoed, as one would judge

FIG. 32.—Cradle board

by their manner of walking. We can offer no objection to this mode
of caring for children. Their natural growth is not affected thereby.
At least it is the only method they could adopt to answer in extremes
of cold, heat, and rain, with infants on their backs; besides their
lodging affords little room for the conveniences used by civilized
persons for rearing children.

They are as careful of their offspring as their manner of life will
allow. Children are never weaned under 2 or 3 years old, giving for
their reason that it retards their growth, but most likely having
nothing but meat that a child can eat, they are obliged to do so. They
call their mother enaw (mother) and their father at-tai (father).
They address their children ma-chunk-she (my daughter) and ma-
chink-she (my son). No abbreviations are used. They call them
also by their given or proper names when there are several. There
are no terms of endearment further than humming songs and meaningless words, such as white nurses use to very small children.

The domestic government is exercised by both father and mother.
As long as the child is small the mother has the sole charge of it,
but when it begins to speak the father aids in forming its manners.
If a girl, he makes toy tools for scraping skins and the mother
directs her how to use them. She also shows her how to make small
moccasins, etc. Their first attempts in this way are preserved as
memorials of their infancy. When a little larger, the scale of
operations is increased and sewing, cooking, dressing small skins,
and garnishing with beads and quills are taught, together with
everything suitable for a woman's employment. If the child be a
boy the father will make it a toy bow and arrow, wooden gun, etc.

When a little larger he will give him still stronger bows and
bring unfledged birds into the lodge for his son to kill. Larger
still and he runs about with a suitable bow after birds and rabbits,
killing and skinning them. Another stage brings him to learn the
use of the gun, to ride, approach game, skin it, etc., all of which is
taught him by his parent. The rest he acquires from the time and
facility their manner of life affords for practicing these pursuits,
and at the age of 17 or 18 makes his first excursion in quest of his
enemies' horses.

The father never strikes nor corrects his children from their birth
to their grave, though the mother will sometimes give them a slap,
yet it must be done in his absence or she would meet with immediate
punishment. Notwithstanding this they are not nearly as vicious
as white children, cry but little, quarrel less, and seldom if ever fight.

The boys are somewhat annoying when about 12 years old, but
seldom do any serious mischief. The behavior of the girls is shy and
modest.

The traditions related to the young in their lodges are usually extravagant fables and exploits of former warriors, exaggerated, of course, to make them interesting. Many local data and memoirs of events are thus preserved but so mingled with superstition by the different narrators as not to present any reliable truth. Most of the old men and many of middle age tell these stories in the lodges when they are invited for the purpose.

The grandmothers are also well versed in this and night after night the children learn a great deal, as soon as they are able to understand. The lives and actions of former warriors and other events of real life form a portion of the instruction thus conveyed.

These Indians living remote from civilization have no opportunity to steal white children, and we have never heard of one among them possessed by these means.

There are several half-breed children in all these nations, who, being raised with the Indians, are the same in all respects.

Cases of infanticide are very common among the Sioux, Crows, and Assiniboin, perhaps most so among the Crow women. It is not far from the correct number if we state that one-eighth of the children are destroyed in utero or after birth by the Crow women. The same also often is done by the Assiniboin, particularly if the father of the child has abandoned the woman before its birth. A quarrel with the husband or even unwillingness to be at the trouble of raising them are the causes for these actions. We think and have strong reason to believe that in some instances, they are destroyed at the instigation of their husbands, although they will not acknowledge this to be the case.

At all events no punishment is inflicted on the woman for the crime but frequently the means and time they use to produce abortions are the cause of the death of the mother. To produce its death in the womb they use violent pressure and blows upon the abdomen. Frequently they retire to the woods, bring forth the child alone, strangle it and throw it into the water, snow, or bushes. The whole of these measures are publicly talked of among them, and no great degree of repugnance is attached either to the act or to the woman, but the circumstance is laughed at as something ludicrous.

Male children are always desired by the husband. When small we see no difference made in their treatment or any preference shown, but when grown or nearly so the young man always takes precedence and is considered of far greater value than the girl. The feeling increases in his favor as he becomes of use at war or in the chase. Daughters, when matured, are married and sold, and here the greater interest in them ends; but sons are a source of profit and support for a good portion of their lives.

SUICIDE

Widows do not burn themselves on the funeral pile on the decease of their husbands, but frequently hang themselves for that loss, revenge, or for the loss of their children. Three suicides of this kind have been committed within the last few months in this neighborhood among the Assiniboin, one for revenge, the other two for the loss of their children. The first was the favorite wife of a camp soldier, who being scolded and accused of crime by the eldest wife, after telling her purpose, left the lodge, in the absence of her husband, and disappeared. Although search was made, yet a week elapsed before she was discovered hanging to the limb of a tree. She had climbed the tree, tied the cord to the limb, and descending, hooked on the noose standing on the ground, suspending her body by drawing up her legs. She hung so low that her knees nearly touched the ground and she could have risen to her feet at any time during the operation.

Another woman had her son (a young man) killed by the Blackfeet, and immediately afterwards another of her children died from disease. Several persons were appointed to watch the mother, suspecting her intentions; but they all fell asleep and she hung herself at the door of the lodge, between two dog travailles set on end. She was a tall woman and could only produce strangulation by swinging herself off the ground from her feet. She did it, however, and the body was brought to the fort for interment.

The third was a still more unfortunate case. The child of this woman had been sick some time and was expected to die. On the night in question it fell into a swoon and was to all appearance dead. No person being present the mother in the derangement of the moment went out and hung herself. The child recovered, but the mother was dead.

Every year in this way the women hang themselves, sometimes for the loss of their husbands, but more frequently on account of the death of their children, or for revenge. Suicides are also common among the men. They generally use the gun to produce death.

The Mandan and Gros Ventres, as has been stated, suspend themselves on sticks or skewers passed through incisions made in the back, and the motive for so doing has already been adverted to.

Spots are worn on the forehead and the under lip by some of either sex. Those on the women are for ornament. The bodies of some of the men are covered with tattooing to denote the warrior and brave. It is an operation requiring high payment, and is a mark also of the liberality and riches of the person who undergoes it, but no religious sects or opinions are thereby intimated. No rivers are deemed sacred or coveted in death by any of them.

PERSONAL BEHAVIOR

These tribes are not degraded in the scale of being in their ordinary intercourse, connection or apparent actions. They frequently exhibit a delicacy in all these, but some of them, particularly the Crows, are addicted to customs, revolting to humanity, too much so for a lengthened description, among which may be mentioned sodomy, bestiality, etc. They all on occasions eat small portions of human flesh, not as a relish but to evince a savage fierceness toward the dead enemy. The Arikara are said to have devoured several entire bodies of their enemies in late years. We have witnessed a few cases of cannibalism among the Assiniboin, but they happened in time of actual famine, one of which we will describe. About eight or ten years since a great famine prevailed among the Cree and Assiniboin. They separated and scattered everywhere over the plains in quest of game. It happened early in the spring when the ground was yet covered with snow and no roots could be found. A Cree Indian with his wife and three children were stationed near the head of Milk River alone and had been without food for a great length of time. The father took the occasion of his wife being out to kill and cook one of his children, a portion of which he forced her to eat on her return. When this was eaten, after an interval of some days he killed a second and this was likewise devoured. Still no indication of game presented itself. He desired her to go out that he might kill the remaining child, which she absolutely refused to do, offering herself in its stead.

It happened that some Assiniboin in traveling came upon his lodge, and seeing them coming he had barely time to smear himself and his wife over with white clay, the symbol of mourning, before they entered. To account for the disappearance of his children he appeared very much grieved and said they had died from want. The strangers, however, suspected all was not right, and when he had stepped out they inquired of the woman, who told them the truth. The visitors left after directing him to their camp, where some game had lately been found, and he proceeded thither with his lodge. When in the vicinity of the camp, he killed and scalped his wife, throwing her body in the bushes, proceeded to camp, displayed the scalp, stating he had killed a Blackfoot; that they had attacked him and killed his wife. The camp turned out to search for enemies and discovered the body of the woman and no trace of Blackfeet. The Indian in the meantime suspecting he would be discovered absconded, leaving the small child and baggage in camp. Being of another nation with whom they were at peace, he was not pursued and yet lives, but is despised by all.

At the period of the catamenia they sleep alone and are deemed taboo for ten days. The word in their language expressing that flux literally interpreted would mean " she who lives in a lodge alone," and their traditions state that it was formerly the custom to pitch a tent outside for the woman to remain in during this period. After childbirth a woman is deemed taboo for 45 days.

SCALPING

During a battle or whenever an enemy is slain they use no ceremony in taking the scalp except despatch. They are in great haste to get off or out of danger, and have no time for useless delay. A knife is run round the cranium, the foot placed on the dead man's neck and a sudden jerk takes it off. The cultivation of the scalp-lock among the Sioux is a very ancient custom but we know of no mode of tracing its antiquity. The rest of these tribes wear their hair in any form that suits their fancy.

OATHS

The Indians have several kinds of oaths. They will say " Wakoñda hears me," or they will swear by the skin of a rattlesnake, or the claws of a bear, wishing the snake to bite or the bear to tear them if they fail to fulfill their oath. They generally keep their oaths. The name Wakoñda in this is uttered in an audible voice with great solemnity and presenting the pipe to the Sun.

When Indians meet on the plains they halt within a few paces of each other, and if recognized as kin will name the relationship existing in a smiling tone. If strangers, one will inquire, " Where did you come from? " " Where going? " etc., during which they sit down and proceed to light the pipe. While smoking they will exchange news of their different places, make inquiries respecting their friends, about game, and anything of general interest, and when the pipe is finished they separate. No shaking of hands or touching of persons takes place, but if meeting with whites they will extend the hand to be shaken.

SMOKING

This is so ancient a custom that even their traditions do not mention a time when their forefathers or ancestors did not smoke. There are tales among them whence came the tobacco seed and plant, particularly among the Mandan, Crows and Arikara, and perhaps among the Assiniboin, though we are not prepared at this time to relate them.

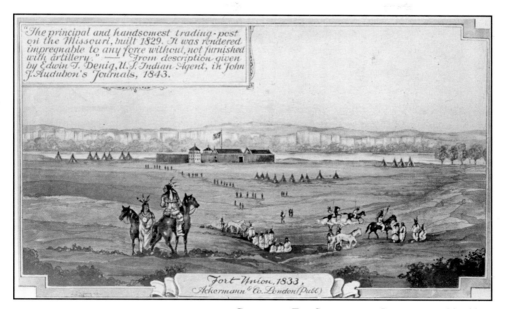

The principal and handsomest trading-post on the Missouri, built 1829. It was rendered impregnable to any force without, not furnished with artillery." —— From description given by Edwin T. Denig, U.S. Indian Agent, in John J. Audubon's Journals, 1843.

Fort Union, 1833,
Ackermann & Co. London (Publ.)

COPYRIGHT THE SMITHSONIAN INSTITUTION: 99-10371

Plate 62: Fort Union as it appeared in 1833.

REPRODUCED FROM BUREAU OF AMERICAN ETHNOLOGY, FORTY-SIXTH ANNUAL REPORT

Plate 63: Edwin Thompson Denig and Mrs. Denig.

REPRODUCED FROM BUREAU OF AMERICAN ETHNOLOGY, FORTY-SIXTH ANNUAL REPORT

Plate 64: Drawings by an Assiniboine Indian.

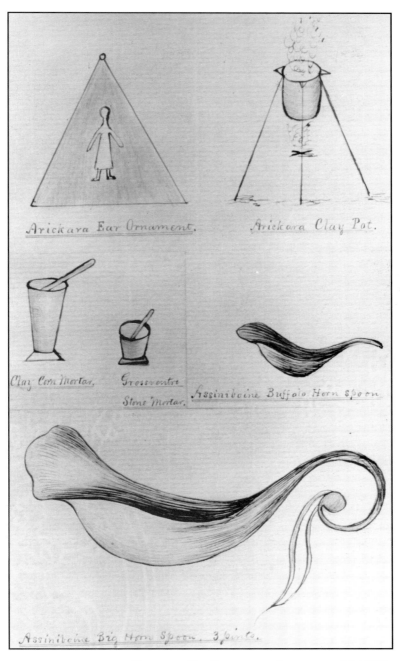

Arickara Ear Ornament.

Arickara Clay Pot.

Clay Corn Mortar.

Grossventre Stone Mortar.

Assiniboine Buffalo Horn spoon

Assiniboine Big Horn Spoon. 3 pints.

COPYRIGHT THE SMITHSONIAN INSTITUTION: 99-10372

Plate 65: Culinary utensils.

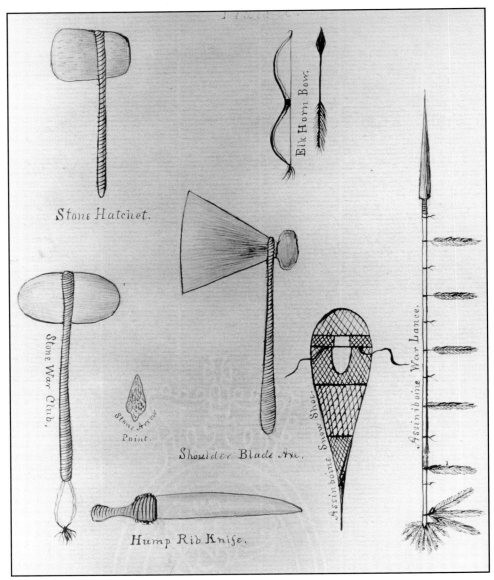

Stone Hatchet.

Elk Horn Bow.

Stone War Club.

Stone Arrow Point.

Shoulder Blade Axe.

Assiniboine Snow Shoe.

Assiniboine War Lance.

Hump Rib Knife.

COPYRIGHT THE SMITHSONIAN INSTITUTION: 99-10373

Plate 66: Characteristic implements of the Assiniboine.

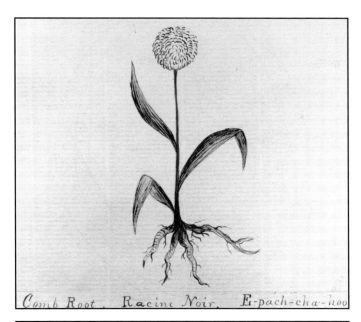

Comb Root. Racine Noir. Ei-pach-cha-hoo

Cat's Tail Hint-káh-koo Racine de Quenoüille

COPYRIGHT THE SMITHSONIAN INSTITUTION: 99-10374

Plate 67: Comb root (above), Cat-tail (below).

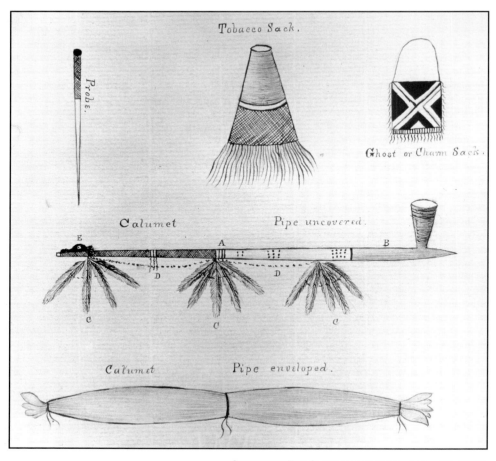

Tobacco Sack.

Probe.

Ghost or Charm Sack.

Calumet

Pipe uncovered.

E

A

D

B

D

C

C

C

Calumet

Pipe enveloped.

COPYRIGHT THE SMITHSONIAN INSTITUTION: 99-10375

Plate 68: The Calumet and its accompaniments.

A: the pipestem of ash wood, garnished about half its length with porcupine quills of various colors; B: a large red-stone pipe; C: three tails of the war eagle, feathers connected with sinew and beads or shells between. The stem or stalk of the feathers is garnished with colored porcupine quills; D: two festoons of beads or shells with a small strip of otter skin on which the beads are tied; E: the head of a mallard duck (male) without the under bill. Sometimes this is the head of a red-headed woodpecker.

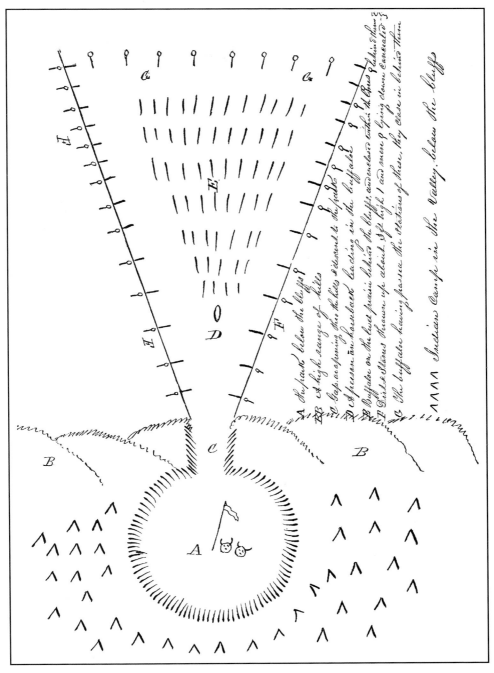

REPRODUCED FROM BUREAU OF AMERICAN ETHNOLOGY, FORTY-SIXTH ANNUAL REPORT

Plate 69: A buffalo park or "surround."

REPRODUCED FROM BUREAU OF AMERICAN ETHNOLOGY, FORTY-SIXTH ANNUAL REPORT

Plate 70: An Assiniboine running a buffalo. Drawn by an Assiniboine warrior and hunter, Fort Union, Jan. 16, 1854.

COPYRIGHT THE SMITHSONIAN INSTITUTION: 42514-E

Plate 71: Scalp Dance. Drawn by an Assiniboine warrior, Fort Union, Nov. 10, 1853.

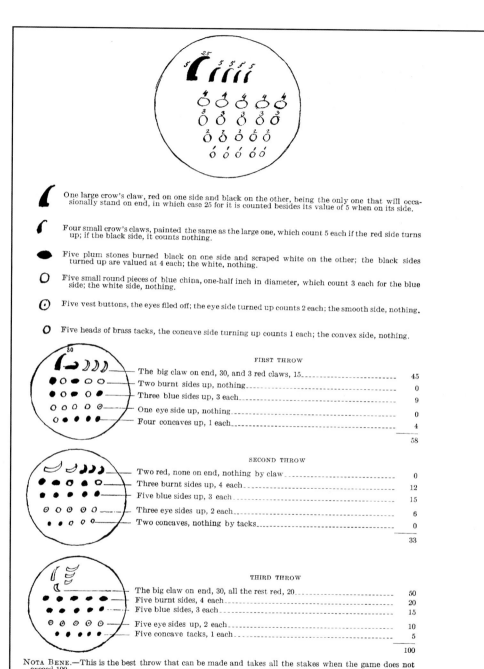

One large crow's claw, red on one side and black on the other, being the only one that will occasionally stand on end, in which case 25 for it is counted besides its value of 5 when on its side.

Four small crow's claws, painted the same as the large one, which count 5 each if the red side turns up; if the black side, it counts nothing.

Five plum stones burned black on one side and scraped white on the other; the black sides turned up are valued at 4 each; the white, nothing.

Five small round pieces of blue china, one-half inch in diameter, which count 3 each for the blue side; the white side, nothing.

Five vest buttons, the eyes filed off; the eye side turned up counts 2 each; the smooth side, nothing.

Five heads of brass tacks, the concave side turning up counts 1 each; the convex side, nothing.

FIRST THROW

The big claw on end, 30, and 3 red claws, 15	45
Two burnt sides up, nothing	0
Three blue sides up, 3 each	9
One eye side up, nothing	0
Four concaves up, 1 each	4
	58

SECOND THROW

Two red, none on end, nothing by claw	0
Three burnt sides up, 4 each	12
Five blue sides, 3 each	15
Three eye sides up, 2 each	6
Two concaves, nothing by tacks	0
	33

THIRD THROW

The big claw on end, 30, all the rest red, 20	50
Five burnt sides, 4 each	20
Five blue sides, 3 each	15
Five eye sides up, 2 each	10
Five concave tacks, 1 each	5
	100

Nota Bene.—This is the best throw that can be made and takes all the stakes when the game does not exceed 100.

REPRODUCED FROM BUREAU OF AMERICAN ETHNOLOGY, FORTY-SIXTH ANNUAL REPORT

Plate 72: Cos-Soo', or Game of the Bowl.

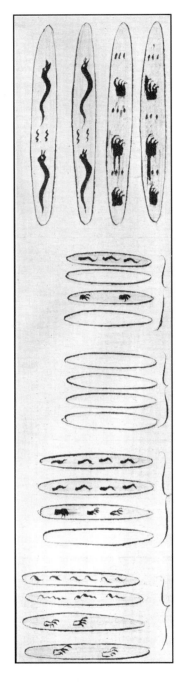

REPRODUCED FROM BUREAU OF AMERICAN ETHNOLOGY,
FORTY-SIXTH ANNUAL REPORT

Plate 73: The Chun-kan-dee' Game.

*Four sticks 12 inches long, flat and rounded at the ends,
about 1 inch broad and one-eighth inch thick, are used.
Two of them have figures of snakes burned on one side,
and two the figure of a bear's foot burned on. All the
sticks are white on the sides opposite the burned sides.*

Throws
Two painted or marked sides and two white count — 2

All the white sides turned up count — 10

Three burned sides up and one white count nothing — 0

Four burned sides up count — 10

*Nota bene: three white sides up and one burned side up
counts nothing.*

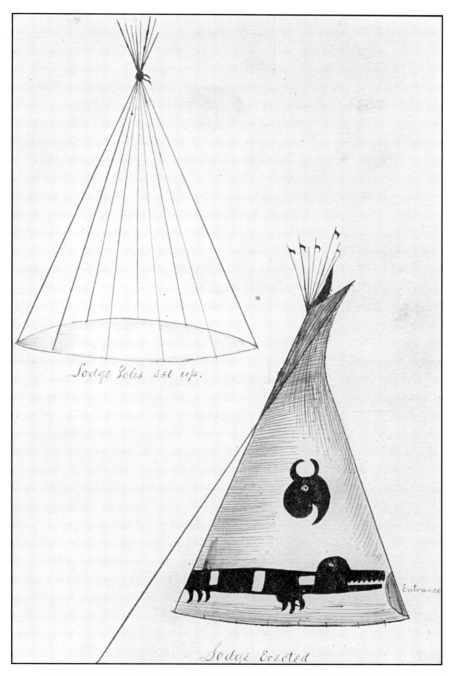

Lodge Poles set up.

Lodge Erected

Entrance

REPRODUCED FROM BUREAU OF AMERICAN ETHNOLOGY, FORTY-SIXTH ANNUAL REPORT

Plate 74: A lodge frame and a completed lodge.

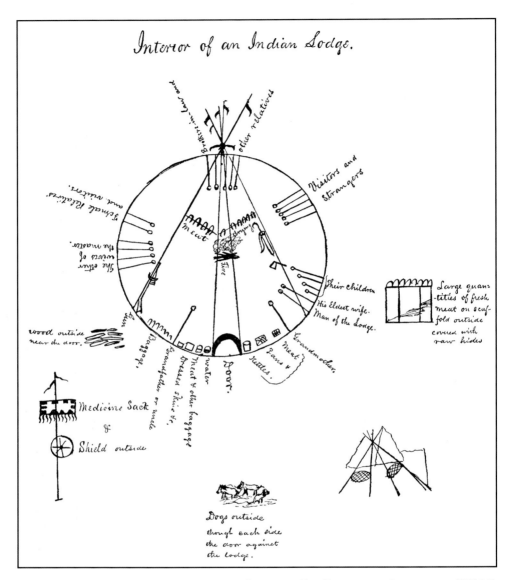

Interior of an Indian Lodge.

COPYRIGHT THE SMITHSONIAN INSTITUTION: 42514-B

Plate 75: The interior of a lodge and its surroundings.

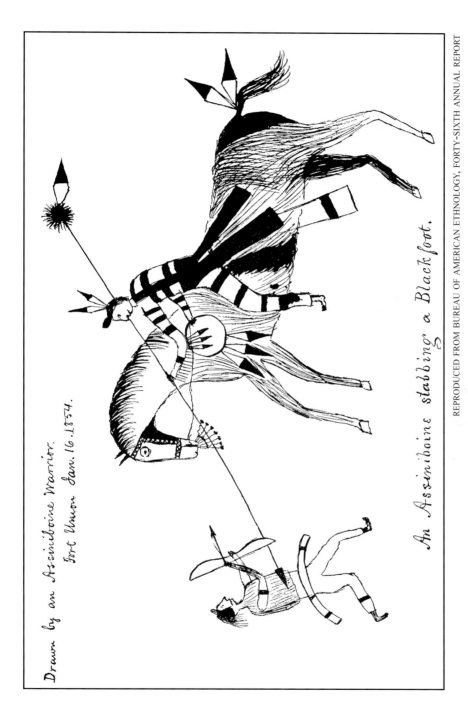

Drawn by an Assiniboine Warrior.
Fort Union Jan. 16. 1854.

An Assiniboine stabbing a Blackfoot.

REPRODUCED FROM BUREAU OF AMERICAN ETHNOLOGY, FORTY-SIXTH ANNUAL REPORT

Plate 76: An Assiniboine stabbing a Blackfoot.

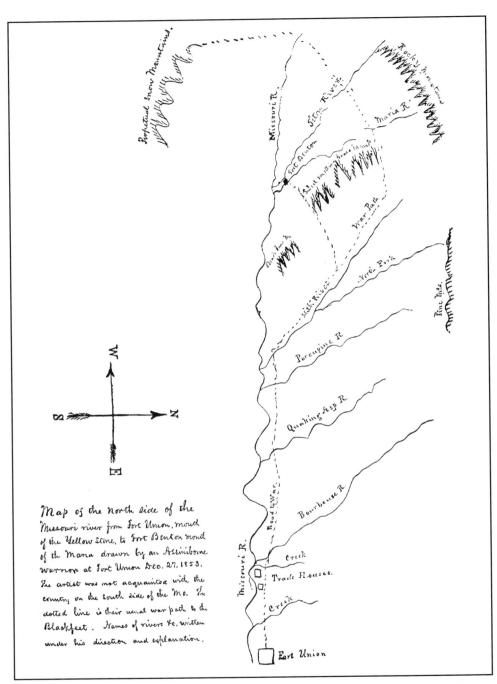

Map of the north side of the
Missouri river from Fort Union, mouth
of the Yellow Stone, to Fort Benton mouth
of the Maria drawn by an Assiniboine
warrior at Fort Union Dec. 27. 1853.
The artist was not acquainted with the
country on the south side of the Mo. The
dotted line is their usual war path to the
Blackfeet. Names of rivers &c. written
under his direction and explanation.

REPRODUCED FROM BUREAU OF AMERICAN ETHNOLOGY, FORTY-SIXTH ANNUAL REPORT

Plate 77: Map of region above Fort Union.

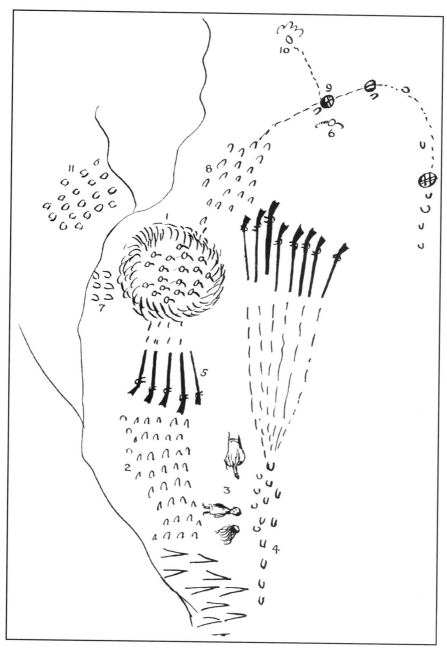

REPRODUCED FROM BUREAU OF AMERICAN ETHNOLOGY, FORTY-SIXTH ANNUAL REPORT

Plate 78: Diagram of a battle field.

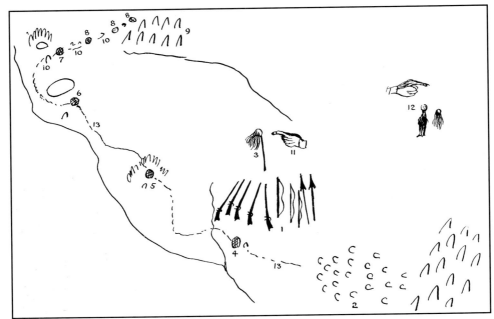

REPRODUCED FROM BUREAU OF AMERICAN ETHNOLOGY, FORTY-SIXTH ANNUAL REPORT

Plate 79: Diagram of a battle field.

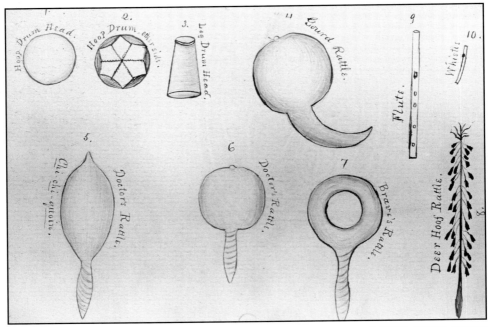

REPRODUCED FROM BUREAU OF AMERICAN ETHNOLOGY, FORTY-SIXTH ANNUAL REPORT

Plate 80: Musical instruments.

COPYRIGHT THE SMITHSONIAN INSTITUTION: 55-B

James Mooney, Ethnologist, Bureau of American Ethnology, was the first editor of the Denig manuscript.

Copyright The Smithsonian Institution: 39-B

J.N.B. Hewitt, Ethnologist, Bureau of American Ethnology, in 1923, shortly after he assumed responsibility for editing the Denig manuscript.

COURTESY OF THE BOSTON ATHENAEUM

Portrait of Henry Rowe Schoolcraft, c. 1850-55.

COPYRIGHT THE SMITHSONIAN INSTITUTION: 2856-53

Rudolph Friederich Kurz's sketch of the packet boat St. Ange.

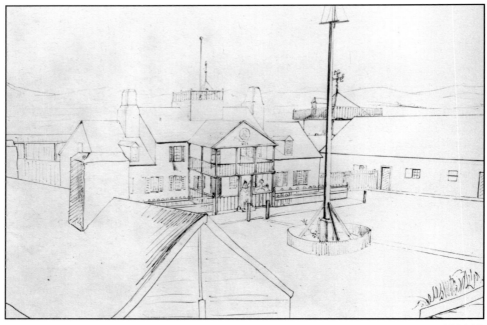

COPYRIGHT THE SMITHSONIAN INSTITUTION: 2856-25

Fort Union in a sketch rendered by the Swiss traveler and artist, Rudolph Friederich Kurz, on 4 February 1852, as it appeared under the administration of E.T. Denig.

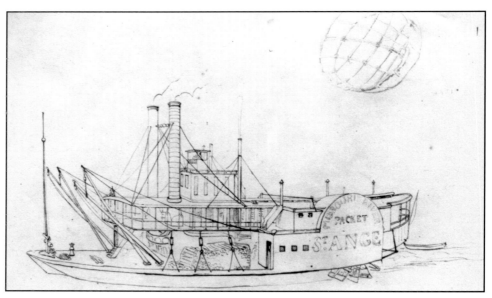

COPYRIGHT THE SMITHSONIAN INSTITUTION: 2856-53

Rudolph Friederich Kurz's sketch of the packet boat St. Onge.

Fame

The principal avenue of fame is the pursuit of war. Other things tend to aid the individual and to render him respectable, as expertness in hunting, powers of prophecy, necromancy, and a name for wisdom, that is, the knowledge of governing, advising, making wise speeches, etc., but all these rather follow than precede the elevation of the man. Success in war is the first step; the others increase the importance of this. Acquiring a good many horses and women, by and means whatever, brings an individual into notice and makes him of importance, as thereby he can distribute many favors that a poorer yet braver man can not. Wealth in this finds him friends as it does on other occasions everywhere. But when rank is boasted, or chieftainship aimed at, bravery and success in war with capacity to lead are the principal requisites, without which all the other qualifications would be of no avail. We are acquainted with no Indian who has arisen to distinction without success in war being the principal cause of his advancement.

Stoicism

The stoicism exhibited by all these nations appears to be partly a natural disposition and partly a bias of their minds produced by their peculiar mode of life. This display of feeling is only seen when the circumstance requires it. It is considered a mark of manliness to treat important subjects, transactions, and conversations with deliberation and decorum. Lighter matters are discoursed upon with appropriate levity. Their constant wants, shifts, and precarious positions induce a thoughtful manner. The knowledge of each other's duplicity and the many ways used to circumvent and deceive to gain each his own ends produces caution. The uncertainty of their lives, liability to be revenged upon, and treacherous conduct generates suspicion. Being subject to severe reverses, extremes of want and danger, etc., a recklessness of life follows. Besides being the victims of superstitious dread, a morbidness of mind is acquired. But even all these would not without some natural peculiar disposition of mind account for their want of excitement and taciturnity and cover a hidden deep and dark design. Even when most expected, no trace of passion would be perceived by a stranger, but among themselves, or those who are well acquainted with their ways, their eye, countenance, smile, and every movement are as true an index to the workings of their mind as are observable among civilized persons in the most violent bursts of passion.

TACITURNITY

Silence is not considered a mark of wisdom. A very silent man is not generally liked and somewhat feared, more so than a talkative one. Their wisdom consists in making apparent their good sense in speeches, advice, and in all their actions. Taciturnity may in some degree arise from their want of sufficient topics of conversation, as when obscene subjects are introduced this faculty is laid aside. All their ceremonies partake of the nature of solemnities, but when these are over and subjects or actions of a lighter nature employ their time they are as jovial and noisy as can be. In general, however, in common conversation Indians are not loquacious. Each sentence appears to be studied and no useless or superfluous words are introduced. They seldom speak twice or argue the point, even in debate in council. Each one states his opinion freely without interruption, and obstinately adheres to it. They never speak earnestly on a subject they do not thoroughly understand. They have a singular faculty of determination in everything they say or do. Even when surprised in extremes of danger their decision to act is made on the instant as if by instinct. No nervousness nor hesitation is evinced. When escape from death becomes impossible they are stolid, stubborn, and die like men.

PUBLIC SPEAKING

Their public speaking is only remarkable for applying their whole mind and soul to the business in hand. They state their opinions in a few words to the purpose, using only such metaphor as has a visible bearing on its elucidation. A great deal of the effects of their oratory is due to posture, gesture, and accent. The importance of the subject to them and their undivided attention bestowed upon it at the time is the cause of their forcible remarks. Some of these speeches are excellent in their way, but only so as they illustrate in a condensed form the opinions they wish to express. They are in fact the real children of nature. The prevailing circumstance governs the mind for the time and produces corresponding words and actions. The young and rising no doubt imitate the elders in some of the forms of set speeches but no pains are taken to learn them.

TRAVEL

When they travel at night and have no moon to afford light they take their direction by the north star with which they are all acquainted, but when stars also are invisible they observe at dark the point from which the wind blows, and shape their course accordingly. By these means they will be able to pursue a right direction until they come to some hill or river with which they are acquainted, and regulate their travel from that point until the sun makes its appearance, and then they are at no loss. Traveling on the plains is much more difficult than in forests. In the terrible snowstorms that sweep over these prairies, darkening the atmosphere and rendering the sun, moon, and stars invisible, or indeed any object a short distance ahead, they are as much at fault to proceed as any other person, and at these times lie down, let the snow drift over and cover them, and remain thus until the storm passes, which is frequently two or three days and nights.

There are many ways of determining within a few hours of the time when an encampment has been deserted and the number of persons composing the party. The camp fires will show how many persons have slept there, the dung of the horses or dogs denotes the time, if the fires have become cool. The tracks of the men and animals and the remains of the meal are also means of judging. If scraps of meat or bone seen around are untouched by wolves or ravens they must conclude that the party has recently left.

In the summer the bending of the grass under their feet, tracks in crossing a stream or any marshy place, and in winter, tracks in the snow, will show to a tolerable certainty how many persons and what time they have passed. A slight rain would determine whether the tracks were before or since it fell. Snow would prove the same; the dew of the morning in summer or fall would reveal the time to within 24 hours. The grass nibbled by the horses by its appearance would denote whether the party had passed within a few days and the hardness of the dung of the animals brings the time to a still greater degree of certainty. A correct judgment is not, however, formed by any one of the above criterions, but by a comparison of the whole, and by following the trail, and observing also the carcasses of the animals killed by the party, their number, state of decay, etc. These with other smaller indications, particularly if an arrow or moccasin be lost or thrown away, will determine the number and nation that have passed and the time. The passage of war parties is distinguished from hunting parties of their own people by the absence of boys' tracks or traces of dog travailles in the former, and by the precautions they take in their encampment.

Senses

There is an extreme acuteness in their sense of sight—that is, to see at a glance, over a wide extent of country, sometimes dotted by bushes, ravines, or hills, and distinguish the living objects when at rest from others. There is a great difference in the faculty of seeing far and what is called "picking up an object"—that is, distinguishing it from the inanimate bodies intervening. The Indians possess this power in so remarkable a degree as to appear a kind of instinct. At a distance of 12 or 15 miles they will distinguish animals from timber, even supposing they are not in motion. If moving they will discern between horses and buffalo, elk and horses, antelope and men, a bear and a bull, or a wolf and a deer, etc. But the greatest mystery is how they make out anything living to be there at such a distance, on the instant, when they themselves are in motion and the animal at rest. This they do when it is surrounded by a hundred other objects as like to living creatures as it is. Once pointed out, the movements are watched and its character thus determined. Their powers in this respect are truly astonishing and must be acquired. They also judge very correctly of the relative distances of objects, either by the eye or to each other. Smoke can be seen rising on the plains at a distance of 60 miles, and they will tell from that or any lesser distance within a few miles of the place where it rises. Their ideas of location are fully as remarkable.

An Indian will shoot 20 or 30 arrows in different directions, and to a distance of 100 yards or more among the tall grass, or in the snow, where no trace of them remains, yet he will pick up the whole without any difficulty; whereas a white man would have some trouble to find any one of the arrows. If they lose a whip, knife, or anything in traveling they can by returning generally find it, though no road marks their steps. Even the boys do all these things admirably. Finding lost horses or a camp from a given direction are also every-day occurrences, even if they have never been in the neighborhood of the place, yet they will find their way.

JUGGLERY AND SORCERY

These people are prone to be deceived in every way. Tricks by jugglers, stories, natural phenomena, or anything, to them unaccountable or uncommon is looked upon with fear. All are so, the priests as well as the others. The former have the address to turn to account their supposed knowledge of these causes—not that they are really any wiser than the others, but impress them with the belief that they are, which is enough for their purposes. The minds of most Indians are disturbed by many useless alarms, such as dreams, omens, and predictions of the priests. Writing or calculations in figures made by whites are among the wonders to which great superstition is attached, and they can be made to believe almost any story, however absurd, if read in appearance from a book. Paintings also, even the nondescript monsters drawn by themselves, inspire them with fear when looked upon. All this has met with sufficient explanation elsewhere.

STRENGTH AND ENDURANCE

Their powers in lifting weights, handling an ox or rowing a boat can not compare to Europeans, yet they equal them in carrying burdens and surpass them in running. It would seem that they have but little strength in their arms, but considerable in the back and limbs. This may be owing to the manner in which they have exercised in their youth. An ordinary Indian can not lift more than 125 to 150 pounds at most, though there are a few very strong men who might be able to raise double that weight, yet most of them will carry a large deer on their backs, traveling at a swift pace for miles without stopping, and this is equal to 170 to 185 pounds weight. The manner in which they put it on their back is by tying the legs together, lying down with their back on the deer, slipping the legs across the forehead, and rising up with the load. The Assiniboin have frequently in this neighborhood and once in our company tired down in a day or two running on foot the best horses we could produce.[22] In running they never "lose their breath" as it is called, do not pant or respire very quickly.

They can not understand why "whites lose their wind in running" and have no name for the idea in their language. They say their legs sometimes fail them in several days running, but their wind never. They are not fast, but constant runners, keeping always at the same pace over hills or on a level, in a kind of short trot about 12 or 15 miles without stopping. They will then rest a few minutes, smoke a pipe, and make as much more at the same rate, and so on, for three or four days and nights in succession if necessary, their speed on these occasions being about $5\frac{1}{2}$ miles an hour. In an emergency, sending an Indian express to the fort to carry a letter for myself, he went 95 miles and returned, being 190 miles, in two nights and one day.

They can not walk as well as strong white men, and never do walk when in haste to get forward. The muscles of their arms do not appear to be formed for very hard work, but it may be that the nature of their labors does not develop them. Upon the whole the European would stand much more hard work in every way, but the Indian would be his superior in active exercise, abstemiousness, and loss of sleep. The greatest burden we have known an Indian to carry any distance, say 3 or 4 miles, was two entire antelope, about 225 pounds.

SPIRITUOUS LIQUORS

No spirituous liquors have been distributed among these nations for many years past, but should it be given them in quantity it would

---

[22] W J McGee noted similar racing ability among the Seri Indians. See Seventeenth Ann. Rept. Bur. Amer. Ethn.

be productive of great poverty and distress. They all drink whenever they can get it—men, women, and children—except the Crow
Indians, who will not taste it. The usual consequence of drinking
spirits is poverty, as they will sell or give away everything they
possess and prostitute their women and children to obtain liquor when
once intoxicated. These Indians have never had a constant supply
of spirits—that is, enough to produce diseases or nervous debility.
Their frolics were made at intervals of months apart and never lasted
more than 24 hours at a time. They are not quarrelsome in their
families when inebriated, generally sing or cry for their dead relations; but among those who are not of kin quarrels often occur
which occasionally result in the death of one of them. It is morally
wrong and productive of great evil, in our opinion, to sell or give
ardent spirits to any Indian.

Hunting

Buffalo are the principal dependence of all the prairie tribes, both
for food and clothing, and are hunted at all seasons; in the summer
when the hair is light and short for clothing, lodges, etc., and in the
winter, when it is long and heavy, for robes. There are three ways
of hunting this animal: by surrounding, by approaching, and by the
parks, each of which we will describe. It may as well be stated that
the buffalo migrate, or take different ranges, and travel all in the
same direction in a given season. Thus in the spring they mostly
move north and northwest, in the fall east and south, in the winter
east, returning west and north toward spring. They keep together
in herds of from 100 or 200 to 5,000 or 6,000, and sometimes the
whole country for five or six days travel is covered with one moving
mass of these animals. News of the buffalo approaching an Indian
camp is received several days before the animals appear, as they
only move forward when the grazing is not sufficient. Where a large
camp is stationed they usually hunt by "surround," which is as
follows:

The soldiers hold a council with the chief in the soldiers' lodge
and prohibit any individual hunting ahead of the buffalo, also send
runners daily on discovery, to observe what progress they are making
toward the camp, their numbers, etc., and when they report them
to be near enough a meeting is held in the soldiers' lodge, the time
for the hunt appointed, and notice given to the camp by the haranguing of the public crier. At daybreak all the horses are caught and
saddled, and each of the horsemen is provided with a bow and a
quiver of arrows. A number who have no horses arm themselves
with guns, and at a signal from one of the soldiers the party moves
off in single file or line. Those who have the fastest horses go in

front, after them the other horsemen. Then the foot hunters, and lastly the women with their dogs and travailles. The soldiers ride along each side the line (which is sometimes a mile and more in length) and observe whether the line of march is preserved, and that no one leaves singly. Were a dog to run out of the line it would be shot with an arrow immediately.

Their march is conducted in silence, with the wind in their faces, consequently blowing the scent away from the buffalo while they are coming near them. The animal is not quick sighted but very keen scented, and a man can, in passing across the wind blowing toward them, raise a herd at the distance of 2 or 3 miles, without their seeing him.

The party proceeds in this order, taking every advantage of concealment the country affords in hills, coulees, bushes, long grass, etc., endeavoring to get around them. As soon, however, as they are close and see a movement among the buffalo intimating flight, they push their horses at full speed, and riding entirely round commence shooting the buffalo, which run in the direction of the footmen, these in their turn shoot, and the animals are driven back toward the horses. In this way they are kept running nearly in a circle until very tired, and the greater part are killed. Those on horseback shoot arrows into all they can at the distance of from 2 to 6 paces, and the footmen load and fire as often as the animals come near them.

A "surround" party of 80 to 100 persons will in this way kill from 100 to 500 buffalo in the course of an hour. As soon as possible the women get to work skinning and cutting up the animals. The tongue, hide, and four best pieces are the property of the one who killed it, and the rest belongs to those who skin it. When the men have stopped killing and turned their horses loose to graze they commence with their women, and the work being divided among so many is soon gotten through with. If any disputes occur as to the right to the hides or meat, they are settled on the spot by the soldiers; but these disputes do not often occur, as they generally all have as many hides and as much meat as they can pack home. The meat is cut in long, thick slices, merely detaching it from the bones, and leaving the carcass on the plains. It is packed home on their horses 'and dogs. Before leaving, however, they all make a hearty meal of raw liver, raw kidneys, raw stomach, and cow's nose, with other parts in the same state, and the blood being thus smeared over all their faces presents a savage appearance.

On arrival in camp if the soldiers wish the tongues, each one throws his down at the soldiers' lodge in passing, or sends it to them. Each also furnishes a piece of meat for that lodge, and all the old and feeble are supplied by their relatives who have been to the hunt. The chief has no interference in all these matters. He sometimes hunts and works the same as the others, but generally sends some of his sons or other relations with his horses for meat. They never use the gun on horseback or the bow on foot after game. The former they can not load while running and the latter is not calculated to shoot with certainty any distance over 10 paces.

THROWING BUFFALO IN A PARK.—This is the most ancient mode of hunting, and probably the only successful one prior to the introduction of firearms and horses, as their bows and arrows are insufficient for killing buffalo on foot. We know of no nation now except the Assiniboin and Cree who practice it, because all the rest are well supplied with horses that can catch the buffalo, therefore they are not compelled to resort to these means to entrap them.

Every year thousands of them are caught in this section by the Assiniboin, and at the time we are writing there are three parks in operation a short distance from this, all doing a good business. When a camp of 30 to 60 lodges find themselves deficient in guns and horses they move to a suitable place to build a park (pl. 69), and there wait the approach of buffalo toward it. Most streams have high bluffs on each side and a valley between. They therefore pitch their camp in the valley opposite and near a gap of perpendicular descent through the hills; a high level plain being beyond the bluffs. They cut timber and plant strong posts in the ground nearly in a circular form and fill up the openings between with large logs, rocks, bushes, and everything that will in any way add to its strength, inclosing an area of nearly an acre of ground. This enclosure is run up the sides of the hill to the gap or entrance C, though neither it nor the camp is visible from the place beyond. The whole is planned and managed by the master of the park, some divining man of known repute, who is believed to have the power of making the buffalo come into it by his enchantments.

On the plains beyond, and commencing where the wood mark leaves off, are thrown up piles of earth, about 3 feet high and large enough to conceal a man lying behind them, which are about 18 paces apart and extend in angles to the distance of a quarter to half a mile in proportion as there are people to man them. When these arrangements are completed, four fast running young men are selected by the manager whose duty it is to scour the country every day or two, making a circuit of about 20 miles in discovery of buffalo, and report to headquarters. The master in the meantime commences his magic arts as follows: A flagstaff or pole is planted in the center of the park, to the top of which is attached a yard or two of scarlet cloth, some tobacco, and a cow's horn. This is a sacrifice to the Wind.

At the foot of the same are placed two or three buffalo Heads which are painted red, decked out in feathers, and new kettles with scarlet cloth and other things placed before them. These are given to the Buffalo Spirits.

Another Head painted and decked very gaudily is placed in the lodge of the master, who smokes and invokes it, at times singing the Bull Song, which he accompanies with a rattle nearly all night, and prophesies as to their appearance of success in the morning. A man is now chosen who is to lead the buffalo within the lines, and there are but few among them who can do it. When the discoverers have reported buffalo to be within 8 or 10 miles of the camp, and the wind is favorable, the master, after great ceremonies to the Heads, and making them other sacrifices, gives notice that a throw must be made, sending all the camp to take their stations behind the piles of earth, lying down; he remains in camp, keeping up a singing, rattling, and smoking—with invocations all the time. The person who brings the buffalo mounts a horse and meets them a great distance from camp. When within about 150 yards of the herd he covers his body with his robe, lies along the horse's back, and imitates the bleating of a buffalo calf.

The whole mass immediately moves toward him. He retreats toward the pen, always keeping to the windward of them, and about the same distance ahead, renewing the noise of the calf whenever they appear to stop. They generally follow him as fast as his horse can gallop, and in this way alone he conducts them within the lines of the angle. Of course as soon as they are a short distance in, the scent of one of the angles reaches them but it is now too late, they have closed in behind. The animals now take fright and rush from one line to another, but seeing people on both sides (who rise as the buffalo attempt to get through) they keep straight forward. The leader on horseback now makes his escape to one side, and the whole herd plunges madly down the precipice, one on top of the other, breaking their legs and necks in the fall. Into the pen they tumble, those in front having no power to stop. They are forced on by the pressure from behind and frightened by the yelling and firing of the savages. When all have passed into the pen the work of slaughter commences, with guns and bows firing as long as any appearance of life remains. From 300 to 600 are thus thrown in at one time by a small camp, and two or three days are required to skin and cut them up.

Men, women, and children now commence skinning. Each secures as many hides as he can skin. The master of the park claims a portion for his share, indeed all are said to belong to him, but he does not take more than the rest. All the tongues, however, are his, and he also receives other payment for his services in presents, besides the standing of a divining man. Plate 70 will perhaps exhibit the hunt more clearly if we have not been sufficiently plain in the description.

When there is a deficiency of people to man the angles they are made by placing the lodges of the camp in that form, but this can only be done when they have a dozen or two of fast horses to extend the angle of the lodges and force the buffalo within the lines. This is also done, but it does not succeed as well as the way described. Great is the joy and feasting in camp after a large throw.

APPROACHING BUFFALO.—This is done on foot with the gun by a single man. It is indispensable he should have on a skin dress in summer and a white blanket coat over it in winter, or a buffalo robe coat with all the hair turned inside.

Any dark-colored dress is easily seen by them at a considerable distance, but white or light-colored clothing does not attract their notice. The hunter has his gun covered with skin to prevent the dirt or snow from entering the barrel while in the act of crawling. His accoutrements are also firmly attached to his person by a belt. He proceeds toward the buffalo, keeping the wind as nearly in his face as possible, sometimes being obliged to make a circuit of miles to get the wind in the right direction. When near the animals he observes from the top of some hill how they are stationed, which way they travel, and the nature of the ground as regards coulees, gullies, bushes, grass, and any objects that may hide his person from their view and shapes his course according to the means of concealment presented. If he finds the country too level to get them within range of the gun he then commences crawling on his belly toward them, pushing his gun ahead as he goes.

This is a very laborious and slow mode of progressing and often takes one or two hours to come within shooting distance, as the hunter only moves while the animals are eating, stopping the moment their attention is directed toward him. In the snow it is a very cold business, and in the summer difficult on account of the cactus, but they are obliged to do it frequently in both seasons on these level plains. Great precaution is needed to approach buffalo or antelope on a level plain. The hunter covers his head with sage bushes, and sticks the same or grass in his belt; at other times a wolf skin covers his head and back—he lying flat, no form of the man can be perceived—and the animals being accustomed to these objects do not affright so easily. When by any of these means he has arrived within shooting distance he fires without rising, elevating his piece by support of the elbows. After firing he remains motionless a few minutes during which the buffalo, after recoiling a few paces, and seeing nothing on the move, commence grazing. He now turns over on his back and reloads his gun (lying in this position) by putting the butt against his foot—and when ready will turn over on his belly and fire again, and so on, sometimes killing six or eight without changing his place, or with very little movement.

As soon as he rises the herd runs off and he commences skinning. Some hunters mimic the bleating of a calf and thus decoy the buffalo to them, but this is a rare talent, and only practiced by a few good performers; in hilly places or where there are gullies and bushes to hide the hunter, neither buffalo nor antelope are difficult to kill, but on the barren and level plain it requires great exertion, time and patience.

Another method by which great numbers of both buffalo and antelope are slain is, when the snow has drifted in the gullies, forming banks 10 to 15 feet deep. The animals are pursued on foot, with raquettes and snowshoes. The hunter goes over the snow, but the animals become embedded and are killed with ease. In the summer if several animals are killed, the meat is placed in a pile covered with the hides, and a portion of the hunter's clothing left on it, the scent of which prevents the wolves from coming to it. Occasionally the bladder of the animal is inflated, small pebbles put in, which being tied to a stick and stirred by the wind, will keep off the wolves and foxes.

But in the winter the usual way is to bury the meat in the snow, which effectually prevents the wolves from eating it, as they have no power of smell through a foot of snow. Meat can be left in this way in perfect security for a month or more, but they usually return with their dogs and take it away the next day. If the hunter goes out on horseback he leaves his horse near the buffalo, and after having killed in the manner stated, packs him home with the meat and hide, but in the deep snow horses can not travel, the dogs do not sink much in the snow and the men and women go over it on snowshoes.

Antelope are hunted in the same way as the preceding, also sometimes decoyed by tying some portion of clothing to a pole, the man lying down and raising and lowering the pole at intervals, or by kicking up his heels, one after the other. They have great curiosity to see the strange object, and after making many circles will come near enough to get a shot, though as soon as they make out the man they are off. A wolf skin is decidedly the best disguise when hunting any of the animals on foot.

It may as well be recorded here that all young hunters sacrifice the first game they kill by cutting it up and giving it to the crows, magpies and wolves, saying to each, " I give you this that I may always be able to kill and feed the wolves, that I may be successful in war."

The bull's head is often painted and bound round with scarlet cloth, with painted feathers or sticks stuck in, and an address made to it announcing that it is done by the hunter to prevent the animal from goring him. Likewise the Assiniboin, when they undertake to swim the Missouri, will tie to a stick some dried buffalo guts, grease, and bladder, and stick the same in the water, say to it, "This is to enable me to cross without accident, let no wind blow, nor pain take me in crossing." They are not expert swimmers like the Crow Indians, and the fear of the undertaking causes the sacrifice. In all these things they are very particular and superstitious, asserting that if these ceremonies are neglected some accident will certainly happen to the person who despises these powers.

DEER HUNTING.—A good deer hunter must use the rifle. Shotguns do not shoot with certainty. This is the reason why all these Indians are poor deer hunters. They use the northwest shotgun altogether except a few of the Sioux, who hunt antelope and bighorn with the rifle. The art of deer hunting may be thus divided: Finding the deer, approaching it, shooting it, cutting it up, and carrying it home. They are hunted in the timber by a man alone and on foot. He must be well acquainted with the habits of the animal, where it is to be found at different hours in the day, what it feeds upon at different seasons, to know by the tracks if it is traveling, grazing, running, retiring to rest, or going to water; he must be quick sighted, a good walker, and go cautiously through the bush when near the game. The morning and evening are the best times to hunt them, as they are then on the edge or borders of the woods where grass is found, or in open places in the bottoms; returning into the thick bushes for a few hours in the middle of the day. The hunter travels fast until he comes near the place where he judges a deer is to be found, then proceeds very slowly and silently, looking in every direction, always keeping the wind in his favor until the animal is seen. He then approaches it stepping from tree to tree, bush to bush, crawling and creeping, hiding himself entirely from its view, by every means, and making no noise. When he thinks he is within range he rises and fires quickly and the deer falls. It is then skinned and cut up, the meat packed in the hide, and it tied in a bundle by the skin of the legs, in such a way as to form a collar, which is drawn over his forehead, by lying or sitting down, and slipping it over, then rising up with the weight between his shoulders he starts homeward. If more than one is wanted he hangs the first on a tree thus cut up, and proceeds in quest of others, sometimes killing three or four in a day, which he returns for with his horse or dogs the next day.

Whistles made of wood like the mouthpiece of a clarinet are used to call both deer and elk in hunting seasons, and are then a useful decoy. They do not catch them in traps or pits.

ELK HUNTING.—This is done on foot, with the gun, but by parties of men. Elk go in droves of from 100 to 300 each and are found in the large timbered bottoms of the Missouri and Yellowstone. There is some ceremony required in hunting this animal. In the first place some divining woman who is said to be an "elk dreamer" states she has had a favorable dream for hunting them. The woman is then stripped to the waist and also barelegged, the body and face painted a bright yellow, and a wreath of bushes with leaves on projecting two or three feet on each side is placed on her head in imitation of the horns of the elk. Thus decorated she starts at the head of a party of 15 to 25 men. When in the vicinity of the place, where, according to her dream, the elk are to be found, she stops and commences her incantation song, while the others continue in quest of the game. As soon as the herd is discovered the party separate, and outflanking them on either side, commence firing and running toward them, loading and firing while running, in quick succession, when the elk become confused, scatter and turn in different directions, presenting at times a mark for each of the hunters.

Every shot bewilders them the more, and instead of running in any one direction they keep turning every way until a great many are killed.

They are then skinned, cut up, and the meat and hides packed home on horses brought for the purpose, which having been left behind in charge of some women and boys, are brought up during the fixing. The skins are used for clothing and the meat, though eaten, is not relished much by most of the Indians.

Elk are also approached singly and at those times the same precautions are used as stated under the head of deer hunting, though they are not so shy and timid an animal as deer.

GRIZZLY BEARS.—This animal is not hunted but often found when not desired, and mostly passed by unmolested by a single Indian when on foot, though on occasions they do kill them in this way, which exploit ranks in bravery next to killing an enemy, but the thickets and mauvaise terre which they inhabit makes the pursuit too dangerous for ordinary hunters. They are more frequently killed in their dens in winter.

The grizzly bear in the beginning of cold weather and snow seeks some hole in the side of a hill in some solitary place, and carries in a quantity of grass and brush to make his nest, lies all winter apparently asleep and eats nothing, though they are said to derive some nourishment by sucking their paws. The nest or wash is always within a few feet of the entrance and they can easily be seen from the outside. Generally a den contains two to four bears, or one large male and two yearling cubs, or one large female and two yearlings. Sometimes, however, they are found singly. When a den is discovered six or eight Indians go to attack it, approaching the hole so close as to see the foremost bear, when three of them fire, the others reserving their shots. They all run off some distance and if the animal, or any others pursue them, the rest fire. If the first one has been killed and there are others the smoke of the guns drives them out, when they receive a volley from the hunters. If they see nothing after waiting a sufficient time for the smoke to escape from the hole they again approach as before and see if the animal be dead. If so, they make a smoke within the entrance with the view of driving out any other that may be within. Should nothing appear they conclude there is but one, enter, and drag him out.

Frequently two or three bears are killed in the same hole at the same time, and at others some of the hunters get dreadfully mangled. Bears are also run on horseback, when found on the plains, and shot with arrows. This is the least dangerous manner of killing them. No pits or traps are used, though we have known forked sticks to be placed before the hole so that when they came out they were caught by the hind part and detained a short time. When a bear is killed he is skinned, all except the head, which is covered with scarlet cloth, the hair smeared over with vermilion, handsome feathers stuck around it, and new kettles and tobacco laid before it. It is presented with the pipe to smoke and a long ceremony of invocation takes place, purporting that they give him this property and pay this attention to have pity upon their wives and children and not tear them when they are hunting after fruit and berries. They say if this is not done the bear will certainly sooner or later devour some of them or their children.

BEAVER.—None of these Indians trap the beaver to any extent except the Crow and Cree Indians. The steel trap is used by them, set under the water, and a stick dipped in the musk or oilstone of the beaver, placed behind the trap, though above the surface. The animal, smelling the bait, will come to see what it is, and in swimming around is caught by the foot. Oils of cinnamon, cloves, and rhodium are also used for bait by white trappers.

WOLVES AND FOXES.—Wolves and foxes are caught in deadfall traps made by planting sticks in the ground with a crosspiece supporting a heavy roof of stone laid on sticks. The whole is propped up with a stick, and the wolf going in to eat the meat displaces the prop and the whole weight falls upon him and breaks his back. The Cree catch them in a pit or hole dug for the purpose—covering it with a revolving trap door with a bait of meat on each end above and beneath. The animal in endeavoring to reach the bait is turned in by the revolving of the door under its weight, which brings the other bait on top. A second revolution turns up the first bait and turns down the second wolf.

In this way they will catch as many as the pit will hold, especially as when a few are turned in they commence fighting; and the noise attracts others. Wolves are also sacrificed to and small presents given them, with the view of avoiding their being bitten by them when mad, or as the Gods of War.

The chase does not vary much at any season, except that in the summer, no skins being seasonable but deer in the red, only enough animals are killed to suffice for food, clothing, lodges, etc. From the middle of September to the middle of March the hair and fur of all animals become merchantable. They are then hunted for the hide, though all prime furs are taken off in the middle of the winter. Pelts are judged by the thickness of their skin and fur. In the warm months all animals shed their hair. A little observation enables a person to determine to a certainty in what month the animal has been killed.

Hunting parties not decided on by council in the soldiers' lodge are formed by any respectable hunter sending invitations to those he wishes should accompany him.

The spoils of smaller game belong to him who killed it but they share the meat with all who are there, and but little difficulty occurs on this point. When but few animals are killed it is always known who killed them, and when many are slaughtered all have enough. Disputes arise occasionally, however, but it is not a matter of sufficient importance to proceed to extreme measures, and one of the party usually relinquishes his claim.

The morning and evening are the best hours for approaching small game, as at those times they are found feeding, but buffalo can be easier approached in the middle of the day when they lie down for an hour or two, and if not asleep their range of vision is much diminished by that position and intervening grass. Light and shade are not of much consequence in approaching game. The object of the hunter is to keep out of sight entirely until the moment of firing, and when that is not possible to make use of some skin, branches, grass, etc., to deceive the animal, move very slowly, and keep the wind in his favor.

The manner in which animals are decoyed has been pointed out, but is not always successful, and only resorted to by those who are adepts in the art of mimicry, as in the rutting season. This is the reason why he who leads the buffalo into the parks is supposed by the mass to be possessed with some supernatural power which forces the buffalo to follow him, when in fact it is nothing more than a correct imitation of the bleating of a calf or a noise as though a calf was being devoured by a wolf and crying for help. The buffalo never get near enough to the man to make him out, as he is covered with his robe, the hair turned outward, and he always keeps the wind in his favor. It is, however, a rare talent.

The hide of the buffalo, to make a robe, is taken off in two halves, by slitting the animal down the middle of the back and the middle of the belly. The first process it undergoes afterwards is taking off the portions of meat and membrane adhering to it, so that it will present the smooth clear skin. This is done with a tool made from

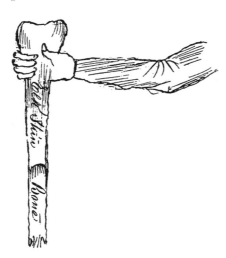

FIGURE 33.—Tool for fleshing the hide

the shin bone of an elk. (Fig. 33.) The lower end is cut to an edge and small teeth made therein. The skin is hung up at one corner to a pole and the meat is dug off by hoeing down with the instrument, which is held firmly at the upper end. A woman will finish this operation on two whole skins or four halves in one day. Next the skin is stretched to dry. Holes are cut through it near the edge. In summer it is pinned to the ground by wooden pegs, or in winter when the ground is frozen, stretched on a frame of four poles tied together, and a small fire built to dry it. When dry the next thing to be done is to scrape it, that is, to hoe off about one-third of the thickness of the hide. This is done with an iron tool about 3½ inches long, 1½ inches wide, and ⅛-inch thick. Formerly a flint stone was used for this purpose, but the iron tool answering better, is now substituted. This piece of iron being sharpened at one edge is tied on a handle made of elk's horn (fig. 34), cut off at one of the forks, so as to afford a projection to fasten it, being held in both hands. The hide is laid on the ground, the woman stands upon it, and, stooping, digs off the hide in shavings, until of the proper thickness.

This occupies about half a day to each whole hide and is a very fatiguing employment. Grease is then melted, sprinkled sparingly over the skin, and it is suspended over a small fire for a few hours that the grease may penetrate; then taken down and smeared over with the brains or livers of some animals boiled in water, being soaked thoroughly and left all night in this state. In the morning it is again stretched on the frame, the liver scraped off, clean water thrown on and scraped off until the hide becomes white. A fire is then made near and the skin slowly heated and rubbed with pummice stone or porous bone until it is about half dry, then taken out of the frame and drawn backward and forward round a strong cord of sinew which is tied at each end to the lodge pole. Every few minutes the skin is held a short time to the fire, then rubbed, and this operation continued until it becomes perfectly dry and soft. This is also hard work. A good hand will rub two whole skins or four halves in a day. The skin is now dressed. The holes made for stretching it around the edges are cut off and it is sewed up along the back with an awl and sinew, which takes about half an hour to each two halves of the buffalo.

The robe is now fit for sale and is packed away. Deer and elk skins undergo the same operations, and in addition the hair is scraped off with the same tool that the hide is shaved with, though they are skinned whole and not in halves like the buffalo hides. It

FIGURE 34.—Tool for scraping hides or shaving the skin

will thus be seen that at least three days are required to prepare one buffalo robe for market, but by their division of time in attending to several skins in different stages of advancement the labor would be about equal to two days for each buffalo skin. Twenty-five to thirty-five robes is considered an excellent winter's work for one woman. The average is about 18 to 20 each. Wolf, bear, fox, rabbit, beaver, hare, ermine, lynx, otter, rat, mink, etc., are not dressed for market, and all these are skinned, stretched and dried by the men and boys. A wolf or fox skin is now and then dressed for the use of a woman or hunter to wear round his head, and undergoes the preceding operations, though the skin being small and light not much labor is required. Robes and skins are packed up in small bundles, the hair side out, each bundle weighing 30 or 35 pounds, and when a sufficient number are collected for supplies, one of these bundles is tied on each dog travaille and they go to the trading house to dispose of them.

INSTRUCTION IN HUNTING.—As stated in a former place, boys commence with archery as soon as they can run about after birds and rabbits, enlarging the size of the bow to suit their strength, until they attain the age of 16 years, when the full-sized bow is used. About this time they are taught by their father or other relations the use of firearms and the different modes of approaching game. At this age they may be considered fit to engage in the active labors of the chase on foot, but seldom run buffalo on horseback so early. About 18, however, they can hunt in every way, though before this age they can and do assist in supporting their parents. Even when much younger they follow to the hunt and aid in skinning and packing home meat. They are perhaps of more service in this way when young than at a riper age, when the pursuit of war and the possession of women occupy the greater part of their time. Women are never known to practice any part of the hunter's art when left alone. They generally find some relative to remain with them when deserted by their husbands, and their labor always secures them a home.

When they desert the camp on account of some quarrel they travel alone for days, subsisting on roots, berries, or fruit, if the season affords them, shaping their course toward the fort or some other band of their own people.

The bow and arrow is used altogether by all these tribes when hunting buffalo on horseback and the Northwest shotgun is the only arm employed in killing any and all game on foot. A few Sioux, perhaps a dozen in the whole nation, use rifles in hunting antelope, bighorn, and other small game. A warrior has if possible both gun and bow. Ammunition is sold at the rate of 3 pounds of powder and 1 pound of balls for one buffalo robe, which is enough for a month's hunting by any Indian. Traps, metallic instruments, arms, or anything they want, also persons to repair their guns, kettles, and axes and to make tools to dress robes, etc., can be furnished them at any time; but they will not pay for these things. We have kept in constant employment, mostly for their benefit, a blacksmith, a gunsmith, and a tinsmith at all the forts for 20 years past and are heartily tired of the business, as no profit arises from their labor.

It is not designed hereby to produce an impression that these labors have been performed by us from charitable motives, but thereby to put the Indians in a position to hunt and collect skins for the trade. Every Indian without a horse or gun, or only with his bow and arrows is an idler; his time is a loss to us. We therefore lend him a gun and furnish him with ammunition free of charge. He commences hunting and realizes to us from $60 to $80 in skins that would otherwise have remained upon the backs of the animals. True he never returns or pays for the gun, but he has it, or some other has, and it is in our active service. As long as the buffalo are as numerous as they now are these tribes will have no difficulty in maintaining themselves by the chase. Traders are too observant of their own interests to let them suffer for the means of hunting, but should the buffalo fail the very reverse would be the case. In that event the trade not being of sufficient profit would be discontinued, and the Indians thrown upon their own resources, which are extremely deficient.

They are no deer hunters, and besides only a small portion of their country along the rivers is stocked with deer and elk and the greatest famine and distress imaginable would follow, as they are entirely unacquainted with agricultural pursuits.

There appears to be an anxiety exhibited on this point in many of the queries, viz, whether the chase is sufficient for the support of the Indians, and whether they would not be benefited by the introduction of agriculture. It does not admit of a doubt; neither are any arguments required to prove this. Having witnessed their eating their own children during a temporary absence of buffalo in 1845–46 is enough to satisfy any person on this head. Any railroad or emigration of whites through their country would ruin it at once as a buffalo country, and the misery above alluded to would as surely follow as night succeeds day.

We think, however, that attention on the part of white friends is not enough directed to pastoral pursuits instead of agricultural and mechanical. It appears to us that the former occupation would suit the Indian better to commence with. He would thereby gradually emerge from his savage state into another which would lead to agriculture in the end. The tilling necessary for the support of his stock would be increased in proportion as he saw the advantages arising therefrom. It would be expecting too much of the Indian to suppose that he would suddenly change his indolent life for one of hard and constant labor, but it seems reasonable that the raising of horses, cattle, hogs, and sheep, for which their country is admirably adapted, would be to them both interesting and profitable employment, particularly as they could unite these operations with the chase when game came near. This state would be but the chrysalis in the present generation, to merge into agriculture, mechanical arts, and civilization in the next.

Another argument in favor of this is that they are accustomed to animal food entirely, therefore grain of any kind could not replace this; but domestic animals, fowls, eggs, etc., would—and in the meantime a relish would be formed for breadstuff and vegetables, the want of which is not now felt. The course to be pursued (that is if any be in contemplation) by persons in high stations appears to us to be very plain, and must be apparent to any one who makes himself acquainted with their real character as set forth in these pages.

FISHING

These tribes take no fish in quantity by any means whatever.

WAR

The raising of a war party is always a subject of discussion in the
soldiers' lodge, not to choose the persons, but whether the time is
suitable; if men, arms, and ammunition can be spared from camp,
or if they are required for defense; if it is advisable to keep up the
war; how they are situated with regard to their enemies as to locality, numbers, and general prospects of success as presented at the
time. It being determined in favor of hostilities, the partisan soldier or chief who intends leading the expedition proceeds to fast,
sacrifice, and dream in the manner before pointed out in these pages,
and having had favorable visions makes a feast of dog in his own
lodge, and invites thereto the persons he wishes to accompany him,
opening to them the object and plan of the expedition, after the
feast has been concluded. Should he not be able to obtain a sufficient
number of recruits in this way he sends runners with tobacco to
other camps conveying an invitation to join within a given time.

War is made either to steal horses from their enemies or to take
their scalps. For the first object but few people are required, as concealment and avoiding battle is aimed at, and parties for this purpose are comprised of from 10 to 30 men, whereas a party starting
expressly for battle often contains two, three, or four hundred warriors. We will endeavor to follow up the first description of parties,
supposing stealing horses to be the object, which is the most common
kind of war excursions. The partisan or captain, as has been
stated, after dreaming, sacrificing, etc., to Wakoñda, the Sun, and
Thunder, makes his last offering, consisting of some scarlet cloth
and tobacco, to the Wolves, which are considered the war fetishes,
and viewed in the light of the special Gods of War. The day for
starting being appointed, all his followers are assembled the night
before, when the business is again considered, and they consent to
follow him as the leader during the time they are out, obey his instructions, without, however, acknowledging any right in him to
punish in case of disobedience, also reserving to themselves the privilege of leaving him at any time and under any circumstances they
think proper.

It is a voluntary action and those who will not obey or are dissatisfied leave and return home at any stage of the march, but do
not separate and remain to thwart the intentions of the others. No
harm being done by their desertion, no punishment follows. At all
events he is obliged to be contented with these precarious terms of
enlistment. The night previous to their departure they assemble

(say 20 men) in the soldiers' lodge, where a dance called the Crow dance is performed by them, and the next morning they all start together, singing the Wolf Song as they leave, their faces usually being painted with vermilion at all times and particularly at this time. All go on foot; no order or file of march is taken up; neither is it necessary. Each one has six or eight pairs of good strong-soled moccasins on his back. Some are armed with bows and arrows, some with guns, and some with lances and war clubs. Battle not being sought, a profusion of arms is not desired and might prove cumbersome. Every man furnishes his own ammunition and war implements.

Though guns are sometimes borrowed and ammunition begged of their friends and relatives, yet there is no tax laid on the camp for supplies nor any public arrangement whatever for providing arms, etc. No provisions are taken; they hunt it on their way. The partisan takes his fetish Wolf Skin, which is an entire skin of that animal dressed with the head, ears, legs, etc., complete, so that by lying down or standing on his hands and knees and covering himself with the skin, drawing it over his head, he might easily be passed as a wolf by any person within a short distance. His other charm or fetish is also secured about his person. A good many, and sometimes the whole party, have wolf skins of the above description on their backs.

During their march through their own country but little precaution is used. They stray along at random and toward evening look around for some game for supper, kill whatever presents itself, take enough for the night and the next day and encamp.

They proceed in this way, if no signs of enemies appear, until entirely out of their usual hunting grounds, the leader in the meantime consulting his dreams, smoking to his fetish wolf skin. A bad dream, or any unpropitious omen, such as the howling of a single wolf in a peculiar manner, breaking his pipe, letting fall his fetish, very severe thunder and lightning, would suffice to turn back the expedition. When large parties start we find two or three returning almost every day from the time of leaving until the attack, caused by dissensions, omens, or other dissatisfaction, but no disgrace or remarkable comments are attached to this fact, though the excuses some of them give look very much like fear.

Having arrived at their enemy's country, the greatest possible precaution and vigilance are now exercised.

According to the orders of their leader they proceed slowly, scatter in different directions for miles around, lie about on the tops of the hills covered with their wolf skins, or headdresses made of bunches of wild sage, examining the country in every direction for hours

before they move. If nothing is seen they signal to each other the
result by imitating the howling of wolves, the barking of foxes, or
the hooting of owls, as the signals agreed upon require. Assembling
in some hollow, they compare notes, receive new directions, and proceeding a few miles, separate again and reconnoiter as before. They
now shoot very seldom, and only when meat is absolutely wanted,
and the wind blows in a direction to carry the report away from their
enemies, or toward that part of the country already explored. By
observing the movements of crows and wolves, in which direction
they travel, where they stop and light, they will find out the carcass
of some animal killed by the hunters of the camp. The state of its
decay, tracks, and other signs around will determine the probable
direction of their enemies, and they steer for that point.

When advanced thus far—that is, to know they are in the vicinity of a camp—the real science of their manner of warfare exhibits
itself. Night marches commence, and separating as before about
daylight they occupy the hills, lying motionless all day, watching
in every direction some signs of their enemies. They are placed so
as to be within call of each other, and the signals for different discoveries being agreed upon by imitating the howling of wolves, etc.,
as has been stated, they can communicate with each other all the time
without rising to their feet. They never expose their persons to
view on a hill. If necessary to assemble they crawl down and meet
in some ravine well covered with thick bushes. They now never
shoot, make no fire, eat nothing, keep very quiet, and travel in the
night. Of course, by these measures they must soon perceive some
one belonging to the camp, and by observing his direction will find
where it is.

Having discovered the camp, the last rendezvous takes place prior
to the attempt upon the horses, and here several things are determined—a place is agreed upon where they will all assemble after
the attack, a direction for the return chosen in case of separation,
smoking, and invoking the different fetishes are performed, and
general directions given by their leader as to the manner of approaching the camp.

There can be no plan of operations laid down, as they are as yet
unaware of the position of the camp, how their horses are kept,
what surrounding objects afford concealment, etc. In the night
they approach the camp in a body under cover of the hills and
bushes, and when near enough to see the horses, and judge of the
opportunities of getting to them unobserved they again separate,
and each pursues his own way of proceeding from different points,
as the nature of the ground affords. The best horses of the Crows
and Blackfeet are usually picketed near the lodge of their several

owners and the rest grazing near. Sometimes pens are made around the lodges, the horses driven in at dark, and cottonwood bark thrown in for them to eat. The risk of extracting horses from the interior of a camp is very great, as young men are moving about from lodge to lodge all night in their various prosecutions of schemes on women; but the horses must be had, and the venture must be made.

Near daylight, when all the people of the camp are supposed to be asleep, but when yet dark (and the darkest kind of nights are chosen) each warrior creeps slowly and silently toward that portion of horses apparently the best situated to be taken off unperceived. Should he in this way be so fortunate as to reach them without discovery he cuts the cords with which they are tied and works them gradually into the shade or darkness, then mounting one, drives the whole to the appointed place of rendezvous. But owing to the many obstacles in the way of each, the probability of some one being observed is great, and in that case the whole camp is alarmed on the instant, each rushing toward his horses. Shots are fired and the warriors seek safety in flight, with or without horses as it happens. If there be snow to show their tracks the enemy pursues them the next day, but if no trail can be found to follow they abandon it. In either case the warriors shape their course individually toward the appointed place of meeting, and if all are not assembled, leave some token for those not arrived to know they have passed, and continue their flight.

The horses are put to full speed day and night for several days in succession until entirely out of reach of pursuit, and now begins a series of quarrels as to the right of possession of the animals. Some who have been disappointed and drove none off take from those who have. The leader takes several, combinations of two or three to rob another are entered into, horses are killed in the quarrel, or stolen from each other, and unless a great haul has been made very little satisfaction appears. These differences are mostly gotten through with before reaching home and they make known their approach by setting the prairie on fire. When arrived in the outskirts they shoot and sing, but do not black themselves for stealing horses, unless they have brought a scalp also, which occasionally happens. If any of their party have been killed they arrive uttering loud lamentations.

The whole camp turns out to meet them. The old women cry over their sons, rubbing the hand down their face, a great deal of flattery is used by some of the elderly men, shouting the name of some one of the warriors in a loud voice, stating his bravery, greatness of heart, etc., until overwhelmed by glory, he presents him with one of the horses. Great is the joy and tumult, and it frequently happens before the warrior has arrived at his own lodge, that all his horses are given away, and he retains nothing but the glory of the action. In this event, however, his name is sung around the camp by the persons who have received these gifts, accompanied with the song of thanks, and loud and prolonged praises of his bravery and strength of heart.

War parties for battle are a long time in contemplation, frequently occupying a whole winter in preparing for the campaign, and in counseling regarding it. Usually large parties are led by some chief of a band, and invitations are sent by him to different chiefs of other bands of the same nation and to those of another nation with whom they are at peace.

In the beginning of the summer they all assemble with their lodges at the place appointed, and a great deal of debate, feasting, and private consultation takes place, with sacrifices by the chiefs and soldiers, and also by many of the warriors to the several supernatural powers before referred to. It appears to be the misfortune of these large expeditions to fail in executing anything like what is anticipated at the start. Here also, the cause of their failure appears to be due to their insubordination. There is no one man to lead, no one source of authority in carrying out any plan decided upon. The nominal leader as chief is only chief of his band, and even among these there are others who are his equals in war. There are several chiefs of bands, and also many other chiefs; every one's advice, although asked, can not be taken, which produces dissatisfaction. The soldiers of one band will not be commanded by those of another, rank on every side is interfered with, old grudges renewed by meeting with old delinquents, in short though all looks pretty fair on starting, yet difficulties and disputes from various causes take place every day after, which results in their leaving and returning home in detached parties.

When, however, the ranks have by these means become purged of the most turbulent and unruly characters the others proceed in the following order: Chiefs, warriors of note and soldiers, dressed in deerskin shirts and leggings trimmed with ermine, horse, or scalp hair. A war eagle feather cap is on his head, a shield of bull's hide covers his arm, a bow and quiver of arrows is carried on his back, a short gun stuck in his belt with pouch and horn across his shoulders and scalping knife in its sheath, the powder horn and ball pouch are carried on the middle of the back, the connecting strap reaching across his breast and the upper parts of both arms. These are the mounted men, and the most distinguished for their former deeds. The footmen consist of young warriors and new recruits without any peculiar insignia, but well armed if possible. The soldiers are men holding that rank in whichever camp they reside, and their duty is to ride on the outside of the main body to keep any person from straying away and prevent any useless noise or manner of travel.

The scouts are appointed by the leader and changed daily; their duty being to separate and keep 5 or 6 miles ahead of the main body. These scouts or discoverers are footmen and use the same precautions as before stated. The main body moves slowly forward after reconnoitering has commenced, without any order, and only passing whatever ground has been rendered secure by the reconnoiterers. During the time before arriving in their enemies' country, or at least before any signs of enemies have been perceived, they run buffalo with horses, kill enough meat for present use and dry and pound more to be used when hunting is not advisable. When signs of the camp are perceived, sentinels are posted every night, who lie down around the camp within 200 or 300 yards of the main body, and 50 or 60 steps from each other. All the horses belonging to the expedition are picketed within this circle and near the place where their several owners sleep. These sentinels are changed every night.

When by means of scouts and other observations they have discovered the camp it is approached in the night and the several advantageous positions which the ground affords around it are occupied by different detachments of the party, who are to attack from various quarters as nearly as possible at the same time. About daybreak a rush is made by the mounted men, shouting the war whoop and firing into the lodges as they pass through. The attention of the horsemen is directed toward driving off every horse found in camp. These, although picketed, take fright at the noise, snap their cords and are driven away. This rush only passes through the camp, and the enemy being raised and armed turn out and pursue and a battle now takes place near the camp. Indian fighting is individual fighting, each one for himself, without any military order, line, or file. Orders are given by any of the chiefs or soldiers in a loud voice when some advantage presents itself. Both parties endeavor to cover their bodies by any objects which are in the way. A thicket is much desired, small trees, stones, bunches of grass, or hollows made by the rain are all occupied, and those who cannot find any shelter jump from side to side, never standing still a moment to avoid any certain aim for their enemy's fire.

The whole is accompanied with a terrible yelling on both sides. When one falls on either side the war whoop is sent forth by the party who killed and a simultaneous rush is made by the enemy to obtain the scalp and the friends of the fallen man to rescue the body. In these mêlées of small parties take place the terrible savage struggles for which they are remarkable. It is hand-to-hand fighting by a few on each side over the body of the fallen man.[23]   Knives, lances, and war clubs are the arms then used and frequently several fall on each side before one party recoils.   These scenes are going on over several parts of the field at the same time.   The war whoop is sounded from either side whenever any success is visible, and when any disproportionate loss takes place the flight of that party is the consequence.   This is the great aim of either party, as a massacre of the scattered fugitives then takes place.   It should be remembered that when the contending parties are nearly equal very little damage is done.

The firing is at such a distance that only a random shot takes effect, and after abusing each other and firing hundreds of shots all day, perhaps only three or four are killed.   There must be a great superiority of numbers and position on one side where there is any great destruction.   The greatest loss of life happens when some 200 to 400 warriors surprise a camp of 20 or 30 lodges, or when the war party is too large to effect concealment for stealing horses, and too small for defense.   In this case when pursued by the whole camp they are brought to a stand.   If on the prairie they take up a position on the top of some hill covered with stones with which they make a barricade or seek a gully or cluster of bushes.   Here they fight as long as one of them is living, but being surrounded by a superior force are all killed in the end.   Three years since 52 Assiniboin who were discovered in an attempt to steal horses from the Blackfeet were pursued and brought to bay in a sink hole, or gully, where they were surrounded by about 800 men of the latter nation and fired upon until all were killed.

Their enemies, however, lost 34 men before they succeeded.   A retreat is ordered in words to that effect and the movement being perceived is followed by all, which generally ends in downright flight.   A very common exhibition of individual bravery is, when the parties are equally divided, and slow skirmishing going forward, each party having good positions, a single warrior rides forth near the place where the other party is stationed, and riding slowly within reach of their fire along their front, sings his war song and calls out his name, presenting a mark for the whole of his enemies to fire at.   Either he or his horse is generally killed, or if he escapes he is considered a brave man ever afterwards.   In either case he is followed by one of the opposite side in the same manner, and in this way often three or four are killed.   They eat no root supposed to have the power of deadening pain or inspiring courage.

---

[23] Such fierce struggles over fallen heroes recall similar combats engaged in by the stalwart figures in Homer's Iliad.

The divining men are consulted as to the nature of their dreams before they set out, and on the march, but not in regard to their operations in battle.

Battles are planned as soon as they can determine the position of the enemy, which plans are changed according to circumstances afterwards, but the fighting is done at random, each loading and firing when he chooses, and using any measures of concealment of his person.

No general orders are conveyed or aids employed, although whenever a cluster of men occupy a position some soldier or chief being there gives orders to the others, individually or collectively, as the danger is apparent. The chiefs and soldiers retreating would be a signal for all to run. The leader gives advice occasionally as to dislodging the enemy, etc., but all his orders partake of the nature of requests. They rally often during a retreat if the party be large, and keep up a running fight for 10 or 15 miles.

A favorite device to decoy enemies is to send but few to make an attack on their camp and drive off the horses. The camp, following, are led to where the main body lies in ambush.

The war whoop is the signal of advance and also of encouragement during the fight. It is also a cry of joy when any of the enemy fall, and at all times a defiance, but never used in retreat or under any humiliating circumstances. They speak to and abuse each other during the fight, adding their former deeds to exasperate the enemy and induce some one of them to step forth that he may be killed.

They never quit a masked wood and take the level plain unless their party is greatly superior in numbers and no danger of pursuit is apprehended; but if they are few they remain in the wood until burnt out, which is done by setting fire to the grass on the prairie, which in a wind will communicate with the undergrowth of the woods. If this can not be done by the surrounding party the besieged party defend their position until night and then make their escape under cover of the darkness.

The Gros Ventres and Crows are the only nations who take women and children prisoners and spare their lives, though they kill all males able to bear arms.

All the wounded left on the field are tortured to death in every possible way, mostly by mutilation, are seldom burned, perhaps for the reason that death would be too soon produced by that manner of proceeding. The Assiniboin burn children prisoners.

The Crow Indians a few years since, after killing all the men and large boys of 50 lodges of the Blackfeet, took prisoners upward of 200 women and children. One of our gentlemen now in charge of that nation was with the Crow camp when the battle took place, and for two or three months afterwards, during which time he sought occasions to liberate about 50 women and send them home to their people. Most of these prisoners, it appears, are treated well, particularly the children, who are adopted into families who have lost their own. When a child is thus adopted it is painted and dressed very gaily, a horse given to it to ride, and to all appearances treated as affectionately as their own.

A grown woman, however, is not adopted. They are retained to work, or if young and handsome are kept as one of the wives of their owners, though not abused or made to bear any unusual hardships. It is singular that when these women prisoners have remained a few years with the Crow Indians they will not return to their own people, even if liberty be given them. Indeed, after the first few months they are not watched and have it in their power to leave at any time, and many do during the first year of their captivity, but after having learned to speak the language, mostly remain, which proves that nation to be much more lenient toward their women than the Blackfeet and others. The children prisoners become identified with them and never desire to leave when grown.

Every male fit to bear arms is put to death by the tribes. The Assiniboin, Blackfeet, Sioux, Cree, and Arikara also kill women and children and sing and dance as much for their scalps as for those of men. The horrid manner in which they put the small children to death exceeds description. Some are stuck through with wooden skewers, like a rabbit, while alive, and roasted before the fire.

There is but little subordination in all large war parties of Indians. There appear to be jealousies on every side between soldiers and chiefs or between the warriors and soldiers. No penalties being attached to disobedience, it has no limit, and they are often in as much danger from each other as from their enemies. Once in a century a chief arises who can lead large parties to war, but it is only when his success and capacity as a warrior is accompanied by his art as a prophet and he has gained entire ascendancy over all his people. Small parties succeed better—say from 80 to 100 men. These an ordinary chief can command tolerably well, because they are for the most part chosen from his own band and composed of his own relations. This kind of party always proves most successful, as the leader only attacks when success is certain from the numbers on each side. All Indians carry off their wounded if possible, and the dead also if not scalped, interring the latter in some secure place not likely to be discovered by their enemies.

As stated, no grown male prisoners are retained alive by any of these tribes, and only two preserve the lives of the women and children. These, of course, are obliged to work, though not exactly in the character of slaves. All the women work and these pursue the same labors, though no doubt a greater share falls upon them than upon others. No description of labor, such as carrying burdens, drying hides, cooking, or procuring fuel, etc., is considered disgraceful or menial. They all do it, even the wives of the chiefs, and the prisoners would be compelled to employ their time to the advantage of their owners; or if young and handsome would be kept as wives, yet still be made to work as the rest. They are not beaten nor brutally treated, but forfeit their lives by an attempt to run away. Female chastity is always violated on prisoners [24] if they are even tolerably young and good looking, and often in such a degree as exceeds the possibility of description or belief, but we are not aware that any superstitious opinions are connected with the act.

COSTUME OF A WARRIOR.—The ordinary costume of a mounted warrior of known bravery has already been described. The headdress, however, differs in form according to the fancy and standing of the individual. The tail feathers of the war eagle are the only mark of rank. These are attached to scarlet cloth or otter skin in many ways, sometimes merely encircling the head, at others extending in a ridge along the back, reaching below the horse's belly when mounted. The shirt and leggings are made of clean white dressed deerskin, antelope, or bighorn skin, with black stripes painted around the arms and legs and fringed with the hair of the scalps taken by him, occasionally also with ermine skins, or horsehair. The horse's head and tail are adorned with the same kind of feathers, as also his lance and shield. The latter is a piece of dried raw bull's hide, very thick, round, and about 18 inches in diameter. The feathers are sewed or tied on around near the edge, and two or three in the center. Frequently this is painted with the figure of some animal, either real or imaginary, and is impervious to arrows, though a ball will perforate within the distance of 100 yards if it be held steadily.

The manner in which it is slung on the left arm and being bowed in the middle the ball is apt to glance off to one side and often in this way his life is saved. Arrows will stick in but not go through, and he can with it cover most of the vital parts, at the same time using his arms with ease. A good many of the renowned warriors wear necklaces made of the claws of the grizzly bear, worked or tied on a strip of otter skin, and chiefs wear their medals if they have any. These fine dresses are not worn on the march, but packed on

---

[24] It appears that the violation of the chastity of female prisoners was unusual among other tribes who were highly organized socially. It was repugnant to the Iroquois.

their horses in bundles, and put on when the attack is about to be made.

The faces of most of them on starting or in battle are painted with vermilion, the entire face being a bright red, though no orders are given to this effect. Indians generally paint on all public occasions, but no other parts of the body are painted at this time.

The costume of those on foot does not differ from that of a hunter, except he has both gun and bow, if possible, sometimes adding a shield, and a bundle of moccasins on his back, which, with a blanket, or skin capot, leggings of the same and breech flap, completes the dress.

No great display of dress can be made on foot and is not often seen except among the Blackfeet, when it is the same or nearly the same as the mounted warriors. The hair of the young warriors is dressed out and adorned in many ways, sometimes enclosing small portions in front with beads, shell, or wampum, which hangs down on each side of the face. The Crows have small portions combed up in front and the whole of the rest tied in a queue behind, which is spread out and stiffened with patches of gum, spotted with white clay, and looks like turkey feathers. The elder warriors generally tie up their hair in a knot in front, which projects out from the forehead like a thick short horn. During the march not much attention is paid either to painting or ornaments, but on the eve of battle, if possible, it is done. Nothing uniform appears, however, in their costume, ornaments, or hair dressing, each one suiting his fancy in these particulars, except the acknowledged marks of warriors are not worn by untried and inexperienced recruits.

The back dress, if not a continuance of the headdress, is mostly a wolf skin thrown over his robe, the tail trailing on the ground and the snout on his shoulder. Crow-skin headdresses are also worn by young warriors, and owl feathers are worn by new beginners. No portion of their war dress is constructed so as to emit jingling sounds, though such are worn on other occasions. Every Indian has either a blanket, buffalo robe, or dressed skin of some kind covering the whole person, and these are painted with their battle scenes or garnished with beads and porcupine quills in many ways. His robe is his bed by night and his cloak in the day, under which in the winter is worn a blanket capot, made with a hood to cover the head. In the large summer war parties, portions of lodges of two to four skins each are taken along with which they make cabins to protect themselves from the rain, but in the winter no shelter is made. When parties are too small to admit of proceeding without fear of night attacks from their enemies while in their country, they make small forts every night of dry timber along some stream, or of rocks when timber is not to be had.

WEAPONS.—Firearms are certainly much valued by warriors. Indeed, they are the principal arms, but bows and arrows are used fully as much by mounted men. The difficulty appears to be the loading of the gun on horseback. If possible they carry both on their war expeditions, also some are armed with lances, war clubs, and battle axes. The last three instruments are used only in mêlées at close quarters. Indians are often so situated in battle that neither gun nor bow can be used, and in these emergencies the tools last mentioned stand them in great need. Guns are therefore only additional weapons, aiding and facilitating their mutual destruction, but have by no means been substituted altogether for the bow and arrow. The metal arrow point is superior to the flint one formerly used, and more easily procured. The arrows for battle are barbed and tied on loosely, so that an attempt to withdraw the arrow invariably leaves the iron in the wound, which makes many of their wounds dangerous that would not be so if the metal could be extracted.

The stone war club is the most efficient weapon in battle of any we know of. A drawing of one is shown in Plate 65. The weight of the stone is about 5 pounds. The handle is made of elastic sinew and can not be broken. Any attempt to ward off the blow must be attended with a broken arm, and if the stroke is not fended the strongest man must fall beneath it. Tomahawk and battle axes are not thrown at their enemies, as generally represented, but are secured to the wrist by a strong cord, and only used at close quarters; as also the lance and knife. The scalping knife is of English manufacture, a logwood or Brazil wood handle, and soft steel blade about 8 inches long and 1½ inches wide, sharp on one edge, and with the point turned like a butcher knife. These are the kinds of knives mostly used by all Indians for hunting and all purposes, though Willson's butcher, Cartouche, eye dagues, and other knives can be had. Most Indians at all times carry knives of some kind and scalps are taken off with whatever knife they happen to be in possession of at the time.

In loading the gun in battle it is first primed from the horn, then a charge of powder put in, and a few balls being held in the mouth of each man, one is dropped in wet on top of the powder, without any wad between or on top. In this way they load and fire very quickly, four or five times in a minute, but not with a very certain aim.

When scalps are taken without loss on their side the whole party on their way back paint their faces a jet black with a mixture of grease and charcoal. This is the symbol of joy, and on arrival in camp the scalp song is raised. The whole population turns out to meet them. Whichever person the warrior touches also blacks himself and commences singing. If the party has had any one killed, the relatives of the deceased smear their faces and clothes with white clay, the symbol of mourning, wear old, ragged skins on their backs, go barefooted, cut their hair, arms and legs, and cry in loud howlings.

In this event the camp presents a scene of mingled rejoicings and lamentations, which are kept up for many days and nights in succession. If the loss on the part of the warriors is greater than the gain—that is, if they have lost two or three men and taken but one scalp—no faces are blackened, no dancing is done, and the scalp song is sung throughout the camp, at the end of which all set up a howling cry.

It often happens that the party have all, except a few, been killed, and should the partisan in that case have escaped he does not return immediately to his own camp but remains in another for some time, until the grief for the dead has in a manner passed, for should he come home with the report of a general massacre of his party he would run great risk of being put to death by the relatives of the persons who fell while under his charge.

DANCING AND AMUSEMENTS

Dancing must be considered as a characteristic mode of expressing popular opinion on most, if not on all, occasions and is generally done with the view of swaying the multitude, and conforming their actions to certain measures. It is also one of their principal means of publishing and handing down to posterity the remembrance of their gallant actions, of inspiring the young with a desire for distinction, and of awarding the praise due all brave warriors. Dances are usually performed by the different kins, such as the Wolf-pups, Braves, Bulls, Foxes, Mice, Comrades, Ducks, and Crows. All these are societies, formed by different young men, some of which we have had occasion to mention in a former answer, and all have for their object combination in love or war. There is also the Soldier's Dance in which none but these officers act, and several dances in which all promiscuously take part, or in which the distinction of the different clubs named is not recognized. Of this nature are the scalp dance, dance in the diviners' lodge, and others got up for begging purposes.

Most Indians after having passed the degree of soldier and emerged into that of chief or councillor seldom perform in any dances, though they encourage it by their presence. There are but two dances in which the women join the men, which are that in the diviners' lodge and on the occasion of taking a scalp. There is also another in which women alone perform, aided by a few young men, say, five or six. The principles of all these are imbibed by the youths, from their being always publicly exhibited, and from their natural talent of imitation, but they do not join in the circle until at the age of maturity, except a few girls in the scalp dance. Each one of these performances has some motive independent of amusement, as will perhaps appear from the different descriptions of them which follow, and are to them often matters of deep interest and importance.

SCALP DANCE (WAH-KITTAI WACHE).—When a scalp is taken it is during the return stretched on a small hoop, and left in this manner; the hoop is attached to the end of a rod about 5 feet long. These are handed by the warriors on arrival to those in camp who have recently had some of their relatives killed by enemies and is an intimation that revenge for the dead having been taken, their mourning must be laid aside, their faces blackened, and they to rejoice with the others in the dance, which is always done. Moreover, this mark of politeness on the part of the warrior to those in mourning is always remunerated by a suitable present—a gun, a blanket, or some other piece of property. Often a horse is bestowed in the excitement of the moment. The dance is then called by an old man going round the camp singing the song and beating a drum, calling on all who feel disposed to join in celebrating their triumph by a dance, and each one makes the necessary preparations. (Pl. 71.)

Both men and women paint their faces entirely black, except the tip end of the nose, which is not touched, dress in the gaudiest and best style they can afford, and at a signal by the yelling and drumming of the music assemble in the area or public square with which most villages are furnished, being an open space in the center of the camp, near the soldiers' lodge. In this dance the men carry no arms of any kind. Some of them have in their hands a rattle with which they keep time, but most of the women hold in their right hand some weapon, such as a tomahawk, bow, pakamāgan, lance, or stick. The scalps also are held by the females. Being attached to the rod, they are shaken up and down to the taps of the drums. When ready they form nearly a circle. Old men with drums come first, next all the rest of the male dancers, and afterwards the women, the whole ring standing so close as to press a little against each other, and the scalp rods, and other things held in the hand, are extended out a little in front.

The scalp song is now struck up by the music, and joined in by the whole circle, the women singing only in the second part of the tune. In this song the name of the warrior who has killed the enemy is introduced, with a few words alluding to the circumstances, though without any violation of the tune or time. The part of the tune at which the women commence is when the names or words are

sung. The rest consists in a loud chant by all the ring. After
swinging to and fro a moment they all move round in a circle by
short side steps, lifting their feet together and keeping the exact
time with the drums, and after describing one or two circles by these
movements the song concludes with a general shout from the men,
the scalp is forcibly shaken, and some warrior stepping forth from
the ring recounts in a loud voice either his share in the present glory
or some of his former brave deeds. This is received with a loud
shout of approbation, the drums beat up, the song commences and
another round or two is performed.

Then some other makes a speech of a like nature, either in praise
of himself or of those who brought the scalps, and in this way it continues for several hours. Occasionally some old woman will take
the scalp in her teeth and shake it like a dog, or throw it on the
ground and trample on and abuse it as though it were a living enemy,
concluding with a short speech in praise of the warriors, and the
dance proceeds as before, the music going round with the dancers.

During the night, or rather all night, nothing but the same dancing and song is heard. They make small fires outside the lodges and
a dozen or so of young men and women, with a drum or two, sing
and dance around each fire, with or without the scalp, and without
public speaking. Sometimes 20 or 30 of such dances are going on
in different parts of the camp at the same time, all night and nearly
all day, for weeks in succession, until they grow tired of it, or some
new excitement supersedes. Their faces are blackened all this time
and the color left to wear off but never washed off.

The opportunity is not lost by the young men during these night
dances to make love, in all the various ways that passion is susceptible, and many runaway matches are concluded at these times, when
the young warriors having the advantage of the battle glory are most
likely to be successful. Portions of the scalp are also sent by runners
to the different camps, with the news of the battle. The tenor of
the song includes the names of the warriors who struck the enemy,
and if any of their names have been changed on this occasion it is
also mentioned, so that the new name by the time the dancing is concluded in the different camps is thoroughly known by all the nation.
This dance is not attended with any violent gesticulation or eccentric
motions, as has been represented, but is an orderly affair, and seri-
ously performed. Unless a scalp has been brought no singing or
dancing can take place. Even if many enemies were seen to fall, yet
the enemy must be struck, which is the coup, and the hair produced,
which is the proof.

BRAVE'S DANCE (NAPPAISHENE).—This is performed by the group
or club of Indians bearing this title, who are tolerably numerous

and composed of men from 20 to 30 years of age, whose organization has already been alluded to in these pages. No one is admitted in the ring but those who belong. The women, say 8 or 10, stand behind as many drummers and join in the chant but take no part in the dance. All sing, both dancers and musicians. The men form in a ring completely naked.[25] Their bodies are painted in various ways. Yellow and red stripes from head to foot is a favorite manner of painting, red face and yellow body, or red face and body striped with white. Sometimes the face is dotted with white, yellow, or red spots, and to their moccasins are attached skunks' or foxes' tails. Guns, spears, bows, and other implements of war are held in their hands and some have rattles with which they keep time to the taps on the drums.

The step is done by jumping off both feet and striking them forcibly on the ground, one a moment sooner than the other, always keeping the exact time. No words are used in the song, and when the round is about half finished it suddenly ceases, though the drumming and dancing is continued, accompanied by a low simultaneous grunt by all at each step. They commence the dance in the form of a ring but do not go round. Dancing for the space of a minute in the same position, they bend their bodies forward and press all to the center of the circle, turning and looking in every direction without any order, and when all are huddled very close, and that part of the song arrives where the chorus is discontinued, all except the tune on the drums, they keep it up for the space of about a minute afterwards, when a sudden and general yell by all finishes that round, and the form of the ring is resumed.

This is the principal occasion taken by those concerned to recount their former deeds of valor or coups. The whole camp being spectators, and the bravest of them present, also many in whose company the acts now about to be published had been performed, makes it indispensable that the boasts of the warriors should be confined to the limits of truth. After one round has been danced a warrior (one of the dancers) steps forth in the middle of the ring and speaks in a loud voice to this effect, using his gun or lance in gesticulation: " One or two years since, he, in company with 15 others, went upon the Blackfeet and succeeded in bringing away 40 of their enemies' horses." [here the drum is tapped once]. " On another occasion in a battle with the Crow Indians six years since he struck an enemy the first " [here follows two taps on the drum]. " At another time he struck two enemies the second, took a gun and a tomahawk from the dead enemies " [four taps on the drum].

---

[25] The prepuce of the penis is drawn forward and tied with a sinew, to the end of which floats a war eagle feather. Others not sufficiently advanced as to merit that mark of distinction tie the same with some grass.

"Also that in battle he took an enemy's horse" [one tap]. "That he fired fifteen shots" [one tap]. "Four years since, being near the Blackfeet camp with six others in quest of horses, they were discovered and pursued but succeeded in making their escape" [one tap on the drum]. "Alone and on foot he, three years since [naming the place] killed and brought to camp a full-grown grizzly bear" [one tap on the drum]. "Behold where one of the balls of the Blackfeet broke my arm" [one tap]. "Here an arrow pierced my thigh" [another sound of the drum], etc., until he has run through the catalogue of his meritorious acts, when he is honored with a general shout of approbation, the music strikes up, the song commences, and another round or two being performed, another warrior recounts his coups in the same manner. In this way they continue until all who wish have had an opportunity of renewing the remembrance of their past deeds, and reestablishing their importance as braves in the eyes of their countrymen. It takes some hours to prepare for and perform this dance and it is only done twice or thrice a year. Although the performers are naked, yet there is no idea of indecency [26] attached to this fact. They are in a manner obliged to appear in this state so that they may publicly expose and point out any wound they may have received in battle.

Wounds behind are fully as honorable as those before. Running away where success is impossible is more commended than death or defeat by remaining. The number of shots a man has fired during the fight, if over 10, counts a coup, inasmuch as it shows he has stood his ground long enough to fire that many.

Killing an enemy counts nothing unless his person is touched or struck. The first who strikes the dead foe counts the best coup, although each succeeding one counts as far as the fourth.

Scalping does not count more than striking. Taking an enemy's gun or horse or bow by any means counts a coup, likewise killing a grizzly bear alone and on foot. Scalps are very little valued by him who takes them. They are mostly cut up in small pieces and sent to the different camps. The hair seen on the warrior's leggings is sometimes really the hair of the enemies slain by him, and at others his own, or horsehair. In either case it is the symbol of having killed.

If he has struck even one enemy he is entitled to wear hair on his shirt and leggings, but it is not absolutely necessary that it should be the same hair as that which he took from his enemy's head. Any human hair or black horsehair will answer the purpose fully as well if he has a right to wear it.

[26] This viewing of the nude human figure without a feeling of a sense of indecency is confirmed by the Swiss artist, Frederick Kurz, in his Journal, already cited in the preface.

Fox Dance (To-kah-nah Wah-che).—This is done by those who belong to the band called Foxes, who are pretty numerous among several nations. It is got up with the view of publishing their feats as in the preceding one, and also to display themselves as a body. Their costume consists of a deer or antelope skin, shirt, and leggings painted a bright yellow, and their faces painted with yellow stripes, besides other forms. A dressed fox skin being slit in the middle, the head of the man is thrust through, the skin spread out on his shoulders, the head of which lies on his breast, and the tail hangs down his back, the whole skin being fringed round with colored garnishing of porcupine quills, bells, and polished buttons placed in the eyeholes of the animal in the skin.

A headdress of foxes' teeth, bored and strung, is stretched across the middle of the head from ear to ear, a lock of their hair is tied in front, which projects out several inches, and the rest, combed straight down behind, to which at about the middle is attached four war eagle feathers. Their lances are wrapped with fox skins cut in strips, and the tails of that animal sewed on the handle every 12 inches or so. Some also carry their bows and quivers of arrows at their side during the performance.

After having been warned of the meeting, and preparing in the above manner, they assemble at the sound of several drums and whistles at the spot appointed, being generally near the center of the camp. Here they form in line during the drumming and singing, which is kept up by five or six men and women who are invited for the purpose (this music) taking their stand to one side, the women as usual behind the drums, who sing, but take no part in the dance.

When ready they all start off at a swift pace and describe the movement of the coiling of a snake, and when wound up in this form, all commence jumping up and down, striking one foot immediately after the other on the ground, keeping exact time, and all singing with the music for the space of about a minute, when a general flourish on the drums and a shout or yell from the dancers concludes that round, and their places in line are resumed.

Some one of them now steps forward and counts his coups in the same manner as pointed out in the Brave Dance, which is succeeded by another movement in dancing, which is again followed by another speaking, and so on until all who wished have spoken, the drum denoting by taps the value and number of coups thus counted by each.

The whole concludes by a feast given by one or more of the most distinguished members of this club, during which their professions of amity and assistance are renewed, and presents often exchanged; the musicians also partake of the repast.

This club is composed of men from 20 to 25 or 28 years of age.

DUCK DANCE (PAKHAN'TAH WAH-CHE).—This is done by the band who bear that name and are not so numerous as the others. The same principles govern their proceedings, being to seek this occasion to publish and perpetuate the memory of their past deeds on the battle fields. The dancers are all naked, except the breech-cloth, which hangs down before and behind one or two yards. Their bodies are painted in various ways, principally striped, according to the fancy of the individuals. No arms are carried in the dance, but they hold in their hand a flat striped painted stick about 2 feet long, with which they keep the time. Women are excluded from the ring but form a portion of the music. All sing, both dancers and drummers. The evolutions are: Commencing in a ring, they mingle together for a few minutes and conclude with a general shout, after which coups are counted by those who wish, or who are able, as in the preceding. The time, step, and figure of every dance differ, but we can not describe them so as to be understood.

BULLS' DANCE (TAH-TUN-GAH WAH-CHE).—The kin called Bulls is perhaps the most numerous among them, and a good many middle-aged men and chiefs are found in this dance who do not figure in the others. Their headdress is the skin of a buffalo bull taken off as low as the shoulders of that animal, and dressed with the head, horns, hair and snout complete. Around the holes where the eyes were and in the nostrils and mouth are sewed pieces of scarlet cloth. The skin is then sewed up along the back of the neck. The head of the man is thrust in this, and the rest of his body being naked except the breechcloth and moccasins, is painted with black and red stripes. They carry guns and powder horns in the dance, moving without any order, jumping about, snorting, and shaking their horns at each other, and firing among their feet with powder. The song is the Bull Song. They usually are attended by six or eight drummers and singers, all males, who are not dressed in any remarkable manner.

No speeches are made by the Bulls during the dance, but they seek the occasion of other dances, such as the Braves or Soldiers to which most of them belong, to perpetuate the remembrance of their chivalrous deeds. This kin give a good many feasts to each other and are said to be remarkably faithful in the observance of their promises of mutual aid and protection.

SOLDIERS' DANCE (AHKITCHETAH WAH-CHE).—This body of men having already been fully described in these pages it will, of course, be understood that their dance must include the most important personages in camp. They seldom perform, and only with a view of exhibiting their force as a body; and in the presence of strangers or visitors to count their coups or when a war party is in contemplation, with the intent of stimulating the ardor of the young to follow them to battle. They must have some object to dance for, as they are not men to expend much time merely for the sake of amusement and display; besides their characters and acts are so well known as to need no repetition.

Their costume is as nearly as possible that of warriors equipped for battle. From the nose up their faces are painted a bright red, and from thence down to the neck a jet black. The dancers form the ring on foot but are attended by a guard of mounted soldiers, dressed in very gay battle array, who ride round outside the ring all the time, striking, and keeping at a respectful distance either man or beast that is found in the way. A select band of drummers and female singers is chosen and placed apart, who having struck up the song, the dance is led off by a soldier alone, who moves out by short steps toward the center of the circle, is soon joined by all the rest, jumping and keeping the time, which round concludes with a loud yell and discharge of firearms, and the one who led off the dance counts his coups on his enemies in the manner before related. This is also accompanied by taps on the drum denoting the number and value of the coups and the speech, honored with a general shout of approbation.

The warrior resumes his place, another leads off, and the same behavior is repeated until all get through, the whole ending with a feast of dog meat given by the chief of the soldiers in the Soldiers' Lodge, to which the strangers, if any in the camp, are invited. This is the most imposing and warlike dance they have, and is well calculated to inspire the young with a desire for glory. Their dresses and appointments are very gay and complete according to their rank, their gesticulation and oratory fierce and bold.

WHITE CRANE DANCE (PAI-HUN-GHE-NAH WAH-CHE).—There is no band of this name, but the dance is got up by some divining man, most probably for some begging purposes. He is the principal figure, being painted yellow and wearing a dressed elk-skin robe on which a large two-headed crane is painted. The costume of the others is whatever their fancy dictates, and, of course, they put on the gayest attire they can afford. The dancers are young men of any and all kins who choose to take part, except women, who join the chorus. The evolutions are different from any of the rest, as also the song, but can not be described so as to be understood. The only one who speaks during the performance is the divining man, and the tenor of his speeches differs according to his object in introducing the dance.

CROW DANCE (CONG-GHAI WAH-CHE).—This dance is performed by the kin called Crows. Neck and head dresses of crow skins taken off the bird entire with wings and head on are worn by all, and crow feathers adorn their lances, shields, and other war implements. For the rest, it proceeds much in the same way as the others. These are mostly young warriors.

DANCE OF THE MICE COMRADES OR PROVISION STEALERS (WOK-E-PO MAUN NOOMP-PE).—This is done by a band of young men bearing the above name. The dance is kept up all night and during it some of them take by stealth the provision bales from the rest of the camp who are asleep, on which they feast all night.

The dance is performed in a large lodge, or rather several lodges thrown into one for the purpose. The bales or other property thus obtained are kept until daylight, when the haranguer of the camp publishes that those who have lost anything will go and redeem it, and the several owners of the provision sacks present a piece of tobacco to the dancers, who deliver them their property. By visiting many lodges in the night a good deal of provisions, robes, etc., are secured, which often take the best part of the next day to distribute. The dress of this club, though gay, is not remarkable in any way except they hold in their hands the skins of stuffed mice or have the same attached to different parts of their attire. To describe the whole of their dances in detail with the different costumes would occupy too much space and perhaps not be required. We think enough has been written to present a general idea of these performances and their use with the Indians.

WHIP DANCE (ETCHAP-SIN-TAI WAH-CHE).—This dance is performed by as many warriors as choose to assemble with whips ornamented with eagle feathers and horse-skin wristbands tied to the whips. In this the number of horses they have stolen from their enemies at various times is boasted of.

DIVINING DANCE (TEE-CHAGH-HAH).—The divining dance is a complicated religious ceremony occupying a whole day and that part of it appropriated to dancing is done by men and women promiscuously, headed by some of the divining men without any distinction of kin or speeches regarding their coups. Their bodies are also scarified and pieces cut out of their shoulders.

WOMEN'S DANCE (ISH-KUN WAH-CHE).—This is a dance in which women alone perform. They are painted in many ways and very gaily dressed. The men drum and sing for them and the dancers are ranged in two parallel lines opposite, dancing forward until they meet, and then resuming their places. Besides the foregoing, there are several other dances, all of which have for their object swaying popular feeling in some way. Very little is done by Indians in any form merely for amusement, and their dances in this respect partake of the nature of the rest of their employments.

GAMES

Most of these tribes, particularly the Sioux, are fond of ball playing in parties. The principal game at ball is called *Tah-cap-see-chah*, being the same denominated shinny or bandy by the whites. It is generally got up when two different bands are camped together and a principal person in each having made a bet of a blanket or gun, they choose from their bands an equal number of young men, who are always the most active they can select, the number varying from 15 to 40 on each side. Sometimes the play is headed by the chief of each band betting, though they take no part in the game, which is usually played by men 20 to 30 years of age. Each of the players stakes something against an equivalent on the part of one on the opposite side and every bet is tied together separately, which consists of shirts, arrows, shells, feathers, blankets and almost every article of trade or their own manufacture, and as fast as the bets are taken and tied together they are laid on a pile about the center of the playground, being given in charge of three or four elderly men who are chosen as judges of the sport. After this has been concluded two posts are set up about three-quarters of a mile apart and the game consists in knocking the ball with sticks toward these posts, they being the limit for either party in different directions.

They strip naked except the breechcloth and moccasins and paint their bodies in every possible variety of manner. Each is furnished with a stick about $3\frac{1}{2}$ feet long, turned up at the lower end, and they range themselves in two lines, commencing at the middle of the ground and extending some distance on either side. The ball is cast in the air in the center of the course, struck by some one as soon as it falls, and the game begins, each party endeavoring to knock the ball to the post designated as their limit. The game is played three times and whichever party succeeds in winning two courses out of the three is judged conqueror. When the players are well chosen it is often an interesting game, and some splendid specimens of foot racing can be seen, but when one of them either intentionally or by accident hurts another by a stroke with the play stick a general shindy takes place, and the sticks are employed over each other's heads, which is followed by a rush for the stakes, and a scramble. We have seen them when this was the case arm themselves and exchange some shots, when, a few being wounded, the camps would separate and move away in different directions. Supposing, however, the game proceeds in its proper spirit and humor, each bet being tied separately, the parcels are handed out to the successful

party by the judges.   This game is not often played by large parties
of men, or if so it is very warmly contested and very apt to break
up in a disturbance.

We have seen it also played by both men and women joined, a
few men aiding two parties of women.   This was among the Sioux,
but with the other tribes it is generally played by men only.

Another mode of playing the game is by catching the ball in a
network over a small hoop a little larger than the ball attached
to the end of a stick.   They catch it in this net as it flies through
the air, and throw it from one to the other toward either goal.   The
man who catches can run with the ball toward the limit until he is
overtaken by one on the other side, when he throws it as far as he
can on its way, which is continued by the others.   The women play
hand and foot ball, also slide long sticks on the snow, or billiards
with flat stones on the ice.   We know of no other game at ball
worth mentioning being played among them.

Foot racing is often practiced by the Mandan and Crows.   The
former nation before they were so much reduced by smallpox had a
regular race course 3 miles in length, in which any and all, who
chose, could try their speed, which they did by running three times
around this space, betting very high on either side.

They still practice the amusement, but not so much as formerly.

RACING

Foot races among the Crow Indians are usually contested by two
persons at a time, a bet being taken by those concerned, and many
more by the friends and spectators on either side, consisting of
blankets, buffalo robes, or some other article of clothing.   They
mostly run about 300 yards and in starting endeavor to take every
advantage of each other, a dozen starts being often made before the
race begins.   These Indians also run horse races, betting one horse
against the other.   The same trickery and worse is displayed in
their horse races as in their foot races, and often the loser will not
pay.   The Sioux also have foot races in which any one may join,
provided he bets, which, if they have anything to stake, they are sure
to do.   The name of being a fast and long runner is highly prized
among them all; indeed, after being a warrior and hunter that of
being a good runner is next to be desired, but the principal aim in
all these amusements appears to be the winning of each other's
property.   They, of course, occupy and enable them to pass agreeably some of the long summer days, but we never see these things
introduced without the bets or prospects of gain, and from this fact,
together with the earnestness exhibited in betting, and in the contest,
we conclude it to be no more than another mode of gambling, to
which they are all so much addicted.

GAMBLING

Most of their leisure time either by night or by day among all these nations is devoted to gambling in various ways, and such is their infatuation that it is the cause of much distress and poverty in families. For this reason the name of being a desperate gambler forms a great obstacle in the way of a young man getting a wife. Many quarrels arise among them from this source, and we are well acquainted with an Indian who a few years since killed another, because after winning all he had he refused to put up his wife to be played for. Every day and night in the Soldiers' Lodge not occupied by business matters presents gambling in various ways all the time; also in many private lodges the song of hand gambling and the rattle of the bowl dice can be heard. Women are as much addicted to the practice as men, though their games are different, and, not being in possession of much property, their losses, although considerable to them, are not so distressing. The principal game played by men is that of the Bowl or Cos-soo', which is a bowl made of wood with a flat bottom, a foot or less in diameter, the rim turned up about 2 inches, and highly polished inside and out. A drawing and description of the arithmetical principles of this game is now attached in this place. (Pl. 72.) The manner of counting therein mentioned is the manner in which we learned it from the Indians, but the value of each of the articles composing the dice can be and is changed sometimes in default of some of them being lost and again by agreement among the players in order to lengthen or shorten the game or facilitate the counting. However, the best and most experienced hands play it as it is represented. It can be played between two or four, that is, either one on each side or two against two. The game has no limit, unless it is so agreed in the commencement, but this is seldom done, it being usually understood that the players continue until one party is completely ruined.

The bowl is held by the tips of the four fingers inside the rim and the thumb underneath. The dice being put in, they are thrown up a few inches by striking the bottom of the bowl on the ground, so that each counter makes several revolutions. It is altogether a game of chance and no advantage can be taken by anyone in making the throws. The counters or dice never leave the bowl but are counted as the value turns up. One person having shaken it and the amount of his throw having been ascertained a requisite number of small sticks are placed before him, each stick counting 1. In this way the game is kept, but each keeps his adversary's game, not his own; that is, he hands him a number of sticks equal to the amount of his throw, which are laid so that all can see them. Each throws in turn unless the big claw stands on end, in which case the person

is entitled to a successive throw. By much practice they are able to
count the number turned up at a glance and the principles of the
game being stated on the drawing, we will now describe how it is
carried on. It has been observed in these pages in reference to their
gambling that it is much fairer in its nature than the same as carried
on by the whites and this is worthy of attention, inasmuch as it
shows how the loser is propitiated so that the game may not result
in quarrel or bloodshed, as is often the case.

The game is mostly played by the soldiers and warriors, and each
must feel equal to the other in courage and resolution. It is often
kept up for two or three days and nights without any intermission,
except to eat, until one of the parties is ruined.

Example.—A plays against B; each puts up a knife, and they
throw alternately until 100 is counted by the dice; say A wins. B
now puts up his shirt against the two knives, which is about equal in
value; say A wins again. B then stakes his powder horn and some
arrows against the whole of A's winnings. Should B now win, the
game commences again at the beginning, as A would only have lost
a knife; but supposing A wins. B now puts up his bow and quiver
of arrows against all A has won—the stakes are never withdrawn but
let lie in front of them. Say A again wins. B then stakes his
blanket and leggings, which are about equal in value to all A has
won, or if not, it is equalized by adding or subtracting some article.
Supposing A again to be winner, he would then be in possession of
2 knives, 1 shirt, 1 blanket, 1 powder horn, 1 bow and quiver of
arrows, and 1 pair leggings, the whole of which the Indians would
value at 8 robes. B now stakes his gun against all the above of A's
winnings. Now if A again wins he only retains the gun, and the
whole of the rest of the property won by A returns to B, but he is
obliged to stake it all against his gun in possession of A, and play
again. If A wins the second time he retains the whole and B now
puts up his horse against all of A's winnings, including the gun.

A wins, he retains only the horse, and the gun and everything
else reverts again to B, he being obliged to stake them again against
the horse in A's possession. If A wins this time, he keeps the whole;
but if B wins, he only gets back the horse and gun, and all the rest
of the property goes to A. Supposing B again loses and continues
losing until all his personal property has passed into the hands of
A, then B, as a last resort, stakes his wife and lodge against all his
property in the hands of A. If A wins he only keeps the woman;
the horse, gun, and all other property returns again to B with the
understanding, however, that he stakes it all to get back his wife.
Now if B loses he is ruined; but if A loses he gives up only the
woman and the horse, continuing the play with the rest of the
articles against the horse until one or the other is broke.

At this stage of the game the excitement is very great, the spectators crowd around and intense fierceness prevails, few words are exchanged, and no remarks made by those looking on. If the loser be completely ruined and a desperate man, it is more than likely he will by quarrel endeavor to repossess himself of some of his property, but they are generally well matched in this respect, though bloody struggles are often the consequence. We have known Indians to lose everything—horses, dogs, cooking utensils, lodge, wife, even to his wearing apparel, and be obliged to beg an old skin from some one to cover himself, and seek a shelter in the lodge of one of his relations. It is, however, considered a mark of manliness to suffer no discomposure to be perceptible on account of the loss, but in most cases we imagine this is a restraint forced upon the loser by the character of his adversary.

Suicide is never committed on these occasions. His vengeance seeks some other outlet, in war expeditions, or some way to acquire property that he may again play and retrieve his losses. There are some who invariably lose and are poor all their lives. A man may with honor stop playing with the loss of his gun; he has also a second opportunity to retire on losing his horse, and when this is so understood at the commencement they do, but when a regular set-to takes place between two soldiers, it generally ends as above described.

Ordinary gambling for small articles, such as beads, vermilion, rings, knives, arrows, kettles, etc., is carried on by playing the game of hand, which consists in shuffling a pebble from one hand to the other and guessing in which hand the pebble lies. They all sit in a ring on the ground, each with whatever stake they choose to put up before them. Both men and women join in the game and a song is kept up all the time by the whole with motions of the hands of him who holds the pebble. After singing about five minutes a guess is made by one of the parties as to which hand the pebble is in, and both hands are opened. If the guess has been correct, the one holding the pebble is obliged to pay all the rest an equivalent to the stake before them; but if the hand not containing the pebble be picked upon, all the ring forfeit their stakes to him. Either one man can thus play against the whole or he has it in his power to pass the pebble to the next, he betting like the others.

This is a very common game, and a great deal of property by it daily changes hands, though seldom such large articles as guns, horses, or women.

The usual game which women play alone, that is, without the men, is called *chun-kan-dee'*, and is performed with four sticks marked on one side and blank on the other, as described in Plate 73. The women all sit in a circle around the edge of some skin spread

upon the ground, each with her stake before her.   One then gathers
up the sticks and throws them down forcibly on the end, which makes
them rebound and whirl around.   When they fall, the number of
the throw is counted as herein stated.   Each throws in turn against
all others, and if the whole of the marked sides, or all the fair sides
of the sticks are turned up, she is entitled to a successive throw.   The
game is 40, and they count by small sticks as in the preceding.   In
fine weather many of these gambling circles can be seen outside their
lodges spending the whole day at it instead of attending to their
household affairs.   Some men prohibit their wives from gambling,
but these take the advantage of their husband's absence to play.
Most of the women will gamble off everything they possess, even to
the dresses of their children, and the passion appears to be as deeply
rooted in them as in the men.   They are frequently thrashed by their
husbands for their losses and occasionally have quarrels among themselves as to the results of the game.

Another game is played by the boys and young men which consists of planting an arrow in the snow or ground and each throwing
other arrows at it until struck, and he who strikes the planted arrow
is winner of all the arrows then on the ground.

Death and Its Consequences

When a warrior dies the body is straightened and dressed in full
war dress, as for battle, the face being painted red.   It is then
wrapped up in a blanket, which is again enveloped in scarlet cloth,
or his flag, if he has one; then his bow, quiver, sword, gun, powder
horn, battle ax, war club, tomahawk, knife, and his medicine or
charm are laid alongside and the whole baled with the body in his
buffalo robe, being the one on which his coups on his enemies are
painted.   The last covering is the raw hide of a buffalo, hair inside,
which incloses all, and is strapped up tightly by strong cords passed
through holes cut around the edge of the skin, the whole presenting
the form of a large oblong bale.   All this is done by some old men,
often some of the divining men, though not those who attended him
while sick; and the persons who pay this attention to the corpse
know they will be well paid by the relatives of the deceased, as it
is the greatest honor one Indian can confer on another and is a
claim on the patronage of the relatives during their life.   Before
enshrouding the body some one of the persons who officiate cuts off
a lock of the dead man's hair, which he retains a year.   At the end
of that time the nearest relatives of the deceased buy the hair from
him at a very high price in horses, blankets, etc.   This is another
long ceremony and should be described, but our limits do not
admit of it.

When the body is thus dressed and prepared for interment it is the wish of the relatives to get it out of sight as soon as possible, or in a few hours after dissolution, but it often happens that there is no suitable place in the vicinity for burial and they are obliged to carry it along for several days. Most of these tribes prefer scaffolding the corpse on trees, which is the most ancient method of disposing of them, arising from the want of tools to excavate, particularly in the winter season, when the ground is frozen to the depth of 5 feet as solid as a rock, and for the reason that they wish the dead to be placed where they can at all times feast and speak to them. Of late years, however, they prefer their being interred by the whites at the different trading forts if possible, but as this can only happen to a few the others either scaffold them or inter them, when the weather admits, on the tops of hills, covered with large stones, which being rolled on the grave after it is filled prevent the ravages of the wolves and foxes. In either case the clothing, arms, medal, or other trinkets not bequeathed are deposited with the body, and as the sanctum of the dead is never disturbed nor these articles renewed, they must present a sure criterion whereby to judge of their state of arts and arms at the time of the interment as far as it is possible to be determined by the nature of the materials thus deposited. Supposing they are near the timber, and the man has died in the night, the funeral takes place next day, or if he has died during the day it is disposed of the following morning.

At the moment life becomes extinct the relatives set up a loud howl, cut their hair and legs, and the neighbors crowd into the lodge, each endeavoring to excel the other in the violence of their lamentations, which are kept up without intermission from that time until the funeral is over, by all, and during this interval the whole of the property of the deceased, except his war horse and arms as mentioned, is given away by the relatives to those who lament. All his horses, skins, clothing, provisions, and a good part of that of his relatives (brothers, father, etc.) must pass into the hands of strangers; even the blankets off their backs, arms, and cooking utensils are seized and carried away by those who aid in mourning. If he has made a will, which occasionally happens, it is sometimes carried into effect, but usually the nearest relatives sit around the body howling, with their heads down, and pay no attention to the general pillage which then takes place, or if they do, it is only to tell each of the mourners which of their horses or other property to take away, giving the horses to those who have aided in laying out the dead man. Their custom is to make themselves as poor as they can be made on these occasions, either in property or with regard to their persons.

The body being placed on a horse travaille crosswise, it is conveyed to the spot for scaffolding by leading the horse, the whole following without any order and uttering loud howlings, both men and women. Several men now ascend the tree and draw up the corpse with strong cords attached to it, placing the feet as near toward the south as the fork of the tree will admit, and elevating the head part of the bale so that it may face in that direction, after which it is secured by the cords being tied round the limbs of the tree many times, to prevent the wind from blowing it down.

When this is finished they recommence cutting their legs and howling, calling on the deceased by the tie of relationship which bound them, thus: " My brother " or " my son," adding, " remain in peace where you are; let your spirit go to the south and not be troubled; we will feast you; do not visit us in spirit; you are happy; and we are miserable." These words are not distinguishable on account of the noise, and most probably muttered; as, having witnessed many of these funerals in every way, we have never heard any other words than lamentations; but they say they do pronounce them either mentally or very low, and that if it is neglected some more of their relatives will die; consequently we are bound to believe they utter these and other words in an audible voice. At this stage of affairs his war horse is led under the tree and shot, in addition to which, among the Crow Indians, a finger or two of each of the near relatives are chopped off and the blood smeared over their faces, left to dry there, and remain until it wears off. The deceased's shield, lance, or other implement, too long or unwieldy to be enveloped with the body, are now tied at his head on the tree, and the mourners retire. Some of the near relatives, however, often remain all day and night, naked and barefoot, exposed to cold, snow, or rain, for several days and nights without eating until they are completely exhausted, and for a year or more afterwards wear nothing but an old torn skin, which, with their bodies and faces, is smeared over with white clay, and present a miserable appearance.

This is the most general custom among all the tribes of which we write of disposing of their dead, and nine-tenths of them are scaffolded in this way. Yet occasionally some, either by request or desire of surviving relatives, or in the event of their dying where no timber can be found, are interred on the top of a hill. In either case the mourning and ceremonies are the same. When interred, the hole or grave is excavated to the depth of about 5 feet, and made large enough to contain the implements before referred to, which are all buried with the body, the grave filled up and large rocks rolled upon it. In either way no inscription or device is made to mark the spot, nor any hieroglyphics carved on trees denoting the age, name of the person, or anything else. No consolation is offered to Indians at the time of the funeral, nor for several days afterwards. Those who wish to console must aid to mourn, but say nothing. In a few days, however, many elderly men invite the relations to feast and console them by the usual arguments the nature of the case dictates. The reason why the feet are placed southward and the face turned in that direction is that the Indian paradise is supposed to be in that quarter, and the soul is thus given to the South Wind to be carried off to that point. Very brave and formerly renowned warriors sometimes requested not to be interred in any way, in which case they are placed inside their lodge propped up, in a sitting posture, dressed and painted, the door of the lodge is closed tight, and the outside around the lodge inclosed by a hedge of thick branches and dirt to prevent the wolves from entering, and the whole is thus left on the plains.

In the course of time the lodge rots away, the wolves enter, and the bones are scattered about or carried away by them. This is the manner in which the Chief Wah-he-muzza, or The Iron Arrow Point, ordered his obsequies to be performed, giving for his reason that he wished to remain above ground in order to see and hear his children all the time and to have the spot rendered remarkable by his being there.

The death of ordinary Indians is attended with like results, though if not warriors of note they are merely enveloped in their ordinary clothing and blankets or skins with their implements, but no horse is killed over their grave. When women die their favorite dogs are killed and all their tools for scraping and dressing hides, with their pillow and porcupine quills, are enveloped with them. If she be the wife of a chief or man of importance she is also wrapped in scarlet cloth, formerly in painted skins. There is as much mourning and distress observed on the death of their children, perhaps more, than when grown. On these occasions often some one of the parents destroy themselves, and all other Indians are very attentive to them for several days until the most violent grief is over. Should anyone offend the parent during this time his death would most certainly follow, as the man, being in profound sorrow, seeks something on which to wreak his revenge, and he soon after goes to war, to kill or be killed, either of which being immaterial to him in that state.

The reason the implements are deposited in the grave is that they are supposed to be necessary to his being in the world of spirits. It is a very ancient custom, perhaps coeval with their existence.

We know of no tumulus or barrow erected either in former or later times through this country containing many bodies or possessing the character of a charnel house, but are in the knowledge of the graves of many chiefs either on scaffolds or on hills.

Bodies are never interred in a sitting posture, though that manner
is sometimes observed when deposited in the lodge above ground and
the posture preserved by stakes driven in around the body with forks
on the end supporting the different members and equilibrium.

There are no herbs or spices placed with the corpse, neither is it
submitted to any process analogous to embalming. It is enveloped,
as before mentioned, in skins to which those who can afford it add
scarlet cloth and blankets.

Scaffolding of corpses is the general manner of disposing of them
with all the prairie tribes, and the way they are prepared has been
alluded to. They would prefer having them boxed instead of baled,
but have no tools to prepare timber, and even if they had can not
at all times procure it, which together with their lack of means to
excavate in these frozen regions were no doubt the original causes
of this mode of burial. When bodies are brought to the trading
houses for interment or scaffolding they are always boxed by the
whites, the coffin being made large enough to contain the implements
and ornaments enveloped with the corpse. This in former times
was a great honor done the Indians and highly recompensed, but
of later years is a great bore and expense.

This method of securing them can, however, only be embraced
when death takes place near the houses, and consequently happens
to few. The Mandan and Gros Ventres, being stationed at the fort
with those nations, have their dead boxed by the whites and placed
on a scaffold made of posts planted near their villages. The Arikara
prefer interring them in the ground, and all the rest of the tribes
place their dead, secured in the manner described before, in the forks
of trees, which in a year or two, as soon as the cords rot off and
the envelopes fall to pieces, are blown down, and the bones are found
scattered beneath. Carnivorous birds, such as eagles, ravens, and
magpies, often pick at the envelope until they get at the body, but if
it is well strapped in rawhide it is generally secure from either birds
or beasts as long as it remains in the tree.

It is the custom of the Assiniboin to put up a funeral flag over
the graves of their dead, particularly children, which at this time
is composed of some such fabric as red flannel or calico tied to a pole,
but which was formerly made of feathers and light skins. This is a
very ancient custom, arising, we are told, from the necessity of
having some such object thus raised which, fluttering in the wind,
frightens away the beasts and birds of prey.

The custom of collecting and reinterring the bones is very general at the present day among all these tribes; indeed, it is seldom
neglected if when they visit the scaffold they find the body to have
blown down and the bones exposed.

The bones are picked by any one of the party, not related, in the presence of some of the relatives of the deceased, and this time buried in the ground, with demonstrations of grief and some scarifying, though they do not go into mourning dresses further than some white clay about the face, and no property is confiscated by others, as in the case of the first funeral, but those who aid are paid with some smaller articles. On these occasions a feast is made for the dead which, being eaten, and the spirit propitiated by prayer and invocation, the whole concludes, those concerned resuming their usual dress and occupations.

There is no such thing as charnel houses or receptacles for the dead in all the district of the upper Missouri, neither are there any appearances of such things having been, each individual being buried or scaffolded separately at the most convenient place and as soon as possible after decease.

Incineration of bones is not practiced by any of them, neither do their traditions mention this custom to have ever existed among them; they have a horror of the idea.

Their symbols of mourning have been referred to, which are cutting short their hair, scarifying their legs, cutting off their fingers (Crow Indians), wearing an old tattered robe or skin on their back, the rest of the body being naked except the breech flap of the men, or body dress of the women, bare legged, bare footed, the face, hair, body, and robe smeared with white clay, often intermixed with their blood.

When the lock of hair of the deceased has been redeemed by the relative by high pay to him who took it, which is done in a year or two after demise, this relic is inclosed in a small sack and carried on the back of some of the female relatives. A piece of tobacco is wrapped with it, which is used on several occasions, as before mentioned. There are periodical visits to the grave, twice or thrice a year for the first year, and afterwards for several years whenever they happen to be in the vicinity, and on these occasions takes place the feast to the dead, so often referred to in these pages, which is one of their principal ceremonies. A repast is made of corn or pounded meat mixed with grease and sugar, sometimes a dog is cooked by some medicine man, and a crowd of people being assembled round the grave after lamenting the dead by howling, smoke, and pray to the spirit, leave a portion of the feast for it, and the rest is eaten by those who attend the ceremony. One of their prayers at these times is recorded in a former page, together with the reason of these observances. Fires are kindled near the grave or under the scaffold, but do not appear to be of further use than to light the pipe by while smoking to the dead, and are suffered to expire at their leisure.

No gravestones or posts are planted to mark the place, or any inscriptions or devices painted or carved by any of these tribes, denoting the age of the deceased or any other thing.

As has been frequently stated, there are no large mounds perceived on the upper Missouri, the work of Indians, as have been discovered in some of the western States, but were it an object or custom to bury the dead in that manner we believe there is energy and power sufficient among any of these tribes to accomplish a work of the kind, even with the rude tools they have, in a loose soil, free of rock, and in the summer season. These mounds have most probably been national or public depositories for the dead of Indians in stationary huts; and as great superstition is attached to all funeral rites, it is not improbable they were excavated in a length of time by the united efforts of the nation. Being a work in which both women and children could join, and which could be executed with the most primitive tools, they no doubt worked at it in favorable seasons, stimulated to exertion by the directions and commands of the divining men. These marks of antiquity only prove the nation to have been numerous, stationary, and unanimous in the undertaking. The materials disinterred from these receptacles must show beyond doubt the state of arts and advancement of the tribe at the time the interment was made, supposing the articles thus exhibited to be of their own manufacture and not traded from Europeans. Bones reburied are not accompanied with a new deposit of instruments.

Those articles first enveloped with the body, if found, are reinterred with it, which, having been the property of the deceased, are valuable, but to none other. It is only when the corpses fall from scaffolds or the bones of the dead by some means have become exposed that a second burial takes place; otherwise no Indians disturb the repose of the dead.

Orphans and the Aged

The care of orphan children and the aged devolves upon the nearest relatives of their deceased parents, but neither the chiefs nor any other persons not of kin pay them the least attention, unless they are adopted into their families. The aged and infirm are supported by their sons and other relatives until they become helpless and a burden, and are then left in some encampment to perish. There are no very old people without some relatives. The fact of their being old presumes that some of their lineal descendants are living, and it is with these they reside; but should there be no kin whatever acknowledged they would only the sooner die, as neither chiefs, hunters, nor any others would take the least interest in them, much less furnish them with provisions or be troubled by packing them along in traveling. Should an aged person of this description die in camp the body would be wrapped in the skins composing its bed and stuck on a tree by some of the men, without the least symptom of mourning. The life of the aged of both sexes, even with their own children, is one of drudgery and misery, and when entirely helpless they are in a manner obliged to get rid of them in some way, as their manner of traveling and conveniences of lodging are not adapted to the infirm.

A very near and correct view of their means and disposition warrants the opinion that it is more through extreme necessity than hardness of heart that they resort to the inhuman alternative above mentioned. Age without power is never venerated even by sedentary Indians, though these can and do treat the infirm better than the roving tribes, because, being better prepared with commodious lodges and not obliged to travel, the burden of useless and aged persons is not so much felt. They are therefore tolerated for their talents in story telling and other qualifications, exciting more their laughter than their abuse or neglect. But it is always a hard fate. The others will say they have had their day, their youth, and their prime, have enjoyed much and should now die and remove the burden of their care. They all know and expect this to be their own fate if life be prolonged, and hence we find the influence of chiefs, once renowned, declining with age or debility. Their gallant acts and services are forgotten or laughed at, later incidents of the same nature replacing theirs in the memory of their friends; they are neglected, ridiculed, imposed upon, and, being helpless, submit.

It does happen with some divining men that the older and uglier they become the more they are feared for their supernatural powers, and these, as long as they can sing and drum, are well off, because they can always command property for their services and pay their way for any attention or assistance, besides their supposed supernatural powers prevent any practical jokes or petty torments from being inflicted as on ordinary aged persons.

There are but few old people of either sex. Their lives are too laborious, precarious, and exposed to secure an advanced age.[27]

LODGES

The lodges of the Sioux, Crows, Assiniboin, Cree, and Blackfeet are made of buffalo skins, hair shaved off and dressed, then sewed together in such a manner that when placed upright on poles it presents the form of an inverted funnel. The skins are dressed, cut out, and the lodge made up altogether by the women. When cut and

[27] There is some tautology in treating the foregoing subject of death and its incidents, but it could not be helped without omitting some portions of the subject.

sewed and laid on the ground it is in shape nearly three-quarters of a circle, with the two wings of skins at the small end to serve as vanes, which are changed by moving the outside poles with the wind, to prevent the lodge from smoking. The tent is stretched on poles from 12 to 20 feet in length according to the size of it, each family making one to suit the number of persons to be accommodated or their means of transporting it; therefore their sizes vary from 6 to 23 skins each, the one being the smallest, and the other the largest size in general use, the common or medium size being 12 skins, which will lodge a family of eight persons with their baggage, and also have space to entertain two or three guests. The area of a lodge of 12 skins when well pitched is a circumference of 31 feet, and the space each grown inmate requires for bed and seat would be about 3 feet in width. People seldom stand upright in a lodge. They enter in a stooping posture, and moving forward in this way to the seat opposite, sit there until they leave. (Pls. 74, 75.)

When sleeping the feet of every one is turned toward the center of the lodge, where the fire is made, the smoke escaping at the opening in the top. The material will last with some repairs about three years, not longer. They usually make new lodges every third summer and cut up their old ones for leggings and moccasins. Their lodges are always carried along when they travel with the camp, being packed on a horse in summer, or on a travaille in winter, in default of horses, and when the snow is deep they keep out wind and rain and answer all their purposes, but are cold, smoky, and confined. Families of from 2 to 10 persons, large and small, occupy tents of different dimensions, say, one of 6 skins for the former and one of 16 skins for the latter number. Lodges of 36 skins are sometimes found among the Sioux, owned by chiefs or soldiers. These when carried are taken apart in the middle in two halves and each half packed on a separate horse. When erected, the halves are again joined by wooden transverse pins, the poles are dragged on the ground, being tied together in equal-sized bundles, and slung to each side of the horses. A tent of this size will accommodate 50 to 80 people on an occasion of feast or council, as they can sit in rows three or four deep; about 30 persons, however, could sleep therein with ease, independent of the space required for baggage, provisions, and utensils. The females, young and old, aid in making them, and the eldest of them erects, removes, and arranges the locations of the interior in the manner described in a former answer.

They are never vacated and left standing, but are needed wherever they go to protect themselves and property from the weather. The skins are put up when sewed together in proper form without being smoked, as the smoke from the fire in the inside soon penetrates them and renders them impervious to rain. The men have nothing to do with the construction, erection, removal, or internal arrangement of the lodges.

The Mandan, Gros Ventres, and Arikara live in dirt cabins made by planting four posts in the ground, with joists on the top. From this square descend rafters to the ground in angular and circular shape, the interstices being filled with smaller sticks and willows; then grass is laid on, which is covered with mud, over which is thrown earth, and the whole beaten solid. An opening is left in the top for the smoke and a door in the side, which is extended into a covered passage of a few steps and will admit a man upright. These are large and roomy huts, will accommodate 30 or 40 persons each, but are generally occupied by one family, who frequently have their beds and bedsteads, corn cellar, provision room, and often a horse or two under the same roof. They are said to be damp and unhealthy.

The figures and representations of animals, etc., painted on their skin lodges are those of monsters seen by them in their dreams; also the hand is dipped in red paint mixed with grease and its impression made in many places over the tent. This denotes the master of the lodge to have struck an enemy. The same impression is also made on their naked bodies in some of their dances and has the same signification.

CANOES

Skin canoes are the only watercraft used by these tribes, and these are only to be found among the Mandan, Gros Ventres, and Arikara. They are made of the skins of one or two buffaloes with the hair on, not dressed, and stretched over a basketwork of willows. The women make, carry, and propel them with paddles, one person only paddling in front. A canoe of one buffalo skin will contain four persons and cross the Missouri, but they must sit very quiet or they will upset. The women carry these canoes on their backs along the bank to the place where they wish to cross, and on their return bring them to the village and turn them upside down to dry. A canoe of this kind is made in two or three hours and will last a year. Bark canoes are used by the Chippewa, but we are not well enough acquainted with their construction to describe them. When no skin can be found to make a boat war parties will cross any river on a raft.

MENTAL AND ETHICAL ADVANCEMENT

There is no doubt but most of these nations are disposed to advance from the barbaric type, though as yet they have made but little progress. Indeed, when we consider their mode of life, wants, and situation with regard to each other we can not imagine how they can well be anything more than what they are. Harassed by internal wars, pinched by necessities that compel them to constant exertion, discouraged by the ravages of diseases, and overwhelmed by innumerable superstitious fears, their condition is not one calculated to prepare either mind or body for the arts and habits of civilization. The whole tenor of an Indian's life, and the sum and substance of all his labors is to live, to support his family, and rear his children, and he must bring them up in such a way that they in their turn can do the same. For this all is risked, and to this end the whole of their occupations, even their amusements, tend. They would be most willing to embrace any mode of life by which this main object could be realized with less risk and toil than the one they now pursue, but they must first be convinced of the certainty of success in the strange pursuit to which their formed habits must give way before they would apply themselves.

Their present manner is certainly precarious, but they would not abandon it unless some better way to live was made manifest, not by tales and speeches but by actual experiment. Indians (men) will not work. Even the slight attempt at agricultural labor by the few nations on the upper Missouri who raise corn and other vegetables devolves solely upon the women to perform them, and the men hunt as the other tribes. Meat must be had, and as yet no relish has been formed by any of them, except the Sioux, for the flesh of domestic animals. Notwithstanding all this, we see in many things a desire to change for the better, exhibiting itself in a general feature of improvement when compared with that of 20 years since. Within that time and within our acquaintance with these people the Sioux, Assiniboin, and other nations were much more savage than they now are. At the period to which we allude it was almost impossible for even the traders, much less strangers, to travel through their country without being robbed and often killed. Horses were stolen from whites on all occasions; every person outside the fort was liable to be abused, imposed upon, flogged, or pillaged, and even their dealings with each other were no better. Murders upon slight provocation, robberies, and misdemeanors of all kinds were common among them. Even whole bands armed against each other and skirmishes took place whenever they met.

All these things now, if not obsolete, are very rare. Whites move about among most of the nations with security of life and property, and the Indians are better clothed, provided for, armed and contented than formerly. For these happy results so far we are indebted to the unmitigated exertions and good counsel of a few white traders of the old stock, some good Indian agents, the entire abolishment of the liquor trade, and lately the humane endeavors on the part of the Government by the treaty at Laramie in 1851.

MEDICINE; DRUGS

Most of them are beginning to see the superiority of drugs and treatment of the sick as exhibited to them by whites and are becoming aware that their drummings and superstitions are of no avail, but it is only a perception of truth, not as yet leading to any change in their superstitions, because no person instructs them in aught better. As it stands at present and to come to the point of this matter, we would say a disposition to emerge from barbarism is apparent among most of these tribes, though as yet no great advancement has been made. The small improvements alluded to only show the desire to exist, but their present organization, knowledge, and relative positions to each other as nations do not admit of further improvement, which must necessarily unfit them for their ordinary pursuits and successful contention with enemies.

FOOD

Their provisions, cooking utensils, manner of cooking, serving the meal and eating assimilates yearly more to that of the whites. Their conversation, desires, and willingness to listen to counsel for their benefit all convince of a disposition to advance toward civilization and exchange their present mode of life for one more certain in its resources, provided they could follow these employments secure from the depredations of neighboring tribes yet their enemies; but here is the difficulty, they are obliged to be always in readiness for war, also to make excursions on their foes to replace their stolen horses or revenge the death of their relatives.

They usually eat three times a day, morning, noon, and night, if meat is plenty, but the number of meals depends altogether on the supply of food, as has already been stated. Clay pots and other earthen vessels are still in use among the Mandan, Gros Ventres, and Arikara, being of their own manufacture, though they also have metallic cooking utensils.

The flesh of buffalo and other animals is cut in broad, thin slices and hung up inside the lodges on transverse poles over the fire, but high up in the lodge and in the way of the smoke, which soon penetrates it, and in a few days the meat is dried and fit to pack away. In the summer it is dried by spreading it in the sun, being cut up as above, which soon cures it. They employ no salt in curing any meat.

The parts of the buffalo eaten in a raw state are the liver, kidneys, gristle of the snout, eyes, brains, marrow, manyplies, or the omasum, testicles, feet of small calves in embryo, and glands of the calf envelope. Meat when cooked is either boiled or roasted, princi-

pally the former, and always rare in either way, not overdone.
They have no salt for seasoning, but are fond of a little in the
bouillon. In former times meat was boiled in the rawhide, in holes
in the ground smeared with mud, and heated stones dropped in, or
in pots made of clay and soft stone, but metallic cooking utensils,
consisting of kettles of every size and description, have entirely replaced these. Tin cups and pans, with some frying pans, wooden
bowls, and horn spoons, are yet common.

The tongues of buffalo sent to market are salted by the traders,
who secure them from the Indians during the winter in the hunting
season, and when frozen, salting them before the spring thaw comes
on. None of these tribes preserves meat in any other way than above
mentioned, some of which when dried is pounded and mixed with
berries and marrowfat. It is then called pemmican, or in Cree
pim-e-tai'-gan. Dried meat will keep but one year if free of wet,
as afterwards the fat turns rancid and the lean tasteless.

The tail of the beaver is first turned in the blaze of a fire, the outside skin scraped off, then incisions are made each side lengthwise
along the bone, and it is held in boiling water for a few minutes to extract the blood. It is then hung up in the lodge or in the
sun and left to dry.

All inquiries regarding fish are inapplicable to these Indians, as
they take none in quantity. The few catfish that are hooked by the
Gros Ventres and Arikara are boiled in water, no salt added, and a
horrid mess of bones and fish mixed together is produced, which
no one but an Indian could eat. They eat but do not relish them.

All the hunter tribes rely greatly on the spontaneous roots and
fruits found in the country and collect, dry, and pack them away,
to be used in times of scarcity of animal food. We have known hundreds of Indians to subsist for one or two months on the buds of the
wild rose boiled with the scrapings of rawhides. At all times the
different kinds of roots and berries are a great resource, are used in
their principal feasts and medicine ceremonies, are of great assistance when game is not to be found, are easily packed, and contain
considerable nourishment. The following is a catalogue of those
found among all the nations of which we treat, though there are
several others whose names in English are unknown to us, and some
of these now named peculiar to the most northern latitudes.

ROOTS, BERRIES, ETC., EATEN BY THE INDIANS OF THE UPPER MISSOURI

English name	Assiniboin name	Method of preparation
Prairie turnip (pomme blanche)	Teep-se-nah	Dried and pounded.
Service berries	We-pah-zoo-kah	Dried.
Bull berries (grains des boeufs)	Taque-sha-shah	Do.
Chokecherries	Cham-pah	Pounded with seeds and dried.
Red plums	Caun-tah	Stones extracted and dried.
Wild grapes	Chint-kah	Not preserved; eaten ripe.
Currants	Wecha-ge-nus-kah	Do.
Gooseberries	Chap-tah-ha-zah	Do.
Wild rhubarb	Chan-hn-no-ha	Tops eaten raw or boiled.
Fungus growing on trees	Chaun-no-ghai	Not dried; found in winter.
Artichokes	Pung-ghai	Eaten raw or boiled; not preserved.
Berries of the red willow	Chau-sha-sha	Eaten raw only in great need.
Antelope turnips	Ta-to-ka-na Teep-se-nah	Boiled and dried.
Wild garlic	Ta-poo-zint-kah	Raw; not preserved.
A berry called	Me-nun	Not dried; eaten ripe.
Acorns [27a]	Ou-tah-pe	Roasted and dried.
Strawberries	Wa-zshu-sta-cha	Not dried.
Inner bark of cottonwood	Wah-chin-cha-ha	Resorted to in time of actual famine.
Berries of the smoking weed	She-o-tak-kah	Not preserved; eaten ripe.
A root resembling artichoke	Ske-ske-chah	Dried, pounded, and boiled.
Buds of the wild rose	We-ze-zeet-kah	Found everywhere all winter on the stalk.
Red haw berries	Tas-paun	Not dried; eaten in fall and winter.

[27a] Found only along White Earth River.

ANIMALS EATEN BY INDIANS

Buffalo (wo-ta-cha { bull	Ta-tun-gah.		Mink	E-koo-sa.
cow	Petai.		Beaver	Chap-pah.
Antelope	Tah-to-ka-nah.		Muskrat	Sink-pai.
Elk	Opoñ.		Glutton	Me-nag-gzshe.
Deer	Tah-chah.		Lynx	Ega-mo'.
Bear	Wah-ghuñ-kseecha.		Mouse	Pees-pees-anah.
Wolf	Shuñkto-ka-chah.[28]		Ground squirrel	Tah-she-ho-tah.
Foxes { red	Shunga shanah		Water turtle	Kai-ah.
gray	To-kah-nah.		Terrapin	Pat-kah-shah.
Porcupine	Pah-hee.		Horns of elk in the velvet.	Tah-hai.
Badger	Kho-kah.		Horse	Shungatun-gah.
Skunk	Man-gah.		Mule	Sho-shonah.
Rabbit	Mushtinchanah.		Dog	Shunka.
Hare	Mushtincha ska.		Snake (not eaten except by Cree).	
Ermine	E-toonka sun.			
Otter	Petun.			

[28] Literally, the other kind of dog.

BIRDS EATEN

Crow	Ah-ah-nah.	Crane	Pai-hun.
Raven	Con-ghai.	Pelican	Mid-dai-ghah.
Magpie	Eh-hat-ta-ta-na.	Small bird of any sort.	Sit-kap-pe-nah.
Owl	He-hun.		
Duck	Pah-hon-tah.	Eagles are not eaten.	
Goose	Man-ghah.		

PARTS OF BUFFALOES NOT EATEN

Glands of the neck.	Bull's pizzle.
Sinews.	Horns, hoofs, and hair.

Every other part, inside and out, is eaten, even to the hide.

Sugar is made from the sap of the maple. Wild rice is gathered by the Cree and Chippewa on Red River and the adjacent lakes, but not by the upper Missouri tribes. In times of great scarcity old bones are collected by the nations of whom we write, pounded, and the grease extracted by boiling, and eaten together with any of the foregoing roots or berries that can be found. But these sad times always happen when the snow is deep, the ground frozen, and they can not be found. Then those who have not laid up a stock of some of these roots the previous summer are driven to the necessity of killing and eating their horses and dogs, which being exhausted and nothing more to be found they are compelled to eat human flesh.[29]

GARMENTS; DRESSES

In the materials of their clothing, as far as the cold climate will admit, articles of European manufacture have been substituted for their skins, but there being no fabric as yet introduced equal to or even approaching the durability and warmth of the buffalo skin, all hunters and travelers in the winter season must be clothed with the latter to preserve life or prevent mutilation by frost. Still in the summer season these are laid aside, being full of vermin and saturated with grease and dirt, and the Indian steps proudly around in his calico shirt, blanket, and cloth pantaloons. Their hair also, formerly tangled and matted, has been unraveled by the use of different kinds of combs, and the livestock, which found "a living and a home there," has, by these instruments, been torn from their comfortable abode, thus rendering useless their original method of disposing of these vermin, viz, extracting them with their fingers and masticating them in turn for revenge.

Most of the clothing used by these tribes is made of skins of their own procuring and dressing, the process of which has already met with attention. They have different dresses for different seasons, also various costumes for war, dancing, and other public occasions, some of which have been described. In the summer seasons, when comparatively idle, the clothing traded from the whites is preferred on account of its superior texture and color, but in their usual occupations, in winter, at war, in the chase, or any public ceremonies among themselves, very few articles of dress thus obtained are seen, if we except some blankets, undercoats, scarlet cloth, and ornaments.

---

[29] We have only witnessed one season in 21 years where they were driven to this necessity.

Their own dresses of skins fancifully arranged, adorned with feathers, beads, shells, and porcupine quills, are much more highly prized by them than any article of dress of European manufacture introduced by the traders.

We will now detail a few of the most common or everyday dresses among them, in different seasons, male and female, estimating the cost of each in buffalo robes at $3 each, their value in this country.

SUMMER AND FALL DRESS FOR MEN

No. 1

A buffalo robe, thin hair, or a dressed cowskin robe on the back	1	robe
Dressed deer or antelope skin leggings	1	robe
Cloth breech flap and moccasins	½	robe

2½ robes at $3= $7.50

No. 2

A scarlet blanket	4	robes
Beads worked in same	10	robes
Deerskin shirt and leggings fringed and garnished with beads and porcupine quills	5	robes
Breech flap of scarlet cloth and moccasin	1	robe
Necklace of bear's claws	5	robes
Moccasins and handkerchief for the head	1	robe

26 robes at $3=$78.00

No. 3

White blanket	3	robes
Calico shirt	1	robe
Neckerchief and cloth breech flap	1	robe
Cottonade pantaloons	1	robe
Muskrat cap	1	robe
Moccasins	0	robe

7 robes at $3=$21.00

No. 4

White blanket	3	robes
Blanket capot	3	robes
Skin leggings, plain antelope skin	1	robe
Breechcloth and moccasins	½	robe

7½ robes at $3=$22.50

No. 5

Scarlet or Hudson Bay blanket	4	robes
Beads worked on same	10	robes
Scarlet laced chief's coat	6	robes
Black fur hat and three cock feathers	2	robes
Silver hatband and plate	2	robes
1 pair silver arm bands	2	robes
Scarlet cloth leggings and hawk bells	1	robe
Black silk handkerchief and cloth breech flap	1	robe
Silver gorget, ear wheels and hair pipe	2	robes
Moccasins garnished with beads	½	robe

30½ robes at $3=$91.50

WINTER DRESS FOR MEN

Hunter's winter dress of the Plains

No. 7

Buffalo robe coat, hair inside_____	1 robe
Buffalo robe over it_____	1 robe
Skin cap and mittens, hair inside_____	½ robe
Blanket breech flap, robe, moccasins, belt knife, and fire apparatus_____	½ robe
Dressed cowskin leggings_____	½ robe
1 pair snowshoes_____	

3 ½ robes at $3=$10.50

No. 2

White blanket coat with hood_____	3 robes
White blanket over it_____	3 robes
Flannel or calico shirt_____	1 robe
Blanket leggings_____	1 robe
Soled rope moccasins_____	
Blanket breech flap_____	1 robe
Skin mittens, hair inside_____	

9 robes at $3=$27.00

No. 2 is the dress of a wood hunter, ordinary warrior in winter, if we take away the blanket and substitute a buffalo robe; or it is worn in traveling, and is occasionally used by hunters in the Crow and Sioux Nations, but the Cree and Assiniboin mostly wear No. 1 winter on the plains. Other ordinary dresses are only variations of the foregoing, adding some articles and withdrawing others, but none of them are used when in full dress, on public occasions, among themselves, except sometimes No. 5. All their fancy dresses for dances, war, and feasts have their peculiar marks and distinction in rank; also the robes worn by chiefs, soldiers, or warriors in stated assemblies have their battle scenes painted on them in rude drawings, though intelligible to them. When merely designed to be ornamental the drawing consists of a representation of the sun, made by a large brilliant circle painted in the middle. Sometimes a calumet is pictured, and other devices, such as guns, bows, lances, horses, etc.

The dresses of the divining men are not distinguished from those of ordinary Indians by any marks, unless they are able and wish to renew the remembrance of their former coups on their enemies by wearing a robe on which they are drawn, but being generally old they seldom make any display in dress, though wearing a cap or piece of bearskin round the head is common with them. The rest of their clothing in summer would answer to No. 1 and in winter to No. 2, abstracting the blanket capot.

WOMEN'S SUMMER DRESSES

No. 1

Dressed cowskin cotillion	1 robe
Leggings of same	½ robe
Dressed cow or elk-skin robe	1 robe
Moccasins	0 robe

2½ robes at \$3=\$7.50

No. 2

Colored blanket	4 robes
Blue or scarlet cloth dress	3 robes
Garnishing of beads on same	5 robes
Scarlet cloth leggings ornamented with beads	2 robes
White deerskin moccasins worked with beads	1 robe
Heavy bead earrings and necklaces	4 robes
Brass-wire wristbands and rings	1 robe

20 robes at \$3=\$60.00

No. 3.—CROW INDIANS

Fine white dressed elk-skin robe	1 robe
Fine white bighorn skin cotillion adorned with 300 elk teeth	25 robes
Neck collar of large brass wire	1 robe
Fine antelope skin leggings worked with porcupine quills	3 robes.
Brass wire wristbands and rings	1 robe.
California shell ear ornaments	3 robes.
Very heavy bead necklaces	3 robes.
Mocassins covered with beads	2 robes.

39 robes at \$3=\$117.00

No. 4.—SIOUX

Fine white dressed elk skin robe, painted	1 robe.
Fine white dressed antelope skin cotillion heavily ornamented with beads or shells on breast and arm	30 robes.
Leggings of same ornamented with beads	3 robes.
Bead or wire necklace	2 robes.
Garnished mocassins and brass breast plate	1 robe.
Ear bones	3 robes.

40 robes at \$3=\$120.00

No. 5.—COMMON SIOUX, ASSINIBOIN, OR CROW DRESS

White blanket	3 robes.
Blue cloth cotillion or green cloth	2 robes.
Scarlet cloth leggings	1 robe.

6 robes at \$3=\$18.00

No. 6.—Winter Dress

Buffalo robe_____	1 robe.
Dressed cowskin cotillion_____	1 robe.
Dressed cowskin leggings and shoes_____	1 robe.

3 robes at $3=$9. 00

No. 7.—Winter Dress—Crows

Buffalo robe much garnished with porcupine quills____	4 robes.
Big Horn cotillion trimmed with scarlet and orna- mented with porcupine quills_____	3 robes.
Leggings of elk skin, fringed and worked with quills__	2 robes.
Wrist, ear, and neck ornaments, say_____	3 robes.

12 robes at $3=$36. 00

There are many other dresses worn, differing in cost according to the ornaments or labor bestowed on them, and the foregoing are varied with their fancy and means; some therefore would cost high and other merely a trifle. Those of mounted warriors, for dances, soldiers, etc., are still more valuable owing to the war eagle feathers and other decorations. It is difficult to determine the cost and durability of each costume. The cost has been stated, but every Indian can dress only according to his means, which, if sufficient, will adorn his clothing with ornaments to a great extent; but if limited, he must be contented with such materials for covering as are yielded by the skins of the animals that furnish him with food; consequently every shade and variety of dress is visible among them. Some portions of these dresses are only worn on occasions, while others are retained all the time, and wear out the sooner. As an ordinary rule, Indians, both male and female, renew their clothing of European manufacture every spring, though the portions discarded are cut up for leggings, breech flaps, hunting caps, gun wadding, etc.

It may be said to last six months if worn while hunting, or a year if only used at times, in traveling and while idle, as is comparatively the case in the summer season. A complete suit of skin will last the whole year round, its actual cost being only the labor of dressing, and as time in the summer is of no value to them it may be said to cost in reality nothing if not ornamented. Blankets and cloth are not damaged by wet but do not resist the cold. Skins are impervious to cold and wind but are destroyed by being wet, hence the necessity and advantage of wearing the one in summer and the other in winter, independent of the filthy nature of skins when long worn, and of the capability of woolens to be cleansed by washing. The dress of a mounted warrior (pl. 76), as in battle or in the dance, would be as follows, the cost being estimated as before:

Mounted Warrior's Dress

Buffalo robe painted with battle scenes and garnished with porcupine quills; best; 6 robes	$18.00
Skin shirt and leggings garnished with human hair and porcupine quills, valued at 1 horse or 10 robes	30.00
War-eagle feather cap, largest kind; price, 2 horses, 10 robes each	60.00
Necklace of bear's claws wrought on otter skin, 6 robes	18.00
Feathers of the war eagle on shield, lance, and horse, 10 robes	30.00
Garnished moccasins, 1 robe	3.00
Shell ear ornaments, 4 robes	12.00
Total	171.00

Another fancy dress would cost as follows:

Scarlet blanket, 4 robes, at $3	$12.00
Beads on same, 10 robes	30.00
Skin shirt and leggings garnished with porcupine quills and trimmed with ermine, 20 robes	60.00
Bear's-claw necklace, 6 robes	18.00
Soldier's cap of magpie feathers, tipped with red and fringed with ermine, 10 robes	30.00
Brass-wire arm bands, 3 robes	9.00
Eagle feathers on lance and shield, 6 robes	18.00
Shell ear ornaments and moccasins, 4 robes	12.00
Total	189.00

Both of the above dresses are principally of their own manufacture; yet if a trader wishes to purchase them he has great difficulty in doing so, even by paying the above prices in merchandise, of which they always stand in need; indeed, they seldom can be induced to part with them on any terms unless forced to sell to supply some reverse by loss of property which has happened to their families. The reason is that they are scarce, difficult to replace, and also it is the wish of the warriors to wear them during their lives on all public occasions and to be clothed with them when they die. Two tails of the war eagle of 12 feathers each would be worth two horses if wrought into a cap, or something more than a horse without. Usually the value of the tail feathers of this bird among any of the tribes of whom we write is $2 each in merchandise in this country, or 15 feathers for a horse.

Ten ermine skins will also bring a horse among the Crow Indians, and 100 elk teeth are worth as much, there being but two teeth in each elk which are suitable, and the tail feathers of the war eagle are the only ones used. The elk are not killed in great numbers by any one hunter, so that much time and bargaining are required for an individual to collect 300, the number usually wrought on a Crow woman's dress. The eagles are scarce and difficult to catch; hence the value of these two ornaments.

THE ASSINIBOINE

196

590   TRIBES OF THE UPPER MISSOURI   [ETH. ANN. 46

The men in their homes in their own country at night divest themselves of their moccasins, leggings, and blanket capot (if any),
retaining only the breech flap, and covering themselves with their
robe or blanket; but when traveling, at war, in the chase, or encamped on the borders of their enemy's country no portions of clothing are taken off at night; even their arms and accouterments are
retained while sleeping. In the summer season the women lay aside
their leggings and moccasins when going to bed, reserving only the
petticoats, or cotillion, as it is called in this country, and covering
themselves with the robe, but in the winter, or in traveling, no part
of their clothing is taken off. Young unmarried and as yet untouched women take the precaution at night to wind around their
dress a strong cord, strapping the same tightly to their body and legs.

This is done by some of their female relatives, the cord being well
tied and wrapped around many times to prevent the consequences
of any mistakes on the part of young men as to the location of their
bed, which might happen if they entered during the night, or if they
were guests. It is considered a great credit to a young woman never
to have slept unbound as above previous to marriage. Saddles,
billets of wood, and parts of clothing taken off serve as pillows for
the men. Provision bales, wooden bowls, and baggage sacks answer
the same purpose for the women. Rawhides, saddle blankets,
apishimos,[30] skins in hair, with grass and twigs beneath form the bed,
which is seldom longer than two-thirds the sleeper, and about 3 feet
wide.

ORNAMENTS

All Indians are excessively fond of display in ornaments. Indeed,
as may have been gathered from the preceding, the value of their
dresses depends entirely upon the nature and extent of these decorations. Small round beads of all colors are used in adorning every
portion of their dress, as also agate for their ears, hair, neck, and
wrists, but these are by no means as valuable as several kinds of
shells or as their ornamenting with colored porcupine quills. A
shell, called by the traders Ioquois,[31] is sought after by them more
eagerly than anything else of the kind. They are procured on the
coast of the Pacific and find their way to our tribes across the mountains through the different nations by traffic with each other until the
Crows and Blackfeet get them from some bands of the Snake and
Flathead Indians with whom they are at peace.

These shells are about 2 inches long, pure white, about the size of a
raven's feather at the larger end, curved, tapering, and hollow, so
as to admit of being strung or worn in the ears of the women, worked
on the breast and arms of their cotillions, also adorn the frontlets

[30] This appears to be a word adopted from the Cree or Chippewa language. It means
anything to lie on, as a bed.
[31] Ioquois appears to be a loan word.

of young men, and are worth in this country $3 for every 10 shells. Frequently three or four hundred are seen on some of the young Crow or Blackfoot women's dresses. The large blue or pearl California shell was once very valuable and still is partially so. It is shaped like an oyster shell and handsomely tinted with blue, green, and golden colors in the inside. One of these used to be worth $20, but of late years, owing to the quantity being introduced by the traders, the price has depreciated to about half that amount. These shells they cut in triangular pieces and wear them as ear pendants. Silver is worn in the shape of arm and wrist bands. Hat bands, gorgets, brooches, ear wheels, finger rings, and ear bobs are mostly in use among the Sioux, the upper nations preferring shells. Other ornaments consist of elk teeth, colored porcupine quills, and feathers of the white plover dyed. Feathers of ravens, owls, hawks, and eagles, furs cut in strips and wrought in various parts of their dress, besides a great variety of trinkets and paints furnished by the traders, among which are brass rings, brass and iron wire, beads, brass hair and breast plates, brass and silver gorgets, wampum moons, hair pipe, St. Lawrence shells, spotted sea shells, hawk bells, horse and sleigh bells, cock and ostrich feathers, thimbles, gold and silver lace, etc.

PAINTS AND DYES

The principal paints sold them are Chinese vermilion, chrome yellow and verdigris. Out of all these an Indian can please himself, and either buy such as are mentioned, or use the shells, feathers, furs, etc., their own country and labor produces.

The native dyestuffs for coloring porcupine quills and feathers are as follows: For yellow, they boil the article to be colored with the moss found growing near the root of the pine or balsam fir tree. For red, they in the same way use the stalk of a root called we-sha-sha, the English name of which is unknown to us. They have also some earths and ochers, which by boiling impart a dull red, violet, and blue color, but we are unacquainted with the process and their names in any other language except the Indian. Their native dyes, however, with the exception of the yellow, are superseded by those introduced by the traders, with all but the Crow Indians, who living near and in the Rocky Mountains find several coloring herbs and mineral substances unknown to the other tribes, which produce much better colors than these mentioned. At the present day they all mostly use the clippings of different colored blankets and cloth, which by boiling with the substance to be dyed, communicates the tint of the cloth to it in some degree. Thus rose, green, pale blue, and violet colors are obtained. For black they boil the inner papers in which Chinese vermilion is enveloped.

TATTOOING

Tattooing is much practiced by all these tribes, and a great variety of figures are thus painted, sometimes in spots on the forehead, stripes on the cheeks and chin, rings on the arms and wrists; often the whole of the breast as low down as the navel, with both arms, is covered with drawings in tattoo. It is a mark of rank in the men, distinguishing the warrior when elaborately executed, and as the operation is one requiring the pay of one or two horses, it proves the person's parents to have been sufficiently rich to afford that mark of distinction imprinted on their children, whether male or female. It is usually done on females at the age of 12 to 14 years, is only exhibited on them in the form of a round spot in the middle of the forehead, stripes from the corners and middle of the mouth down to the chin, occasionally transversely over the cheek, and rings around the wrist and upper parts of the arms. On them it is merely designed as ornament. Men are tattooed entire after having struck their first enemy, but smaller marks of this kind are also only ornamental. The material employed and the modus operandi are as follows: Red willow and cedar wood are burned to charcoal, pulverized, and mixed with a little water. This is the blue coloring matter. From four to six porcupine quills or needles are tied together with sinew. These are enveloped in split feathers; wrapping with sinew, until a stiff pencil about the size of a goose quill is had, with the quills or needles projecting at the end. One of the priests or divining men is then presented with a horse and requested to operate. At the same time a feast of dried berries is prepared, and a considerable number of elderly men invited to drum and sing. When all are assembled the feast is eaten with much solemnity and invocations to the supernatural powers.

The person to be tattooed is then placed on his back, being stripped naked, and the operator being informed of the extent of the design to be represented, proceeds to mark an outline with the ink, which, if correct, is punctured with the instrument above alluded to, so as to draw blood, filling up the punctures with the coloring matter as he goes along, by dipping the needles therein and applying them. The drumming and singing is kept up all the time of the operation which, with occasional stops to smoke or eat, occupies from two to two and a half days, when the whole of the breast and both arms are to be tattooed; and the price for the operation is generally a horse for each day's work.

BADGES OF OFFICE

There are no badges of office that we are aware of. These marks belong to kinships and appear only in their dress in the different dances, apart from which nothing is seen denoting official station. Rank is known by the devices drawn on their robes; that is, to a warrior who has struck an enemy and stolen horses is accorded the privilege of wearing a robe adorned with a representation of these acts; he is also entitled to make the impression of a hand dipped in red paint on his lodge or person, to wear hair on his shirt and leggings, and two war eagle's feathers on his head. After making many coups he arrives at the degree of camp soldier [32] and is known on public occasions by the addition to the above of the war-eagle cap or bear's claw necklace, which, together with the advantage of publishing his feats in the dances and other ceremonies, establishes his standing among his people.

A still further progress, so as to rank with chiefs or councillors, is not attended with any additional display or mark of distinction; indeed, in that event their coups are seldom boasted of, that being rendered unnecessary from the fact of the whole nation's being aware of the cause of his advancement, and although chiefs and councillors generally have appropriate dresses, as already described, they never wear them unless on the most important occasions, such as a battle, council with other nations, great religious assemblies, or an approaching dissolution. It is their greatest desire when arrived at the head of the ladder of fame to receive a flag or medal from some whites in power, which are worn or displayed on all ordinary convocations and councils. In like manner a sword would be the mark of a soldier in camp, but we see no other badges of office except what have already been referred to as existing in kins, which are laid aside as soon as the ceremonies which caused this display are concluded.

BEARD

As has before been observed, these tribes have naturally little or no beard. What few hairs and down make their appearance on the face and other parts of the body are extracted by small wire tweezers of their own make. They have no method of killing or dyeing the hair; they cultivate it, and consider to cut it a great sacrifice. It is only clipped short or torn out by handfuls in excessive grief, but is never shaved, and until modern times but seldom combed.

INTELLECTUAL CAPACITY AND CHARACTER

Laying aside the advantages of education, of knowledge acquired by conversation with superior men, and the increase of ideas gained in travel by the European, and drawing a comparison between the

---

[32] This is the term explained in footnote 10, p. 436.

ignorant white and the savage, we feel bound to award preference to the latter. In all their conversation, manners, government of families, general deportment, bargaining, and ordinary occupations they exhibit a manliness, shrewdness, earnestness, and ability far superior to the mass of illiterate Europeans. Even their superstitions and religion present a connected, grand chain of thought, having for its conclusion the existence of a Supreme Power, much more satisfactory and sublime in the aggregate than the mixture of bigotry, infidelity, enthusiasm, and profanity observed in the actions and language of the lower class of Christians. An excellent opportunity offers in this country to draw a comparison between the Indians and the engagees of the Fur Company, and what can never fail to strike the mind of the observer is the superior manliness and energy of the Indian in thought, word, and action, as evinced in their patience, contempt of death and danger, reverses of fortune, in their affection for their children, government of their families, their freedom from petty vexations, and useless bursts of impotent passion.

The Indian reverences his unknown God in his way. Though the principle be fear and the object Creation, it leads to reliance and resignation when his own resources fail, whereas the whites spoken of vent their displeasure for most trifling grievances and accidents in eternal curses on the Great Disposer, the Virgin Mary, and all other holy persons and objects they deem worthy of their execration. These Indians are capable of pursuing a logical train of reasoning to a just conclusion. If the subject be one with which by experience they have become acquainted, they can argue it point by point with any person. Even the Assiniboin, who are the most ignorant of all these tribes, can pursue a satisfactory mode of conversation. Clear sightedness is more observable in matters touching their own personal or national welfare, the utility and expedience of war or peace, camp regulations, or the advantage of trade. Not many years since the Cree and Assiniboin combined against the Hudson Bay Co. at Red River for the purpose of forcing that powerful house into more reasonable prices for goods and a less distressful policy of trade or to abandon the country.

The case was as follows: It was then and still is in a measure the custom of that company to make credits to those Indians in the fall for nearly the entire amount of their winter hunts, taking advantage of their necessities in putting exorbitant prices on the supplies thus advanced, so that when an Indian came to pay he found himself with nothing left to clothe his family or meet his wants; in fact, as poor as before, and consequently obliged to contract other debts on the ensuing year, being in this way kept always poor, more especially so if by some accident his hunt should fail.

Even those who were not indebted bought supplies at such enormous rates as with difficulty to support themselves. In order, therefore, to reform these proceedings they assembled in council at various places, sent runners to all the camps in the two nations, and decided to convene at the Hudson Bay Co.'s fort and make known to them their determination, which was to hunt no more at such prices, or if they did hunt, to seek some other market for their furs on the Mississippi or Missouri. The company being aware of their proceedings and knowing the inexpedience of being forced into measures, besides dreading the effect such a large body of discontented Indians might have on the settlers and property, sent their half-breed runners to the different camps on the advance toward the fort with orders to turn them back with stories that the smallpox had appeared in the settlement. The fear of this terrible infection disbanded the expedition, the Indians traveling in haste the contrary direction, which gave the company time to alter in detail their manner of dealing with them, apparently of their own accord. Things of this kind prove the Indians to be capable of looking into their own interests, also of acting in a body when they are concerned, in cases where rank is not interfered with nor subordination required, while gain is the object and public opinion unanimous.

On subjects in which their actual experience and observation are at fault, even if supported with good arguments, they are suspicious and incredulous. They listen, doubt, but say little. On all such topics their minds receive a bias from their superstitions and lack of appreciation of motive. They can not conceive of any efforts made through motives of charity, benevolence, or pity, nor realize any other disinterested action, even if it be for their benefit, because all they do is in expectation of reward, and being destitute of the above principles of actions are disposed to attribute interested views to everyone else. In reviewing such subjects with them, and supporting the moral principle by argument, they are silenced, though not convinced; they do not grasp it, but will not contradict, for the thing may be so. Hence their thoughtfulness and apparent apathy, also their uninterrupted deliberations in councils and conversation, all arising from a desire to hear the subject in all its bearings, either with the view of forming an opinion or of the propriety of expressing it.

Regarding their temperament, it is peculiar and general. We see none of those great differences ·in disposition observed among the European races.

There appears to be a uniformity of individual feeling and action among them. Being all the same on like occasions, it would seem a national and natural feature, calling forth corresponding feelings

and actions with circumstances as they arise, exhibited in overwhelm-
ing demonstrations of grief or joy, in seriousness in business, ceremonies, and worship, excessive gayety in their amusements and
lighter conversation, with earnestness in matters of personal interest.   They have strong powers of memory and forecast, are of a reflective habit, their physical propensities predominating over the
moral, in their general conduct grave, can be and are very gay on
occasions, but upon the whole are rather of a cold than a fervid
temperament.   We are unable to say whether their reasoning powers
are brought out or strengthened by education, never having witnessed
its application to any of these tribes, but see no reason why they
should not be as capable of improvement in these respects as any
other race of people.   Their ideas are by no means groveling, nor
is their form of government to be derided.   Neither can we conscien-
tiously assign to them a lower place in the scale of creation; perhaps not so low as any other race of uneducated sentient beings.

We are not well enough acquainted with the capacity and history
of the oriental stock to say whether these assimilate in any great
degree; most likely the inference can be drawn from what has been
written in these pages.

We may state that as yet no person has appeared among them noted
for his natural or acquired powers as a real physician, though many
have risen to eminence in this department from their supposed supernatural powers in curing the sick.   Neither does their history produce
any person who has evinced ability as a linguist,[33] moralist, or in the
cultivation of any of the exact or moral sciences.

They use no studied maxims of expression in conversation, nor are
there observed any compositions partaking of the nature of laments,
unless the speeches made to departed spirits and the universal monot-
onous mourning chant [34] would be construed in that light.   Their
ordinary talk is pretty much the same as that of other men, though
perhaps the Indians use fewer words in conversation, selecting only
those which have a direct reference to the subject.   They do not
evince a quickness in repartee, even in their jokes, and all conversation, except the obscene, is carried on more deliberately and concisely
than among other races.   The effect of their oratory is a great deal
enhanced by the position, bearing, and gesticulation of the speaker,
yet it is not without its merits; simplicity, clearness, and strength of
language are its distinguishing traits.   We have heard and understood some hundreds of speeches on every subject of interest among
the Sioux, Assiniboin, and Cree Nations, and must confess we can not

---

[33] Denig seems to refer here to grammatic analyses rather than to the mere learning of languages.

[34] The song for the dead contains a few words suitable to the occasion.

discern the figures and tropes attributed to their oratory by fiction writers. Metaphor is sometimes used, but not often. Their eloquence lies in the few words, bold assertions, and pointed questions with which they clothe their ideas, added to fierce expression of countenance and earnestness of gesticulation.

Everything they say in a speech has a tendency to gain their object if they have any, and Indians seldom speak otherwise. No set forms are followed, their thoughts finding utterance as they arise, or rather according to their feelings, and consequently make an impression on their auditors. The principal aims of the Indian speeches we have heard were to gain something or to impress the mass with the spirit of emulation, a desire for war or peace, and for the better regulation of their national affairs. One or two addresses of this kind have already been inserted and now follow two more, both heard and interpreted by myself and copied from our records. We fear in reading them a woeful disappointment on the part of novel writers and romantic authors of Indian tales, but such as they are they exhibit true samples of Indian eloquence at the present day, however much it may differ from that in the time of the celebrated Logan and others. In interpreting these speeches, the exact and entire ideas of the Indians are preserved, though the words chosen to express them are not always the same. We have had occasion to remark on this head before that no Indian language admits of being translated word for word; to do so, the purport desired by the Indian would fail, injustice be done to his ideas as realized by him, and a futility of words presented so devoid of order as to make no impression on the person for whom they are intended.

Nevertheless it is not to be inferred that the ideas have been improved upon. They are entire, and only so because clothed in the only kind of words sufficient to convey the real extent of their signification.

The occasion which produced the following speech by the Crazy Bear was this: In the summer of 1837 the Assiniboin, with other nations, were invited to attend the treaty at Laramie. It was with great difficulty any of them could be persuaded to go, as the road along the Yellowstone was beset with Blackfeet war parties; but this man with three others went in company with A. Culbertson, Esq., who was authorized to conduct them. The Crazy Bear was, while at the treaty, made chief of the Assiniboin Nation by Col. D. D. Mitchell, the United States commissioner, and on his return to his people repeated to the nation the stipulations of the treaty, together with the "talk" held at the rendezvous, but, as usual with Indians, was not believed. It also happened that in the ensuing spring, by some delay, the merchandise intended for the Indians and promised them at the treaty did not arrive in the West in time to be forwarded, so that summer passed and the Missouri froze over without any appearance of presents forthcoming. The Indians became dissatisfied, thought they had been trifled with, abused Crazy Bear and me for deceiving them, raised war parties, and bid fair to break the treaty and become more troublesome to whites than ever.

Amidst all this clamor and disturbance the chief stood firm and, being supported in office by the fort, all hostile demonstrations were for the time averted. At this juncture, in January, 1853, Mr. Culbertson arrived from St. Louis with orders from the superintendent to supply the amount due the Indians as per treaty from the merchandise of the fur company in this country. The nation therefore being called together and placed in order in the interior of the fort, the goods as per invoice laid in front of them, the Crazy Bear rose and said:

" My children and friends: The clouds that have hitherto obscured the sky are brushed away and a fine day appears before you. The time has arrived when all the turbulent and discontented must be convinced that the whites have but one tongue; that our great father, the President, is rich and powerful. But a few days since most of you were violent in your reproaches against myself and the whites. If you have any more abuse left, heap it on now, disburden your hearts at once of all complaint, make the pile of your abuse as large as the pile of goods before you. The whites have kept their word and your heads should hang in shame.

" When you were invited to the treaty you were afraid to go, some to leave their wives, others their children, others to cross the warpath of the Blackfeet. I went. I appeared among nations in your name and am the cause of the present smiling pile of goods being laid before you.

" When I returned from the treaty after an absence of three moons and repeated to you the words of our Great Father, what was my reception? How was I listened to? When, by some accident the goods promised did not arrive, how did you act? What now do you think of yourselves?

" I hold in my hands the words of our Great Father. They are scored on my heart, were poured into my ears, did not run out, and now is the most fitting time to repeat what I have so often told you without being believed. Your Great Father does not want your lands; he seeks your welfare. You are a few poor miserable beings; he is rich, his people are numerous as the leaves of the cottonwood. He desires to stop the bloody wars heretofore existing between Indian tribes, to make all one people, to enable all to hunt and visit together in peace and friendship. He wishes you to refrain from all depredations on whites, respect your chief as a chief, and listen to his words. For this he sends you these presents which will be repeated every year for 15 years, unless by your misconduct you incur his displeasure. I have heard the words; they are true. I have seen his soldiers and know he has the power to punish those who have no ears.

"A great deal of what you do and say is foolishness, the work and talk of children, not of men. Last fall in despite, you raised war parties, made threats against myself and the whites, gave me trouble. You now see the rashness of your proceedings. Who gives you these goods?

"Do you pay for them? Have you traded them? Do you intend to recompense your Great Father in any way? If so, listen to his words. It has been said I have sold you to the whites—bartered for your lands. I now tell you it is no such thing. There are no stipulations made for your lands in these papers. They were not even mentioned in the treaty. They are too cold for any persons except Indians, or any animals other than those with heavy hair.

"The Blackfeet are yet your enemies, but are to be spoken to by our Great Father; therefore let us refrain from war upon them to advance the views of our Great Father. Since the treaty I have had a son and a son-in-law killed by these people, and all my horses stolen twice. I can count seven times damage they have done me and my nation, but still I am disposed to remain quiet so that our Great Father may be pleased. All of you do the same. The day is coming when the Blackfeet will have ears given them.

"There are many poor people in this assembly that will be greatly benefited by this distribution of goods. Indians are born poor; they are always poor. Whatever they get for nothing is a great help and they should be thankful.

"I now appoint you six men, soldiers, for the equal distribution of these goods. Let all have a fair share. Your duty as soldiers does not end here. In the camp when you hear of war parties being assembled, stop them.

"If any one breaks the treaty stipulations with regard to the whites or other nations I desire you to punish them. If you are not able to do so you are no soldiers, and such disturbers shall be taken down by the whites in irons.

"The President of the United States has thought fit to appoint me your chief. Here is my medal; there are my papers. This makes some of you jealous. You should have thought of it before and plucked up courage enough to be seen at the treaty, that he could have chosen a better man than I, if there be one. As it is, as long as I can stand and my voice holds good I shall never agree to what is wrong nor be deterred from doing what is right.[35] I have spoken."

It is the custom of most of the upper Missouri tribes when at the fort for trading purposes for the principal men to make what are called presents; that is, a portion of the buffalo robes are brought into the office and with much ceremony laid at the feet of the gentleman in charge of the fort, which action is followed by a speech. To a spectator only viewing the act as a gift, and only understanding the literal meaning of their speeches on the occasion, they would appear to be the most liberal people in the world, as often 100 to 150 buffalo robes are laid down and carried out to the store without any merchandise being produced in payment at the time, besides each Indian distinctly states many times in his speech that it is absolutely for nothing he makes the present.

But unfortunately for this generous appearance it has quite the contrary signification. The trader during the course of this harangue receives hints enough as to the compensation for the present and the Indian fully expects both the honor done to the trader and the skins given to be paid for; in fact, requiring in return nearly double the amount in value had the skins been handed, as is usual by the mass of the Indians, to the clerk of the store without any ceremony. It is at these times that the principal men make the speeches, such as the one which follows, which, though not distinguished for beauty of allegory or force of argument, may serve to show their shrewdness and cunning, also their reliance on flattery to gain their ends. It was necessary to premise this much so that the speech could be understood in all its bearings.

SPEECH OF LE CHEF DU TONNERRE TO THE GENTLEMAN IN CHARGE OF
FORT UNION, JANUARY, 1850

"My friend, my Father, look at me. You see standing before you one of the poorest of his nation, but one who has a good heart and open hand. Our Great Grandfather, the Earth, is the parent of us all—Indians and whites. When Wakoñda created man he made two sorts; one clothed, comfortable, rich, plenty to eat, and endowed with wisdom; these were the white men. The other he produced naked, in a cold climate, poor, ignorant, obliged to hunt for their meat. to labor, to starve, to suffer, to die; these were the red men.

"Who receives the profits of their labor? The whites. Who protects them from their enemies? Themselves. When your Great Grandfather across the sea sent you to reside with Indians, what did he say? Did he pour no good words into your ears? Did he not

---

[35] Literally "my road shall be in a straight line with my talk and not frightened to one side."

tell you, you will behold a poor, naked, starved nation, have pity on them? I believe he did, he was a chief, a man of sense, a rich man, and no doubt said, 'Give away a portion of your good things to the Indian, let him feel something soft on his back. He is not an animal, his body is not covered with hair like the buffalo, but he is a man like yourself and requires clothing to protect himself from the cold. Are you not aware Indians freeze to death?'[36]

"When this big fort was built, when the first whites opened the road up the Missouri, they found us with bone knives, stone axes, clay pots, stone arrow points, bone awls, and nothing but the bow and arrow to kill game; they had pity on us, and exchanged for our skins iron arms and utensils.[37] In this they did well; they bettered the Indian; they made themselves rich. They had sense. They also gave us good words, and I have recollected them; they have been handed down to us when children, and all good Indians remember. I was told if you meet a white man give him your hand, take him to your lodge, give him to eat, let him have lodging, show him the road. I have done so.

"If you meet him while on the warpath, do not steal his horse or rob him of his property. If others steal his horses, bring them back; if any of the fort property is damaged, pay for it. I have done so. I was told to hunt, make robes, trade the skins for blankets, arms, and ammunition. All this I have continued to do from my youth to the present time. My part has been fulfilled. Yet you see me before you still a poor man. I stand nearly alone in the village, like an aged tree whose tops are dead. The bones of my friends and relatives are piled around the fort or scattered over the plains. All the good, all the wise, all the handsome, all the brave were rubbed out by the smallpox. Young men are growing, but they are not like those of the old stock.

"The road to the fort gates has been swept free of grass by the feet of my people in coming to trade. Each year we have loaded your boats with the skins of our animals, and I now bring a few more. The 10 robes laid before you are a present, for which I desire nothing. I wish to make your heart glad and to have my name remembered on the large books.[38] I know very well you are a chief and will have pity on me. Let me feel something soft over my shoulders.[39] Bestow some glittering mark on my back,[40] cover my

---

[36] Four Indians had at this time been frozen to death near his camp in a snowstorm.
[37] When the trade of the Missouri was opened the Assiniboin were the poorest of all nations, and have remained so to this day.
[38] It is customary to keep a list of men who behave well and make large trades.
[39] A blanket is wanted.
[40] Hint for a chief's coat.

bare head [41] and let something gay [42] appear there, that my young men may know that I am respected at the fort.

"My leggings [43] are worn out and the cold enters, and my breech flap no more covers what is beneath. My body [44] and neck [44] are laid bare in hunting skins in this cold weather. I lack some mark [45] of my standing with the fort to make my young men listen to my words to be good to the whites and hunt. If you wish many robes, recollect the young men are hunters and can not kill buffalo without ammunition.[46] The women have hard work dressing skins; their arms are sore; some beads and vermilion [47] would give them strength; and the tobacco [48] you will no doubt furnish me will be smoked by all my people in talking over matters for the good of the fort and in the councils for hunting. I know you are a chief and good father to your red children and will never refuse them what they ask. Remember our hardships, dangers, and exposures in hunting for you. Open your heart and lengthen your measure and reduce,[49] if ever so little, on the prices of trade. Indians suffer for everything; even the tobacco chewed and spit out by the whites is picked up and smoked by them. Your store is large; let your heart be so also. Let me be able to sing your praise;[50] your name is in the clouds; your father was a chief; you will be greater than he. Listen to the words of your poor friend. I have spoken."

The Sioux make better speeches and use more figures than the Assiniboin, but none of the many we have heard among both and other nations are as replete with metaphor as is represented by fiction writers. Either the Indians treated of by them were of a superior order or the speeches have been liberally interpreted. The foregoing presents their style as it now exists among all the upper Missouri tribes, though subjects of more importance, such as war, peace, or religious rites, are accompanied by a proportionate earnestness of oratory and boldness of gesture. They do not pride themselves on making fine or flowery speeches, but bold, pointed, and sensible ones, and, if begging be the object, will descend to the grossest flattering of their auditor, and vainness of their own merits.

---

[41] Hat desired.

[42] Feathers desired.

[43] Leggings wanted.

[44] Shirt and neck handkerchief desired.

[45] Medal or gorget.

[46] Hint for general present of ammunition to the party.

[47] Some to each woman.

[48] An intimation that tobacco is not only wanted but plenty of it.

[49] This is an invariable request, and would be so no difference how long the prices were.

[50] Whoever makes a liberal present to Indians has his name sung around the camp or fort in a song of thanks.

PICTURE WRITING

Picture writing can not be said to be much practiced by any of these tribes, though it is to some extent by all, principally by the Crow and Sioux Indians. The former of these nations are incessant in the war expeditions against the Blackfeet, and in the absence of the warriors the camp from which they departed moves in quest of game, but pursue a direction made known to the warriors before they leave. It often happens that the trail made by the camp is effaced by rain or covered with snow before their return, also that they (the camp) are obliged to diverge from the route agreed upon, and in these cases leave intelligence in pictorial devices in some of their encampments as guides to the returning absentees, who, if they find them, can not fail to reach their friends by following the instructions

FIGURE 35.—Picture writing. Key: "We are a camp of 13 lodges (1); encamped on a creek above the forks (2); started hunting with eight horsemen (3) and two women on foot (4); slept two nights out (5); found buffalo beyond the second creek from the camp (6); killed some, and made travails (7); and slept but one night on our return home (8)

pointed out by these means. (Fig. 35.) Another occasion where it is useful is where a war party, after having made an attack, whether successful or not, have reason to believe more of their own people are out for like purposes, wish to convey to them the intelligence that their enemies are on the alert, and prevent if possible their falling into their hands, as would happen if they attempted to steal the horses before the late excitement caused by their own appearance had subsided. The information, together with the success or failure of their own expedition and any other matters they wish their friends to know, are pictured in some place likely to be found by those for whom it is intended.

There is, however, this danger in these records, that if they are stumbled upon by their enemies in their war excursions they are as certain a guide to them as to their own people, and this is one of the reasons why it is so seldom done. But the Crow Indians, who rove through the spurs of the Rocky Mountains, frequently making long and rapid marches, are compelled to leave such marks behind, or some of their warriors would ramble about for months searching for their homes, which would be extremely inconvenient should they be driving before them a herd of their enemies' horses. The information conveyed by this system of writing is complete as far as it is intended, which is only to represent leading and general facts, and is not nor could it be applied to minute details. All warriors read and understand the devices of their enemies and most of them practice it when necessary, but the direction to war pursued by the Cree and Assiniboin in the summer, being over plains, there are no places noted as their usual encampments, and timber is seldom found; they therefore practice this manner of writing less than the others, owing to the probable uncertainty of their being found by their friends. In the winter, however, it is occasionally done by them when their way lies along some river, and their encampments are found by the small forts in which they have slept every night being left standing.

The same species of intelligence is sometimes left in hunting grounds with the view of announcing to any of their own nation who are supposed to pass the same way that the game, as denoted by the carcasses round, has been killed by friends, not war parties of enemies, intimating to them the direction and situation of their camp, that meat may be had there, that a juncture of forces is desirable, etc. The number and kind of game taken are not painted as the heads of the animals around would show that, but it, too, could be explained if wished.

These devices are generally drawn on some dry tree without the bark, the characters being cut in the wood and filled up with vermilion mixed with grease to prevent it being washed off by rain. Pieces of bark and portions of skins are used, and in default of either soft stone will answer. Powder dissolved in water is used to mark on the skin, the impression being made with a pointed stick, inked and pressed forcibly on the skin.

The meaning of every mark is fixed and exact, understood by the mass of warriors of all tribes, not confined to or practiced by the priests unless their situation in traveling be the same as the warriors or hunters and they desire in like manner to convey some information to the nation. The foregoing purposes in different forms are the only ones to which we have had the opportunity of witnessing the application of these devices. Perhaps they are the only cases as yet necessary for their present operations, but there would be no difficulty in their picturing the passage of whites or other nations through their country should it be required, and the same be intelligible to them.

Another form, and the one in which this manner of writing appears to be of more importance among them, is the devices drawn on the robes, exhibiting their standing as warriors whenever they appear. The height of distinction in an Indian, and his greatest ambition, is to impress upon his own people or strangers the idea of his being brave, of his having done acts that entitle him to appear among men, of his superiority in this respect over others in the crowd; therefore the actions which lead to these impressions are pictured on his robe; his biography is carried on his back so that "he who runs may read." It insures him respect through life, an honorable shroud at his death, and is believed to merit reward in futurity. A further use these devices are made to serve is the representation of monsters said to be seen by them in dreams, and supposed to have the effect when painted on their lodges of averting strokes of lightning, disease, etc.

In like manner buffalo heads are pictured to bring those animals in the direction of the camp, besides a great variety of smaller devices are seen on their shields, drums, medicine sacks, and envelopes of their amulets, to all of which appropriate and general meanings are attached corresponding with their superstitious belief or to insure success in domestic affairs. In conversation with most elderly Indians regarding locations, travels, or to explain battles and other events, resort is had by them to drawing maps on the ground, on bark with charcoal, or on paper if they can get it, to illustrate more clearly the affair in question. In this way the chief of the Crow Nation three years since made and left with us a map (pl. 77) of his intended travels during the entire fall and winter succeeding, embracing a circumference of 1,500 miles, with the different encampments to be made by that nation in that time, and so correct was the drawing that we had no difficulty in finding their camp the following winter in deep snow, one month's travel from this place. It is regretted that those Indians are not now in this neighborhood, as in that case some specimens of their charts and devices could be inserted, but in default of better we present in this place some Assiniboin drawings, with their explanations, which will serve to give a general idea how they are managed, and other pictorial devices are attached in several parts of this work.

These are the only forms the pictorial art of the Indians takes. It is more largely applied to the designs represented on their robes and mythological subjects when appearing on their lodges, fetish envelopes, etc., as has been stated. Songs can not be recorded in this or any other form. The value it may be to a people who are without letters is mostly apparent in the instances where it denotes the rank and standing of individuals when painted on their robes. The in-

formation intended only for their friends when cut on trees is liable
to be interpreted to their disadvantage by enemies, which would
consequently be a bar to its general practice. None of their drawings are executed with neatness, but occasionally have some pretensions to proportion. It appears to be the meaning only that is
desired, for paintings done by whites correctly are not more appreciated as work of art, perhaps not so much, as their own rude representations, but are looked upon with more superstitious dread.

The explanation of the drawing (pl. 78) would be as follows:
" We were a party of 20 men (1) and stole 39 horses (2) from the
Blackfeet " (see the 29 horse tracks so marked going away from the
camp). " The camp turned out, killed one of us " (see the picture
of a hand pointing toward their enemy's camp (3) and a scalped
man drawn) " and recaptured from us 14 horses (4) " (see the 14
tracks going back to camp, each track always standing for a horse).
" We forted and fought with them " (see (1) representing a brush
fort and the men therein; the guns pointing toward the fort (5)
are those of their enemies and the others signify the firing kept up
by themselves).

" In the battle three of us were wounded and six horses killed "
(see 6 representing a wounded man, and six horses stationary, seven;
that is, going neither way, proving them to be unable to travel).
" We got off with 19 horses " (8) (this being the tracks of horses leaving the fort) ; " the first night we encamped on the plains near a
spring " (9) (the dotted line shows the path, and 9 is intended to represent a small fort or sleeping place, with another dotted line to the
left where the spring (10) is marked). " In the encampment we left
a wounded man (6) ; we made two more encampments after that, when
we now leave this painting and intend pursuing our course home to
the right. A band of buffalo (11) was seen on the opposite side of
the river on a creek while the battle was going on, which are all we
have yet seen." (These marks mean buffalo tracks.)

The end of the dotted line is as far as they have then gone, and
other marks show the road they intend to pursue, but if they expect to
get home without sleeping the dotted line is made as far as the lodges.

Explanation of Plate 79.—" We are a party of 10 men (1), have
stolen 21 horses (2) from the Blackfeet and taken a scalp (3), but
lost one of our own party. The first night we forted on a creek (4),
the second night we slept on the prairie in a small fort at the foot
of some timbered hills (5), the third night we slept at a lake (6),
the fourth at a spring (7) where we are now. We intend to make
three more encampments to get to our lodges, which are on the head
of the next river (8). These figures (9) represent the lodges of their
enemies, and the horses' tracks going from the lodges, indicating

them to have been stolen, each single mark (10) counting a horse. The guns, bows, and lances show the party to be 10 (1). The hand pointing the direction in which they are traveling and toward a scalp (11) intimates that they have killed an enemy. The hand pointing the other way with the scalp (12) explains they have lost one of their party. The dotted line is their path home along a river and only extends as far as they have traveled to the place where the painting was left. The number of days they expect yet to travel to reach home are indicated by these characters (8, 10), the one a brush fort, signifies the number of encampments, and the horse track with it means it is the road they intend to travel."

MYTH TELLING

As has been several times mentioned in these pages, one of the principal ways of passing time at night in an Indian camp is the recital of fables for their amusement. Most old men and women can recount these stories, but there are some particularly famed for their talents in this respect, and these are compensated for their trouble by feasting, smoking, and small presents. At night, when all work is over, a kettle is put on containing some choice meat, tobacco mixed with weed prepared, the lodge put in order, the family collected, and the story-teller invited, who often prolongs his narrations the greater part of the night. Some of the tales are of a frightful kind, and to their impression on young minds is no doubt mainly to be attributed the fear of ghost monsters and other imaginary supernatural powers exhibited by most Indians when grown.

We have taken some pains to call together a few of the most famed and sensible story-tellers and listened with much patience to a great many of their allegories, but find nothing in any of them bearing on their ideas of a future state.[51] The circumstances and actors portrayed do not reveal the actual notions of the tribe on their religion as it now exists but are founded on their ancient mythology and handed down complete in their details through successive generations, and their real signficance, if they ever had any further than amusement, is now lost or absorbed in their manner of worship as referred to in these pages.

Nevertheless, we can discern in them a probability of their being the real belief of their ancestors in their primitive ignorance, before their superstitions and religions had assumed a systematic form and tangible shape. This much may be inferred by the tacit acknowledgment of their truth apparent in the auditors and the unwilling-

---

[51] This inference on the part of Denig indicates that he was not cognizant of the facts, poetically expressed, conveyed by native Indian myths, and so he reached the false conclusion that all myths are no more nor less than simple fictions, when, in fact, except in their verbal dress, they are true. He failed to interpret rightly the metaphorical diction.

ness evinced by all to hear them ridiculed or contradicted. We think the truth of the matter is these tales were believed and formed a portion if not the greater part of the religion of their ancestors, are reverenced for their antiquity and originality, together with a lingering uncertainty as to their having actually transpired in times long passed. This may be deduced from the evident veneration with which some of them are regarded, and from the fact that there are no new fables made at the present day, nor any one who possesses or professes the character of a myth maker. These stories are not added to or diminished, for if in the telling the least circumstance be omitted the narrator is reminded of the error and corrects it. In none of them is the creation of animals or other objects, animate or inanimate, reasonably attempted, though such things are alluded to in many absurd forms and grotesque imaginings according with the general tenor of the tale. These, though often trifling in their details, present a connected chain of events and often contain a kind of moral, that is, a double meaning as observed in the one relating to the formation of the Ursa Major and Polar Star, before inserted.

None of these serve to demonstrate to the young the power and ubiquity of Wakoñda.[52] This awful principle is too much feared to be lightly introduced in common conversation or connected with amusing tales, though inferior demons and minor supernatural powers with a great variety of figures of the imagination, such as monsters, ghosts, giants, beasts with reasoning powers, transformation, and works of necromancy, are represented.

There does not appear to be much useful instruction conveyed by any of these oral tales, but they are resorted to as a source of amusement. Stories related by us to them from books, such as the fables of Æsop or those from the "Arabian Nights," are listened to with great attention and sought after as eagerly as their own fiction. Moreover, they can, when these fables are plainly narrated, not only comprehend the literal meaning but appreciate the moral when it is pointed, not in its moral sense but as a necessary conclusion arising from the circumstances related. The only objection to recording many of these tales is their interminable length, one frequently occupying two or three hours in its recital. So remarkably long are they that the auditors are apt to become sleepy, and the narrator, if not responded to occasionally to convince him of their attention, breaks off and abruptly takes his leave. We now subjoin some of these stories that may serve to show the scope of imagination involved and that others may form their own opinions regarding their interest and utility.

---

[52] This statement is highly questionable, since these Indians show a deep reverence for Wakoñda, the highest God of their pantheon, as may be learned from various passages in Denig's own report.

FABLES

RELATED BY "THE EAR RINGS OF DOG'S TEETH," AN OLD ASSINIBOIN

A long time ago there lived a great chief of a powerful nation, but he was a fearful and desperate man. He had killed six of his wives at different times in fits of passion, and at the time of our story had separated from his people, being jealous of his wife, and placed his lodge alone on the bank of a small stream. His family consisted of his wife, a boy say 12 years old, and a girl about 10 years, both his children by the woman now with him. The man went out hunting, and the game being far off did not return for several days. In the meantime the woman continued her domestic duties at home. Being in the timber in quest of wood, she struck her ax on a hollow tree and a great many snakes came forth, one of which [53] was large and handsome, had a fascinating eye and horns upon his head, spoke sweet words to the woman, and in the end succeeded in seducing her. Her husband returned and inquired of her " What had become of the paint on her face, which he put there before starting? She made some hesitating answer and he suspected all was not right and determined to watch. In the course of a few days he gave out that he was again going hunting and might be absent some time, as he had not yet seen game. He as usual painted his wife's face and departed. In place of going to hunt he hid in the bushes to watch his wife, who made her visits to the snake's nest, striking on the tree and calling on the horned snake in terms of endearment to come forth. The snake came out, and the husband witnessed the infidelity of his wife.

He remained a day or two near the place, and each day observed his wife to repair to the snake's den for like purposes. He then returned home. She was absent, but returned in a short time. " My wife," said he, " I have killed a deer some distance off; go and get the meat." After having received instructions as to where the meat was to be found, the woman departed with her dogs to bring it. In the meantime her husband went into the bushes, struck with his battle ax on the snake's house, saying, "My husband, come forth," imitating the voice of his wife. The reptile sallied out with all his family and the Indian destroyed them all with his battle ax. Gathering up the snakes, he carried them home and cooked them by boiling them to a jelly. His wife returned without finding any meat (as indeed there was none), and found her husband sitting down sharpening a huge flint ax. He invited her to sit down, and observing that she must be hungry after such a long travel, poured into a bowl the mess of snakes, which he handed to his wife, who, thinking it was some

---

[53] The Fire Dragon or Mateor—Son of the gods.

other kind of meat, ate the whole. After she had feasted, the man said, " You have eaten your beloved husband, the snake, and now you shall follow him." He rose up and cut her head off at one stroke of his sharp ax. A storm arose, the wind blew, the thunder rolled, and the man disappeared in a whirlwind of dust and was caught up in the air. The children, much frightened at all this, ran out of the lodge over the prairie, never ceasing their speed until they were at some distance.

On stopping to rest themselves they looked back and beheld the Head of their mother rolling after them, calling on them to stop.[54]

This frightened them more and they continued their flight. The Head rolling after them was now very near and the children were very tired. The boy threw his knife behind him and immediately the prairie was bristling with knives, through which the Head on endeavoring to pass was cut in a dreadful manner, and stopped in its course. The children continued their way. A fox came to where the Head lay, and the Head said, " My friend, I am in want of a husband, will you marry me?" " You are too ugly," replied the fox and disappeared into his hole. The Head followed the fox, who being afraid of it, when he arrived at the end of the burrow commenced digging farther in great haste, the Head still following and calling on the fox to stop. But the animal dug very fast, and finding he could not escape from the Head in this way came out to the surface of the earth near where the children were. The Head also came out and, perceiving them, rolled after them, coaxing them to stop, but they ran forward until they arrived at the top of a hill. The little girl said, " My brother, I am tired, throw something else behind you, the Head is close upon us." He threw his awl and up rose innumerable awls on the prairie which, pointing toward the Head, formed a barrier which it could not pass. The children continued their flight. A badger appeared alongside of the Head. The Head said to it, " My fine fellow, I wish to marry you. Will you be my husband?" " Your face is too ugly and bloody for me," said the badger, and disappeared in his hole.

The Head followed the badger, who like the fox continued digging underneath the ground, making a road underneath the awls in the direction the children were going, so that the Head came out again to where they were seated resting themselves. On seeing it they again ran forward, the Head after them calling on them to stop, but they were afraid. Again did the little girl get tired and ask her brother to save them by throwing something behind him. He threw his tinder or spunk, and immediately the prairie took fire, spreading out behind them, burning the Head to a cinder, leaving

---

[54] The Whirlwind that took up her husband.

nothing but the bones. The children traveled on. A wolf this time came near the Head and, as with the fox and badger, was desired by the Head to become her husband. "You are nothing but a frightful ghost," exclaimed the wolf, and ran into his hole. The Head followed, the wolf dug, and in the end the Head again came out near the children. They ran forward and arrived at the bank of a large river. Two cranes were standing on the bank. The boy requested the cranes to carry them over. One of the cranes asked the boy, "How does my breath smell?" "Very sweet," said he, "as though you had eaten service berries." "Good," replied the crane, "now both of you get on my back." They being seated, the bird flew across and landed them in safety on the opposite shore. In the interim the Head came to where the other crane was standing and commanded it to bear it over immediately, as it was in a great hurry to overtake the children. The bird proposed the same question. "How does my breath smell?" "It smells of stinking fish," replied the Head. "Good," said the crane, "now get on my back."

The Head having placed itself, the bird flew, and when about the middle of the stream shook the Head off its back in the water, which on falling cried out, "Now, I go to dwell among the fishes!"

The children perceiving they were freed from their tormentor continued their route more at leisure, and after traveling some days they arrived at a large camp very hungry and very tired. It was the camp of their father, and he was there as its chief. When he saw his children he abused them for having a bad mother, would not let any person give them food nor take them into their lodge. He brought cords, bound the children's hands, and taking them outside the camp raised them into a tree, tied them both together and to the top limb of a large tree. He then ordered the whole camp to move off and thus left his children to perish. After all had gone he again looked that his children were secure and examined the camp to see that no one remained behind, but perceived nothing but a little old dog lying on an extinguished fire, with his head in a large shell for a pillow, apparently sick. "Why do you remain behind the camp?" inquired the man. "Because I am sick and can not travel," answered the dog. The man was enraged, told the dog to begone, kicked it, but he only howled and would not raise his feet. The chief after beating the old dog so that he thought him dead left and followed his people. As soon as he departed and was out of sight the dog rose and sought the tree where the children were, commenced gnawing at the root of it, and in four days and nights it fell to the ground.

He then gnawed off their cords, which occupied two nights more, and the children found themselves free but so very weak they could not travel. The little old dog rambled through the ground where the camp had been placed, discovered a piece of rotten wood afire, and brought it to where the children were. He gathered other branches and made them a comfortable fire, at which they warmed themselves. The little boy covered his eyes with his hands and hung his head, his sister cried, they were very hungry and very miserable. "Look, my brother, what a fine herd of elk is near!" the girl exclaimed as about 50 of those animals came walking toward them. The boy looked at them, wishing they were dead so that they might have meat, and as soon as he looked upon them they all fell dead. They went to them, and, having no knife wherewith to skin them, the boy wished them skinned, and in a moment they were so. He now began to see the power granted him, which was to look upon and wish for anything he desired. By the same means he produced the elk skins dressed and made into a large lodge, far larger than any of his people, which was erected, and the meat of the elk piled around the lodge on scaffolds outside. In the interior was an apartment for the little old dog. They were now happy.

Day after day large herds of buffalo came near the lodge, and on looking at them the boy killed them, skinned them, and placed the meat on scaffolds, cut up and dried.

When he thought he had enough he made a feast to the magpies and desired one of them to take along some fat meat and fly in the direction of the camp to endeavor, if possible, to overtake them. The bird left and after flying some days arrived at the camp. They were all starving, having had no meat for a long time. Some of the men were playing ball in the middle of the camp. The magpie advanced and dropped a large depouille among them and all scrambled to get a share. They inquired of the bird where he got the meat, and received the information, together with the news, that a great deal of meat was on scaffolds, enough to feed the whole camp. The father of the children was the chief; he called a council and determined on going back to the large supply of food, but knew it belonged to his children from the description given of them by the magpie. In due time the camp arrived at the boy's lodge and placed their tents. The boy sat in his lodge, his head down, and his eyes covered with his hands. All the camp with his father at their head came around begging him for meat. But the boy answered not a word, neither did he look up. The rest had no power to take the meat, not even to approach the scaffolds. The second day after their arrival his sister said, "Do, my brother, come out and look what a fine camp of our people are here." He went, looked, and all fell dead in their lodges, or wherever they happened to be. At this the little old dog began to cry and besought the boy to revive his (the dog's) relations, who fell with the others. "Show me them," said the boy. "They shall live."

He went with the dog through the camp, who pointed out his sisters and brothers, all lying dead. The boy revived them by looking upon them.[55] After a short time the little girl said, "My brother, it is a great pity so many fine men and women should die. Look upon them and let them live again." The boy did as desired and the whole camp was again called to life and motion.

He then made a feast, called all of them together, distributed the meat, and told them of the conduct of their father toward them. The boy was made chief of the camp, the little old dog was transformed into a man and became the first soldier, and the father was degraded to be a scullion and bearer of burdens for the whole.

BY A WOMAN

An old woman lived in a lodge alone except her children, and raised corn in a garden. One of her little boys was shooting birds with arrows in the garden, when on a sudden appeared a sack full of rice, which, dancing up and down before the boy, sung out, "My nephew, shoot me and eat me, my nephew, shoot me and eat me." (This part is sung by the narrator.) The boy shot an arrow into the sack and all the rice spilled on the ground. Here the story ends with a general laugh.

BY TAH-TUN-GAH-HOO-HOO-SA-CHAH, OR "THE BULL'S DRY BONES," AN OLD AND FAMED PRIEST OF THE ASSINIBOIN

The whole surface of the earth was at a time covered with water; in fact, no land existed but at the bottom of this great ocean. Seven persons were on a raft, viz, five men and two women. These were the first Gros Ventres, besides whom the only living objects visible were a Frog, a Muskrat, a Crow, and a Spider. The men, wishing for land and being informed in a dream how to act, told the Muskrat to dive to the bottom of the water and try to bring up a portion of earth. The being plunged, remained a long time under, but appeared without any. He was ordered to try again, and dived still farther, remaining under a much longer time, but reappeared with nothing. Again and again he plunged and at last disappeared for such a length of time that all thought he was drowned, but he rose to the surface, stretching out his claws to those on the raft, saying, "I have brought it," and immediately expired from exhaustion. They drew in the being and scraped from between his claws a small portion of earth which they made into a flat cake, set it on the water, and behold it spread rapidly in every direction.

---

[55] In Chippewa and cognate Algonquian dialects the Life God, Nanabozho (i. e., Inabi'ozio'), was created, mythic tradition explains, by a look of the Great Father Spirit in the heavens, gazing down through the Sun as His shield. Such is the literal meaning of this illuminating designation.

They then called the Crow, gave it directions to fly as far as the earth extended. The bird departed but did not return, from which they concluded it to be so extensive that the Crow could not come back.

Being in possession of land, and seeing all was damp and cold and barren, they wished for spring to make something grow, and inquired of the frog how many moons remained until spring would come. The Frog said, " Seven," but the Spider contradicted it, called him a liar, on which a quarrel ensued, and the Spider beat the Frog to death with a stick. The latter, on dying, stretched out his legs toward the men, indicating seven by the claws thereon. The eldest of the party and head of the whole, whom they called their father, not being certain whether the Frog told the truth, started two of the others (brothers), both very brave and venturesome, with orders to travel in quest of spring. They set out eastward and in six months arrived at warm weather, where they found spring bundled up and placed on a scaffold, the packages consisting of flowers, seeds, turnips, roots, etc. Two large Cranes were standing beneath the scaffold, which the brothers loaded with the " spring season " and ordered them to fly back to their people. The birds started, and in another month arrived with their cargo safe, thus verifying the predictions of the Frog, which so enraged the men against the Spider that they put him to death, and he is to this day despised and crushed by all, while the frogs every spring sing forth the praises of their truthful ancestor.

The travelers, having accomplished their mission, bent their course westward to explore the new country, and after a long time came to the Rocky Mountains.

In one of the valleys between the mountains they perceived a motion in the earth at a certain spot as though it was boiling or as though some animal was endeavoring to get out. One of the brothers proposed shooting an arrow into it, but the other objected and requested him to let it alone. The former was, however, a very obstinate, reckless man who never would listen to good advice, and shot an arrow into the spot. A whirlwind gushed out, and rose up in the air in a round black column, bearing the two men up along with it. Higher and higher they rose until so far above the earth that they could not see it. The wind now carried them eastward for several days, when at length they descended to earth on the other side of the sea. Here they rambled about some time and found an old woman working in a cornfield from whom they begged something to eat. She gave them a mess of corn and potatoes. After having eaten they inquired of her if she could inform them how they could get back to their family. She said she could, but they must implicitly follow her directions or some harm would befall them. After they

had made the required promises she took them to the seashore, made
a sacrifice of some corn to the water and invoked the appearance
of the Wau-wau-kah. Immediately afar off appeared an object moving over the surface of the water, spouting it out high in the air,
and, approaching with great rapidity, soon arrived at the place
where the travelers stood. The being thus conjured up had the head
of a man, though of monstrous size, and out of which projected two
horns as large as the largest trees.

The body was that of a beast covered with long black hair, the tail
was like that of a very large fish and covered with scales, and it was
endowed with a spirit. To this monster the woman gave directions
and made two seats in its horns like large birds' nests, one in either
antler, in each of which she placed a man, in one a sack of corn
and in the other a sack of potatoes. Spreading out her hands and
invoking the sun, the monster at her desire departed with its cargo
and in a great many days arrived at the opposite shore in safety.
The old woman had instructed the travelers that immediately on
landing they should sacrifice to the waters, by throwing in a little
corn. One of them did so, but the obstinate brother would not.
Being reproached by the monster for not following the advice of the
woman he shot an arrow into it and was immediately swallowed up
by the beast. The remaining brother was in great distress at this,
and, recollecting the conduct of the old woman, made a sacrifice
of some corn. Stretching out his hands he invoked the Sun to his
aid. Immediately a dark round spot appeared in the west which
came forward with terrible velocity and a whistling sound, increasing in size and speed as it approached. This was a thunder
stone, which, with an awful report and bright flash, struck the
monster on the back, separated it in two, and the man was liberated.
A terrible storm arose, the sea rolled, and the monster disappeared.

They now bent their course westward and after many days came to
a lodge inhabited by an old man and his family, from whom they
begged something to eat. He showed them immense herds of buffalo,
apparently tame, and all black except two, which were milk white.
He told them to kill whichever they wished, but not to destroy more
than they wanted for food or clothing. The good brother killed a
fat cow, which, being more than they wanted, he took the rest of the
meat to the old man's lodge. The other remained behind and shot
arrows into a great many buffalo uselessly, for which the old man
reproached him. After having feasted they were about departing
when the old man showed them a great number of ducks and geese.
" These," said he, " with the buffalo, are our life; treat them well."
On the old man's leaving the Indian who had no ears commenced
killing the birds with a club and made great havoc. The old man

returned and said, " You have done wrong, you are a bad man, evil
will befall you, the Wau-wau-kah shall bar your road home to your
people. But your brother is a good man, has ears, and for his sake
some of my buffalo will follow him home to his people, and the white
cowskin shall be his fetish to remember me by." They separated;
the travelers pursued their journey and encamped on the prairie at
the foot of what they supposed was a mountain, but which was the
Wau-wau-kah lying across their road. In the morning they advanced
to go around it, but, turn whichever way they would, the monster
turned with them and obstructed their way, so that the whole day
was spent in useless efforts to get forward.

The good brother proposed sacrificing some corn to appease it,
but the other became very angry and would not listen to any peaceful
measures. He collected immense piles of buffalo dung all around
the monster and set it on fire, by which the Wau-wau-kah was
roasted alive. The smell of the roast being savory he cut out a
slice and ate it, offering some to his brother, who, however, would
not taste thereof. In the morning they continued their way, the
buffalo following at a distance. At rising the ensuing morning the
one who had eaten the flesh of the monster said, " Look, my brother,
what handsome fine black hair is growing from my body." The
other looked and beheld the hair of the beast. On the next morning he said, "Look at my head, my brother, horns are coming out
upon it," and so it was. On the third morning he said, " Look at
my legs, my brother, fish scales are growing there." Each and every
morning when they arose the Indian was assuming more and more
the shape and apearance of the Wau-wau-kah. In the course of a
few days his body was completely covered with hair, his head was
furnished with horns of a monstrous size, and his legs were growing
together in the form of a fish. They traveled on, the body and
entire shape of the Indian rapidly increasing in size and appearance
to that of the monster whose flesh he had eaten. They now proceeded slowly, owing to the difficulty the one experienced in walking
by the change he was undergoing, and this impediment increasing
in proportion as his extremities gradually assumed the form of a fish.

In the course of time they arrived at the mouth of the Yellowstone and encamped for the last time together. The change was
now nearly completed, and when they arose in the morning behold
a complete Wau-wau-kah was presented, who said to the other,
" Depart, I am no more your brother; I am no more a man; I am
either your friend or your enemy, according to the way you treat
me. Leave. You will find your people several days' travel down
on the banks of the Missouri. Take them the corn. Yonder stand
the buffalo you have brought; they will follow you home. You will

become a powerful nation. Each and every year they must sacrifice
some corn to me by throwing it into the Missouri, or the wind shall
blow, the rain fall, the water rise and destroy your crops. As for
me, I shall be separated here; my head will go up into the clouds
and govern the wind, my tail fall into the water and become a
monstrous fish to disturb it. My body will rove through the Rocky
Mountains; my bones may be found, but my spirit will never die.
Depart, you have ears and a good heart."

At the close of this speech the winds blew, the thunder rolled, the
lightning flashed, and a terrible storm arose, amidst which the monster disappeared. The other returned to his people, told them the
story of his travels, and to this day corn is sacrificed to the Missouri
by the Gros Ventres to appease the spirit of the Wau-wau-kah.

Songs; Music [56]

The construction of the Indian flute and music produced by it have
already been described, although we are not able to state in what
manner, if any, it resembles the Arcadian pipe.

Most ceremonies, dances, public domonstrations of joy or grief,
and other matters of general interest are accompanied by songs, which
have appropriate names, but these chants are for the most part only
tunes or modulations of voices in concert, with the introduction of a
few words in some of them. They are in fact a continued chorus
consisting chiefly in repeating the meaningless syllables " Hai-yah,
hai-yah, hai-ai-ai-yah-ah-ah, hai-yah, he-e-e-ah, hai-yah," etc., fast or
slow as required by the nature of the song. Where words are introduced they are composed of five or six syllables or three or four
words, bearing some relation to the event which is honored with the
song, but are of no consequence, so that all question regarding their
rhyme or poetical compositions may be passed over in silence. The
tune is generally begun by one person pitching it, who after singing
a few notes, is joined by the whole choir, or sometimes, as in the
scalp song, the women add their voices in the second part of the tune,
where the name of the warrior who killed the enemy is mentioned.
The modulations are bold and wild, by no means discordant or disagreeable, and they are remarkable for keeping very exact time
either with the voice, drums, or feet, and where words are added they
are so few, and the syllables so separated to accord as scarcely to be
understood or distinguished from the rest of the chant.

The songs are measured, accents occur at fixed and regular intervals, being mostly the same in beats as the Scotch reel time. The
effect intended is produced by action, energy of voice and motion,

---

[56] For the recording and interpretation of Siouan music see Miss Frances Densmore,
Bull. 61, Bur. Amer. Ethn.

costume, and the wild intonations of the tune, not from words repeated. These songs are suitable to the occasion, and the whole when well got up has a decidedly unique appearance, singularly correspondent in all its component parts. These chants are very difficult for us to learn and scarcely less so to describe, but are preferred by them to any music, vocal or instrumental, of white performers yet presented to them. The length of a tune is about equal to eight bars of our common time, and the syllables to each beat vary from four to eight, but in some of the medical songs the intonation is so rapid as scarcely to admit of being counted. Songs for dancing, medicine (that is, the practice of healing), and on other assemblies are generally accompanied with drums, bells, rattles, flutes, and whistles, of all of which the drum is the principal instrument, for though on some occasions all of them and several of each kind are used, yet there are none in which the drum is not used, but several where the rest are dispensed with.

Independent of public songs, singing is a very common amusement for the young men at nights, principally to attract the attention of the females, and often intended as signals for secret assignations.

Subjoined is a list of most of their songs, in reading over which it will be observed that there are none denominated "Hunting songs," that employment not being celebrated in song in any way, either for success or failure, unless the incantative song by the Master of the Park to bring the buffalo toward it would be construed in that light. The uses of the others can be traced in their names, taken in connection with what has already been written concerning their ceremonies. The words " do-wan " attached to all means " a song."

SONGS OF THE SIOUX, CROW, AND ASSINIBOIN NATIONS

Indian name	Interpretation	Occasion, etc.
Wah-kit-tai' do-wan	Scalp song	More than ten different kinds.
Chan-du'-pah do-wan	Incantation Pipe song	Two or three varieties.
Tah-tun'-gah do-wan	Bull song	In the Bull dance; also used in the park.
Te-chagh'-ah do-wan	Incantation Lodge song	Religious.
Cong-ghai' do-wan	Crow song	In Crow dance and before starting to war.
Pai-hun-ghe-nah do-wan	White Crane song	Incantation—in the song of that name.
Nap-pai'-she-ne do-wan	Song of the Braves	In the dance of "Ceux qui sauve pas."
Ah-kitchetah do-wan	Soldiers' song	Used at the soldiers' dance.
To-kah-nah do-wan	Foxes' song	In the dance of that band.
Ah-do-wah	Diviner's song for the sick	About 20 different kinds.
At-to-do-wah	Tattooing song	Sung while performing that operation.
Opah-ghai do-wan	Gathering of the kins	Called also the thunder song (incantation).
Och-pi-e-cha-ghah do-wan	Buffalo Park song	Incantation.
Shunga-tunga do-wan	Horse song	In the whip dance.
Shunk to-ka-chah do-wan	Wolf song	Sung on starting to war.
To-shan do-wan	Drinking songs	More than ten varieties.
We do-wan	Sun song	Religious.

SONGS OF THE SIOUX, CROW, AND ASSINIBOIN NATIONS—Continued

Indian name	Interpretation	Occasion, etc.
We-chah-nauge do-wan	Song to the dead	Lament.
Hoonk-o'-hon do-wan	Song of thanks	Several.
Wah-ghunh'-ksecha do-wan	Bear song	Medicine.
We-coo-ah	Love song	About 10 varieties.
Nap-pai-e-choo do-wan	Hand gambling song	
Hampah-ah-he-yah	Moccasin gambling song	
We-hhnoh'-hhnoh	Incantation song and feast	
Tsh-kun do-wan	Women's dance song	Where women only perform.
Opon do-wan	Elk song	Medicine for elk, religious.

Their drums are of two kinds. The most common is made like a tambourine without its bells, the skin forming the head being stretched over the hoop while wet and kept there by sinews being passed through it and the hoop a few inches apart. (Pl. 80, fig. 1.) The inside portions of the skin have cords made of sinew extending across from several places, meeting in the middle and forming a handle to hold it up by (2). It is held up in one hand and beaten with a stick by the other, no more beats being made than are necessary to correspond with the accents of the notes, thus preserving the time.

The other kind of drum is made of a piece of hollow dry tree about 2½ feet long, scraped to a shell and smooth inside and out, resembling in shape a staff churn (3). The head or skin is stretched on the smaller end with a hoop, which is retained in its place by sinews passed through. The other is left open. When beaten but one stick is used, the drum being set on end. Both are often painted with different devices. The rattles, wag-ga-mó (Sioux) or Chi-chi-quoin (Cree), were originally and in a measure still are gourds dried with the seeds in, or after being dried the seeds, etc., are taken out and pebbles put in (4). Others are made of the rawhide of elk stretched over a slight frame of woodwork while wet and dried in that shape, pebbles being put therein at holes left in the top or in the handle (5 and 6). No. 7 is the rattle used by the " braves " in their dance. It is made of rawhide like the rest, but in the form of an open ring.

No. 8 is the rattle made out of deer and antelope hoofs scraped thin and light, reduced in size, and a number of each attached to small strings, so closely that they clash together when shaken. The flute (9) is made of wood, and the whistle (10) is the wing bone of a swan. These have before been described. From what has preceded it will be understood that there are no verses in their songs evincing their patriotism, or other chants representing their triumphs; that all is chorus and tune. Their laments for the dead are of the same description, adding a few words and calling upon the departed by stating the degree of relationship, the few mournful words to deplore their loss, and the rest of the chant is in meaningless ejaculations.

Their music is never recorded nor have they such things as music boards or bark songs. In their bacchanalian songs they often repeat catches of whatever comes into their minds at the time, adapting the words to the song, but these words or any particular expressions do not properly belong to the songs, which, in their original are of the same description as the others.

Many lullabies are sung to children by their mothers, but as usual but few words introduced, consisting mostly of humming of different tunes to put them to sleep, adding sometimes, " Sleep, sleep, my pretty child," or " Red fox come here; you will get a marrow bone to eat "— this when they are 2 or 3 years old.

There is nothing in their painting or sculpture worthy of notice. All are rude drawings and carvings scarcely intelligible without explanation.

PRESENT CONDITION AND FUTURE PROSPECTS

The nations we write of are as yet in their savage state. But few steps have been taken by them in the path of knowledge. Their original manners and customs, if not entire, are but slightly changed, their superstitions the same as their ancestors, and their minds deplorably void of moral truth or useful science. Their idol worship remains undisturbed by religious teachers, and the humane efforts in this respect, extended to China and the South Seas, are withheld from the coppered brethren residing next door.

There are some points not to be overlooked, inasmuch as they have a general bearing upon the whole race, involving a subject of great interest to which the foregoing details form but the prelude. The principal of those to which we allude is this: " How far has knowledge, art, and commerce, and the progress of civilization, affected the improvement of the Indians, and changed or modified their original manners, customs, and opinions? "

As art and knowledge are yet in their infancy among them and as has been stated but little improvement in their moral condition is visible, yet great and important changes have been brought about by the commerce of trade, without which any plan for their future advancement would be retarded a century, and by correct appreciation of which views can be formed regarding contemplated measures for their prosperity.

In the foregoing pages, which present their savage life in detail, nothing speculative has been ventured upon, no conjectures hazarded,
us or by anyone well acquainted with the wild tribes, nor will any

new opinions be perceived. The whole is merely a collection of facts, thrown together in the form of answers to certain questions without further comment than necessary for their illustration and clothed in the simplest garb of verbiage to facilitate their comprehension.

When we entered the fur trade in the spring of 1833, now 21 years since, all the Indians herein treated of, from the Sioux to the Blackfeet, inclusive, were much more ignorant in everything, degrading in their habits, slovenly in appearance, and barbarous in their actions than they now are. Life was then held by a slight tenure, crime was frequent, atrocious disorder and family feuds were general, and their occupations confined to slaughtering their enemies, murdering each other, and providing for their families only in extremes of necessity.

The traders of the Columbia Fur Co. and after them those of the American Fur Co. were men of ability, honesty, and truth. In the course of their dealings, intermarriages, and conversations with the Indians, the minds of the latter were enlarged, a different train of thought and action engendered, new desires created which gave a stimulus to industry, which raised the Indian from the level of the brute to the standing of an intellectual being.

The enmities formerly existing between different bands of the same nations, arising from the petty jealousies of chiefs or private family animosities, were soldered up by the traders. To be sure their object in this was personal gain, but that is immaterial, the beneficial results arising from their traffic, etc., were consolidation of force and interest of the Indians, unity of purpose and action, entailing order in their government, a great diminution of family feuds and private quarrels, and an application of their time to the comfort and welfare of their families instead of its being spent in bloody contention or domestic idleness or discord.

The introduction of firearms, metallic cooking utensils, and other tools gave them a greater reliance on their own powers, increased their hunting operations, and with them their domestic comfort, by these means withdrawing their attention from their barbarous practices and opening a new field for their exertions. With the substituting of European instruments and clothing arose a different kind of pride than that of olden time. The distinguishing features of the original savage were fierceness, obstinate will, and bloody determination, leading to barbarous and disgusting practices. Their women were worse than slaves, the extent of their labor was more than they could bear. With the stone ax, the bone awl, the clay pot, the rib knife, and all their primitive tools, even their most pressing wants were met with great difficulty. The process of procuring fuel alone

was one of much toil, and occupied most of the time of one female
to a lodge.   On account of their inadequate instruments for dressing
hides their clothing was wretched, often insufficient to protect from
cold or to cover with decency.

Commerce has changed all this by facilitating their means, and the
character of their women has risen from a state of intolerable slavery to one of ordinary labor scarcely more servile than that of
European female operatives. Their persons are cleanly dressed,
combed, and adorned, a desire to appear genteel is manifested, a
neatness in their lodges and domestic arrangements perceptible, proving the transfer of their time and ideas to these ends from those of
original filth and savage recklessness.

In former times the trade was carried on in their different camps
by paying a number of desperate men (Indians) to restrain the
populace from robbing the trader.   This force was effective and necessary at the time, because the wants of the Indians were so numerous
and pressing, their cupidity so great, that it was impossible for the
trader publicly to display his goods or deal with them on anything
like fair terms. And the Indians thus employed considered it an
honorable station; it flattered their pride to rely for protection on
their bravery, and no robberies could be committed nor the traders
insulted without killing these men at the door of the lodge, which was
never attempted. This gave rise to a body of men called soldiers,
and the power first invested in them by the traders formed a nucleus
around which collected a superior and coercive force, which, in the
course of time, was applied to their own civil organization, producing
order in their government, unity of action, and rendering effective the
decisions by council.

The original natural authority was centered in the chiefs of small
bands, supported only by their family connections, who could not
or would not enforce decrees for general welfare nor interfere in
any public differences not touching their private interests. Power
being thus confined and circumscribed, separations into small camps
took place and minor subdivisions into heads of families, resembling
in this elementary form of government that of the ancient patriarchs
who as their interests jarred or covetousness increased made war
upon each other and were insufficient for any general purpose.
But when the body of soldiers was established and their efforts
united to support the chief and council, they soon collected in large
bands, from two to four or six hundred lodges each, entered into
effective measures of defense from the surrounding tribes, regulated
their hunts to advantage, and by this consolidation of interest extinguished the principal sources of private discord. This was a
great step in advancement produced by the traders and their com-

merce, for through the chief and council as the organ of public opinion and soldiers as its support the nation could be spoken to, their interest consulted, their feelings known, and the mass made to advance toward a further point of improvement.

Property by means of commerce having been acquired, rates of exchanges established, and hunting operations enlarged and facilitated, other things besides scalps became valuable in the eyes of the Indians. Each having something to lose, perceived the necessity of respecting the rights of others, giving rise to a spirit of compromise in difficulties, so that arms were less resorted to in settling disputes, payment in most cases superseding that ancient and barbarous custom; also they evinced a disposition to aid each other in times of need, which minor obligations bound still closer their hitherto feeble bonds of society.

These were some of the effects of the introduction of commerce. A still further improvement is visible in their expansion of ideas arising from association with white traders, exhibited in their amelioration of manners, desire for knowledge, doubts of their own superstitions, increase of their vocabulary and modes for expressing thought, reason supplying the place of passion, and the general usefulness of the whole, resulting in their minds having been made capable of comprehending religious or scientific instruction and their time and talents to be applied to either their moral or spiritual welfare.

This is the point to which these wild tribes are supposed by us to have arrived, but no further. Their future condition depends more upon their white allies than themselves. Traders have instilled education enough to serve their purposes and let them alone. It would be inexpedient for them to do more.

It is also apparent, if their present attainments be not improved upon by those in power, that they must recede, and in case of a discontinuance of trade or a worse influx of whites, their now to them useful organization must dissolve. In this event they must become more miserable than at first, because the desires and necessities induced by their partial elevation can not be satisfied from their original resources, these having been lost and abandoned during their advancement, consequently their present support withdrawn, their hunting ruined, distress, famine, and dissolution as nations must certainly follow.

If they are left in their present condition until the tide of emigration has reached their as yet undisturbed hunting grounds, and the green plains, now covered with multitudes of buffalo, shall be strewn with innumerable grog shops, occupied by nests of gamblers, and hordes of outlaws, bringing with their personal vices a host of infectious diseases, where will the poor Indian be then? Bitter would and should be the reflections of our great national reformers that they had not in time stretched out a saving arm to the aborigines.

It may be said, point out a way, state some feasible plan. Heretofore our policy has been lame, and our efforts retarded by our being but partially informed as to their capacity of improvement, or the practicability of bettering their condition.

To all this we would answer the course to be pursued is plain and can be easily gathered from these pages, which, like other productions of the kind, most probably will be thrown aside as soon as read or disbelieved because the facts recorded do not coincide with preconceived notions of Indian character.

We do not feel ourselves called upon by the inquiry to present a plan of operations, neither do we feel capable of instructing superior men. A plain statement of facts is sought and herein presented, though more could have been done had it been requested. Extensive establishments having for their object the civilization of the Indians have already been commenced with several nations within the boundaries of the United States and have met with success. Let others be tried, adapting the means to the situation and necessities of the roving tribes. A sudden revolution of feeling, an entire change in their habits and occupations, can not immediately be expected, would not be natural, neither would it be durable, but a gradual change brought about in their present employments, by combining them with pastoral and agricultural pursuits, a judicious introduction of mechanical arts, their superstitions carefully undermined and replaced by moral truth, their temporal welfare consulted, and a certain chance of subsistence presented; these things being accomplished, the eyes of the present grown generation would close in the rising prosperity of their children.

We perceive in the closing remarks of the inquiry these words: "In all questions where the interests of the tribes clash with those of the persons whom you may consult, there is much caution required."

Now, our personal interests and those of every trader are at direct variance with any innovations in the present employments or organization of the Indians. Any improvement in their condition mentally or the introduction of other pursuits such as arts and agriculture, even the inculcation of the Christian religion, would immediately militate against the trade and unfit the Indians for being only hunters or being regarded only as a source of profit. We are perfectly aware that the policy advised in these pages, if acted upon, would effectually ruin the trade and with it our own personal interest and influence in that capacity. All these things have been well considered and had they any effect would only have led to our remaining silent on the subject; but, having written, we prefer placing things in their proper light, aiming at great general good, and thus without further comment the whole is left in the hands of those for whom it is intended.

INTERMARRIAGE WITH WHITES

The prairie tribes have not been much affected by intermarriages with Europeans except the Cree. Most of the Red River settlement of half-breeds are of Cree and Chippewa extraction, who though not generally having the advantage of education, are, however, a bold, hardy, and fearless people, invariably good-looking, active, and brave. They unite hunting with agricultural operations but prefer the former, the indisposition to work showing itself equally in the descendant as in the original stock. Their parents and the Cree Nation generally have been, if not benefited, much instructed by these people, and are superior in intellectual acquirements to any of the other tribes. The history of this settlement is no doubt well known to all, so that we need not describe it here.

As far as these other tribes are concerned the only intermixture has been of the fur traders and engagees of the fur company. Of these, all that can afford it take their children to the States to be educated, who usually make intelligent and respectable men. If it were not for the popular prejudice existing, or if it were possible, we would advise amalgamation of the races as the most efficient means for saving the remnants of the Indian tribes.

POPULATION

Regarding the comparative population of these tribes with the years 1833 to 1854, the decrease is very great. Smallpox, cholera, measles, and influenza, together with other diseases and wars, incidental to the climate and their pursuits, have reduced the Sioux about one-third, the Mandan three-fourths, the Arikara one-fifth, the Assiniboin one-half, the Cree one-eighth, the Crows one-half, and the Blackfeet one-third less than they were at the former period. They—that is, from the Sioux up—are now slowly on the increase.

LANGUAGE

To answer the queries on this head would require a volume of itself, but the Assiniboin being the same or nearly the same as the Sioux, and as the Sioux has already been translated into the English letters, books published in it, and the same taught in schools on the Mississippi, it is presumed that any and all answers to these queries can be obtained by procuring the books printed in the Sioux language

and by examining their manner of instruction. We have seen the
New Testament in that language, also several letters, and believe it
to be well adapted to the purpose of Christianity or general usefulness. Should, however, it be the desire of the department that extensive vocabularies be made out and explanations of their language
given, or should any other information regarding these tribes be
sought, we will at any time satisfy it on these topics, provided the
efforts now made for their instruction regarding the prairie tribes
meet with the success it is presumed to deserve.

BIBLIOGRAPHY

The following bibliographical list of works is submitted to enable the student to verify and extend the work of Mr. Denig.

BACQUEVILLE DE LA POTHERIE, C. C. LE ROY DE LA. Histoire de l'Amérique Septentrionale. Tomes I–IV. Paris, 1722. (Same, Paris, 1753.)

CATLIN, GEORGE. Illustrations of the manners, customs, and condition of the North American Indians. Vols. I–II. London, 1848.

> [To be used only with caution.]

CHITTENDEN, N. M., and RICHARDSON, A. T. Life, letters, and travels of Father Pierre-Jean De Smet, S. J., 1801–1873. Vols. I–IV. New York, 1905.

COUES, ELLIOTT, ed. New light on the early history of the greater Northwest. The manuscript journals of Alexander Henry and of David Thompson, 1799–1814. Vols. I–III. New York, 1897.

DE SMET, FATHER PIERRE-JEAN. *See* Chittenden, H. M., and Richardson, A. T.

DORSEY, GEORGE A., and KROEBER, A. L. Traditions of the Arapaho. (Field Col. Mus. Pub. 81, Anthrop. ser. vol. v, Chicago, 1903.)

DORSEY, J. OWEN. A study of Siouan cults. (Eleventh Ann. Rept. Bur. Ethn., pp. 351–544, Washington, 1894.)

——— Siouan sociology. (Fifteenth Ann. Rept. Bur. Ethn., pp. 205–244, Washington, 1897.)

DOBBS, ARTHUR. An account of the countries adjoining to Hudson's Bay in the north-west part of America. London, 1744.

FLETCHER, ALICE C. The Elk mystery or festival. Ogallala Sioux. (Rept. Peabody Mus. Amer. Archaeol, and Ethn., vol. III, pp. 276–288, Cambridge, 1881.)

——— Hae-thu-ska Society of the Omaha tribe. (Journ. Amer. Folk-Lore, vol. v, pp. 135–144, Boston and New York, 1892.)

FRANKLIN, JOHN. Narrative of a journey to the shores of the Polar Sea. Philadelphia, 1824.

HANDBOOK OF AMERICAN INDIANS NORTH OF MEXICO. Bur. Amer. Ethn., Bull. 30, pts. 1 and 2, Washington, 1907–1910.

> [The tribal and other articles in this work are arranged in alphabetical order.]

HAYDEN, F. V. On the ethnography and philology of the Indian tribes of the Missouri Valley. (Trans. Amer. Philos. Soc., n. s. vol. XII, pt. 2, Philadelphia, 1862.)

> [Largely based on information supplied him by Edwin T. Denig.]

HENRY, ALEXANDER. Travels and adventures in Canada, and in the Indian Territories, between the years 1760 and 1776. New York, 1809.

——— *See also* Coues, Elliott, ed.

HIND, HENRY YUEL. Narrative of the Canadian Red River Exploring Expedition of 1857, and of the Assiniboine and Saskatchewan Exploring Expedition of 1858. Vols. I–II. London, 1860.

JESUIT RELATIONS. Relations des Jesuites contenant ce qui s'est passe de plus remarquable dans les missions des pères de la Compagnie de Jesus dans la Nouvelle-France. Embrassant les années 1611–1672. Tomes. I–III. Quebec, 1858.

——— Jesuit Relations and allied documents. Travels and explorations of the Jesuit missionaries in New France, 1610–1791. Reuben Gold Thwaites, editor. Vols. I–LXXIII. Cleveland, 1896–1901.

628   BIBLIOGRAPHY

KELSEY, HENRY. A journal of a voyage and journey undertaken by Henry
     Kelsey ... in anno 1691. With an Introduction by Arthur G. Doughty
     and Chester Martin. *In* The Kelsey Papers, published by the Public
     Archives of Canada, ..., Ottawa, 1929.
          [He mentions " ye Stone Indians " and also has an "Account of these
     Indians beliefs and superstitions," which seems to be the first sketch of
     the life and customs of the Plains Indians.]
KROEBER, ALFRED L. Ethnology of the Gros Ventre. (Anthrop. Papers Amer.
     Mus. Nat. Hist., vol. I, pt. 4, New York, 1908.)
———— The Arapaho. (Bull. Amer. Mus. Nat. Hist., vol. XVIII, New York,
     1902.)
          See also Dorsey, Geo. A., and Kroeber.
LEWIS, MERIWETHER, and CLARK, WM. Original journals of the Lewis and
     Clark Expedition, 1804–1806. Reuben Gold Thwaites, editor. Vols.
     I–VIII, New York, 1904–1905.
LA POTHERIE. *See* Bacqueville de la Potherie.
LONG, JOHN. Voyages and travels of an Indian interpreter and trader, de-
     scribing the manners and customs of the North American Indians. Lon-
     don, 1791.
LOWIE, ROBERT H. The Assiniboine. (Anthrop. Papers Amer. Mus. Nat. Hist.,
     vol. IV, pt. 1, New York, 1909.)
MARGRY, PIERRE. Decouvertes et etablissements des Francais dans l'ouest et
     dans le sud de l'Amerique Septentrionale (1614–1754). Memoires et
     documents originaux. Pts. I–VI. Paris, 1875–1886.
MAXIMILIAN, ALEX. P., PRINZ ZU WIED. Reise in das innere Nord-America in
     den Jahren 1832 bis 1834. B. I–II. Coblenz, 1839–1841.
MOONEY, JAMES. Mescal plant and ceremony. (Therapeutic Gazette, 3d ser.,
     vol. XII, Detroit, 1896.)
———— Calendar history of the Kiowa Indians. (Seventeenth Ann. Rept. Bur.
     Amer. Ethn., pt. 1, Washington, 1898.)
———— The Ghost-dance religion and the Sioux outbreak of 1890. (Fourteenth
     Ann. Rept. Bur. Ethn., pt. 2, Washington, 1896.)
PERROT, NICOLAS. Memoire sur les Moeurs, Coustumes et Relligion des Sauvages
     de l'Amerique Septentrionale, publie pour la premiere fois par le R. P. J.
     Tailhan. Leipzig et Paris, 1864.
RADISSON, PETER ESPRIT. Voyages of Peter Esprit Radisson ... with his-
     torical illustrations and an introduction by Gideon D. Scull. Publ.
     Prince Society. Boston, 1885.
SCHOOLCRAFT, HENRY R. Historical and statistical information, respecting the
     history, condition, and prospects of the Indian tribes of the United States.
     Pts. I–VI. Philadelphia, 1851–1857.
          [In his fourth volume he publishes Denig's Assiniboin vocabulary.]
SCULL, GIDEON D. *See* Radisson, Peter Esprit.
THWAITES, REUBEN GOLD, ed. Early western travels 1748–1846. Vols. I–XXXII.
     Cleveland, 1904–1907.
WISSLER, CLARK. The Blackfoot Indians. (Annual Archaeol. Rept. for 1905.
     App. Rept. Min. Ed. Ont., pp. 162–178, Toronto, 1906.)

                               MANUSCRIPT

KURZ, FREDERICK. Journal. Copy of translation in the archives of the Bureau
     of American Ethnology, Smithsonian Institution. 1,076 typewritten pages
     with 125 drawings.

—— Index ——

— Appendix —

**Inquiries, Respecting the History, Present Condition and
Future Prospects of the Indian Tribes of the United States**

— Henry Rowe Schoolcraft

History

1. ORIGIN. — What facts can be stated, from tradition, respecting the origin, early history and migrations of the tribe; and what are the principal incidents known, or remembered since A.D. 1492? Can they communicate anything on this head, of ancient date, which is entitled to respect? What is the earliest event, or name, in their origin or progress, which is preserved by tradition, and from what stock of men have they sprung?

2. TRIBE AND GEOGRAPHICAL POSITION. — By what name are they called, among themselves, and by what name, or names, are they known among other tribes; and what is the meaning of these respective names? State the various synonyms. Where did the tribe dwell, at the earliest date; what was its probable number, and the extent of territory occupied or claimed by it? How has their location, numbers, and the extent of lands or territories, varied since the earliest known period; and what are the general facts, on these heads, at the present time?

3. ANCIENT OR MODERN LOCATION. — Are they of opinion, they were created by the Great Spirit, on the lands, or are they conquerors, or possessors through the events of war, or from other causes? Can they recollect the first interview with whites, or Europeans — the first sale of lands, or treaty made by them — the introduction of fire-arms, woollen clothing, cooking vessels of metal, ardent spirits, the first place of trade, or any other prominent fact in their economical history?

4. VESTIGES OF EARLY TRADITION. — Have they any tradition of the creation, or the deluge, or of their ancestors having lived in other lands, or having had knowledge of any quadrupeds which are foreign to America, or crossed any large waters, in their migration? Is there any idea developed among them by tradition, allegory, or otherwise, that white people, or a more civilized race, had occupied the continent before them?

5. HAVE THEY ANY NAME FOR AMERICA? — If there be no direct term applicable to the entire continent, search their oral traditions in the hope of detecting the name.

6. REMINISCENCES OF FORMER CONDITION. — Did they, before the discovery, live in a greater degree of peace with each other — had they formed any ancient leagues, and if so, of what tribes did they consist, how long did these leagues last, and when and how were they broken? Did they build any forts or mounds in their ancient wars, or were the earth-works we find in the West erected before they arrived, and by whom, in their opinion, were these works erected?

7. NAMES AND EVENTS AS HELPS TO HISTORY. — What events have happened, in their history, of which they feel proud, or by which they have been cast down? What tribes have they conquered, or been conquered by, and who have been their great men? Have they suffered any great calamity in past times, as from great floods, or wild beasts, from epidemic or pestilential diseases, or from fierce and sudden assailants? And have they, in such cases, had any renowned or wise leader, or deliverer?

8. PRESENT RULERS AND CONDITION. — Who is their ruling chief? Who are their present most noted chiefs, speakers, or war captains? State their names, and give brief sketches of their lives. When did the tribe reach their present location, and under what circumstances?

9. LANGUAGES SPOKEN AS A MEANS OF INQUIRY. — Does the tribe speak one or more dialects, or are there several languages spoken, or incorporated in it, requiring more than one interpreter, in transacting business with them? Are there aged persons who can state their traditions?

International Rank and Relations

10. WHAT RANK AND RELATIONSHIP DOES THE TRIBE BEAR TO OTHER TRIBES? — Do their traditions assign them a superior or inferior position in the political scale of the tribes; and is this relationship sanctioned by the traditions of other tribes? To what mode can we resort to settle discordant pretensions to original rank, and affinities of blood? Are their names for themselves, or others, any clue in the latter case, and if not, must the languages be essentially relied on, to prove original affinities? Is the relative rank or kindredship of the tribe, denoted by terms taken from the vocabulary of the family ties, as uncle, grandfather, brother, &c.? If so, what tribe is called grandfather, &c.?

11. PROOF FROM MONUMENTS. — Are there belts of wampum, quippas, or monuments of any kind, such as heaps of stone, &c., to prove the former existence of alliances, leagues, or treaties among the tribes? If so, describe them, and the places where they are to be found.

12. PROOF FROM DEVICES. — What is the badge, or, as it has been called, the totem of the tribe — or if it consist of separate clans, or primary families, what is the number of these clans, and what is the badge of each? And do these totems, or badges, denote the rank, or relationship, which is sought to be established by these queries?

13. MAGNITUDE AND RESOURCES OF TERRITORY, A CAUSE OF THE MULTIPLICATION OF TRIBES. — Have geographical features, within the memory of tradition, or the abundance or scarcity of game, had any thing to do with the division and multiplication of tribes and dialects, either among the Atlantic or Western tribes? Are there any remembered feuds, family discords, or striking rivalries among chiefs, or tribes, which have led to such separations, and great multiplication of dialects?

14. PROOFS FROM GEOGRAPHY. — What great geographical features, if any, in North America, such as the Mississippi River, Alleghany Mountains, &c., are alluded to, in their traditions, of the original rank and movements of the tribe; and was the general track of their migrations, *from* or *towards* the NORTH or the EAST?

Geography

15. FIGURE OF THE GLOBE. — Have the Indians any just ideas of the natural divisions of the earth, into continents, seas and islands? What ideas have they of the form of the earth?

16. LOCAL FEATURES OF THE COUNTRY INHABITED. — What are the chief rivers in the territory or district occupied by the tribe? State their length, general depth and breadth — where they originate — how far they are navigable; what are their principal rapids, falls and portages, at what points goods are landed, and into what principal or larger waters they finally flow.

17. LAKES AND SPRINGS. — Are there any large springs, or lakes, in the district, and what is their character, size and average depth; and into what streams have they outlets? If lakes exist, can they be navigated by steamers; if gigantic springs, do they afford water-power, and to what extent?

18. SURFACE OF THE COUNTRY. — What is the general character of the surface of the country occupied by the tribe? Is it hilly or level — fertile or sterile; abundant or scanty in wood and water — abounding or restricted in the extent of its natural meadows, or prairies? What grains or other products do the Indians raise in the district, and what are its general agricultural advantages, or disadvantages? What are its natural vegetable productions?

19. FACILITIES FOR GRAZING. — Are cattle and stock easily raised — do the prairies and woods afford an abundant supply of herbage spontaneously — are wells of water to be had at moderate depths, where the surface denies springs, or streams, and is there a practicable market for the surplus grain and stock?

20. PHYSICAL EFFECTS OF FIRING THE PRAIRIES. — Has the old practice of the Indians of burning the prairies to facilitate hunting, had the effect to injure the surface of the soil, or to circumscribe, to any extent, the native forests?

21. WASTE LANDS. — Are there any extensive barrens, or deserts, marshes or swamps, reclaimable or irreclaimable, and what effects do they produce on the health of the country, and do they offer any serious obstacles to the construction of roads?

22. EFFECTS OF VOLCANIC ACTION. — Is the quantity of arable land diminished by large areas of arid mountain, or of volcanic tracts of country, with plains of sand and cactus? If so, are these tracts wholly arid and without water, or do they afford a partial supply of herbage for horses, sheep, or mules?

23. CLIMATE. — Is the climate generally dry or humid? Does the heat of the weather vary greatly, or is it distributed, through the different seasons, with regularity and equability? What winds prevail? Is it much subject to storms of rain with heavy thunder, or tornadoes, and do these tempests of rain swell the streams so as to overflow their banks, and destroy fences and injure the crops? State the general character of the climate, giving meteorological tables if you can.

24. SALINE PRODUCTIONS. — Does the district produce any salt springs of value, any caves, yielding saltpetre earth; or any beds of gypsum, or plaister of paris; or of marl, suitable for agricultural purposes?

25. COAL AND OTHER MINERAL PRODUCTS. — Has the country any known beds of stone coal, or of iron ores, or veins of lead, or copper ores, or any other valuable deposits of useful metals, or minerals? State localities and transmit, when opportunity offers, specimens.

26. WILD ANIMALS. — What is the general character and value of the animal productions of the district? What species of quadrupeds most abound? State their number and kind, and what effect the fur trade has had in diminishing the value of the country for the purposes of hunting. What kinds of animals decreased earliest, and what species still remain?

27. ANCIENT BONES.— Do the Indian traditions make any mention of larger, or gigantic animals in former periods? Is there any allusion to the mastodon, megalonyx, or any of the extinct races, whose tusks, or bones, naturalists find imbedded in clay, or submerged in morasses?

28. TRADITIONS OF THE MONSTER ERA. — What species are we to understand by the story, on this head, told to Mr. Jefferson, or by the names YA-GA-SHO, QUIS QUIS, WIN-DE-GO, BOSH-CA-DOSH, or others, which are heard in various dialects?

29. ANIMALS WHOSE FIGURES ARE MUCH USED AS THE CHIEF ARMORIAL MARKS OF TRIBES. — Have they any peculiar opinions, or striking traditions, respecting the serpent, wolf, turtle, grizzly bear, or eagle, whose devices are used as symbols on their arms, or dwellings, and how do such opinions influence their acts on meeting these species in the forest?

30. ERA OF THE IMPORTATION OF THE HORSE. — Have they any tradition respecting the first introduction of the horse, upon this continent, and from what qualities, or properties, do they name this animal?

31. CHARTS ON BARK, &C. — Are they expert in drawing maps or charts of the rivers, or sections of country, which they inhabit? State their capacities on this subject, denoting

whether these rude drawings are accurate, and whether they evince any knowledge of the laws of proportion, and transmit, if you can, specimens of them.

Antiquities

32. FIRST EPOCH OF MAN ON THE CONTINENT. — Are there any antique works, or remains of any kind, which are the result of human industry in ancient times, in your district? And what traditions, or opinions, have the tribes, on the subject?

33. MOUNDS, PYRAMIDS, TEOCALLI. — What is generally thought by men of reflection, to be the probable origin and purpose of the western mounds? Are they of one, or several kinds — of one, or several eras — and were they erected by one, or several nations, who lived, at various periods, in the country, at the same locations? Were they places of observation — of sacrifice, of burial, or of military defence? Is the mound *sui generis* with the Aztec or Toltec type of pyramids, or teocalli of the earlier periods? Were the later Indian structures in Mexico, improvements upon these rude earthen pyramids of the North, or did the knowledge of these more magnificent structures, or the power to construct them, degenerate in the more Northern latitudes of the continent, where the chase absorbed attention? State your views on this head, and give plans and descriptions of the mounds examined, carefully noting the bearings of the compass, the elevations of the mounds, and of the plains or hills on which they are based, their exact geometrical figure, and the relative position of the nearest rivers, or streams. State also, whether there be any ancient articles of sculpture of stone or shell, or any vases or other forms of pottery, from which the state of arts and character of the builders may be inferred; and what time has probably elapsed from an examination of the forest growth, since these structures were deserted.

34. ANCIENT FORTIFICATIONS OR MILITARY WORKS. — Has the progress of settlements west of the Alleghanies, and the felling of trees and clearing up of lands, disclosed any ancient embankments, ditches, or other works of earth, or stone, having the character of forts, or places of military defence? If so, note whether such works manifest in their structure, any of the modern or ancient principles of engineering. Are there any features resembling the Roman, Grecian, Carthaginian, or Libyan modes of circumvallation, or evidences of military art in the approach to fortified places before the discovery of gunpowder, and the invention of firearms? Are there any ancient missiles of stone, flint, chert, or other fossil and hard bodies, or adjunct antiquities which may throw light on the main subject? Describe accurately such works, and give therewith complete topographical sketches of the country, denoting the strength and importance of the supposed positions of defence. Observe also, whether there be anything answering to a horn-work, or redoubt, or any spring, or well, by which water could be supplied to a besieged place.

35. CIRCULAR WORKS. — Are there any circular, or ring-forts, and how do these differ, in the principles of defence they disclose, from the angular or irregular works? Were these forts circular parapets with wooden pickets — were they pierced for gate-ways? How were these gate-ways crowned and defended, and what are the characteristic features of this species of ancient earth-works?

36. IMITATIVE MOUNDS. — In examining the western mounds, are there any of an imitative, or allegorical character, or resembling an elk, serpent, deer, wolf, or other animate object in their shapes?

37. PROOFS OF ANTIQUE AGRICULTURE OR HORTICULTURE. — Does the level surface of the prairie country, which is now partially over-run by forest, preserve any traces of a plan or design as of ancient furrows or garden-beds, which appear to have been abandoned at a definite period?

38. OLD ARTIFICIAL LAND-MARKS, OR PSEUDO MONUMENTS. — Is there any ancient or noted mark on rocks, or any artificial orifice or excavation in the earth, or other land-mark known in local tradition, which denotes historical events?

39. ANTIQUE IMPLEMENTS AND VESSELS OF POTTERY. — What is the general character of the antique implements, ornaments, or utensils of earthenware found in your district of the country? If vases, kettles or pots, or other vessels of clay are found — of what kind — how were they formed, on a potter's wheel, or by hand — how were the materials compounded — was the ware burned completely or partially — was it glazed, or unglazed? Is it ornamented, and how? Does it resemble the ancient Etruscan ware, the terra-cotta, or any ancient rude form of earthenware. Transmit drawings and descriptions of each species of article illustrative of the potter's art.

40. PIPES. — If pipes are found, what is the material, is it stone, steatite, or clay — how are they formed — to admit a stem, or to be smoked without, and what are their shapes, sizes and ornaments?

41. UTENSILS OF STONE. — How many kinds were there? Describe them, and give figures. How was the axe usually formed, and from what materials? What was the shape and construction of the stone tomahawk? Was it always crescent-shaped, and pointed? What was the range of forms of the ancient implements for pounding corn, roots, and their rude bread-stuffs; and of their instruments for fleshing skins, and for removing charcoal from timber, &c., cut by the process of fire? Do these instruments denote a people advanced in the arts, or still in the rude state of mere hunters? Are there ornaments of bone, spar, gems, mica, copper, silver, gold, mosaic, or glass, denoting a higher degree of skill than the preceding; and are there any evidences, in the examination of this branch of antiquities, which prove the makers to have understood the mechanical processes of boring, turning, polishing, moulding, or making impressions in clay, or cutting hard substances?

42. MANUFACTURE OF DARTS, ARROW-POINTS AND OTHER MISSILES. — What was the process of manipulation of these, often delicately wrought, articles? What species of mineral bodies were chiefly used — and how was the cleavage of them effected? Did the art constitute a separate trade, or employment? If darts abound, what is the material and size? Do they differ much in size, and apparent object, some being for war and others for hunting; and are there any elongated in the shape of spear-heads, or javelins? How many species of darts, spears, &c., were there? Describe them and give figures of the size and descriptions of the uses of them.

43. DISTRIBUTION OF SEA-SHELLS AND OTHER MISSILES. — What species of sea-shells have been found, in ancient graves, or mounds, at remote points from the ocean? At what localities, on the sea-coasts, do these species now abound, and do they furnish any light on the probable track of migration?

44. SHELL-COIN, WAMPUM, ANCIENT CURRENCY. — How many kinds of wampum were there? What shells were employed? What was the value of each kind? How was it estimated? *Vide* 61.

45. ANCIENT USE OF METALS. — Was iron, copper, tin, or any other metal used by the aboriginal tribes in America, for the purposes of art, prior to the discovery of the continent by Columbus? In the copper armbands or other implements, of old graves, are there any evidences of the arts of hammering, polishing, soldering, or engraving?

46. HIEROGLYPHICS, OR ANCIENT ALPHABETS. — Do the rocks of America, or any ancient architectural structures, disclose any ancient alphabet, hieroglyphics, or system of picture-writing, capable of interpretation, which promises to reflect light on the obscure periods of American history?

Astronomy

47. THE EARTH AND ITS MOTIONS. — What is the amount of their knowledge on this subject? Do they believe the Earth to be a plane, a globe, or a semi-circle? What relation does it bear, in their opinion, to the sun and moon and planets? Do they believe the planets to be other worlds, which are inhabited by men? Some of their oral tales denote this. Extend the inquiry.

48. CREATION. — Have they any idea of the universe, or other creations in the field of space, which have in their belief been made by the Great Spirit?

49. THE SUN. — What is their opinion of the nature and motions of the sun? Do they believe it to be a place of fire? Can they be made to comprehend that the sun does not daily rise and set, and that this *apparent* motion arises from the diurnal revolution of the earth?

50. THE SKY, OR FIRMAMENT. — Why do we observe, in their picture-writings, the sky drawn in the form of a half circle, resting on the plane of its truncation? Do they believe the sky, or heavens, to be circumscribed by a material mass of some kind, having orifices, through which the stars and planets shine?

51. ECLIPSES. — How do they account for eclipses? Do they believe, as the Aztecs did, that they arise from the shadow of some other body interposed? What is implied by the term *Gezis Nebo,* or dead sun?

52. LENGTH OF THE YEAR. — How may moons, or months, compose the Indian year? Have they made any approach to the astronomical knowledge of the ancient Mexicans, who determined the length of the year at 365 days, 5 hours and 29 minutes? Have they made any attempt to compute a solar year? If, as has been said, the Indian year consists of thirteen moons of twenty-eight days each, their year would consist of 364 days. If of twelve moons of thirty days each, it would consist of 360 days. How far is either statement correct, or fanciful? Or have the Indians of these latitudes any definite or exact notions on the subject?

53. SOLSTICES. — Do they notice the length of the summer and winter solstices, and of the vernal and autumnal equinoxes?

54. CYCLES. — Have they a cycle of 52, 60 or 120 years, or of any fixed or stated length, at the end of which they believe, with the ancient Aztecs, that the world will come to a close; and do they believe that it is the power and efficacious supplications of the Indian priests to the Great Spirit that causes its renewal?

55. DIVISIONS OF TIME. — Have they any name for the *year*, as contradistinguished from a winter? Have they any division of time resembling a *week*? The Aztecs had a division or month of thirteen days, and a week of five days. Are there any analogous divisions among our Indians? Is the day divided into hours, or any other sub-portions of time?

56. NAMES FOR STARS. — Have they names for any considerable number of the stars? If so, which stars, and what names do they give them?

57. ASTROLOGY. — Have they anything resembling the ancient signs of the Zodiac? Do they attach personal or other influences to the stars? Is the moon thought to influence men, plants, or animals? Is corn planted at particular times of the moon's phases? What superstitious opinions are believed to affect its growth?

58. METEOROLOGICAL PHENOMENA. — What are their opinions of the Aurora Borealis? Have they any definite notions of the Milky Way? What is their theory of the origin and nature of clouds, rain, hail, and winds and tornadoes? What is thought of meteors? Have

they formed any opinions of comets? Do they connect any superstitions with the phenomena of falling stars? How do they account for the rainbow?

59. ORIGIN OF ASTRONOMICAL OPINIONS. — Are there any coincidences with the oriental
system of computing time? Have they any peculiar notions respecting the cardinal points?
Are there any opinions expressed which may have been derived from any of the ancient
and peculiar theories of cosmogony? Must we look to their fictitious tales and allegories
for their notions on this and other abstruse subjects, respecting which they are unwilling,
or unable, to communicate direct information?

60. INDIAN PARADISE. — In what part of the heavens, or the planetary system, do the
Indians locate their paradise, or their happy hunting grounds, and land of souls?

Arithmetic

61. NUMERATION. — Does the tribe count by decimals? Are there any tribes who use the
ventigissimal system of the Aztecs? Do any of the tribes count by fives? How high can
they, with exactitude, compute numbers? What are the Indian names of the digits? State
them. State also, in what manner the computation is carried from 10 to 20, and what are
the terms for each additional decimal up to 100? How is the process continued from 100
to 1,000, and to 10,000? Are the generic denominations carried on, with exactitude, to a
million? Give the extent of their power of computation, with examples of their appreciation of high numbers.

62. COIN. — Was the wampum or any form of sea-shells, referred to in No. 44, anciently
used, or is it now used, to represent numbers and value, and to constitute a standard of
exchange? Had the tribe originally, or has it now, any thing whatever of the nature of a
currency? If a grain of *seawan*, *peag*, or *wampum*, was the lowest fraction, of value, or
unit, in computation, did not the decimal system mark accurately the entire scale, and
denote accurately, by the addition or multiplication of decimals, the price of any com-
modity, up to hundreds, tens of hundreds, &c.? Do they understand federal money?

63. KEEPING ACCOUNTS. — How were accounts formerly kept? And how are they now
kept? If the terms, *skin*, *plue*, and *abiminiqua*, or others, are employed in the interior trade
as synonymous, and as the standard of value, in which accounts are kept, what is *the scale*
of the computation? How are musk-rats and other smaller furs, for instance, computed
into "skins" of the standard value? Are large beaver-skins, or skins above one pound
weight, valued above a technical or standard *plue*, or skin? Are otter-skins, cross foxes, or
any other skins, exempted from this rule? How are deer and buffalo skins valued?

64. PICTORIAL HELPS TO MEMORY. — Are signs, or pictorial devices, used to any extent, in
keeping the accounts in commerce; or in denoting numbers in their pictorial records?

65. ELEMENTS OF FIGURES. — Did a single perpendicular stroke stand for 1, and each additional stroke mark the additional number? Are the ages of deceased persons or number of
scalps taken by them, or war parties which they have headed, recorded on their grave-
posts, by this system of strokes? Is the cross used, as it is said to be among some of the
Algonquin tribes, to denote 40? Did the dot, or full comma, stand as a chronological sign
for a day, or a moon or month or a year? Or was its meaning fixed by adjunct figures?

Medicine

66. GENERAL PRACTICE. — What is the general character of their medical practice? Are
they careful and tender of their sick, and is this attention more marked in relation to children and youth, than to the aged and decrepid?

67. ANATOMY. — Have their professed doctors and practitioners of medicine any exact knowledge of anatomy; of the theory of the circulation of the blood, or the pathology of diseases?

68. TREATMENT OF COMPLAINTS. — How do they treat fevers, pleurisy, consumption of the lungs, obstructions of the liver, deranged or impeded functions of the stomach, constipation, or any of the leading complaints?

69. MEDICINES. — What species of plants or other roots are employed as emetics, or cathartics? How are they prepared or applied? How are their medicines generally preserved from the effects of heat, or humidity?

70. DEPLETION. — Do they bleed in fevers? And what are the general principles of the application of the Indian lancet? Is the kind of cupping which they perform with the horn of the deer efficacious, and in what manner do they produce a vacuum?

71. STOPPAGE OF BLEEDING IN ANEURISMS OR CUTS. — Have they any good styptics, or healing or drawing plasters? Are bandages and lints skilfully applied, and timely replaced, or removed?

72. HEALING ART. — Is the known success with which they treat gun-shot wounds, cuts, or stabs, the result of the particular mode of treatment, or of the assiduity and care of the physicians?

73. AMPUTATION. — Do they ever amputate a limb, and how, and with what success? Are the arteries previously compressed? Have they any surgical instruments? Are they skilful in the use of splints, and the necessary supports to the injured limb? What mechanical contrivances have they for removing the sick, wounded, or maimed, from the woods, or in their lodges?

74. THEORY OF DISEASES AND THEIR REMEDY. — What is the state of the Indian *materia medica*? Have they any efficacious remedies for female complaints? Do they employ, understandingly, any metallic medicine? Do they understand the nature of an oxyde? Are their compound decoctions made with such knowledge of the principles of combination, or admixture, as to insure their efficacy? State what is known of their medicines, elementary or compound, and the theory of diseases.

75. VAPOR BATHS, PARALYSIS, &C. — How do they treat imposthumes, and eruptions of the skin? What is the cause of their known and general failure to treat small-pox, or varioloid? Do men ever interpose their skill in difficult cases of parturition; and what is the general character of the medical treatment of mother, and children? Have they any treatment for paralysis? Do they employ vapor baths efficaciously for the health of their patients?

Tribal Organization and Government

76. INTERNAL CONSTITUTION OF TRIBE. — Does the tribe consist of one or more clans, or sub-divisions? Are the rights of the clans clearly defined, and what are the general principles of the organization and government of the tribe? Is it organized on the *totemic* system, that is to say, is it divided into separate clans, or classes, bearing the name of some bird, quadruped, or other object in the animate or inanimate kingdoms? If so, of how many clans, or totemic classes or bands, did it originally consist? How many does it now consist of, and what is their present relative strength? State the name of each clan, or sub-division, with its signification and origin.

77. OBJECT OR UTILITY OF DIVISIONS INTO CLANS. — What is the apparent object of these devices, where they exist? Are they indicative of the original families or distinguished

chiefs of the tribe? Are they a sign of kindred? If they denote original consanguinity in the individuals of the bands or tribes, bearing these marks, or devices, what is the degree of the affinity, past or present? If they denote primary families, or chiefs, were these devices their *names*? Is there any pre-eminence in the clans? Are the turtle, wolf, and bear clans, as it has been said, more honorable than others? Is each clan entitled to one or more chiefs? And if not thus organized, what other principles of division, or association, or distinction, exist?

78. CHIEFTAINSHIPS — THEIR TENURE. — Were the chiefs originally hereditary or elective? If hereditary, is the descent in the male or female line? If in the female line, as among the Iroquois, how can the son of a chief become the official successor of his father?

79. WHAT ARE THE GENERAL POWERS OF THE CHIEFS IN COUNCIL? — To what extent is an Indian Council a representative assembly of the tribe, and how far are the chiefs invested with authority to act for the mass of the tribe? What invests their verbal summons, or decision, with a binding force? How is their authority derived? Is this authority tacitly committed to them, as a common and general function of their office as chiefs or sachems, or is it delegated by the mass of the tribe for each particular occasion? Or are they open, at all times, to popular opinion, and the mere exponents of it?

80. IF THE CHIEFS BE ELECTIVE, IS THERE ANYTHING BEYOND THE TACIT ELECTION OF POPULAR OPINION? — If elected by their distinguished deeds, does the tenure of their office continue beyond the continuance of such deeds? If hereditary, have the rights of the chieftainship any force beyond the continued ability or capacity of the incumbent, or his descendant, to execute or obey the popular will? Whether, therefore, they be elective, or hereditary, is not the disapproval of the mass, or body of warriors, an effective bar to the exercise of their powers and functions?

81. IS THE DEMOCRATIC ELEMENT STRONGLY IMPLANTED? — Do the chiefs, in public council, speak the opinions and sentiments of the warrior class, previously expressed by the latter in their separate or home councils; or do they particularly consult the old men, priests, warriors, and young men composing the tribe? Are they much subject to be influenced by extraneous opinions? Do they pursue their interests with shrewdness and intensity? Is their right to sit in council ever exercised in a manner which is equivalent to giving a *vote*? Are persons for and against a proposition counted, and if so, by whom? If votes are given, is this a modern or an ancient exercise of power, and has it resulted in giving more certainty and satisfaction in decisions? Are any powers in fact exercised by the chiefs in advance of public opinion in the tribe?

82. WHAT PRINCIPLES GOVERN THE ULTIMATE DECISIONS OF A PUBLIC COUNCIL? — In what manner are the deliberations opened, conducted and closed? Is there much respect to the ancient ceremonies? Is the weather regarded? Are there any official personages who exercise duties equivalent to a crier, secretary, or other legislative or legal functionary? Are questions deliberately considered, or decided off-hand? Are decisions made on the principle of majorities, or pluralities? Were they originally or are they now, required to be made, in any case, on the principle of absolute unanimity? Or is the voice of a leading chief taken as the expression of the will of the tribe?

83. WHAT IS THE SCOPE OF THE CIVIL JURISDICTION AND THE ORDER OF SUCCESSION OF THE CHIEFS AS MAGISTRATES? — Are decisions, made by single chiefs, or by a body of chiefs in council, carried implicitly into effect? If a man have forfeited his life, and the question be decided in a council of chiefs, is an executioner appointed? If so, does he use a tomahawk, or club, or arrow? Is the time, and mode, and place, decided by the chief, or council, or left to the executioner, as it was in the case of Myontonimo? Are the results of

questions of the restoration of property communicated to the parties at once, or sent by a messenger?

84. HOW ARE RANK AND SUCCESSION IN OFFICE REGULATED? — Is the succession of a chief to an office vacated by death, or otherwise, debated and decided in council, or may a person legally, in the right line of descent, forthwith assume the functions of the office? Are new chiefs created by election, and how? May a chief be deposed from his office, and for what offence? Is the custom of wearing medals to mark the distinction of office, an ancient or a modern one? How many chiefs has the tribe, and how many has each clan composing it?

85. WHAT IS THE POWER OF THE PRIESTHOOD, AS AN ELEMENT IN THE DECISION OF POLITICAL QUESTIONS? — Do they constitute a distinct power in the government? If so, do they exercise this power by sitting in council, or in other modes? Are they, in fact, counsellors, and what influence do they exercise in questions of war or peace, the advance or retreat of a war party, or the the sale and cession of land?

86. DEFINE THE POWER OF THE WAR CHIEFS — Does their power come in as an element in the political organization of the council, or in the exercise of the civil power of the village chiefs or magistrates, in cases where both powers are not concentrated in the same hands? Are the powers of a war and a civil chief often united in the same person? If the war chiefs be exclusively designated by the popular voice among the warrior class, at what age can a voice in their favor be exercised? Is there any limit, or time, when a young man may appropriately express his opinion?

87. WHAT ARE THE RIGHTS OF THE MATRONS IN COUNCIL? — May this right be exercised for any purpose but that of peace? Are they permitted, as in the ancient institutions of the Iroquois, to a separate seat in Council? And have they, as in that nation, a prescriptive right of being heard by an official person, who bears the character of a messenger from the women? State the general impression with respect to the political power of the matrons in the tribe, and inquire whether the widows of distinguished chiefs, or of those of acknowledged wisdom, are ever admitted to sit in council?

88. WHO HAS A RIGHT TO GENERAL COUNCILS? WHAT TRIBE? — Are there, among the various tribes, any who possess the power to summon such councils, as a prescriptive right? If so, designate them, and state the extent of this right, the supposed occasion or era of its origin, and the general nature of the subjects that may be brought before them. Are such rights to be regarded as vestiges of ancient confederacies, or the result of causes which have been in operation only since the discovery of the continent? What occasions of such general councils can be referred to? In the Wyandot tribe, and in the Delaware tribe, what are the grounds of the ancient right formerly or at present claimed, in this respect, by each? And in what manner did the growing Iroquois supremacy operate to interfere with, or break down, this right, or render nugatory its exercise?

89. PRIVATE RIGHT TO TAKE LIFE, OR LAW OF RETALIATION. STATE IT. — How is this right exercised — is it with or without the assent of the chief presiding over the village, or band? And when does the right stop? Is it terminated at one, two, three, or more repetitions of its exercise? If there be no male next of kin in a direct line, or of the same *totem*, to the person murdered, may the right be exercised by collateral branches, and to what extent? Is the right to take life for life, in any case, compromised by accepting presents? What is the usual amount? Does it depend upon the means or ability of the person who is to suffer the penalty of the law of retaliation, or on those of his friends? Does the intervention of a long time, and the fleeing of the murderer, generally allay resentment, and lead to negotiations for compromises? What period is sufficient for this change of feeling, and spirit of compromise? Are efforts for this purpose often utterly rejected? Is there

any recognized principle of escape, or place of retreat, analogous to a town, or place of refuge, as among certain of the Shemitic tribes? Are females, in cases of deaths from the feuds of polygamy, &c., vindicated? Are their lives estimated as high as those of males? Are questions of Indian debts due to traders commonly brought before the chiefs, to be settled, or adjusted; and have the chiefs, or people, who are committed to your official charge as an agent, sufficient knowledge of the power of numbers to enable them to act with prudence? Is a message accompanied with wampum, &c., invested with anything like the equivalent authority of a *legal summons*, in cases of private disputes, or controversies?

90. GAME LAWS, OR RIGHTS OF THE CHASE. WHAT ARE THESE? — Has each family of the tribe a certain tract of country, within the circle of which, it is understood and conceded, that the head or members of this family have a particular or exclusive right to hunt? Are intrusions on this tract the cause of disputes and bloodshed?

91. TRESPASSES ON THE PRESCRIBED BOUNDARIES. — Are furs thus surreptitiously hunted, on another man's limits, subject to be seized by the party aggrieved? If such a cause of quarrel be brought before the chiefs, or wise men, is the right awarded according to a fixed rule and understanding, respecting the parcelling out, into families, of all the hunting grounds of the tribe?

92. NOTICES OF LOCAL INTRUSIONS. — Are warnings of such intrusions frequently given? Or is injury to property redressed, privately, like injury to life? Is a forfeit of life often the result of continued intrusions? Or is seizure of the furs hunted deemed sufficient?

93. RULES OF HUNTING, AND DIVISION OF GAME. — If hunting parties or companions agree to hunt together, for a special time, or for the season, what are the usual laws, or customs, regulating the hunt? If one person start an animal, and wound it, and another pursue and kill it, how is the meat divided? Is the game equally divided? Does each retain the skins and furs of the animals actually killed by him? What is done in cases of thefts from traps?

94. DISPUTE BETWEEN TRIBES. — If a tribe, or band, pass over the lines and hunt on the lands of another tribe, and kill game there, is it deemed a just cause of war? Do messages pass, in the first place, between the chiefs; and is there a spirit of comity, and diplomacy exercised?

Indian Trade

95. WHAT ARE THE PRINCIPAL FACTS, NECESSARY TO BE KNOWN, TO REGULATE THE INDIAN TRADE AND COMMERCE, AND TO PRESERVE PEACEFUL RELATIONS ON THE FRONTIERS? — Has commercial intercourse promoted the general cause of Indian civilization? How is the traffic in furs and skins conducted, throughout its operations? What are its general principles — the place of outfit and supply — the place of exchange, the difficulties and risk attending it, and the general chances of profit and loss?

96. CAPACITY AND FIDELITY OF THE INDIANS, AS CUSTOMERS. — Are the chiefs and hunters shrewd, cautious and exact in their dealings, making their purchases with judgment, and paying up their debts faithfully? Are they moral, sober, and discreet? Do they rely on memory wholly, in keeping the sum of their indebtedness, and the number of skins paid, or are they aided by hieroglyphics, or devices of any kind, on the clerk's blotter, or in any other manner? Are they exact herein? If not successful, at the first or second hunt, or but partially so, are the credits required to be renewed? Are they freely renewed?

97. NECESSITY OF THE TRADERS TO LOOK AFTER THEIR CREDITS, AND THEIR LIABILITY TO LOSS FROM FLUCTUATIONS OF CLIMATE. — Is it necessary for the trader to send runners to the Indian hunters' camps, or private lodges, to collect their debts? Are these runners faithful,

honest men? Is the result of unsuccessful, or deficient hunts, often caused by the migration, to other parts of the country, of some of the furred animals relied on, owing to excessive local dryness, or redundant moisture of the season? Do losses flow from these causes?

98. RATES OF BARTER — PERMANENCY OR VALUE OF DEBT, AND TAX OF LOCAL RESIDENCE. — Is the tariff of exchanges such as, generally, to protect the trader from loss? Is it just and fair? At what period after the credits are given, is an Indian debt deemed bad or lost? Are they bad at two years? Are the traders who conduct the interior exchanges, subject to onerous calls on their charity, or hospitable feelings, by sickness, or suffering in the villages adjacent to their trading houses? And if so, does this circumstance come in, as a just element, in summing up the results of a series of years' trade, with the tribe?

99. WHAT HAVE BEEN THE LEADING EFFECTS OF THE DISCOVERY ON THE HUNTER PERIOD? — Have the purposes of commerce, since the discovery of the continent, had the effect to stimulate the hunters to increased exertions, and thus to hasten the diminution, or destruction of the races of animals whose furs are sought?

100. DIMINUTION OF ANIMALS. — Have the different races of animals declined rapidly since the prosecution of the trade? What animals flee first, or diminish in the highest ratio, on the opening of a new district of the remote forest, to trade? Is the buffalo first to flee? Is the beaver next?

101. REFUSE HUNTING GROUNDS. — Are the lands, when denuded of furs, of comparatively little value to the Indians, while they remain in the hunter state? Is not the sale of such hunted lands beneficial to them?

102. AREA REQUIRED TO SUBSIST A HUNTER. — What quantity of territory is required to be kept in its wilderness state, in order to afford a sufficient number of wild animals to sustain an Indian family?

103. QUESTION OF THE ULTIMATE RFFECTS OF THE FAILURE OF GAME ON THE RACE. — If the diminution or failure of wild animals lead the native tribes to turn their industry to agriculture, is not the pressure of commerce on the boundaries of hunting an efficient cause in the progress of Indian civilization? Has not the introduction of heavy and coarse woollen goods, in place of valuable furs and skins, as articles of clothing, increased the means of subsistence of the native tribes?

104. MORAL CONSEQUENCES OF CIVILIZED INTERCOURSE. — What evil effects, of a moral character, have resulted from the progress of the Indian trade? Has not the traffic in ardent spirits been by far the most fruitful, general and appalling cause of the depopulation of the tribes? How has the introduction of gun-powder and fire-arms affected the principles of the trade, and what has been the general influence of this new element of destruction, on their history and civilization? Have internal wars or peace been promoted thereby? What has been the prominent cause of discord on the frontiers, arising from the transactions of trade and commerce? Finally, can this trade be placed on better principles, and what are they?

105. PROBLEM OF THEIR CIVILIZATION. — Are there any serious or valid objections, on the part of the Indians, to the introduction of schools, agriculture, the mechanic arts or Christianity? If so, state them. Specify the objections — examine their bearings, and state the results which are reached by your best observation, reflection, and judgment.

Legislation of Congress

106. WHAT IMPROVEMENTS CAN YOU SUGGEST IN THE EXISTING INTERCOURSE LAWS OF THE UNITED DTATES AS LAST REVISED, WITH THE INDIAN TRIBES? — Are these laws efficient in

removing causes of discord, and preserving peace between the advanced bodies of emigrants or settlers on the frontiers, and the Indian tribes? Do they provide for difficulties between tribe and tribe? Is this at all practicable?

107. SOURCES OF DISCORD. — Whence do causes of difficulties and war usually arise, and how are they best prevented?

108. RIGHTS OF THE INDIANS. — What provisions of existing laws appear susceptible, in your opinion, of amendment, in order to secure more effectually the rights or welfare of the Indians?

109. FISCAL MEANS. — Could important objects be secured by the introduction of any modifications of the provisions respecting the payment or distribution of annuities, the subsistence of assembled bodies of Indians, or the investment or application of the treaty funds?

110. CHANGE OF LOCATION. — Is there any feature in the present laws which could be adapted more exactly to their present location, or to the advanced or altered state of society at present existing in the tribe?

111. ALCOHOLIC DRINK. — What provisions would tend more effectually to shield the tribes from the introduction of ardent spirits into their territories, and from the pressure of lawless or illicit traffic?

112. TREATY SYSTEM. — Is there any feature in the present system of negotiation with the tribes susceptible of amendment and improvement? Can the tribes, at this particular phasis of our settlements, and with their present increased means, and the consequent temptations to frontier cupidity, be as well negotiated with, in the forest, where all the means of improper influence are in full force, as they could be at the seat of Government? Are not the expenses of the subsistence of masses of men, women and children, at remote points on the frontier, unavoidably heavy? Does not an actual intercourse with the Executive Head of the Government, tend to give the tribes better views of its character and influence?

113. CAN THE TRIBAL RIGHTS OF THE INDIANS BE BETTER PROTECTED, AND THE TRIBE BE INCITED TO HIGHER EFFORTS IN CIVILIZATION? — Are the game, and wood and timber of the tribes subject to unnecessary or injurious curtailment or trespass from the intrusion of emigrating bands abiding for long periods on their territories? Are there complaints of any such trespasses?

114. THEIR ULTIMATE INDEPENDENCE. — Are any of the tribes in your district sufficiently advanced to have their funds paid to a treasurer of the tribe, to be kept by him, and disbursed agreeably to the laws of their local legislature?

115. QUESTIONS STILL BEARING ON THE LESS ADVANCED TRIBES. — Are payments of annuities to chiefs, or to separate heads of families, most beneficial? Should the principal of an Indian fund be paid in annuities to Indians at the present period, under any circumstances; and, if so, under what circumstances? Are members of the tribe generally capable of the wise or prudent application of money?

New Indian Governments West of the Mississippi

116. WHAT ARE THE DISTINCTIVE PRINCIPLES OF THE GOVERNMENTS ASSUMED, OF LATE YEARS, BY THE MORE ADVANCED OF THE SEMI-CIVILIZED TRIBES WEST OF THE MISSISSIPPI? — How is the elective franchise expressed and guarded? In giving a vote, are there any qualifications required by their laws as to property, the rendition of prior public services, or any prescribed condition of the voter arising from other pre-deterinined general causes? What

individual rights are surrendered, in these schemes of government, to the central or governing power, as a boon or equivalent for the general security of life, liberty, and property?

117. HOW DO THESE NASCENT GOVERNMENTS PRACTICALLY WORK, AND WHAT HAS BEEN THEIR PROGRESS? — Have original defects been remedied by adapting them more exactly to the genius and character of the people than they were, apparently, in the first rough drafts? What has been the progress in establishing a judiciary, and in the development of their national resources by wise and well-guarded laws?

118. WHAT IS THE PRESENT STATE AND FUTURE PROSPECTS OF THESE GOVERNMENTS? — Have the legislative assemblies adopted a practical system of laws for the enforcement of public order, the trial of public offences, the collection of debts, the raising of revenue, the erection of public buildings and ferries, school-houses and churches, or the promotion of education, the support of Christianity, and the general advancement of virtue, temperance, and the public welfare? Has this new phasis of these ancient communities had the effect to amalgamate the ancient clanships and sectional divisions, so far as these were founded thereon, or to obliterate them, together with their traditions — to dispel superstition, and ameliorate, in any marked degree, the condition of society in its humbler walks, and throughout the general mass? State the present condition of the tribes which have established these governments, the difficulties yet to be surmounted, and the probable progress which they may be expected to make.

Property

119. WHAT IDEAS HAVE THE INDIANS OF PROPERTY? — How do they believe private rights accrued? Have they any true views of the legal idea of property? Are they capable of clear and exact considerations of this character? In what manner do they suppose that property in things was first acquired by man? If possession gave this right, did the right continue, as long as the possessor was able to defend it? If the starting and pursuit of a deer gave a man a right to it, was this right affected by another's killing it? Did building a wigman, or planting corn on a vacant, or distant part, of another tribe's territory, make the land his? And if so, how many years must it be held undisputed, to make the right valid? An Indian of the British dominions applied to an Indian Agent of the United States some years ago, for the allowance and payment by the United States of a private debt contracted in, and by a North Briton, resident in Hudson's Bay. How did the mind operate in this case, and how does it operate generally, in tracing the claim of right and title in property, and of obligation in the affairs of debtor and creditor? Endeavor to trace the process of individuality in rights and property.

120. HOW DID TITLE ORIGINALLY ACCRUE TO TERRITORY? — Was the right of a nation to the tract of country originally possessed by it, acquired by its occupancy of it by them, to the exclusion of all others? Did the Great Spirit make a gift of it to them, and why to them alone? If he gave to each tribe a portion of the country, and thus parcelled out the whole continent, and gave them, at the same time, a right to defend it, who gave one nation a right to invade the territories of another, for the purpose of dispossessing them? How can they justify this? If the Indians have no clear or fixed views on the subject, it will be sufficient to state the fact; if they, on the contrary, evince exactitude, pursue it, and illustrate the topic.

121. ARE THERE ANY TRACES OF THE LAW OF PRIMOGENITURE? — Is the descent of property fixed? Is the eldest son entitled to any greater rights, or larger share of property, than the other children? Does a parent express his will, or wishes, before death, as a descendant of Uncas did, how his property should be disposed of? Does a chief designate which of his

children is to wear his medal; or is there ever made a legacy of a choice gun, an ornamented tomahawk, or other article? State the general usage of parents, and of chiefs, on this head.

122. WHAT ARE THE OBLIGATIONS FELT BY THE INDIANS TO PAY DEBTS? — Does time greatly diminish, in their view, these obligations, and how? Does the Indian fancy that ill luck in hunting, is a dispensation from the Great Spirit, and that he is exonerated thereby from the obligation? Are the Indians prone to sink individuality in their debts, after a time, into nationality, and to seek to provide for them in that manner? Is the tribe punctual in the payment of their debts, and what is their general character on this subject? Do they set a high value on real property, exacting for it its real worth, or do they part with it readily, and for small and inadequate sums? Do they ever make more than one conveyance of such property, and are the questions of decision arising therefrom often complex and difficult?

Crime

123. WHAT CONSTITUTES CRIME? — Has man a right to take his fellow's blood? Is the taking of life an offence to the individual murdered, or to the Great Spirit who gave him his life? In the estimation of the Indians, did the Great Spirit, in forming the world and placing mankind upon it, give all an equal right to life; and if so, was not murder, from the beginning, a very great crime? If a crime, can the spirit of a hunter or a warrior, in their view, go to the Indian paradise, without satisfying the justice of the Great Spirit? How can this be done? Does the law of retaliation (vide 89) please or satisfy the Great Spirit? Can one, or two, or three murders expiate the crime of an original murder? Do they not make the offence to the Great Spirit the greater? State the common notions of the Indians on this point, and endeavor to learn whether they believe at all in punishments after death.

124. CAN THE DEITY BE OFFENDED? — Is a man under high obligations, by the fact of his creation, to worship the Great Spirit? And if he is, and yet he do not worship him, has he thereby committed a crime? What crime? Will the Great Spirit remember it, and how is it to be expiated?

125. WHY IS FALSEHOOD A MORAL OFFENCE? — Is it because the Great Spirit abhors it, or because injuries may result to man? If the Great Spirit abhors a lie, how can he excuse it? Has he not a character to reward truth, and to punish falsehood?

126. IS THE WANT OF VENERATION IN THE INDIANS A CRIME? — Are greater veneration and respect paid to parents than to brothers and sisters? Is an Indian priest, or a chief, more venerated than a common man? Is age, under any circumstances, the object of veneration? Is it a crime to strike a parent, as it was in the Jewish tribes? Is there any known instance of such an offence? Is it punishable, and how? Did the Indians ever kill by stoning a person?

127. WHAT CAN THE SAGES AND WISE MEN OF THE TRIBE SAY IN DEFENCE OF THE INDIAN CODE, DOING LIKE FOR LIKE? — If a bad deed is returned for a bad deed, is the Great Spirit pleased, or satisfied thereby? Try to arouse a moral sensitiveness on this point, in order to bring out their reasons, if any they have, for crimes against humanity, good neighborhood, property, chastity, &c.

Religion

128. DO THEY BELIEVE THAT THERE IS A DEITY PERVADING THE UNIVERSE, WHO IS THE MAKER OF ALL THINGS? — What ideas do they possess of the Great Spirit? Is he believed to be self-existent, eternal, omnipresent, omniscient, omnipotent, and invisible? When the Great Spirit made the earth, and furnished it with animals and men, did he, according to

their traditions, give man power over the animal creation, and did he, by any messenger or angel, or priest, give to man any definite rights, message or moral rules or laws, to be kept? If so, what rules of life did he give? Do they believe that they are responsible, to keep these laws or rules, and if so, why?

129. IS THE GREAT SPIRIT, OR DEITY, REVEALED IN THE PHYSICAL CHARACTER OF THE EARTH? — How does he manifest his presence on the earth, or in the sky? In what forms is he recognised? Is thunder considered his voice? Are storms regarded as his acts? Are cataracts evidences of his power?

130. WHAT ARE THE MORAL PRINCIPLES OF HIS GOVERNMENT, AND HOW ARE THESE PRINCIPLES MADE KNOWN TO THEM? — Is death the act of the Great Spirit? Do war and peace happen according to his will? Is he the author of evil in the world, and what object did he, in their opinion, purpose to accomplish thereby? Do they believe, with the Wyandots, that the Great Spirit created two great personages, subordinate to himself, with general powers in the world, called *Good* and *Evil*, and set them in perpetual opposition? (This, it will be recollected, was the belief of Zoroaster and his followers.) Have these prime spirits, lesser spirits of benign or malignant character, who are subject, respectively, to them? Did the Great Spirit create the great Evil Spirit, as he is generally called, and make him subject to himself, or is this malignant spirit, so universally feared by the Indians, of an independent nature, and may he be worshipped? If he is not independent in his existence and attributes, how do they expect to escape the displeasure of the Great Spirit, for offering sacrifices and worship to so evil a being? Do they indeed worship the Evil Spirit? Is not taking another person's goods, or denying the truth, or doing any act of wrong or unkindness between man and man, displeasing to the Great Spirit? And a proof of obeying the voice of his evil adversary? How do they excuse this?

131. HOW ARE THEY EXCUSED FOR OFFENCES AGAINST THE GREAT SPIRIT? — Is there any provision, in their religious system, by the intervention of their priests, or sacrifices, or fasts, or in any way whatever, by which cases of disrespect, or neglect of the Great Spirit, can, in their belief, be excused or pardoned? Are hunger, cold, or human sufferings of any kind, satisfactory and acceptable, as some of them believe, for offences against the Deity?

132. ARE THE INDIAN SACRIFICES COMPENSATIONS FOR EVIL DEEDS? — Have they any idea whatever of an atonement, or a belief or expectation that some great personage was to come on earth, and answer for them, to the Great Spirit; and if not, is such an idea readily explained, and made reasonable to them? What do the missionaries report on this subject? Can they discern in their rites, or mythology, any name, or feature, having allusion to the atonement, and thus denoting their connection with nations of the Shemitic stock, who embraced this idea prior or subsequent to the opening of the Christian era? Do they sacrifice animals to appease the *justice*, or to acknowledge the *goodness* of the Great Spirit? Did they or their ancestors ever offer *human* sacrifices, as it is known that the Aztecs of Mexico did? Were prisoners — who were burned at the stake by the North American Indians — offered only to satisfy the spirit of vengeance, or to gratify the thirst of warlike glory? Is it *certain* that there was *no* religious rite, or feeling, mingled with these barbarities? What is the latest period of such practices? Are not sacrifices of female prisoners now made by the Pawnees, and some of the Upper Missouri tribes, to a divinity analogous to Ceres, or the supposed goddess of corn?

133. WHAT IS THE MORAL CHARACTER OF THE INDIAN PRIESTHOOD? — Are they virtuous, sober, truthful, or ascetic? Do they bear any badge of their office? How many different classes of priests, or prophets, are there in the tribe? What are their names, and in what manner and with what ceremonies do they exercise their several powers? Are these priests

hereditary, or may any person assume the functions? Are the offices confined to males, or may they be assumed by females? Do they affect to reveal future events; to direct where lost articles may be found; to bring down a blessing, or invoke a curse from the Great Spirit? Have the tribe, or the pagan or unconverted portions of it, general confidence in their power? When an Indian dies, does an Indian priest attend his sick bed, or his funeral? For what purpose does he attend? What office, or functions does he perform? Does he make an address, or anything resembling a prayer? If the man dies, who draws the devices on his grave-post? Give specimens of such devices or inscriptions, if in your power, with their interpretation. What, in the Algonquin tribes, is a *Jossakeed*, a *Meda*, and a *Wabeno*?

134. WHAT GENERAL BELIEFS AND SUPERSTITIONS PREVAIL? — Are there some points in which all agree? Do they believe in angels, or special messengers of the Great Spirit? Are guardian spirits supposed to have the power of shielding individuals from the power of evil? Is there a supposed class of spirits, or agents, who can assume the forms of animals or men, and who have the power of thwarting the will of the Great Spirit? Does the evil spirit thwart his will?

135. NECROMANCERS AND SORCERERS. — Have they a class of persons, who affect to wield the power of necromancy or sorcery? Do they affect to remove diseases, or to inflict them? Do they believe in witchcraft? Are witches and wizards supposed to have the power of transforming themselves into other shapes? What is the theory on this subject? Do witches or wizards invariably exercise their powers for evil and not for good purposes? Have persons accused of those acts been burned? When were the last executions for this offence made? Did Tecumthe avail himself of this superstition to remove rivals from the Indian nations; did he condemn the noted chief Tarhe?

136. VARIOUS BELIEFS, PARTLY OF ORIENTAL, AND PARTLY OF WESTERN ORIGIN. — Do they believe in vampyres or in premonitions from the dead, or in the theory of ghosts? Do they trust in charms and amulets? What is the Indian theory of dreams? Are dreams regarded as revelations of the divine will? Do they exercise much influence over the practical affairs of the Indian life? Are good dreams courted under the influence of abstinence? Are guardian spirits selected under the like influences? Are they prone to regard themselves as doomed, or spell-cast? Are they easily alarmed by omens?

137. WHAT IS THE ACTUAL CHARACTER OF THEIR WORSHIP WHEN CLOSELY ANALYZED? — What species or degree of worship do they, *in fine*, render to the Great Spirit? Do they praise him, in hymns, chants, or chorusses? Do they pray to him, and if so, for what purpose? Is it for success in hunting, war, or any other avocation of life? Give, if you can, a specimen of their prayers.

138. RITES OF FASTING AND FEASTING. — Do they fast that they may acquire mental purity, or cleanliness to commune with him? Are the general feasts at the coming in of the new corn, and at the commencement of the general fall hunts, of a religious character? Are these feasts of the nature of *thanksgivings*? Are any of the chorusses, or songs of the priests, sacred, or of hieratic character? Is the flesh of the bear, or dog, which is sacrificed, used to propitiate his favor? Is it true, that *all* the flesh, bones, and the "purtenance" of the animals sacrificed in the feast, must be eaten, or burned, as in the institution of the paschal supper?

139. SACRED CHARACTER OF TOBACCO. — Are the leaves of the tobacco plant, which are cast on the waters or burned in the pipe, offered as sacrifices to the Great Spirit?

140. HAVE YOU OBSERVED ANY TRACES OF THE GHEBIR WORSHIP, OR THE IDEA OF AN ETERNAL FIRE? — It is seen in their pictorial scrolls of bark, that they draw the figure of the *sun* to

represent the Great Spirit. Is the sun the common symbol of the Great Spirit? Do they now, or did their ancestors, worship him, through this symbol? It is stated by General Cass, after visiting the Indian tribes in the north-west, in 1820, that there formerly existed an order of men, whose duty it was to keep alive an "eternal fire." Is there anything of this nature now existing, or known in the traditions of the tribes best known to you? The French described the Natchez as sun-worshippers. State the traditions and existing opinions of the Indians on this topic.

141. WHAT ARE THE NOTIONS OF THE TRIBE ON THE NATURE AND SUBSTANCE OF FIRE, OR CALORIC? — Is fire obtained from the flint, or from percussion, deemed more sacred than from other sources? Is this the reason why councils are opened for public business, among the far tribes, with fire thus obtained? Is there in this custom of burning tobacco with fire so obtained, accompanied by gesticulations to the Great Spirit, any vestige or evidence of the ancient prevalence of fire-worship among the North American tribes? Are there any other evidences of the estimation of fire known to you, which denote the former prevalence of such worship, in the latitudes of this continent north of the ancient Aztec empire of Mexico?

142. IDEA OF A HOLY FIRE. — Did the Indian priests, at former periods, annually, or at any set time, direct the fire to be extinguished in the Indian lodges, and ashes cast about to desecrate them, that they might furnish the people new and sacred fire to re-light them?

143. WHAT NOTIONS HAVE THEY OF THE PLANETARY SYSTEM? — In speaking of the moon, as some of the tribes have, as being the consort of the sun, do they regard it as the shadow or effusion of the sun, or as deriving its light therefrom? Are the stars or planets regarded as parts of a system? Are they supposed to be occupied by the souls of men? State their ideas of the planets, generally, in connection with number 47.

144. HOW DO SIGNS AFFECT THEM? — Do omens and prognostications exercise a strong sway over the Indian mind? Do they ever influence councils in their deliberations, or war-parties on their march? Are predictions, drawn from the flight of birds, much relied on? Are auguries ever drawn from the sombre line, shape or motions of the clouds?

145. IS THERE REASON TO BELIEVE THE INDIANS TO BE IDOLATORS? — Are images of wood or stone ever worshipped? or is there any gross and palpable form of idolatry in the existing tribes, similar to that of the oriental world? What superstition or purpose is denoted by setting up water-worn stones, or boulders, resembling images, on the shores of the rivers and lakes? What objects are enclosed in the arcanum of the medicine-sack? Has this sack, or secret depository of sacred things, any of the characters of "an ark," which have been attributed to it by writers? What deductions are to be drawn from idols which have been discovered?

146. IMMORTALITY. — Do they believe in the immortality of the soul, and the doctrine of moral accountability to the Creator? Do they believe in the resurrection of the body? A conception has appeared in the traditions of the Chippewa tribe, of the existence of duplicate souls, as if there were one soul of the body and another of the mind. Are there any traces of such a belief of the tribe, whose customs you are acquainted with? Do they believe, at all, in the doctrine of rewards and punishments in a future state? Do they represent the future and unknown state, as, in fact, a phantasmagoria, or shadowy image of the present world — its topography, and its productions and enjoyments? Is the crossing of a deep stream, in the fancied journey of the soul to the land of bliss, as believed by some of the Algonquin tribes, an allegorical representation of future punishments for acts done in this life? Is this a partial or general belief?

147. WHAT IS THE COMMON NOTION OF THE INDIAN PARADISE? — Do the virtuous and the vicious alike, expect to enjoy its fruitions? By taking the idea of evil, suffering, or punishment from its precincts of expected bliss, do the Indians not reproduce, on the western continent, the exact counterpart of the Mahomedan or oriental paradise? Are there any deaths in the Indian paradise? Or is it a final state? Will there be any giants or enchanters there? Will there be any wars?

148. IS THERE NOT A PERVERSION OF THE DOCTRINE OF IMMORTALITY RESPECTING THE BRUTE CREATION? — Do the Indians believe in the resurrection of animals? Do they believe that the Great Spirit has given the brute creation *souls* and *reasoning powers*, as well as man? An Indian, in 1820, begged pardon of a bear, whom he had shot on the shores of Lake Superior. Did this imply that he was to encounter him, as an immortal being, in another life?

149. WHAT PECULIAR SOCIETIES CHARACTERIZE INDIAN LIFE? — Are these societies bound by the obligation of secrecy? What secret rites exist? Do they partake of a religious, festive, or other character? What knowledge do they profess to cultivate? Among the tribes of Algonquin origin, there are separate institutions or fraternities, called the *Wabeno* and the *Medawin* societies. Is there any extension of these societies, or are there similar fraternities in the tribes you are conversant with? If so, describe them, with their origin and rites, the ties which bind them together, and the object of each, and the influence it exerts. Is the knowledge and practice of medicine confined to the members or professors of these societies? Are they, in any marked manner, the depositories of the traditions of the tribe, or of any department of aboriginal knowledge? Are the members of these societies, more than the uninitiated, skilled in the art of drawing devices, or in the keeping of their mnemonic songs? An opinion was expressed by the late Governor De Witt Clinton, that there was, among the Iroquois, some ancient tie or sign of fraternity and recognition, resembling the Masonic tie. Is there any sign or evidence of such a rite observable in the customs of the tribe known to you?

Mythology

150. WHAT PECULIAR MYTHS HAVE THE TRIBE? — Do they believe that the great spirit of evil manifests himself on the earth, in the form of the serpent? Are the rattlesnake, and other venomous species, more than others, invested with fearful powers? Do the priests sometimes put these into their drums? Is the respect and veneration paid to serpents, the true cause of their lives being spared when encountered in the forest? Do they offer tobacco to appease the spirit of the snake? What theory does this imply? Can the species send disease? Can they charm, or enchant the warrior, so as to bewilder him in his path? Did the great serpent, as he is represented in their mythological tales, produce the flood, which submerged the earth and drowned mankind? Do the great *Coatl* of the South, and *Kenabic* of the North, typify an ark, or vessel of safety? State the various mystical notions they have on this, to the Indian mind, important subject.

151. IS THE BELIEF IN METAMORPHOSIS GENERAL? — Do they believe that various quadrupeds, birds, or reptiles were transformed into men? Does the doctrine, as held by them, reach to objects in the vegetable, or mineral kingdoms, or in the open heavens? Were some of the stars once men? Was Ursa Major a bear? Was the rainbow a snare, or net? Were the thunderers once warriors renowned for their use of the arrow? Was the *zea maize* or Indian corn originally a handsome young man, with plumes, who came from the skies? Was the raccoon once a shell? Was the dormouse a mastodon? Who exercised this power of enchantment, or transformation? Were they magicians, or giants, or spirits of

good or evil kind? What was the era of their reign on the earth? Will the doom of the transformed objects be terminated at death? Will it be reversed, and visited upon the enchanters?

152. DO THEY BELIEVE IN THE PYTHAGOREAN DOCTRINE OF METEMPSYCHOSIS, OR THE TRANS-MIGRATION OF SOULS? — Are the changes of the souls of men into degraded and brute forms the awards of a just or unjust punishment? Were they the acts of malignant or good spirits? Are the souls of men sometimes sent into birds of the upper air, as a reward for their deeds, and their unjust or premature loss of life? How are the souls of infants disposed of? How many changes did the souls of *Papukewiss* undergo, in animals and birds, before he was merged into a rock, that be might withstand the bolts of the Great Thunderer?

153. WHAT PARTICULAR ANIMALS STAND HIGH IN THEIR MYTHOLOGY, AND HOW DOES THIS BELIEF AFFECT THEIR INSTITUTIONS? — Do the respect and honor which are paid to the turtle, wolf, and bear, and to the clans who bear these devices, (*vide* 77) arise from the supposed importance of ancient heroes or valiant men, who fell under the necromantic power of evil spirits or wizards? And what influence has this myth had on the original establishment of the Totemic system of the clans?

154. WHAT FABLED GODS, DEMIGODS, HEROES AND VIEWLESS SPIRITS OR GENII OF THE AIR AND EARTH, HAVE THEY EMBRACED IN THEIR ORAL TRADITIONS? — Who were Inigorio and Inigohatatea? Are they allegorical representations of the Great Spirit's will in the moral world? What demigods, giants or heroes are denoted by the names Quetzalcoatl, Tarenyawago, and Manabozho? What missions did they respectively execute? Did they perform the labors or exploits of a Hercules, a Deucalion, or a Minerva? Are these traditions but a western version of Vishnoo, Budha, or Siva? Or were these persons reformers in manners and arts, government, or religion? Were they merely human or pseudo-divine? Who were the stone giants of Indian tradition? What calamity is prefigured by the fiery-flying heads? Who was Atahentsic? Who were Atahocan and Chebiabo? Who pierced the great elk at Itasca? What gigantic animal was buried under the mountains? Who were the giants Hobomok and Kluneolux? What allegoric personages live in a cave under Niagara Falls? Are there demigods who preside over the four cardinal points? Why is the west wind called the father of the winds? Who are the gods of the vernal and autumnal equinoxes? Who does Nope personify?

155. WHAT ARE THE NAMES AND CLASSES OF THEIR PRINCIPAL LOCAL DEITIES, OR WOODLAND SPIRITS, AND WHAT ANALOGY DO THEY BEAR TO THE MYTHOLOGICAL CREATIONS OF THE OLD WORLD? — Is there a class of creations analogous to fairies? Are there fairies of the water, as well as of the land? Are the Indian *puckwies* visible or invisible? Are they vicious or benign? Do these creations delight to dwell in romantic retreats, or at picturesque points? Are there local spirits, or a kind of nymphs and dryads, who reside in caves or at cascades, or inhabit cliffs or mountains? Do they protect or entrap travellers? Do the natives believe in mermaids or *mermans*? Is there any creation analogous to Comus, Ceres, Saturn, or Morpheus? Is death personified? Have they a Hades, or land of shades? What Indian hero visited it? Are their creations of viewless kind and infinite stature, called *Weengs*, a species of gnomes? Can we recognize in the Indian idea of multiform spirits of a local character, the old Arabic notion of genii, or is this conception to be regarded as one of the original creations of the Red Race found here?

156. ARE THE INDIAN ALLEGORIES, FABLES AND LODGE STORIES, MENTIONED IN TITLE V. FRUIT-FUL IN THE REVELATION OF THEIR MYTHOLOGICAL NOTIONS? — Are such oral tales and relations common? Do they form a species of lodge-lore, which the young early learn? Are the relations confined to old, or privileged persons? *Vide picture-writing, No. 245.*

157. IS THUNDER PERSONIFIED? — How many thunderers are there? Are they located in different quarters of the heavens? What is their various character, and origin?

158. IS THE INDIAN MYTHOLOGY VERY ANCIENT? — What fabled monsters and dragons, with wings or horns, filled the antique epochs of the world; and who killed them, or how were the races extirpated? Has their system of mythology been affected by the introduction of Christianity? Something of this kind is thought to be observable in examining the ancient picture-writings of the Aztecs, written after the conquest of Mexico, and it is important to guard against this intermixture of original and interfused notions.

Manners and Customs
Constitution of the Indian Family

159. ARE THE TIES OF CONSANGUINITY STRONG? — Are there terms for each degree of relationship, and what are they for the different degrees? Do these terms embrace all the collateral branches? Are the affinities of families and clans traced far back, and, as there are no surnames, by what means is the line of descent denoted and rendered certain? Are the same names used for collateral relatives by the father's as by the mother's, side? Are the same terms used for elder and younger brother, and for elder and younger sister? Are the words aunt and uncle by the mother's side the same as aunt and uncle by the father's side? By what terms are the dead alluded to? State any peculiarities which may exist in the terms denoting kindred, age, or sex, or other particulars in the family names, which mark them, or distinguish the principles of speech in the family circle from those of other known nations?

160. IS THE FAMILY ASSOCIATION, OR MARRIED STATE, GENERALLY ONE OF A PERMANENT CHARACTER, AND PROMOTIVE OF DOMESTIC HAPPINESS? — Does the hunter state ensure abundance of food and clothing to the family? How is this state, in its domestic bearings, affected by polygamy, and what are the terms and relative affections of stepmothers and children? Are wives well treated under the actual state of the hunter life? Are they ever interfered with in the household affairs, and management of the domestic economy? Do they participate, in any degree, in the hunter's vocation, or forest labors, and to what extent?

161. ARE THE LABORS OF HUSBAND AND WIFE EQUALLY OR UNEQUALLY DIVIDED? — Is the labor and toil of hunting and supplying the family with meats a just equivalent, in point of time, for the cares and duties the wife bestows on the lodge, including its erection? Does the public security of their hunting grounds, arising from councils and warlike expeditions, enter into the views of the wife, as constituting an acceptable part of the husband's duty? Who makes the arms and implements of war? Who makes canoes, paddles, cradles, bowls, and dishes? Who plants, and hoes, and gathers the fruits of the field? Who makes fish-nets, weaves mats, and cuts rushes and gathers wild rice? Run through the entire class of forest labors, and draw a comparison between the relative industry, or time, devoted by the husband and the wife.

162. WHAT ARE THE USUAL CAUSES OF FAMILY JARS IN THE INDIAN LODGE? — Are domestic discords common? Is the loss of youth and youthful attractions in the wife a cause of neglect? Does barrenness produce dissatisfaction? Do children give their mother an additional power over her husband's affentious? Is jealousy a common cause of discord? In cases of a plurality of wives, does the oldest retain the precedence? Is the Indian character for comity, dignity, and forbearance, in the domestic circle, such as it has been generally represented? Do the Indian women disclose a passion for dress, and is the failure to appropriate a part of the hunt to this object among the causes of discord?

163. HOW IS ORDER PRESERVED IN THE LIMITED PRECINCTS OF THE LODGE? — Casual observers would judge there was but little. Inquire into this subject, and state what are the characteristic traits of living in the wigwam, or Indian house. How do the parents and children divide the space at night? How are wives, and females of every condition, protected in their respective places, and guarded from intrusion? Is there a prescribed or fixed seat, or *abbinos*, as it is called, for each inmate? Who fixes it? On what occasion is it changed, or enlarged; and are the rules governing this subject such as at all times and seasons to secure the local lodge rights and privileges of every inmate?

164. SOCIALITY IN THE LODGE CIRCLE. — Are the inmates taciturn and formal, or do they, when relieved from the presence of strangers, evince a general ease and spirit of sociality? Is this observable particularly when on their wintering grounds in remote parts of the forest? Do they eat at certain hours of the day? How many meals do they take in the twenty-four hours? Do they address the Great Spirit at any meal, or feast, by way of prayer? Are their appetites regular or capricious, admitting of great powers both of abstinence and of repletion?

165. CHARACTERISTIC FACTS RESPECTING MARRIAGE. — Is there any tradition of the institution of marriage? Has it the sanction of the Indian *medas*, or priests, or of the parents only? What are its ceremonies? Is the preparation of an *abbinos* in the mother-in-law's tent, to receive the bride, a part of these ceremonies? Is this act done with parade? Are the mats, skins, clothing, and ornaments, appropriated to it, where the parties can afford it, rich and costly?

166. COURTSHIPS. — How are these managed? Are there regular visits to the lodge, or are the interviews casual? Do young persons, of both sexes, adorn themselves, to become more attractive? Do they use any peculiar paints or ornaments? Do young men play near the lodge, on the *pibbigwun*, or Indian flute? Are these chants appropriate? Do they make presents to the object of their esteem? Are presents made to the parents? How is consent asked? When are the parents consulted? Are matches ever made without their consent?

167. AGE AND CONDITION OF THE PARTIES. — At what age do the Indians generally marry? Are there bachelors, or persons who never marry? Are there beaux, or young men addicted to dress? Do widowers remarry, and is there any rule, or limit of propriety observed? Do young widows usually marry again? Are their chances of marriage affected by having previously had children?

168. HOW DOES A FOREST LIFE AFFECT THE LAWS OF REPRODUCTION IN THE SPECIES? — Does the full or scanty supply of subsistence govern it? Are the changes of location, fatigue, cold, and exposure to the vicissitudes of climate, felt in the general result of Indian population; and at what age do the women cease bearing? What is the highest number of children borne? What is the earliest known age of parturition? Are twins common? Is barrenness frequent?

169. VISITS AND VISITORS. — Are strangers announced before reaching the lodge, and how are visits ordered? Do parties of Indians stop, at a short distance, and send word of their intended visit? How are the ceremonies arranged, and how are guests received and entertained? Is precedence always awarded to guests? Are social visits made, in which these ceremonies are set aside? Is there anything analogous to dinner or supper parties, distinct from the stated feasts? Are small cut sticks sent as invitations to guests? Is hospitality a strong and general trait? Are its rites ever denied, or have they been known to be exercised to cover schemes of perfidy, or for base purposes?

170. BIRTH AND INFANCY. — Are there persons who exercise the office of midwives? Are the labors of parturition severe? Are separate lodges provided? Are arrangements made in

anticipation? Does any female friend attend as a nurse? Are cases of solitary confinement rare? Is there any rite analogous to circumcision?

171. NAMING OF CHILDREN. — Are there any ceremonies at the naming of children? By whom is the name given, and from what circumstance? What number of days are suffered to elapse from the birth to the naming; is there any thing resembling the Hebraic period, or is it done at once? Does the father or mother bestow the name? Is there any Indian priest present? Are these names usually taken from the objects or incidents of dreams, which have impressed the minds of the sponsors, and are supposed to be sacred? What are the usual names of males and females? Give specimens. Are the children familiarly called by these names, as in civilized life, or are they kept secret? If secret, what is the cause? How do the children acquire nicknames? Is this the cause of the multiplicity of names which are often borne by the same individuals?

172. DIVORCES. — Has the wife or husband the right of divorce? Must there be good causes, and what are they generally? Must the chief of the village be consulted? What is the common practice? Which party takes the children?

173. NURSING AND MANAGEMENT OF CHILDREN. — How are children nursed and attended? What is the kind of cradle used — how is it constructed — is it well adapted to the purposes of the forest and the protection of the child from accident? Is it suited to promote the natural growth and expansion of the limbs? How do females become *in-toed?* Are the feet of female infants bound by their mothers in this cradle in such manner as to *turn in,* and do they thus determine their growth? At what age are children weaned? How do children address their parents? Do they abbreviate their words? How do mothers address their infants and children? Are there any terms of endearment?

174. FAMILY GOVERNMENT OF CHILDREN. — Is the domestic government left wholly to Indian mothers? Is it well exercised? Is there any discrimination, in the discipline, between male and female children?

175. INSTRUCTION OF CHILDREN IN THE TRADITIONS OF THEIR TRIBE. — How is the identity of their traditions kept up? Are children initiated in the knowledge, or lore of their fathers, by the mother, in nursery tales, or are they left to pick it up, at later periods, from mingling in dances, congregations and feasts? Do grandmothers exercise any influence in this department; or are there old persons who are privileged to collect evening groups in the lodges, and amuse or instruct them by stories or traditions?

176. STOLEN CHILDREN. — Are families often increased by the addition of white children, or youth who have been stolen in marauding excursions, in the frontier settlements? State any known instances of this kind. Was the incorporation into the family in these cases complete, and were the persons reclaimed in after life?

177. EFFECTS OF INTEMPERANCE IN THE FAMILY CIRCLE. — What are the effects of the introduction and use of ardent spirits, in the lodge, in deranging its order? Does it lead to broils and scenes of intoxication? Does it diminish the means of the hunter to procure food and clothing? Does it impair his capacity of hunting? Does it injure his health? Does it affect his reputation? Does it deprive his wife and children of necessary comforts? Do its excesses lead the victim, in the end, to want, to the murder of friends, killed in states of inebriation, and finally, to his own premature death?

178. WHAT MEANS ARE TAKEN TO PRESERVE THE FAMILY IDENTITY? — If the clan-marks or totems denote affinity, is it not rather the evidence of a general and not a near family connexion?

Customs and Employment at Large

179. HAS THERE BEEN A DECLENSION OF THE TRIBES IN THE UNITED STATES FROM ANY FORMER PROBABLE CONDITION, AND WHAT IS THE TYPE AND CHARACTER OF THE HUNTER STATE, AS IT EXISTS AMONGST THESE TRIBES? — Are any of the tribes quite degraded in the scale of being? Have they degenerated into any customs or practices revolting to humanity? Do they eat human flesh, upon any occasion, and if so, under what circumstances?

180. TRACES OF FOREIGN CUSTOMS. — Is there any proof of the existence of infanticide among the American Indians? Are the lives of female children held in less esteem than those of males? Are widows ever doomed to death on the decease of their busbands? Is there any tradition that they were ever burned, on such occasions, as upon a funeral pyre? Are devotees to religion ever known to sacrifice themselves to their gods, as is done in the East? Do they ever suspend themselves on hooks of iron, with the view of enduring meritorious sufferings? Do they wear particular spots on their foreheads to denote religious sects? Are there any castes among the North American tribes, or any vestiges of such an institution, or belief? Are any of the American waters, or great rivers, deemed sacred, and coveted in death?

181. PRACTICE OF SCALPING. — Do they, in scalping persons slain in battle, use any ceremonies, or adopt any practices which are of oriental character? Is the scalp-lock, which it is customary to cultivate, a usage of ancient origin; and is there any peculiar mode of tracing antiquity in its form and position?

182. TRACES OF THE PATRIOCHAL AGE. — Is the patriarchal feature strongly marked, in the Indian institutions? Note whether there be anything in their manners, customs, or opinions, resembling ancient nations of the eastern world. Observe, particularly, whether there be any customs respecting the sacrifice of animals, or the withdrawal of females, or any other well-known ancient trait, in which the Indian tribes coincide.

183. ASSEVERATIONS. — Do the Indians swear, or use any form of oath? Is the Great Spirit ever appealed to by *name,* or is the name carefully suppressed, or some other substituted for it?

184. FORMS OF GREETING. — What is the Indian mode of salutation? Have they any conventional terms for it? Do they shake hands? If so, is this an ancient custom, or is it done in imitation of Europeans? Do they greet each other by name? Did the Indians anciently rub or fold their arms together, as was witnessed, on the first meeting of the northern tribes with Cartier in the St. Lawrence, A.D. 1535?

185. HABIT OF SMOKING. — Is smoking a very ancient custom? Was there a time when their ancestors did not smoke? Did they bring the habit from abroad? Was the tobacco-plant given to them by the Great Spirit? How and when? State the tale. Was the gift made in the North, or did they bring the plant from the southern latitudes? If this plant will not grow, and come to perfection so as to bear seed, in high northern latitudes, is this not a proof that their general migration was from the southern or central latitudes?

186. APPROBATIVENESS. — Is this strongly developed in the Indian mind; and what forms of exhibition does it assume in the manners and customs? Is the war-path pursued as the chief avenue to fame? Are hunting, and oratory pursued with the same ultimate ends? Are there any other modes in which an ambitious chieftain can gratify the passion?

187. HABITS OF THOUGHT. — Is stoicism of feeling deemed a mark of manliness by the Indians? To what extent is the countenance a true exponent of the actual state of feeling? Does taciturnity proceed from a sense of caution, or is the mere act of silence deemed

wisdom? What general theories of thought govern the manners of the sachems, and to what extent and in what manner are the maxims of conversation and of public speaking taught to the young?

188. QUICKNESS OF SIGHT AND ACUTENESS OF OBSERVATION IN THREADING THE WILDERNESS. — These have excited general notice, but the subject is still a matter of curiosity and further information. How are they guided when there is neither sun by day or moon by night? How is the precise time of the desertion of an encampment, and the composition and character of the party, determined? What are the elements of precision in this knowledge, so far as they are to be found in the plants, or forest, or in the heavens? Is there extreme acuteness of the senses, and a nervous power of appreciating the nearness, or relative position of objects?

189. CREDULITY AND SUSCEPTIBILITY OF BEING DECEIVED. — Are the Indians very prone to be deceived by professed dreamers, or the tricks of jugglers, or by phenomena of nature, of the principles and causes of which they are ignorant? Is not the surrounding air and forest, converted, to some extent, by this state of ignorance of natural laws, into a field of mystery, which often fills their minds with needless alarms? Are their priests shrewd enough to avail themselves of this credulity, either by observing this general defect of character, or by penetrating into the true causes of the phenomena? Do the fears and credulity of the Indians generally nourish habits of suspicion? Do they tend to form a character for concealment and cunning?

190. HOW DO THEIR PHYSICAL POWERS COMPARE WITH THE STRENGTH OF EUROPEANS? — How many pounds can they lift? What are their comparative powers in running, or in rowing a boat? Are they expert and vigorous in handling the axe, or the scythe? What is the greatest burden which you have known an Indian to carry?

Hunting

191. WHAT ARE THE PRINCIPLES OF THE ART OF HUNTING, AS PRACTISED BY THE TRIBE? — How does the chase vary, during the several seasons — what species of animals are chiefly sought in each, and what ceremonies take place on setting out, and on returning? Are there different modes of hunting different species of animals? What is the mode of hunting buffalo? How is still hunting performed? Sketch the various modes.

192. SOCIAL TIES AND SECRET ARTS OF THE CHASE. — In what manner do they form hunting parties, and what social ties unite them? How are the spoils generally divided? How are disputes respecting the division of game settled? (*Vide* 91, 92, 93 and 94, for generic inquiries on the power of the chiefs on this subject.) Are there any secret arts? If so, what are they — who teaches them? Are they paid for? What hours of the day are most suitable for hunting? How is the glare of light managed in hunting up a valley? Do they keep in the shade?

193. DECOYS AND TRAPS. — How are bears and wolves decoyed into falls and traps? How is the antelope approached? How are beaver trapped? Are aromatic baits used? State briefly the arts used by the Indians in deceiving the various species of game by light, by sound, by smell and color, or by cunning appeals to any of their senses.

194. MODE OF DRYING AND CURING SKINS. — This is a very important branch of the hunter's art, and it would be interesting to know the process, the various methods, and the amount of labor and time required. How are they packed and prepared for market? What are the indications of skins killed out of season, and how are pelts judged?

195. HOW MANY MODES HAVE THEY OF TAKING FISH? — Are fish taken in wiers and fish dams? Are they scooped up in nets at the foot of falls and cascades? State the manner of

each method, and any other ingenious mode practised, and whether there is any mode of curing or salting practised at their fisheries.

196. ARE THE ARTS OF HUNTING TAUGHT THE CHILDREN AT AN EARLY AGE? — Do they commence with archery? And at what ages are the boys generally competent to engage in the active labors of the chase? Can widows rely early on their sons for the means of subsistence? Do they ever, during the infancy of them, practise any part of the hunter's art themselves, and if so, what part? Have women, thus left alone, or deserted, ever been known to practise the use of fire-arms?

197. WHAT IS THE PRESENT STATE OF THE ARMS AND IMPLEMENTS USED BY THE HUNTERS OF THE TRIBE? — Have they abandoned the bow and arrows, partially or altogether? Do they use the gun or rifle, in hunting deer or buffalo? Are they well supplied with ammunition, and at reasonable rates? Can they readily command steel-traps, and other metallic implements? Facts of this character are essential in determining their condition, and ability to maintain themselves by the labors of the chase. In cases where tribes have advanced to the agricultural state, that fact alone will be sufficient to be stated, and will supersede any notices of this kind. The laws of the chase, and the civil power of chiefs have been referred to in prior inquiries on the organization and government of the tribe.

War

198. HOW ARE WAR PARTIES RAISED, SUBSISTED AND MARCHED? — Is there anything in the Indian customs equivalent to enlistment? If joining the war-dance be thus construed, for what period is the enlistment or assent good, and how and when may its obligations be terminated or broken? Can a warrior be punished for turning back? Must he furnish his own provisions? Is there any public arrangement, whatever, in an Indian war, for arms, subsistence, or transportation?

199. ORDER OF MARCH AND PRECAUTIONS. — Do men set out for a designated rendezvous, singly, or in what manner? Are there any ceremonies observed before marching? How is the march of the party conducted after they are assembled? Do they move in a body, or separately in files or sub-parties? Do they eat any root, or substance which is supposed to have the virtue of deadening pain, or inspiring courage? What precautions are observed on the march, and in their encampments — are sentinels ever posted? Are the priests or jugglers consulted? What signs or omens are noticed? How do these affect them?

200. SUBORDINATION. — To what extent do the chiefs exercise the duties and rights of officers? Is subordination observed? Have they any right to punish its infraction? Do they command in battle? How are orders conveyed? Have they aids, or runners? Are battles planned? Are different chiefs assigned to different locations? Do they fight in line? Do they ever plan retreats, or appoint a rallying place in rear?

201. STRATEGEMS. — What are the usual devices of attack, resorted to? Are they always planned with a minute knowledge of the topography? What are the usual manoeuvres? Is the war-whoop employed to order an advance, or retreat, or side movement? When, and under what circumstances do they quit a masked wood, or defile, and take the open plain?

202. CAPTIVES. — How are prisoners secured and. treated? Has any captive been burned at the stake, since the burning of Col. Crawford, or offered to appease the spirit of cannibalism, in modern times? When their lives are spared, and it is designed to adopt them in families, what are the usual ceremonies? Are men who are found wounded on the field of battle killed?

203. IS PERSONAL SERVITUDE RECOGNISED? — Are there any persons, who, having lost their

liberty, or forfeited their lives, are reduced to slavery, or placed in the relative position of *peons*, or menials, who are compelled to work, and carry burdens?

204. TREATMENT OF FEMALE CAPTIVES. — Is chastity uniformly respected in war? Is there any known instance of its violation in the marauding parties? Is this trait of character connected with any superstitious opinions?

205. COSTUME IN WAR. — What constitutes the ordinary dress of warriors, on a war excursion? What paints are used, and how are they applied to different parts of the person? What feathers are worn on the head, as marks of former triumphs?

206. HEAD DRESS. — Do they wear frontlets, and how are they constructed? How is the hair dressed? Is the head shaved to form the scalp-lock? Are there necklaces of animals' claws, or other ornaments; are there back dresses? Are there ornaments for the ears, or arms, legs, or feet? Are any of these constructed so as to emit jingling sounds?

207. ARMS AND IMPLEMENTS OF WAR. — How have these varied in the lapse of time? Are fire-arms substituted for the bow and arrow in war, as they are supposed to be, generally, (*vide* 197) in hunting? Are war-clubs, tomahawks and knives, employed? How does the scalping-knife differ from the common Indian knife, if it differs in any respect?

Dancing and Amusements

208. IS DANCING A NATIONAL TRAIT OF THE TRIBE? — Is it confined to males? How many kinds of dances are there? State the peculiarities of the various kinds of war-dances, and dances of honor, triumph, religion, or hunting? Is dancing a characteristic mode of expressing popular feeling or opinion on all subjects, and of thus swaying or confirming the action of the tribe? If females are excluded from the principal dances, are they admitted to the choral band of singers or musicians? Are the principles of the various dances, and the choruses, taught to the youth; and at what age do the latter generally join in the ring?

209. SPORTS AND EXCERCISES. — Are there contests in racing and ball-playing? How many kinds of games at ball have they? Describe them, and the manner in which the contending parties are chosen, together with the rules of the games? Are there trials of skill in wrestling? Are there races at fixed times in which the youth may all engage? Are the stakes high on these occasions, and of what do they consist? Illustrate these amusements by reference to the effects which they have had on their history and manners.

210. GAMES OF CHANCE. — How many kinds of games of chance exist? Is the tribe much addicted to these games? Describe them, with their rules, and the general effect of the gambling propensity, if any exist, on the tribe? What are the arithmetical principles of the games of the bowl and the moccasin? Is there a spirit of private gambling, and if so, are there any instances of its power of infatuation?

Death and its Incidents

211. DEATH AND FUNERALS. — What are the characteristic facts connected with these subjects? When a person dies, how is the corpse dressed and disposed of? What length of time is it kept? Is it addressed, as if living, and capable of hearing, prior to its removal, or at the grave? What is the character of these addresses? What implements are buried with it, and of what material do they consist, and why are they deposited with the corpse? Is this burial of utensils and relics an ancient custom, and if so, does not the examination of old sepulchres and places of burial, to compare these relics, afford a means of judging of the state of arts in the Indian tribes, at various eras?

212. STRUCTURE AND POSITION OF THE GRAVES. — Are burials usually made in high and dry grounds? Have you known any tumulus or barrow to be erected, in modern times, to the memory of a distinguished chief? Are the Indian graves usually well excavated and protected, and in what manner are these objects effected?

213. POSITION OF THE CORPSE WITH REGARD TO THE CARDINAL POINTS. — Are the bodies buried east and west, and if so, what reason is assigned for this custom? Is it an ancient custom? Why are not bodies buried promiscuously, as to their position, and without respect to the cardinal points?

214. STANDING OR SITTING POSTURE. — Are bodies ever deposited in these positions, and if so, what is the mode of interment, and how is the posture preserved?

215. EMBALMING. — Are there any herbs, or spices placed with the corpse? Is it wrapped in barks, or cloth, or submitted to any process analogous to embalming?

216. SCAFFOLDING OF CORPSES. — To what extent, if any, is this custom practised in the tribe? How are the bodies prepared for this purpose? Are they enclosed in barks or put in boxes, previously to their being placed on the branches of trees, or on posts? Are they subject to be depredated upon, in these cases, by beasts of prey or carnivorous birds?

217. FUNERAL FLAGS, OR ENSIGNS OF WAR. — Are displays of this kind made over the graves of distinguished chiefs? Is this a modern custom, or were the Indian feather flags formerly disposed of in this way?

218. COLLECTION AND RE-INTERMENT OF BONES. — It is observed in various places that such deposits were made. The custom, if ever known to the ancestors of the present race, is obsolete. Did they ever practise it, or is it due to a prior race? If practised, how was it done and with what ceremonies? Was it the duty of particular classes of men? What time was suffered to elapse before the bones were gathered? Was there, on these occasions, public funeral ceremonies, attended with wailing, and other demonstrations of grief?

219. CHARNEL HOUSES. — The traditions of the tribes denote such depositories to have existed in ancient times. How were they constructed, and the bodies protected against depredations from wild beasts?

220. INCINERATION OF BODIES. — Is this ever practised? Are there any traditions on the subject?

221. MOURNING AND OBSERVANCES. — Do they scarify themselves for the dead? What is the garb, or sign of mourning? Are the dead lamented, and how? Are visits periodically made to the graves? Do widows ever carry, for a limited period, images or bundles of cloth, as symbols of mourning to represent their deceased husbands? Are long beards ever suffered to grow in consequence?

222. FUNERAL FIRES. — Are fires ever kindled on newly made graves? If so, at what times, how long are these fires continued, and what is the object of them?

223. GRAVE-DTONES, OR MONUMENTS. — What species of monumental structures of this nature are usually erected? Are stones ever employed to mark the place of interment? If posts, or tablets of cedar or other species of wood, be placed at the head and foot of graves, are there any hieroglyphics, or devices put upon these fixtures, and what characters do they consist of, and how are these to be understood? For further inquiries on the devices generally, see "picture-writing," No. 245.

224. IS THERE ANY MOUND NOW IN THE PROCESS OF BUILDING IN THE TERRITORIES OF THE TRIBE, OR WITHIN THE BOUNDARIES OF THE UNITED STATES, PARTICULARLY ON ITS EXTREME SOUTHERN AND EASTERN CONFINES? — More than three millions of cubic feet of earth are

estimated to be contained in one of the antique western mounds. Is there sufficient power and energy in the tribe, or any tribe known to you, to have executed such a labor? Could such works have been erected by the labors of women alone? Is there not denoted an energy and capacity of construction in the antique mounds, superior to any which is now possessed by the tribes?

225. TREATMENT OF ORPHANS. — On whom does the care of orphans devolve? Does the chief of the tribe take any notice of children thus left, if there be no near relatives?

226. THE POOR AND AGED. — Are aged and infirm persons ever abandoned? Who takes care of old and feeble persons destitute of children or relatives, when they can no longer hunt, or attend to any forest labors or care, by which they might have contributed, in part, to their own support? Do the chiefs direct food to be left? Do the village hunters make voluntary contributions? When such persons die, who buries them? Philanthropy seeks to ascertain the bitter necessities of savage society, and any facts or incidents illustrating them, which may serve to guide public opinion, will be important.

227. LODGES, OR DWELLINGS. — What are the materials, form, size and mode of construction of their lodges? If skins or bark be employed, what skins and what species of bark, and how prepared, and how long will the material last? Are the tents, or lodges, easily removed from place to place, or are they of a permanent character, so as to be left standing during their periodical absences, and re-occupied? How many persons will they generally accomodate? Are they graduated in size accurately to the number of the family, and if so, how many square feet of ground-surface does each inmate occupy? Who constructs, removes, and re-erects them?

228. CANOES, OR BOATS. — Of what material are these made, how are they constructed, and what is their usual capacity? If built of bark, are they ribbed with cedar, and built on a frame, and in what manner is the sheathing material attached, and closed, so as to be impervious to water? If made from a solid log, how is it excavated, and what are its comparative properties in river navigation?

229. MECHANICAL APTITUDE OF THE TRIBE. — Are they disposed to advance from the barbaric type? If such advances have been made, what are they, and to what extent are mechanical tools of the most approved kinds employed?

230. MODE OF COOKING AND HABITS OF THE TABLE. — Is raw meat ever eaten? Do they roast their meat done, or is it often the practice to cook it overdone? Have they any peculiar skill in boiling fish? Do they use much salt, or relish milk? Do they ever, or have they in former times, followed the practice of boiling meat or vegetables in vessels of wood, or bark? Do they use metallic cooking vessels, generally, at the present time, and if so, what kinds? Or are the ancient clay pots of the Indians still employed in remote positions? Have they any regular periods for meals?

231. METHOD OF CURING MEATS. — In what forms is smoke applied in the drying and preservation of various kinds of meat, or provisions? Do they employ salt in curing the tongues of the buffalo and the reindeer? How is the flesh of the deer, the moose, and the buffalo preserved? What is the method of curing the tail of the beaver, and to what extent, and in what manner, are the various species of fish, referred to, in 195, as taken in quantity, preserved?

232. SPONTANEOUS FRUITS AND PRODUCTIONS OF THE FOREST. — To what extent do the purely hunter tribes rely on these? Give a catalogue of them, denoting the various kinds of roots, truffles, berries and nuts relied on. Is the wild honey sought, and in what quantity is it afforded? Do they collect and boil the sap of the sugar maple, in its season, and to

what extent does it form an element in the means of their subsistence? Is the wild rice gathered in the interior lakes and rice grounds?

233. PINCHING SEASONS OF NECESSITY. — What species of barks are eaten on these occasions? Do they collect old bones, in times of great hunger, and extract their oily, or acrid juices by boiling? Is the lichen called *tripe de roche* eaten, and how is it prepared? The shifts and necessities to which the hunter tribes are driven in seasons of extreme severity, or want, are such as often to shock, while they create strong appeals to humanity; but the facts are required, to show the fallacy of perseverance in such a precarious mode of life.

Costume

234. WHAT IS THE ORDINARY DRESS OF THE TRIBE, MALE AND FEMALE? — Of what materials is it composed — of what quality and color? If any part of their garments be made of materials the growth or fabric of the Indian country, state the kind of stuff used, and in what manner it is prepared, and the places of its growth or manufacture. How long will such dresses, whether made of foreign or domestic material, last, and what is the actual value or cost of each, distinguishing male from female?

235. ADAPTATION OF DRESS TO SEASONS AND OCCASIONS. — The mode of dress and accoutrement for war is inquired into by No. 207. Are there any other peculiar adaptations of dress, to varying circumstances? Are there summer and winter dresses? Is there particular attention paid to robes designed for public occasions? Is there any thing peculiar to distinguish a civil or war chief from a medicine man, or Indian priest? Are the Indian dresses removed at night? If they be slept in, wholly or in part, what part is retained, and what put off?

236. ORNAMENTS. — Do they attach a peculiar value to ornaments? What kinds of ornaments are most desired? In what shape is silver worn? What species of the decorations of dresses are derived from birds, quadrupeds, and other animate objects? Are shells still worn in their elementary forms, and what species? Is a high value attached to the feathers of the war eagle? What species of ornaments are furnished, at the present time, by the state of the fur trade?

237. DYES AND PIGMENTS. — Are there any native dye-stuffs, or roots or vegetables, employed in coloring parts of their clothing, or ornaments? What are these dyes — how is the coloring principle extracted, and with what mordant is it set? Do they ever tattoo, prick or puncture their faces, breast and arms, and how? Is vermilion still sold to them? What kinds of colored clays and ochres, or native oxydes, are employed? Are white or red clays ever smeared over the hands, and their impress marked on the body, or clothing?

238. BADGES OF OFFICE. — How many kinds have they, and of what material do they consist?

239. PHYSICAL TRAITS, AS AFFECTED BY COSTUME. — What are the customs and fashions of wearing the hair and beard? Is the whole head shaved? Have they any preparations for killing, eradicating or dyeing the hair? Is the beard generally extirpated by the tweezers, or other mechanical means? Are there exceptions to its growth or to the reigning customs?

240. PHYSIOLOGY, AS BEARING ON ETHNOGRAPHY. — What is the geometrical and physical type of the Indian *skin,* as examined under a magnifier? How many pores exist in a square inch, and what is the distinctive shape of them? Note, also, the rugosae, shade of color, and other minute physiological traits.

Intellectual Capacities and Character of the Race

241. MENTAL POWERS. — What is the general scope and capacity of the Indian mind, as compared with other stocks of the human race? Does it bear most resemblance to those of the Asiatic, or of the European group? If it disclose traits more akin to the elder, or oriental stocks, in what do these traits consist? Are their minds of an inductive cast? Are they capable of pursuing logical trains of thought to a just conclusion? Is this faculty observed to be brought out and strengthened by education? Are they naturally possessed of strong powers of memory and forecast? Are they of a reflective habit? Do the moral propensities and affections generally predominate over the physical? Are they of a grave, or light character; a sober, or gay cast of mind; a fervid, or cold temperament?

242. PERSONAL INSTANCES. — Has there appeared, in their history, any individual noted for his natural or acquired powers as a physician, linguist or moralist, or any one who has evinced ability in the cultivation of any of the exact or moral sciences?

243. GENERAL MODE OF THE EXHIBITION OF THOUGHT. — Have they any maxims which are used in conversation? Do they repeat, in their families or at assemblages, any thing of the nature of studied compositions or laments? Does the general state of their oral traditions, as traced in the scenes of private life, evince strong powers of metaphor or allegory, or denote any dawning or vestiges of fancy or invention? Inquire into this department with all the means you can; more particularly in reference to the following topics:

244. ORATORY. — What are the general characteristics of Indian oratory? How is metaphor managed? Are their speeches as replete with figures and tropes as they are usually depicted in fictitious writings? What traits, in the specimens of Indian eloquence which are known, are most remarkable? Do the speakers excel in simplicity, clearness, and strength of language? Do these specimens derive much of their force from the political attitude or important position of the speaker? Are there any continued strains of eloquence, or sustained appeals? Give any authentic specimens known to you, among living orators.

245. ART OF PICTURE-WRITING. — Allusion to this subject is made in Number 156. To what extent do the tribe practise this art? Is it generally in the practice of drawing the figures of animals, birds, or other objects, on trees, pieces of bark, dressed skins, or other substances? What is the general purport of these pictorial devices? Is their meaning fixed or exact? Is there any known system in the annotation? Do they convey different kinds of information to the tribe? And how are the characters interpreted? Is there a system of figures and devices, which the people generally understand, and which the mass of the tribe can interpret and explain? Or are these devices known only to the medicine-men or priests? Are devices and drawings which have been left, by hunting parties at the scenes of their success, designed to inform others of the tribe, who may visit these scenes, of the *names* or *clans* of the successful hunters, and the *number* and *kind* of game taken? Is information conveyed, by this system, to distant parts of the tribe, of travellers, strangers, or others, military or civilians, who have passed through their country, denoting their force and object? What information is generally recorded by these simple inscriptions? And what other forms does this pictorial art of the Indians take? Can the medicine-men or *medas* record their songs by it? Describe the system, and give specimens of the drawings, noting the different kinds of pictorial inscription, the method of its interpretation, and its peculiar character and value to a people who are without letters. How does it compare with the Aztec system? Is it largely applied to mythological subjects connected with their oral legends? (*Vide* Number 247)

246. INVENTION OF THE CHEROKEE SYLLABICAL ALPHABET, OR SYSTEM OF NOTATION. — What are the principles for recording thought, which are developed by this concrete alphabet?

Under what circumstances was it invented? How many elementary and how many compound sounds or syllables does it provide for? Is it applicable to recording the sounds of *other* Indian tongues besides the Cherokee? Is the system it provides generally understood by the tribe, or much employed? Are the Scriptures, which are printed and circulated in this character, generally read in Cherokee families? Is it likely to be of permanent benefit or utility to the tribe, to whose language it appears exclusively adapted?

247. ORAL IMAGINITIVE TALES AND LEGENDS. — What can be stated on this topic? In examining their notions on the immortality of the soul, (numbers 146, 156) the existence of such fables, or allegories, is alluded to. It is desirable to know how general they are. Are stories of giants and dwarfs, and wild adventures of men and genii among woods and forests, related for the amusement of the circle of listeners, around the evening fire-side? Do these tales and oral sagas of the wigwam, reveal the actual notions of the tribe, on their religion and mythology, or their ideas of a future state?

248. DOCTRINES AND OPINIONS REVEALED IN THE SHAPE OF ALLEGORY. — Are these legends found to embody and exemplify their ideas of transformations, necromancy and the power of sorcery? Can we perceive, in these imaginative efforts, the true doctrines entertained of good and evil spirits, fairies, ghosts, or any other form of aboriginal story-craft? Are any of these tales related to demonstrate to the young the power or ubiquity of the Great Spirit?

249. ORAL TALES, A VEHICLE OF INSTRUCTION. — Do the allegories and fables ever convey moral instruction or history to the young? Is there a frequent attempt in their lodge-stories to account for the origin of animals, and other objects of creation, animate or inanimate? And do they thus shadow forth the true Indian philosophy of life? Transmit some of these native tales, which may serve to give a general idea of their mental power and character, and the scope of imagination evolved.

250. MUSIC, SONGS AND POETRY. — What is the character of the Indian music, songs and poetry? How many notes, or finger-holes, have they in their flute, or *pibbegwun,* and by what scale are they varied, and what analogy does this instrument bear to the ancient Arcadian pipe? Are there different styles of music and songs for war, religion and love? Are the chants accompanied by other instruments, and if so, what is the character of these instruments? Is there more than one species of drum? In what manner are the Indian drums made? Is the rattle made in various ways, and how? What resemblance or connection have these instruments, in their mechanical structure, and the power of originating or modulating sound, to the ancient musical instruments of the Aztecs, or other nations of the tropics?

251. WHAT IS THE GENERAL CHARACTER OF THE INDIAN SONGS? — Is there any rhyme in them? Are the words collocated so as to observe the laws of quantity? In other words, are they measured, or are the accents in them found to recur at fixed and regular intervals? Has there appeared any Indian poet?

252. WHAT ARE THE SCROLLS AND TABLETS WHICH HAVE BEEN TERMED "MUSIC BOARDS," AND "BARK SONGS"? — Are these mnemonic records of songs executed in the manner of the Indian picture-writings, referred to in Number 245? If so, describe them, and indicate the mode of connection between the words and music, and the devices?

253. INDIAN CHORUS. — Is the chorus a characteristic part of their songs and music? Are the Indian choruses more fixed than other parts of a song? How many syllables do they consist of in a war-song, a religious song, and a hunting song? Is the name of the Great Spirit, or the Deity, denoted in any of these choruses?

254. LAMENTS FOR THE DEAD. — Is it the custom to call on certain persons to frame these laments? Are the laments, themselves, of a poetic character? Do they bewail virtues, or broken affections? If laments are made by professed persons, who are skilled in the use of their language, are these persons, also, skilled in song-making amd song-singing, generally?

255. WHAT IS THE CHARACTER OF THE WAR SONG? — Do the strains recite former triumphs, or breathe defiance or boasting? Do they evince patriotism and the love of military glory? Do they consist of continuous verses, or broken strains independently uttered? Have they a particular chorus? State, also, the character of the death-song. Do they recite their triumphs in hunting as well as in war?

256. SACRED SONGS. — Are there hymns to the sun, or to the Great Spirit? Do the prophets utter any secret incantations, which are supposed to partake of a sacred character?

257. CRADLE SONGS. — Does maternal affection find any expression in strains analogous to lullabies or cradle hymns? Are there love songs? Have you noticed any bacchanalian songs or catches? The character of a people or race is eminently shown in their songs and recitals at their convivial and social assemblies, whether these be for the exercise of sports, dancing, singing, or any other forms of merry-making; and nothing can be more illustrative of the cast and temper of mind and thought of the Indian race, than well-authenticated specimens of their songs, music, and poetry. If there be any thing deserving of the name of painting or sculpture, it may also be appropriately mentioned and described under the present general head.

Present Condition, and Future Prospects

258. THE RESULT THUS FAR. — How far has knowledge, art, and commerce, and the general progress of civilization, affected the improvement of the Indians, and changed or modified their original manners, customs, and opinions? State the general impressions which have been made, and observe what modes of treatment and policy have done best, and on what points the Indian character, in its advanced or semi-civilized phases, usually breaks down.

259. CROSS OR AMALGAMATION OF RACES. — What are the prominent effects, physical and intellectual, of the intermixture, by marriage, between the European and Indian races? Has the tribe been much affected by such intermarriages? General facts, only, are sought.

260. RATIO OF INCREASE — What is the present rate of progress of the population of the tribe, compared with former periods? Are they advancing or receding? How will it compare with the ratio from A.D. 1800 to 1820, and from the latter to 1840? The census "forms" transmitted will show the existing population, but not its former state, nor the results that may be anticipated in the present location and circumstances of the tribe.

261. HEALTH OF THE TRIBE. — How does the agricultural state, in the cases where it has been embraced, affect the laws of reproduction, and what change, if any, has been noticed in the character of the diseases of the removed tribes? Is their general health better, and how, if to any extent, has it been influenced by full and regular means of subsistence? Are fevers, or affections of the liver, as frequent on the elevated plains west of the Mississippi, as they were in their former positions? How does the change of climate affect pulmonary complaints?

262. COSTUME AND CLEANLINESS, A TEST OF CIVILIZATION. — What general changes have taken place in this regard in the tribe, and in their habits or practices of cleanliness, modes of living, and general housewifery? Details on this head are sought under Nos. 227 to 240;

47

and nothing but the general results on the tribe, as an increment in their advance in the scale of civilization, is here required.

263. FIELD LABOR IMPOSED ON FEMALES. — Is this test of the barbaric or hunter state still tolerated; and, if so, to what extent? The condition of woman, as a laborer in the Indian community, has been asked for, No. 161. It is here wished to ascertain whether there be any whole tribes who have passed beyond this marked phasis.

264. PROGRESS OF CHRISTIANITY. — What is the present state of the tribe in this respect? What progress has been made in delivering it from the dominion and influence of the native priests, prophets, and jugglers? How long has it enjoyed the advantages of Christian teachers? What means were first employed to gain a hearing for the doctrines? Were they found efficacious, or were they varied, and what has been the most successful mode employed?

265. TEMPERANCE. — Are the principles of temperance in the use of ardent spirits on the increase or decrease? What are the prominent causes operating on the minds of persons yet addicted to the use of them, and what are the best means, at this time, of further discouraging the use of such drinks, and of effecting their entire exclusion from the tribe?

266. THE CAUSE OF EDUCATION. — What are the prominent facts in relation to this important means of reclaiming and exalting the tribe? What means have been found most effective in the education of their children and youth? Have females duly participated in these means, and has any part of such means been applied to such branches as are essential to qualify them for the duties of mothers and housewives? Are the ancient prejudices of parents on the subject of education on the wane, and what is the relative proportion of the young population who, in the last period of ten years, have received the elements of an English education?

267. STATE OF THE MECHANIC ARTS. — Forms have been prepared to bring out the existing state of facts in the tribe on this head, but they do not denote the prevalent state of feeling and opinion on the subject, nor the progress which has been made. It is known that the tribes rely greatly on white or hired mechanics, who are provided for by treaties, and paid by Government. Are they beginnning to entertain true views on this head, and do they evince a desire to do their own mechanical labors? In this connection it may be proper to inquire whether the native mechanics are capable of furnishing them their teams and wagons for draught and pleasure, and with chains, ploughs, and bars in the labors of agriculture, and horse furniture and gear, suited to a growing and thriving people?

268. IMPROVED MODES OF AGRICULTURE. — Is there any interest observable on this head? Are there rotations of crops? Are there proper theories embraced in the application of manures? Do they employ marl, lime, or gypsum, on portions of lands adapted to them? Do the number increase who cultivate flax, hemp, tobacco, or cotton, in their respective latitudes? Do they manifest a desire to obtain improved breeds of cattle, horses and sheep? Is there a general desire to plant fruit trees? Are the most approved kinds of agricultural implements used?

269. MEANS OF COMMUNICATION. — Have the tribe provided for the construction of roads, bridges, and ferries, either by an appropriation of their general funds, or by imposing the duty of personal service or tax, on the residents of the several districts?

270. THE ENGLISH LANGUAGE A MEANS OF CIVILIZATION. — To what extent is the English language spoken, and English books read, and what is the tendency of opinion and practice on this subject, in the tribe? In giving replies to these queries, express your opinions freely, and state any fact, or mode of procedure which, in your judgment, would tend to advance the welfare or promote the happiness of the tribe. The general question of the

advance and reclamation of the tribes, as connected with the present state of the Indian trade, has been examined in queries 95 to 105, inclusive. The hearings of these interrogatories on their future state, and the obligations imposed on the people and government of the Union, by their position in the scale of nations, are further called out in an examination of some points in the legislation of Congress respecting them in queries 106 to 115; and the questions on the actual condition of the tribes who are more advanced, and have set up new governments on the territories assigned to them west of the Mississippi, 116 to 118, are designed to complete this view of the changes wrought in the position of the tribes, since their discovery, about A.D. 1600. It is important, as they advance, as many of them now do, in their means and population, and in the progress of education and agriculture, that we should scrutinize the whole class of facts on which this advance depends, in order to give it the greater impetus and permanency. In this view, the subject is commended to your general reflection and scrutiny, in the following subjoined inquiries on their general history and languages.

General History of the American Tribes

271. PROOFS FROM TRADITION. — Who were the earliest inhabitants of America? What is the light of tradition on this subject? Were the ancestors of the present Red Race the Aborigines? What evidences exist, if any, of the occupancy of the country by man prior to the arrival of the Indian race?

272. PROOFS FROM GEOLOGY. — Are there any evidences of the country's having been occupied by man prior to the deposition of the tertiary, or the diluvial strata? Are such evidences confined wholly to the unconsolidated deposits; and, if so, to what deposits, and of what probable eras?

273. PROOFS FROM ANTIQUE BONES. — How deep, in any beds or deposits, local or general, of the upper geological formations, are the bones of extinct or existing kinds of quadrupeds or other animal remains to be found? Have the fortunes of the Red Race, or any prior race, been connected with, or are they illustrated by the extinction of the mastodon, or other large animals whose bones are now found in a fossil state?

274. PROOFS FROM ASTRONOMY. — What are the general conclusions to be drawn respecting the era or eras of the antique settlement of America, from the knowledge of astronomy, the style of architecture, the system of religious belief, and mythology, the state of art, or any other department of historical or antiquarian investigation connected with the history of the tropical or equinoxial tribes?

275. PROOFS FROM LANGUAGES. — Do the American languages offer any proofs, in their grammars, or vocabularies, of ancient connexions with oriental or other foreign nations?

276. PROOFS FROM TOPOGRAPHY AND GEOGRAPHY. — What probable facts or just conclusions can be drawn respecting the ancient point or points of approach to the continent, from topographical and geographical considerations?

Groups of Tribes within the United States

277. WHAT INDIAN TRIBES IN THE UNITED STATES ARE CLEARLY DERIVED FROM THE SAME STOCKS? — How are remote tribes to be traced, and into what number of generic families, or groups, can they be ultimately classed?

278. WHAT IS THE EXTENT OF THE ALGONQUIN FAMILY? — How many tribes of this class yet exist, and how many are known to be extinct? What relation do the ancient Lenni Lenapes, or Delawares, hold in this family?

279. OF WHAT GROUP ARE THE IROQUIOIS, AND HOW IS IT MADE UP? — Are there other tribes besides the Wyandots allied to it? Were the Eries of this group?

280. ARE TRIBES SPEAKING DIALECTS OF THE DACOTA, OR SIOUX LANGUAGE, EXTENSIVE? — Does it embrace many of the prairie tribes of the Missouri? To what extent are they to be traced towards the West and South?

281. WHAT FACTS EXIST FOR FORMING AN APPALACIAN GROUP? — Has such an arrangement advantages over the more circumscribed term "Floridian"? In what manner are we to proceed in assigning the Muscogees and other tribes their appropriate positions in this important group? Was there an early infusion of foreign blood into any branch of this race?

282. WHAT CONNECTION DO THE UNITED STATES INDIANS HOLD, ETHNOLOGICALLY, TO THOSE OF MEXICO? — Are there any proofs of affiliation in the grammars and vocabularies? What lights are afforded by history or tradition? Was the valley of the Mississippi probably settled at the period of the establishment of the Aztec empire, under the predecessors of the Montezumas?

283. WHENCE CAME THE NATCHEZ AND THE UTCHES? — Are they of the true Appalachian type? Were there ever a people called Caribs, inhabiting the part of North America called Florida by the Spaniards? What can be said, historically, of the Appalaches, or Appalachians, proper?

284. COURSE OF MIGRATION. — Is the ethnological chain of migration to be traced into the Mississippi valley, and along the Atlantic coast, from south to north, or *vice versa?* Is this chain denoted by any remains of art, as well as by language and tradition? What proofs of such an expansion of tribes are to be sought in climate and geographical phenomena?

285. APPRECIATION OF REMOTE EVIDENCES IN ESTABLISHING GROUPS. — Is there any evidence of ancient affinities to be found in the arithmetic or astronomy, or in the numerals and mode of computing time of the separate tribes? Are mounds and ancient places of defence supposed to evince a state of art, from which any reliable deductions of the affinities of races may be drawn?

286. ARE RELIGIOUS RITES AUXILIARY AIDS IN THE ERECTION OF GROUPS? — Is the name for the Deity, or Great Spirit, necessarily more prominent than any other? What characters do the sun and the moon generally bear, as types? Are the traces of an ancient fire-worship on this continent extensive and reliable? Is the relative position of the mounds explicable, in some cases, on this theory? Have analogies, in prophetic arts, necromancy, music, picture-writing, and oral fiction, any bearing in denoting similarity of origin?

287. PHILOSOPHY OF CHANGE IN LANGUAGES. — How, or by what process in syllabical mutation, have words changed, so as to assume the character of new dialects and languages, on this continent, while the plan of thought, or grammar, has varied less, or been retained?

288. FIXITY OF RACES. — Have there been any striking changes in the physical type of the Indian race, beyond that produced by latitudes and longitudes, and by their manner of subsistence?

Topical Inquiries Illustrative of General History

289. REMNANTS OF THE NEW ENGLAND TRIBES. — What is the number and condition of the Penobscots? Are the Abenakis, who fled from Norridgwack, still under the care of their original teachers, and what progress have they made in industry and the civil arts, since their withdrawal to Canada? What vestiges of the Massachusetts group of tribes remain

within the boundaries of that State, inclusive of Martha's Vineyard and other Islands? What are the present number and condition of the Narragansetts of Rhode Island, and of the Mohegans of Connecticut?

290. NATIVE TRIBES OF NEW YORK. — What is the present number, location, and state of industry of the Iroquois? Was their confederacy of ancient or modern date; and what were the principles of their government? Are there any of the stock of the ancient Mohegans, Munsees, or other tribes of the Hudson valley, or of Long Island and the adjacent coasts, left within the boundaries of this State? What is the meaning of the word Manhattan? Did Hudson ever land on this Island?

291. WHAT INDIANS STILL RESIDE IN NORTHAMPTON COUNTY, VIRGINIA? — Are they of the Powhattanic stock; and are there still to be found, in other parts of that State, descendants of the Nottoways, or other Indians belonging to that family?

292. WHAT NUMBER OF THE CATAWBAS OF SOUTH CAROLINA REMAIN? — Do the Indians of this tribe, who live in York district, own any lands; and, if not, what annuities do they receive from the State; and are these annuities applied in such manner as to promote their education and industry? What affinities exist between the Catawba and other existing languages?

293. WHAT ARE THE CIRCUMSTANCES UNDER WHICH A PART OF THE CHEROKEES ARE LIVING IN NORTH CAROLINA? — How many persons remain at the location secured to them, and what progress have they made in agriculture and civilization?

294. DO THE SEMINOLES, WHO REMAIN IN FLORIDA, INCREASE IN NUMBER? — Have they made any advance in agriculture or the arts, and is their continued residence in that State best suited to promote their happiness and welfare, and to secure, at the same time, the prosperity of the State settlements?

295. WHO WERE THE MOST ANCIENT TRIBES INHABITING FLORIDA? — Is there any reason to believe that Cuba, the Bahamas, or any of the northernmost groups of the West India Islands, were originally peopled by Indians from the peninsula of Florida? Who were the Appalachites spoken of in Davis' history of the Caribbee Islands? Did a colony of Minoreans ever land, in ancient times, in Florida? What was the fate of the French, who abandoned themselves to the wilderness of Florida, on the failure of Laudonniere's plan of settlement? Are there any evidences of De Soto's expedition to be found in existing Indian names?

296. WHAT REMAINS EXIST OF THE INDIAN POPULATION OF THE STATES SOUTH OF, OR BORDER-ING ON, THE SOUTHERN RANGE OF THE APPALACIAN MOUNTAINS? — In what manner were these tribes originally related; what incidents led them to leave their original sites on the south-ern and southwestern streams, and how are they distributed and located at the present time?

297. HOW FAR ARE THE CLAIMS OF THE NORTH-MEN, AS THE ORIGINAL DISCOVERERS OF AMER-ICA, ENTITLED TO CREDENCE? — If "Vinland" was discovered in the tenth century, what particular latitudes and longitudes of North America are we to understand by this term?

298. WHAT IS THE CHARACTER AND PURPORT OF THE ANCIENT INSCRIPTION FOUND ON THE DIGHTON ROCK, ON THE BORDERS OF MASSACHUSETTS AND RHODE ISLAND? — Is this inscrip-tion in the Runic or any other ancient character, in part, or altogether; or is it *sui generis* with the devices and picture-writing of the North American Indians, referred to by No. 245.

299. DID THE PHOENICIANS, OR ANY OTHER PEOPLE FROM THE MEDITERRANEAN, FURNISH ANY ELEMENT IN THE ANCIENT INDIAN POPULATION OF AMERICA? — Is there any affinity between the Iroquois and Greek languages?

300. IS THERE ANY ASIATIC WORD OR WORDS NOW IN USE BY ANY OF THE AMERICAN TRIBES? — What is the origin of the Aztec word "peon?" What are the elements of their name for the Deity, "teo-tl"?

301. DO WE DERIVE THE TERM ALLEGHANY FROM AN ANCIENT PEOPLE CALLED ALLEGHANS? — Are there any other words of their language remaining in our geography? State them, with their etymology.

302. WHO WERE THE ERIES? — Have we reason to suppose that we may recognise, under this name, the Kahkwas of the Iroquois, or the lost "neuter nation," of the French writers?

303. WHAT TRIBE ARE WE TO UNDERSTAND BY THE TERM "FIRE NATION"? — Is this a synonym for any of the existing western tribes? Were they of the group of the Algonquin tribes, or of a different stock, who were expelled by them?

304. IS THE WORD OREGON AN INDIAN TERM? — If so, in what language, and what are its syllabical elements and meaning? Was it employed, by writers, prior to the time of Carver?

305. IS THE INSCRIPTION FOUND ON OPENING THE GRAVE CREEK MOUND, IN WESTERN VIRGINIA, IN 1839, ALPHABETIC OR HIEROGLYPHIC? — If alphabetic, in what ancient character was it executed, what is the purport thereof, and what bearings has it on the early epoch of American history? Furnish an authentic copy of the inscription, with its interpretation, if known.

306. CINCINNATI ANTIQUE STONE. — What objects are depicted on an antique ornamented stone found in a mound in the town plat of Cincinnati in 1840? Are these ornaments in the Yucatanese style?

307. AT WHAT TIME, AFTER THEY BECAME ACQUAINTED WITH THE GULF OF MEXICO, WAS THE MOUTH OF THE MISSISSIPPI FIRST DISCOVERED BY THE SPANISH? — What name did they bestow on it; what terms were bestowed by others, and in what manner has the present term of Mississippi come to prevail? Is this an Algonquin phrase, and if so, what are its elements?

308. WERE THE EVIDENCES OF ANCIENT CIVILIZATION CONFINED TO TRIBES LOCATED AROUND THE GULF OF MEXICO? — Do the articles and fragments of ancient earthenware, found at Appalachicola Bay, and at other places, in Florida, denote a degree of skill in that art superior to that known to have been possessed, by the northern tribes, on the planting of the colonies?

309. WHAT ORIENTAL CUSTOMS ARE DENOTED BY WESTERN ANTIQUITIES? — Articles of antique pottery have been found in Tennessee, which are stated to denote the existence of the Phallic worship among the ancient tribes who inhabited the precincts of that state. What are the facts on this head; and do they receive countenance from discoveries in other quarters?

310. ARE THERE ANY AFFINITIES BETWEEN THE CARIB AND NORTH AMERICAN DIALECTS?

311. TRIBAL ELEMENT OF ANCIENT CIVILIZATION? — Are the reports we have in Humboldt, which are renewed by later writers, of a tribe of White Indians, called Moques or Mocas in the north-western parts of Sonora, founded truth, and what are the features, habits, and arts of this people? Do this tribe possess blue eyes, flaxen hair, and a white skin? Do they build stone-houses, raise large herds of cattle, and grow and spin cotton?

312. TRIBES OF NEW MEXICO. — What are the character, habits, and state of industry of the Navihoes, Jicarillas, Utahs, Kayaguas, and other native tribes of this intendency?

313. INDIANS OF OREGON. — What are the principal facts respecting the numbers, names, and groups, of these tribes? Are there any analogies between the ancient languages of Mexico or California, and the Pacific tribes in the vicinity of Nootka Sound? And are the tribes of the Columbia Valley, as they are represented to be, destitute of the knowledge of a God, and otherwise degraded in their intellectual character, below those generally located east of the Rocky Mountains?

314. WAS AMERICA KNOWN IN THE FIFTH CENTURY, AS IS NOW SAID, IN THE BIBLIOTHETICAL CIRCLES OF GERMANY, ON THE AUTHORITY OF CHINESE WRITINGS?

Language

315. WHAT ARE THE GRAMMATICAL PRINCIPLES OF THE LANGUAGE? — Do these principles correspond with the ancient or modern class of languages? If with the ancient, with what family, and in what particulars, do resemblances or affinities exist? Are the words simple or compound? If compound, or compound derivatives are used, what are the rules by which these compounds are effected?

316. IS THE VOCABULARY OF THE LANGUAGE FOUNDED ON GENERIC ROOTS OR PRIMARY FORMS WHICH COALESCE WITH ADJUNCTS, IN THE UTTERANCE? — Are these roots numerous? Are they monysyllabic or dissyllabic? Do they express the primary senses of motion, existence, and action, quality, and position, without their relation to objects or persons?

317. WHAT IS THE PROCESS OF SYLLABICAL ACCRETION? — Does more than one substantive and one verb enter into the new compound? If two or more words coalesce, do they both retain their quota of syllables, or are some dropped, or thrown away? What are the rules of this process of discarding syllables? Which syllable is invested with the primary meaning? Give examples of the mode of coalescence.

318. HAVE THE VERBS AND SUBSTANTIVES POWER TO ABSORB INTO THEIR TEXTURE, PRONOUNS, PREPOSITONS AND ADJECTIVES? — If so, does not a word become highly concrete, descriptive, and pollysyllabic, exhibiting rather the force and meaning of an entire sentence?

319. WHAT LAWS OF CONCORD GOVERN THE USE OF SUBSTANTIVES? — Have they variations of form to designate number, gender, and case? How is the plural formed? Is there any dual number? Is there a limited and an unlimited plural, or an inclusive and exclusive plural? Have substantives any inflection to denote the animate or inanimate class of objects?

320. GENDER. — Is there a masculine, feminine, and neuter gender? If the sex of objects require no concords, to what principle of distinction do the inflections of transitive verbs and nouns point? Is the arrangement of matter and masses into animate and inanimate kingdoms observed? By what inflections of the substantives are these classes denoted? Do nouns, animate or inanimate, require verbs animate or inanimate, and *vice versa?*

321. WHAT ARE THE PRINCIPAL CHANGES OF FORM OF SUBSTANTIVES? — Are they declined to form cases? Are they susceptible of local and of adjective inflections? Does the noun precede, or follow the verb? Do they say "give me food," or "food give me?" Are substantives converted into verbs, and how?

322. WHAT ARE THE LAWS OF ACCIDENCE OF VERBS? — Do verbs consist of ground forms, which indicate independent or generic action, passion, or existence? How are these forms varied to denote person and object? How, in the incorporation of pronominal elements, is the actor distinguished from the object? How many moods, tenses, and voices have they? Can they be conjugated positively and negatively? Is there any true infinitive in the spoken dialect, or how is the infinitive denoted? Are there participles? Are verbs formed

from nouns? How are the verbs to speak, to dance, to cry, converted into speaker, dancer, cryer? Conjugate the verbs to love, to see, to burn, through the various moods and tenses.

323. DO ADJECTIVES, AS WELL AS VERBS AND SUBSTANTIVES, OBEY THE GRAMMATICAL DISTINCTION OF ANIMATE AND INANIMATE? — Are the words good and bad, black and white, varied in their terminations to denote the generic classes of objects to which they are applied? Cannot the same adjective term be applied to a man and a rock? Are adjectives declined for comparison? How do they denote the degrees of comparison? If adjectives are not varied for degrees, how is precision imparted? Do substantives admit of adjective inflections, by which the use of a governing adjective is obviated? In the terms a good man and a good gun, need the words man and gun be separately employed? Describe the rule, with its transitions and variations.

324. HOW MANY PRONOUNS HAS THE LANGUAGE? — Are there personal, relative, and demonstrative pronouns, and how many of each, and in what manner are they varied in the plural? Is there any pronoun *she,* as contradistinguished from *he?* Is the number of the third person always indefinite? Are there two plurals for we, founded on the principle of the inclusion or exclusion of the person addressed? How is the Deity addressed under the operation of this anomalous rule?

325. ARE PRONOUNS SUSCEPTIBLE OF INFLECTIONS FOR TENSE, NUMBER, OR TRANSITIVE OBJECT? — In what manner are they varied, and how is the past and future distinguished from the present? Can they be further varied to denote the oblique tenses? Is there more than one class of personal pronouns; and if so, how do the personal prefixed pronouns differ from the suffixes?

326. HAS THE LANGUAGE PREPOSITIONS? — If so, are they employed disjunctively, or as independent parts of speech, as heard in by, to, in, with, if, from, through, or are these senses expressed by inseparable particles, or by alphabetical signs? How is precision given to the phrases, in the water, by the rock, on the tree?

327. WHAT IS THE NUMBER AND CHARACTER OF THEIR ADVERBS? — Can the Indians express the sense which, in the English language, is conveyed by the inflection *ly,* as heard in *badly, rapidly?* In the phrases, *stand up, lie down, go there,* how do the verbs differ from their ordinary forms in the singular of the indicative or imperative present? What are the forms of *yes* and *no?*

328. IS THERE A DEFINITE AND AN INDEFINITE ARTICLE? — How is the want of a definite article supplied? It will be necessary, in examining the subject of the definite article, in the Indian dialects, to guard, on the part of interpreters, against the use of pronouns, in this supposed sense. It is also important to decide whether the indefinite article, where it is given, does not strictly denote the number *one,* and not *an;* and to be sure that the sense of the expression employed is not *an* animal, &c., but *one* animal, &c.

329. CONJUNCTIONS. — How many conjunctions have the Indians? Give the common equivalents for the words, *and, nor, neither, but,* &c., together with the manner in which their equivalents in the Indian dialect, under your examination, are employed. Are there chronological conjunctions?

330. INTERJECTIONS. — Does the language abound in exclamations, and does this part of speech partake of the anomalous transitive character which marks the other forms? If an Indian exclaim *lo!* in relation to a man, and *lo!* in relation to a country, are the equivalents for the word *lo!* the same? Are there any differences in the interjections used by males and by females? Is the word for *alas!* the same in both cases?

331. IS THERE A SUBSTANTIVE VERB IN THE LANGUAGE? — And, if so, what are its elements?

Can the Indians say, *I am, he is, they are,* &c., in a generic or elementary sense, and as declarative of independent existence? If the word exist, as the radix *Iau* is stated to, in the Ojibwa dialect of the Algonquin, does the rule separating the grammatical forms of the language into animate and inanimate classes apply to it? Is the word *Iau,* in the dialect referred to, a verb substantive animate, and *Iëë,* a corresponding verb substantive inanimate? Are there analogous forms in the language known to you, and how are these words conjugated? Are the conjugations based on one root, or, as in the Latin *sum,* on several? If an equivalent for the English verb *to be* exist, is it generally employed in the expression of sentiment or passion in conversation, or is its use limited to an object or objects not present to the senses, or which are deemed mysterious or unknown? Does an Indian say, *I am sick, I am well, I am glad, I am sorry,* or are the several expressions, in these cases, without any declarative syllable, as a prefix or suffix to, or incorporated into the texture of the verbs to be sick, or well, or glad, or sorry, by the absence of which declarative forms, the terms would be, literally, *I sick, I well, I glad, I sorry?*

332. HOW ARE ACTIVE DISTINGUISHED FROM PASSIVE VERBS? — *I carry, I am carried. I lift, I am lifted. I strike, I am struck. I burn, I am burned.* Vary the persons which alternately affect actors and objects of action, so as to exemplify the rule.

333. DERIVITIVE COMPOUND VERBS. — Are active verbs made up, in part, of the generic word in the language for existence, or for the property of independent vitality? Is there a corresponding generic root in neuter or passive verbs?

334. GROUND FORMS OF THE SUBSTANTIVES. — Are the nouns based on a stock of generic particles, implying various grades of matter, in inert or active forms? If so, what are the terms, respectively, of liquid, solid, light, heavy, aerial, or metallic, animal, vegetable, or mineral matter? In analyzing the language, endeavor to eliminate these radical words or particles from their concrete forms. Nothing can tend more conclusively to throw light on the structure of the language, than this process of syllabical analysis, and it is desirable that you should apply it also to the verbs and to other forms of speech. The Indian languages differ so essentially from those best known to us, that we should constantly suspect them to be reproductions of old languages, in which the original radices are hid under a set of combined grammatical forms, which are, after all, very simple.

335. ARE THERE ANY REDUNDANCIES OF FORMS? — Such redundancies have been found in the tensal inflections of pronouns wherein the verbs are supplied with the very same inflections, as if we should say, *I did — love did;* or, *I will — hate will.* It is found in some of the languages, that both substantives and pronouns and verbs must, in order to agree, have the same plural inflections for number, by which a species of verbiage or tensal tautology occurs, as if we should use expressions such as these: *the birds — they approach — do;* or, *he or they did go — did;* instead of simply, *the birds approach* or *he* or *they went.* It is also found that possessive pronouns require possessive inflections in their nouns in regimen, and the expressions are, literally, in these cases, *my horse — mine; his dog — his;* and not, as in English, *my house, his dog.* These forms have the cast rather of an illdigested and crude language, and not one which, according to the general and most approved impressions, exists in a very perfect state. Please extend this inquiry to all apparent redundancies of form.

336. HOW IS DECLARATIVE OR PASSIVE EXISTENCE PREDICATED OF ANOTHER IN THE USE OF A NOUN, CHANGED TO A VERB, WHOSE ACTION IS TRANSFERRED TO ONE'S SELF? — In what manner is the substantive invested with the power of a verb? *There is a bear; I am a bear. A horse; I am a horse. God exists; I am a God.*

337. HOW ARE SUBSTANCE AND MOTION, QUALITY AND POSITION, DENOTED IN CONCRETE WORDS, WITHOUT THE SEPARATE USE OF THE ELEMENTS OF SPEECH ESSENTIAL TO SUCH EXPRESSIONS IN THE ENGLISH LANGUAGE? — *A leaf moves, a bird flies, a canoe glides; a dry leaf moves, a blackbird flies, a white canoe glides; a small dry leaf moves, a great blackbird flies, a beautiful white canoe glides; a small dry leaf moves on the tree, a great blackbird flies in the air, a beautiful white canoe glides down the stream.* How far can this process of combination and accretion be carried? May other senses besides these, be added to the original noun, by inflection, or the transfusion of syllables or alphabetical signs?

338. WHAT FORMS CAN SUBSTANTIVES OR VERBS TAKE TO DENOTE POSSESSION, OR THE OBJECT POSSESSED? — Is there a possessive inflection in the first and second persons? How is this affected, if affected at all, by an objective particle or inflection in the third person?

339. AGREEMENT IN NUMBER. — In English Grammar, nouns singular govern verbs plural. *A man walks, men walk; a robber shoots, the robbers shoot.* Is the rule similar in the Indian, or is it directly the reverse? Do they say, *a man walk, men walks?* thus requiring, in all cases, singular to singular, and plural to plural?

340. HOW MANY MOODS ARE PROVIDED FOR BY INFLECTIONS OF THE VERBS? — In what manner are the indicative and infinitive formed? Is there, in the verbal forms, any of greater simplicity than the third person singular? Is there an interrogative mood?

341. ARE THERE INFLECTIONS FOR PAST TENSE, ADDED TO DECEASED PERSONS' NAMES TO INDICATE THEIR DEATH? — State the rule which is said to govern this delicate practice of allusion to the dead, in some of the dialects.

342. ARE THERE ANY WORDS OF A SEXUAL CHARACTER, OR WHICH ARE EXCLUSIVELY USED BY MALES AND FEMALES? — The Carib language denoted anomalies of this kind, and there are traces of the principle in some of the northern languages.

343. IS THE LANGUAGE ADAPTED TO THE PURPOSES OF CHRISTIANITY? — Have translations of the Scriptures been made in it, and if so, what portions of the Old or New Testament have been translated and printed; and what degree of precision, force and exactitude has been attained? Is the language as well adapted to the disquisitive and argumentative style of the Epistles, as to the Gospels, and narrative portions? Has the language been well and characteristically brought out in these translations, or has the literal verse by verse system, seeking equivalents for verbal terms which are shielded under the concrete forms, loaded the pages of the translations, as has been noticed in some instances, with unnecessary verbiage and redundancies? Is there a word in the language for "virgin," as contradistinguished from "maid," and "young woman" — a point upon which its capacity to narrate accurately the incarnation turns? Inquiries of this character will tend to illustrate and explain the principles of the language, and are important in judging of the literary value of what has already been effected, on the frontiers, in this way.

344. IS THE LANGUAGE ADAPTED, TO ANY EXTENT, AND, IF SO, TO WHAT EXTENT, TO THE PURPOSES OF HISTORY, POETRY AND GENERAL LITERATURE? — What is the relative space occupied by parallel passages of Indian and English? Take, for this purpose the parable of Nathan, and the Lord's prayer. If the principles of the amalgamation of words tend to the concentration of sounds, it is reasonable to anticipate that brevity in the annotation, or written characters, should follow. If it does not, in what *other* manner is the language adapted to the purposes of literature?

345. IS THE VOCABULARY COPIOUS? — Can it readily express, or furnish equivalents for, foreign words? Are there any sounds in the English alphabet which it cannot express? Is

gesticulation essential to carry out some of its meanings? Does it appear to be homoge-
nous in its origin, or does it exhibit a mixture of other and dissimilar stocks, domestic or
foreign?

346. IS THE RADIX OF THE NOUN AND VERB GENERALLY A MONOSYLLABLE? — Can you furnish a vocabulary of one hundred specimens of the radical forms of verbs, nouns, or other
primary parts of speech? It is suspected, from their capacity of concrete expression, that
the North American languages are founded on a limited number of elementary roots, of a
general or abstract character, which derive precision, not from radical changes of sound,
but from relative position, permutation, elision, or expansion. The ear, and the ear alone,
is manifestly the principal guide. The art, which a child early learns by practice, and which
appears to require but little power, inductive analysis, it is conceived, may reach and
explain.

347. WHAT IS THE STATE OF THEIR VOCABULARY? — Place the Indian opposite the English
words in the following vocabulary. It is essential to the purposes of comparison that plurals and pronouns should be omitted, or carefully noted, wherever they are employed.

1. God.	32. Arm.	63. Lodge.
2. Devil.	33. Shoulder.	64. Chief.
3. Angel.	34. Back.	65. Warrior.
4. Man.	35. Hand.	66. Friend.
5. Woman.	36. Finger.	67. Enemy.
6. Boy.	37. Nail.	68. Kettle.
7. Girl, or maid.	38. Breast.	69. Arrow.
8. Virgin.	39. Body.	70. Bow.
9. Infant, or child.	40. Leg.	71. War-club.
10. Father, my.	41. Navel.	72. Spear.
11. Mother, my.	42. Thigh.	73. Axe.
12. Husband, my.	43. Knee.	74. Gun.
13. Wife, my.	44. Foot.	75. Knife.
14. Son, my.	45. Toe.	76. Flint.
15. Daughter, my.	46. Heel.	77. Boat.
16. Brother, my.	47. Bone.	78. Ship.
17. Sister, my.	48. Heart.	79. Sail.
18. An Indian.	49. Liver.	80. Mast.
19. A white man.	50. Windpipe.	81. Oar.
20. Head.	51. Stomach.	82. Paddle.
21. Hair.	52. Bladder.	83. Shoe.
22. Face.	53. Blood.	84. Legging.
23. Scalp.	54. Vein.	85. Coat.
24. Ear.	55. Sinew.	86. Shirt.
25. Eye.	56. Flesh.	87. Breechcloth.
26. Nose.	57. Skin.	88. Sash.
27. Mouth.	58. Seat.	89. Head-dress.
28. Tongue.	59. Ankle.	90. Pipe.
29. Tooth.	60. Town.	91. Wampum.
30. Beard.	61. House.	92. Tobacco.
31. Neck.	62. Door.	93. Shot pouch.

94. Sky.
95. Heaven.
96. Sun.
97. Moon.
98. Star.
99. Day.
100. Night.
101. Light.
102. Darkness.
103. Morning.
104. Evening.
105. Mid-day.
106. Mid-night.
107. Early.
108. Late.
109. Spring.
110. Summer.
111. Autumn.
112. Winter.
113. Year.
114. Wind.
115. Lightning.
116. Thunder.
117. Rain.
118. Snow.
119. Hail.
120. Fire.
121. Water.
122. Ice.
123. Earth.
124. Sea.
125. Lake.
126. River.
127. Spring.
128. Stream.
129. Valley.
130. Hill.
131. Mountain.
132. Plain.
133. Forest.
134. Meadow.
135. Bog.
136. Island.
137. Stone.
138. Rock.
139. Silver.

140. Copper.
141. Iron.
142. Lead.
143. Gold.
144. Maize, or corn.
145. Wheat.
146. Oats.
147. Potatoe.
148. Turnip.
149. Pea.
150. Rye.
151. Bean.
152. Melon.
153. Squash.
154. Barley.
155. Tree.
156. Log.
157. Limb.
158. Wood.
159. Post.
160. Stump.
161. Pine.
162. Oak.
163. Ash.
164. Elm.
165. Basswood.
166. Shrub.
167. Leaf.
168. Bark.
169. Grass.
170. Hay.
171. Nettle.
172. Thistle.
173. Weed.
174. Flower.
175. Rose.
176. Lily.
177. Bread.
178. Indian meal.
179. Flour.
180. Meat.
181. Fat.
182. Beaver.
183. Deer.
184. Bison, or buffalo.
185. Bear.

186. Elk.
187. Moose.
188. Otter.
189. Fox.
190. Wolf.
191. Dog.
192. Squirrel.
193. Hare.
194. Lynx.
195. Panther.
196. Muskrat.
197. Mink.
198. Fisher.
199. Marten.
200. Mole.
201. Polecat.
202. Hog.
203. Horse.
204. Cow.
205. Sheep.
206. Turtle, or tortoise.
207. Toad.
208. Snake.
209. Lizard.
210. Worm.
211. Insect.
212. Fly.
213. Wasp.
214. Ant.
215. Bird.
216. Egg.
217. Feather.
218. Claw.
219. Beak.
220. Wing.
221. Goose.
222. Duck.
223. Swan.
224. Partridge.
225. Pigeon.
226. Plover.
227. Woodcock.
228. Turkey.
229. Crow.
230. Raven.
231. Robin.

232. Eagle.
233. Hawk.
234. Snipe.
235. Owl.
236. Woodpecker.
237. Fish.
238. Trout.
239. Bass.
240. Sturgeon.
241. Sunfish.
242. Pike.
243. Catfish.
244. Perch.
245. Sucker.
246. Minnow.
247. Fin.
248. Scale.
249. Roe.
250. White.*
251. Black.
252. Red.
253. Green.
254. Blue.
255. Yellow.
256. Great.
257. Small.
258. Strong.
259. Weak.
260. Old.
261. Young.
262. Good.
263. Bad.
264. Handsome.
265. Ugly.
266. Alive.
267. Dead.
268. Cold.
269. Hot.
270. Sour.
271. Sweet.
272. Pepper.

273. Salt.
274. Bitter.
275. I.
276. Thou.
277. He.
278. She.
279. They.
280. Ye.
281. We, inclusive/ exclusive.
282. This, animate/ inanimate.
283. That, animate/ inanimate.
284. These, animate/ inanimate.
285. Those, animate/ inanimate.
286. All.
287. Part.
288. Who.
289. What/what person/ what thing.
290. Which person/ which thing.
291. Near.
292. Far-off.
293. To-day.
294. To-morrow.
295. Yesterday.
296. By and by.
297. Yes.
298. No.
299. Perhaps.
300. Never.
301. Forever.
302. Above.
303. Under.
304. Within.
305. Without.
306. Something.
307. Nothing.

308. On.
309. In.
310. By.
311. Through.
312. In the sky.
313. On the tree.
314. In the house.
315. By the shore.
316. Through the water.
317. To eat.**
318. To drink.
319. To laugh.
320. To cry.
321. To love.
322. To burn.
323. To walk.
324. To run.
325. To see.
326. To hear.
327. To speak.
328. To strike.
329. To think.
330. To wish.
331. To call.
332. To live.
333. To go.
334. To sing.
335. To dance.
336. To die.
337. To tie.
338. To kill.
339. To embark.
340. Eating.
341. Drinking.
342. Laughing.
343. Crying.
344. To be, or exist.
345. You are.
346. He is.
347. I am that I am.

---

* Denote whether the adjective be animate or inanimate; put an, for the first, and in, for the second.

** If there be no infinitive to verbs, insert the simplest concrete form here, as, *he eats, he drinks,* &c.

348. ARE YOU ACQUAINTED WITH ANY MATERIAL ERRORS IN THE GENERAL OR POPULAR ACCOUNTS OF OUR INDIAN TRIBES? — If so, please state them.

In submitting the preceding queries on the several subjects named, it is not designed to limit the inquiry to these particular forms. Called upon, by the terms of the act, to embody materials illustrative of the history of the tribes, as well as their statistics, the Department seeks to avail itself of the knowledge and experience of persons in various parts of the country, to contribute their aid. The inquiry is here placed on a broad basis, that it may embrace the general grounds from which we are to judge the history and condition, past and present, of the people whose benefit is sought by future legislative provision; and by the adoption of a course of public policy which shall best subserve the highest interests. It is not supposed that every person who sits down to answer these queries, whether he be in a public or private capacity, will take an equal interest in them, or feel equally prepared, with facts and observations, to reply to all. By denoting the general line of inquiry, and running out the leading questions a little into detail, enough has been done, it is conceived, to serve as hints to the respondents, and little more is, indeed, intended. Facts are sought, and nothing but facts. It is essential that, where the respondent is unknown to the Department, some reference should be given. Many of the inquiries relate to customs and opinions which are believed to be common to most of the tribes; but the excepted cases are important to be noted, and in these cases simple affirmative or negative replies will often be sufficient. Where new facts are stated, or new opinions expressed, which are founded on personal knowledge or study, in any branch of the subject, it is of moment that they should be well vouched. Hitherto inquiries of this kind have been chiefly in the hands of casual visitors or travellers in the Indian country, often of foreigners, who have necessarily taken hasty and superficial glances at their mere external customs and ceremonies. Of the more abstruse view of Indian character — of their religion, tribal government and clanships, their thoughts on death and immortality, their mental capacities, and the leading causes of their action, very little has been observed, which possesses the character of research, while there are essential points of discrepancy. But whatever degree of imperfection has characterized these desultory and casual efforts in describing the Indians, and however much cause we may have had to dissent from some of the conclusions and criticisms respecting our treatment of, and policy towards them, drawn by tourists from abroad, or by over-zealous but mistaken observers at home, it is essential to the just discharge of the duty imposed on the Department, in the present effort, that exactitude should stamp its labors. I will therefore thank you to inquire carefully, and be sure that no deception has been practised. In all questions where the interests of the tribes clash with those of the persons whom you may consult, there is much caution required. There is great prejudice of opinion, and preconception of the Indian character, generally. It is due to them that they should be judged candidly, and from an examination of opinions and statements from the best sources. A few examples of the misconceptions referred to, will be mentioned. It was stated a few years ago, by one of the most popular writers of England, that the United States had borrowed money, in 1837, from a wealthy Indian chief, to pay its annuities to his tribe! and its policy has been deeply censured, in high quarters, in the foreign literary world, on the bases of books of travels, whose least severe censure it is believed to be, to declare, that their authors have relied, in some instances, on hastily gathered, or ill-digested, or unworthy materials. One writer represents the Mandans as practising the arts of self-torture of Hindoo devotees, by hanging from hooks, or cords fastened into the nerves, so as to sustain the whole weight of the body. This, together with the general account of the Mandan religion, by the same author, is contrary to the facts, as understood here. The same writer will also have this tribe to be descendants of the

Welsh, who are supposed to have reached this continent in the twelfth century. Yet the British Druids imposed no such self-torturing rites.

Much inexactitude and uncertainty exist with respect to the class of evidences to be drawn from the antiquities of the area of country now composing the United States. To illustrate this topic, in the Indian history, exact plans and descriptions are required. The state of their traditions is ill-explored, on most of the topics embraced in title V. Their general history and languages, constitute a wide field for remark. The whole subject is one of interest, and in giving the inquiry official sanction, it is designed to collect and prepare a body of facts, which shall present the customs, character, and institutions of the tribes in the simple garb of truth.

THE END.